THE OXFORD GUIDE TO THE MIND

THE OXFORD **GUIDE TO THE MIND**

Edited by
Geoffrey Underwood

Consulting Editor
Richard L. Gregory

OXFORD
UNIVERSITY PRESS

OXFORD
UNIVERSITY PRESS

Great Clarendon Street, Oxford OX2 6DP

Oxford University Press is a department of the University of Oxford.
It furthers the University's objective of excellence in research, scholarship,
and education by publishing worldwide in

Oxford New York

Athens Auckland Bangkok Bogotá Buenos Aires Calcutta
Cape Town Chennai Dar es Salaam Delhi Florence Hong Kong Istanbul
Karachi Kuala Lumpur Madrid Melbourne Mexico City Mumbai
Nairobi Paris São Paulo Shanghai Singapore Taipei Tokyo Toronto Warsaw

with associated companies in Berlin Ibadan

Published in the United States
by Oxford University Press Inc., New York

First published 2001

British Library Cataloguing in Publication Data
Data available

Library of Congress Cataloging in Publication Data
Data available

ISBN 0-19-860083-6

1 3 5 7 9 10 8 6 4 2

Typeset in Bembo
by Kolam Information Services Pvt Ltd, Pondicherry, India
Printed in Great Britain by
Biddles Ltd
Guildford and King's Lynn

CONTENTS

PREFACE

The roots of this guide are planted firmly in *The Oxford Companion to the Mind*, edited by Richard Gregory a decade ago. That magnificent collection of short essays, definitions, and biographical notes was a *tour de force*. The quality was signalled by the identity of the contributors alone—it reads like a list of the notable contemporary thinkers on problems of brain, mind, and behaviour.

This *Guide* presents a selection of entries from the *Companion*, arranged in a series of themes, and each introduced by a short summary of the relationships between the ideas described in the main entries. The organization of the themes reflects current thoughts on our study of the mind using the approaches of the various disciplines that have an interest. An underlying assumption forming the basis of these introductory summaries involves the notion that our minds are grounded in our brains. When the electrochemical activities of our brains work in a certain way, then our minds emerge. If these activities are subject to a malfunction—through the introduction of drugs, or as a result of physical damage caused by a stroke, perhaps—then our minds will also malfunction. Under these circumstances disruption of the normal operation of the brain can result in bizarre perceptual experiences, or the loss of the mental processes associated with highly specific abilities such as reading or recognizing people's faces. When the system closes down we can observe a coma or an anaesthetized patient, in whom no mental processes are observable. In these cases the brain is not being activated in the necessary way.

The generation of minds by the operation of the biological substrate is an interesting phenomenon in its own right, of course. Although philosophers have puzzled over the question of how a physical system can give rise to a mental process, the question has been sidelined by the development of computers that can perform operations that simulate mental processes, and even by the observation that the hardware of a domestic compact disc system can generate music when operated in a particular way. In all of these cases a physical system, when activated, gives rise to a different form of energy. The only difficulty here, in the case of our minds, is to describe the specific operating characteristics that allow mental processes to appear. There is no mystery here, and this is a minor problem in comparison with that of how brains and minds can generate conscious awareness. It is important to distinguish between minds and consciousness here, and the emergence of consciousness is a separate problem from the emergence of minds. Mental processes are those that collect information from the world, organize the inputs to represent objects, encode the objects and events for future use, recognize familiar objects, use our representations to solve problems, and organize our responses to the objects and events around us. These are the processes that involve sensations, perceptions, memories, and cognitions, and it is not only biological brains that perform these functions. Computers can mimic an increasing number of our natural mental processes, and it is this comparison between natural and artificial brains that provides the organizing metaphor for the *Guide*. If our biological brains provide the computer hardware for our minds, then the software that runs in the brains is what produces sensory, perceptual, and cognitive processes. When the hardware is damaged the software may not run normally, and we see cognitive deficits in the form of dysfunctions. When the software responds to its inputs in consistent ways, we talk of it demonstrating a discernible personality, and so on. This is an organizing tool here, and the extent to which biological brains can be likened to the hardware of artificial computers continues to provide the basis for heated argument.

The question of *how* the property of consciousness can emerge from our brains and minds is one that presents us with a special difficulty. We have no answers, but plenty of speculations. Bookshelves are filling with volumes written by physiologists, psychologists, mathematicians, and philosophers, attempting to account for the appearance of the state of subjective awareness. How does awareness emerge, and why has it evolved? It is not clear what awareness adds to our mental processes. There must be some evolutionary advantage for organisms that are aware of themselves and of other objects in the world, over and above registering their presence, but at this point we are again returned to speculation. One approach is through the computer metaphor that provides our organizing theme, and to ask not only whether artificial brains will need to become conscious, but just as critically, how we would know when they were. As is traditional when we start to think about the relationship between brain, mind, and consciousness, we have ended up with more questions than answers.

The major credit for this volume must go to Richard Gregory for his vision of the originating enterprise, and to the eminent contributors who wrote the compelling, informative, and entertaining essays. Michael Cox at OUP was instrumental in taking one idea and developing it into another, and in different ways Alison Jones, Sue Jeffery, and Adèle Brown have helped it materialize.

Geoffrey Underwood
University of Nottingham

August 1999

ALPHABETIC LISTING OF ENTRIES

1: THE SOFTWARE OF THE MIND:
Mental Processes in Sensation, Perception, and Cognition

Colour vision	Perception
Extra-sensory perception	Remembering
Forgetting	Short-term memory
Hearing	Smell
Illusions	Taste
Models of mental processes	Touch

The minds of others are accessible to us only indirectly, through the behaviours that they direct. The only mind whose existence we can be sure of is our own, but it seems reasonable to infer that other people (and perhaps some other animals) are sufficiently similar to us that they also have minds. To say so, however, is to use inference. When we watch someone pick up a pencil and write an answer in a cryptic crossword puzzle, we can see only letters being written in the crossword grid, but we can infer a number of things about the person being observed. One of the simplest inferences is that she can read words, but more relevant is the conclusion that she understands the complicated rules by which groups of words point towards a solution. This person can think, and we might even say that she has intelligence, but all of these attributions are only indirectly observable. This kind of inferential enquiry is the domain of the cognitive psychologist, who describes the characteristics of basic psychological processes such as perception, memory, and thinking. A vital part of this investigative process is the construction of theories in the form of **models of mental processes**. It is not insignificant that our more pervasive models are those that can be described in terms of computer simulations—models that mimic our mental processes by running as computer programs. One of the more powerful families of models uses neural networks or connectionism. It is worth noting that there is a healthy debate between these families and others that depend upon a more symbolic level of description. In a sense then, we can be said to have understood our own minds when we can copy them into computers. It is this form of modelling that lends the analogy that our minds are the software that runs on the hardware of the brain.

Our psychological processes work upon information in the form of sensations, which are gathered from the external world, in combination with previously collected information stored as knowledge in our memory systems. Our senses have evolved to respond to useful physical energy in the environment. We have **hearing** for noises that correspond to changes in air pressure within a specific range of frequency of vibration, and no hearing for air pressure frequencies greater than about 20 MHz. Animals with hearing systems that have evolved under different constraints can hear noises above this frequency, and while this is unsurprising it does indicate the limitations of the information that we can collect about our environment. There are a number of sources of energy that are out of range of our limited sensory systems. In addition to high frequency sound, electromagnetic waves of the frequencies used in radio transmissions are unavailable to human senses. Our detection of light is similarly limited, with our vision restricted to electromagnetic waves in a narrow band of frequencies. Energy in the form of X-rays, ultra-violet rays, and infrared rays is undetectable by our senses. Similarly, for those animals whose range is even more limited there is no **colour vision**. The senses that collect information from a distance—vision and hearing—can be distinguished from those that collect information about our immediate environment—**smell**, **taste**, and **touch**. The immediate senses are used to discover whether things that we are about to touch or ingest are likely to be hostile or friendly. Without these senses we can survive comfortably, if not luxuriously, but other species value them to a greater extent. In contrast, without vision or without hearing our negotiations with the world are critically impaired.

Energy that is available to our senses is the basis of **perception**, the process whereby we interpret signals transmitted from the sensory receptors to the cortex via the neurones. The process of interpretation is one of determining the nature of different classes of phenomena, such as what objects are in visible range, what someone has said to us, or what variety of grape was used to make the wine we are tasting. These are acts of pattern recognition, and they are not conducted using sensory evidence alone. We make use of our previous experiences—our knowledge of the world—when perceiving, and it is this influence of conceptual knowledge upon the interpretation of sensory evidence that can lead to perceptual errors and **illusions**. When we believe that we have perceived an object that is contextually probable, on the basis of either a coincidence of sensory data or impoverished sensory data, then we are going beyond the information presented by our senses and are vulnerable to illusion. Other illusions are perceptual distortions rather than interpretative errors, but all show the extent to which our perception of the sensory world can differ from reality. The possibility of perception without a sensory input, or **extra-sensory perception**, is not one that receives much serious scientific attention. If it is ever established as an authentic phenomenon (as opposed to a stage magician's trick), then it will probably also be demonstrated that the underlying mechanism involves the detection of sensory cues previously unobserved by the investigators, and at this point the perceptions will by definition cease to be extra-sensory. A second challenge to the conventional view of sensation resulting in perception and interpretation comes from investigations of subliminal perception, whereby our minds are influenced by sensory signals of which we are unaware. This is less of a challenge than that of the possibility of extra-sensory perception, in that we need only demonstrate a gap between perception and awareness to confirm the plausibility of subliminal perception. This can be done quite easily in laboratory studies in which words and objects are displayed under conditions that prevent the participants from becoming aware of their presence. Presentation conditions such as duration and illumination can ensure that subjects are unable to report the presence of the words or objects. If the stimulus still has an effect upon behaviour—by influencing the response to some other stimulus, for example—then subliminal perception is demonstrated.

As we process sensory evidence into perceptions these understandings become available for use by higher-order processes that involve language, whereby our perceptual experiences may be described. They are also available to memory, where they may be retained for later use, and in thinking, where the information may be used creatively or to solve a problem. It is at this point that we can appreciate the aesthetics of a painting or a piece of music, having recognised the images or made out a tune. Information that has been perceived can subsequently be recalled using words, and is available to influence our behaviour implicitly. As we report that which we have perceived, we can be said to be using two forms of memory. An immediate or **short-term memory** is necessary to hold the information until a report is necessary, and a long-term memory is used to help recognise events and objects that are familiar. Particularly familiar circumstances give rise to the phenomenon of déjà vu, in which we have such a strong feeling of recognizing a location or set of circumstances, that we feel we have had the experience already. This phenomenon occurs frequently in certain types of psychological disorders, but it is also a common experience in everyday life. Although there is no definitive explanation it seems likely that it arises when a new environment has sufficient similarity to a previously experienced environment to evoke a memory of an actual experience.

Short-term memories have been likened to extended perceptions, but this simple analogy does not take into account our ability to use mnemonics and rehearsal procedures to prevent **forgetting** by circulating information in short-term memory. The mnemonic rules themselves must be retained in long term memory, of course. This means that identifying the separate components of **remembering** as coming from short-term or long-term memory is complicated to the extent that the distinction between these memory systems is questionable. In the nineteenth century William James used the terms primary and secondary memory to distinguish between memories currently under conscious scrutiny and those that are not currently in awareness but are available to be so. The terms fell into disuse for many years, but capture a phenomenological aspect of our memory experiences, and with the current interest in implicit memories that are effective though not recallable, there is a case for reinstating them.

COLOUR VISION. When things are seen, it is usually because light enters the eye and is focused upon the retina, that sensitive membrane at the back. Light consists of electromagnetic vibrations of minute wavelengths—one million waves to the half metre for green light.

Isaac Newton, by his famous prism experiment, showed in 1666 that sunlight consists of a mixture of rays, each bent to a different degree in traversing the prism and thus falling at a different place upon the far wall. He showed that each ray was elementary in the sense that it could not be changed into a ray differently bent. Each elementary ray had a different colour, and the colour of objects depended upon the copiousness with which the various coloured rays were reflected or transmitted from the object to the eye.

Newton's conclusions, though true, met with fierce opposition. To Goethe it was absurd to assert that the mere mixing of all the rainbow colours could appear white since white is without colour. And artists had long known that it was not necessary for them to have a set of seven rainbow paints; a judicious mixture on the palette of a few bright paints—perhaps only three—was sufficient for masterpieces of natural representation.

A person's perception of everything in the world outside him depends upon three factors: (i) the physical stimulus, such as vibrations of light or sound, (ii) the sense organs that respond to particular stimuli in special ways, and send corresponding messages along their nerves to the brain, and (iii) the mind that creates perception out of brain activity. Newton analysed correctly the diversity of light rays that constitute sunlight. But he did not consider the limitations of the eye in responding selectively to these diverse rays. This was done by the physician Thomas Young in 1801, at St George's Hospital, London. He saw that human perception of fine detail implies a 'fine grain' of photoreceptors in the retina, and thought it unlikely that each 'grain' would be selectively responsive to every wavelength of light. Nor was this necessary to explain colour discrimination. Young suggested that each grain consisted of a triad of resonators each thrown into vibration by light waves. The 'green receptor' was moved chiefly by waves from the middle of the spectrum (which looks green), though neighbouring spectral waves also acted upon it less vigorously. The 'red receptor' and the 'blue receptor' respond likewise to waves near either end of the spectrum. Thus light of any composition falling upon the eye will throw these three resonators, R, G, and B, into determinate amplitudes of vibration. Their sum, $R+G+B$ defines the brightness, and their ratio $R:G:B$ defines the colour.

This view, which is essentially what is believed today, is seen not to question Newton's physics but, by taking into account the limited discrimination of the eye, to explain the painter's experience that mixing a few paints will give the whole range of colour. Young's explanation should lead to a simple and striking result. Every colour (including white) should excite the R, G, and B receptors in a characteristic set of ratios. Consequently, a mixture of red + green + blue lights, adjusted to produce this same set of ratios, should appear white, or whatever the initial colour was. In 1854 this was systematically tested by James Clerk Maxwell (1831–79), the great physicist, while a student at Trinity College, Cambridge. He showed that every colour can be matched by a suitable mixture of red + green + blue 'primaries', although sometimes it is necessary for the experimenter to mix one of his three primaries with the colour to be matched rather than with the other primaries. This *trichromacy* of vision was confirmed by Hermann von Helmholtz in Heidelberg and later measured with spectral lights and great accuracy by W. P. Wright at Imperial College, London and independently by W. S. Stiles at the National Physical Laboratory, London.

Visual pigments. What does light do to the photoreceptors of the retina to make them send nerve messages to the brain? Willy Kühne (1837–1900), professor of physiology at Heidelberg, observed in 1877 that a dark-adapted retina removed from a dead frog in dim light and then observed in daylight, was initially pink, but bleached to pale yellow upon exposure to light. This showed that the retina contains a photosensitive pigment, i.e. one that changes its chemical constitution on exposure, as does a photographic film. This pigment, 'visual purple' or 'rhodopsin', is present in the photoreceptors called 'rods' that serve deep twilight vision, which is without colour. Therefore the pigments serving colour vision must lie not in the twilight receptors but in the daylight receptors called 'cones'. And Young was correct in supposing that these are of three types.

Researchers in Cambridge were the first to measure the visual pigments in the living human eye, applying the familiar observation that if at night a cat's eye is caught in the beam of a car's headlamps it shines back with reflected light (Rushton and Campbell, 1954). By knowing the incident light and measuring the reflected light, it is found what light has been absorbed in the eye. And if these measurements are made before and after the visual pigment has been bleached away with strong light, the change in absorption, resulting from the change in amount of visual pigment present, is learnt.

The same measurements may be made in human eyes, though here there is a very black surface behind the retina instead of the cat's shining *tapetum lucidium*. Since the measuring light sent in may not be made very strong (or it will bleach away the pigment that is being measured), the great sensitivity of a photomultiplier tube is needed to measure the faint light that emerges from the eye. Using this technique, it has been possible to measure the spectral sensitivity and kinetics of bleaching and regeneration in the living human eye, first of rhodopsin, then of the red and the green cone pigments. There was never sufficient blue light reflected to measure the blue cone pigment.

This work has been confirmed and extended by Marks, Dobelle, and MacNichol at Johns Hopkins University, Baltimore. They used fresh retinas from monkeys' and human eyes removed at operation, and with superb technique measured the visual pigments in single cones. They found Young's three types of cone and specified the visual pigment in each, confirming the measurements made in Cambridge on living colour-blind subjects who possessed only one of the two cone pigments measurable by the Cambridge technique.

Colour-blindness. Almost all so-called colour defectives have some appreciation of colour, and generally resent being called colour *blind*. The common defective cannot distinguish well between red and green. This is a hereditary defect, something wrong with a gene carried on one (or rarely both) of the sex chromosomes in the female or on the single active sex chromosome in the male. If in the male the gene is missing or abnormal, colour vision will be defective; and 8 per cent of all males exhibit some defect. But in the female it needs *both* chromosomes to suffer the loss before her defect will show, and of course the probability of the double event is much smaller than that of the single one. In fact only 0.4 per cent of females show some abnormality. Even so, women who are abnormal in only one chromosome, though showing perfect colour vision themselves, have a fifty-fifty chance of transmitting their weakness to their children; and half their sons will be 'colour-blind', since the (normal) father holds his normal gene on the one sex chromosome that will make his child a daughter, and he has none for his sons.

Dichromacy. In the extreme conditions of the red-green defect, the subject cannot tell red from green and can match every colour of the rainbow exactly with a suitable mixture of only two coloured lights, for example red and blue. Such subjects are called dichromats, to distinguish them from ordinary people (trichromats) who need also a green primary if every colour is to be matched.

The cone pigments in the red-green spectral range of dichromats have been measured by a reflection technique. It has been shown that instead of the red- *and* green-sensitive cone pigments of normal vision, these subjects have only the red or the green. They lack one dimension of colour vision because they lack one kind of cone pigment.

Anomalous Trichromacy. The majority of colour defectives are not true dichromats, but anomalous trichromats: like normal subjects, they require three variables in a colour-matching experiment, but the matches they make are different from those of the normal. Thus, in matching a monochromatic yellow with a mixture of red and green, some ('Protoanomalous') observers require more red than normal in the match, whereas other ('deuteranomalous') observers need more green. Usually, though not necessarily, the abnormality of matching is associated with a reduced capacity for discriminating colours. It is thought that anomalous trichromacy arises when one of the cone pigments is displaced from its normal position in the spectrum.

Adaptation. Newton's physics of colour was inadequate because it did not take into account the selective physiological action of Young's three cone types. We are now on the way to understanding their selectivity and the sort of nerve signals they generate. But though light waves and nerve signals are factors that lead to colour vision, there is still the miracle of how some nerve signals generate a sensation in the mind. This sensation certainly does not depend exclusively upon the $R:G:B$ excitation ratios of the three cone types. We all know how adaptation to any strong-coloured light leaves the eye, as it were, fatigued to the colour so that some extra light of this colour must be added to any presentation if its appearance is to be the same as it was before adaptation. This adaptation is often called 'successive contrast' to distinguish it from the rather similar 'simultaneous contrast', where two different-coloured objects seen close together have their differences enhanced through their proximity. Some of these effects can be objectively measured by recording from nerves in the visual pathways of animals.

Psychology. Colours are so gay that those with total colour loss cannot but be pitied; and it must be wondered what it is that makes red produce the wonderful red sensation most people perceive. What has been said here explains only what cannot be discriminated, and nothing has been said about how sensations arise from what is seen. Let it be concluded that Newton ended his first paper with these strong words: 'But to determine . . . by what modes or actions light produceth in our minds the phantasms of colours is not so easie. And I shall not mingle conjectures with certainties.'

WILLIAM A. H. RUSHTON

EXTRA-SENSORY PERCEPTION. There are those who hold that man is an exclusively material being, living in an exclusively material universe; and there are also those who hold that he is a spiritual or psychic entity, inhabiting a material body in a universe which has both physical and non-physical aspects. The first view is a relative newcomer in philosophical terms: it has come to be widely held only since the advance of scientific materialism in the nineteenth century. The second view is of course much more venerable, lying at the heart of most systematized religions; and despite the fact that it is scientifically unfashionable, it nevertheless commands wider support, even today, among the population at large. Given our present very limited understanding of the brain and mind, it is possible to support this view without being in any way irrational or unscientific, though most scientists would probably lean toward a more agnostic position, which can be roughly summarized as: 'I will suspend belief in the existence of a non-physical entity such as mind, soul, or spirit until I have good evidence to indicate that it exists.'

Is there evidence that it exists? The non-materialistic view of the universe claims that there is, and that it comes from studies of the various types of phenomena clustered under the heading 'extra-sensory perception' (ESP). This phrase, which was coined by J. B. Rhine, one-time head of the world's first university parapsychology department, retains, despite popular usage, a fairly specific meaning. It refers to any mental faculty which allows a person to acquire information about the world without the use of the known senses. Such faculties are generally classified as telepathy, clairvoyance, and precognition. A fourth phenomenon, psychokinesis, while not involving perception in the recognized meaning of the word, is almost always studied alongside ESP. The systematic investigation of these four faculties is the subject-matter of psychical research or parapsychology. Here we will merely consider what each term implies.

(i) Telepathy refers specifically to the transmission of information from one mind to another, without the use of language, body movements, or any of the known senses. Because of the difficulty of ruling out normal sensory cues when humans are within sight or earshot of each other, most scientists are impressed by telepathic evidence only when it involves two people separated by a considerable distance or when at least one of them is isolated under the most stringent conditions. (ii) Clairvoyance refers to the acquisition by a mind or brain of information which is not available to it by the known senses, and, most important, which is *not known at the time to any other mind or brain*. To give examples, if one could read the pages of a closed book, or give the sequence of a shuffled but undealt pack of cards, then one would be demonstrating clairvoyance. (iii) Precognition refers to the acquisition of information about an event before it takes place. Common anecdotal 'evidence' for precognition comes in the form of dreams about the future which subsequently come true, but evidence in a laboratory setting is, for example, ability to predict the order in which cards will be dealt from a pack, with shuffling carried out *only after the prediction had been made*. (iv) Psychokinesis refers to the supposed power of the mind to manipulate matter at a distance without any known physical means. At its crudest and most dubious level, 'evidence' for this faculty comes from the performances of Uri Geller and others. More serious evidence comes from laboratory experiments into willing the fall of dice from a mechanical shaker.

Establishing the reality of one or all of these faculties would be of great interest to anyone engaged in studying the brain and nervous system. Not only would strictly mechanistic models of psychology—such as those exemplified by Skinnerian behaviourism—have to be scrapped, but many of the assumptions and theories of physical science would need at least to be thoroughly overhauled. Perhaps the least challenging is telepathy, for all that is alleged is that information can pass from one mind to another without the *known* senses. There could be other senses, equipped with appropriate sense organs, hidden somewhere in the brain and acting as transmitters and receivers. It is now established that information can be sent across vast distances by radio—a fact which would have been considered highly improbable a century ago—and perhaps some parallel system, as yet unidentified, operates in human brains. But what of the remaining three faculties? What possible mental mechanism could allow the mind to inspect the sequence of a shuffled deck of cards *before the shuffling has taken place*? Or how could the mind physically operate on matter from a distance, causing a die to fall with one face rather than another uppermost?

Clearly, if ESP exists, in one or more of the forms discussed, then the idea of a non-materialistic component to the universe becomes more plausible. If the mind can roam more or less at will, then it would seem that man is, in part at any rate, a non-physical being, capable of exercising far greater control of his own destiny and of his environment than is usually assumed by science. Fortunately—or unfortunately—systematic laboratory research, once full of promise, has yielded little in the way of concrete evidence for ESP, while anecdotal evidence, however superficially convincing, so often withers away under close inspection.

CHRISTOPHER EVANS

FORGETTING. There are three possible causes of forgetting. First, relevant information may have been lost from the storage system of the brain—'storage loss'. Second, there may be failure to retrieve or to use stored information—'retrieval failure'. Third, insufficient information may have been put into storage to permit of differentiation between wanted and unwanted information—'encoding deficiency'. (Strictly, this is only one form of encoding deficiency. How information is encoded can also affect retrieval, as the success of mnemonic systems testifies.)

Storage loss can occur in several ways. There may be decay of the physical representation of the information. Decay is a plausible explanation for the very rapid forgetting which takes place in the first second or so after an experience has occurred—for example, the fading perception of the visual world that occurs if you close your eyes. Another possibility is that information is displaced from storage by new information; the idea of displacement is used, for example, in the 'slot' theory of the memory span (see **short-term memory**). Or information may be modified by new information rather than be displaced by it, as in Bartlett's 'schema' theory. Modification of schema may underlie the way our memory for a changing feature of the environment is updated, whether the feature is transient, such as our own location in space, or one that changes only slowly, such as the face of a friend. Schema provide a basis for recording abstractions from events without recording the events as such.

There is no direct evidence for storage loss. If such evidence is obtained it will be physiological. However, the total absence of storage loss would mean that, in a sense, nothing is ever really forgotten. This view was popularized by Freud but it is doubtful whether he meant that every trivial detail of every trivial experience remains stored. There is suggestive evidence of storage loss in post encephalytic amnesia, since the amnesia is characterized by unusually rapid forgetting. (Typically, amnesia is characterized by poor learning rather than rapid forgetting.) Suggestive evidence for storage loss, without any association with disease, comes from an extensive investigation of memory for school-learned Spanish: there was forgetting for the first 5 years after study, no forgetting for the next 25 years, and additional forgetting with the onset of middle-age. The interpretation of such evidence is, however, controversial.

Without physiological evidence it is impossible to be sure that storage loss occurs, for retrieval failure can never be excluded as a reason for forgetting. There is plenty of everyday evidence for retrieval failure: for example, we all forget names we know that we know and which we can later recall (the tip-of-the-tongue phenomenon). The likelihood of successful retrieval is greatly affected by the presence or absence of relevant cues—stimuli, logically or associatively related to the information to be retrieved—especially if they were present at the time of learning. Mood, which provides internal cues, has been shown to have quite a powerful effect on retrieval. It is easier to remember happy events when we are happy than when we are unhappy and vice versa (thus reinforcing a current mood state). Hypnosis can be used to alter mood state and can thereby affect retrieval. However, the common belief that hypnosis produces a dramatic increase in retrieval (thereby supporting the notion that there is no true forgetting) has been shown to be false, and the memories produced under hypnosis have proved to be highly unreliable.

An event is difficult to remember if it is one of a number of similar events (What did you have for lunch on Tuesday last week?)—a difficulty which has been extensively studied under the heading of proactive and retroactive interference. The difficulty probably arises partly because insufficient information has been stored to enable differentiation of one event from another—that is, from encoding deficiency. Immediately after an event has occurred, its recency is a sufficient basis for its identification, but later it can be distinguished from similar events only by some form of stored code of adequate precision. The difficulty also arises because retrieval failure becomes more likely; according to cue-overload theory, this is because retrieval of similar memories tends to depend on the same cues, and the effectiveness of a cue falls as the number of memories associated with it rises.

We think of forgetting as undesirable. However, the difficulty of remembering similar events suggests that there is a positive advantage in forgetting, through storage loss, the great majority of our moment-to-moment experiences: such forgetting should reduce retrieval loss for information of importance to us. Can we, then, voluntarily discard information? Experiments suggest that the extent to which we can is very limited and probably confined to ceasing active maintenance of recently acquired information. Sadly, the mind does not seem to have at its disposal anything corresponding to the erase button of a tape-recorder.

JOHN BROWN

HEARING. When an object vibrates, pressure changes are set up in the surrounding medium, usually air, and these pressure changes are transmitted through the medium and may be perceived as sound. Sounds can be categorized into two main classes. Those for which the pressure changes have a random or irregular quality are perceived as noise-like; examples are the sound of a waterfall, or the consonants 's' or 'f'. Those which repeat regularly as a function of time are called periodic sounds, and generally have a well-defined tone or pitch: for example, a note played on a musical instrument. The size of the pressure change is related to the perceived loudness of a sound; the greater the pressure variation the greater the loudness. However, it is inconvenient to express the magnitude of sounds in terms of pressure changes, because the ear can perceive sounds over a huge range of pressures. Hence a logarithmic measure called the decibel (abbreviated dB) is used to express sound magnitude, or level; 0 dB corresponds roughly to the quietest sound which can be heard by a healthy young adult, normal conversation has a level of 60–70 dB, while sounds above about 100 dB tend to be uncomfortably loud and can damage our ears if heard for a long time. Sounds with a level above 120 dB can damage our ears within quite a short time, perhaps only a few minutes. When the level of a sound is increased by 10 dB, the subjective loudness roughly doubles, whereas the sound power actually increases by a factor of 10. The smallest detectable change in level is about 1 dB.

Periodic sounds can also be described in terms of their repetition rate and the complexity of the pressure variation. The repetition rate is related to the subjective pitch; the higher the rate the higher the pitch. Complexity is related to the subjective timbre or tone quality; differences in timbre distinguish between the same note played on, say, the violin and the organ. One of the simplest pressure waves has the form of a sinusoid: pressure plotted against time varies as the sine of time. A sine wave may also be called a pure tone or simple tone, since it has a very 'pure' or 'clean' quality, like that of a tuning fork or the Greenwich time-signal. For a pure tone the repetition rate, the number of complete cycles per second, is called the frequency. The unit of one cycle per second is called the hertz (abbreviated Hz). The Greenwich time-signal has a frequency of 1,000 Hz. The highest frequency we can hear varies from 16,000 to 20,000 Hz in young adults, but tends to decrease with increasing age. The lowest frequency which is heard as sound is about 20 Hz. Below that the pressure changes are felt as a vibration rather than heard as sound. We are most sensitive to frequencies around 1,800 Hz.

Sine waves, or pure tones, are particularly important in the study of hearing. Joseph Fourier showed that any periodic complex sound can be considered as composed of a sum of sine waves with different frequencies and levels. Conversely, any periodic sound can be synthesized by adding together sine waves with appropriate frequencies and levels. This can be very useful, since if we are investigating how some part of the auditory system works, it is often sufficient to measure only the way it responds to sine waves of different frequencies. The response to any complex sound can then be predicted from the response to the sine waves. The same philosophy lies behind the specification of amplifiers or loudspeakers in terms of their frequency response. It is assumed that if an amplifier faithfully reproduces any sine wave within the audible range, and amplifies each sine wave by the same amount, then it will also faithfully reproduce any complex sound composed of those sine waves.

A further reason why sine waves are important in the study of hearing is that the ear behaves as though it carries out a Fourier analysis, although it does not do this analysis perfectly, and is therefore said to have limited resolution. Thus when we are presented with two sine waves which are sufficiently separated in frequency, we are able to hear two separate tones, each with its own pitch. This contrasts with the eye, where a mixture of two different colours (frequencies of light) is perceived as a single colour. The process by which the different frequencies in a complex sound are separated in the ear is known as frequency analysis or frequency resolution.

If we subject a complex sound to Fourier analysis, and then plot the level of each sine-wave component as a function of frequency, the resulting plot is known as the spectrum of the sound. The spectrum is related to the complexity of the pressure variation: the simple sine wave has a spectrum composed of a single point, or vertical line, whereas musical instrument tones generally contain many sinusoidal components, and have a spectrum composed of many lines. The subjective timbre of sounds is more easily explained in terms of the spectrum than in terms of the pressure variation as a function of time. Sounds with many high-frequency components will seem sharp or strident, while those with mainly low-frequency components will seem dull or mellow. This correspondence between spectrum and timbre provides another example of the action of the ear as a frequency analyser. In the following sections we will discuss the physiological basis of this frequency analysis, and some of its perceptual consequences. We will also discuss the perception of pitch. Finally we will describe the major types of hearing impairments, and their perceptual consequences.

The anatomy and physiology of the ear. Fig. 1 illustrates the basic structure of the outer, middle, and inner ear. The outer ear consists of the pinna and the ear canal. The pinna is thought to play an important role in our ability to locate complex sounds. The spectrum of such sounds is modified by the pinna in a way which depends upon the direction of the sound source relative to the head. These spectral modifications are not perceived as changes in timbre, but rather determine the perceived direction of the sound source. They are particularly important in allowing us to distinguish whether a sound comes from behind or in front, and above or below.

Sounds impinging upon the eardrum are transferred by means of three small bones in the middle ear (the smallest bones in the body, called the malleus, the incus, and the stapes) to a membrane-covered opening (the oval window) in the inner ear or cochlea. The main function of the middle ear is to improve the efficiency of transfer of energy from the air to the fluids inside the cochlea. Small muscles attached to the bones contract when we are exposed to intense sounds, reducing sound transmission to the cochlea, particularly at low frequencies. This may serve to protect the cochlea, and it may also help to stop intense low frequencies, occurring in the environment or in our own voices, making higher frequencies inaudible.

The cochlea is filled with fluids, and running along its length is a membrane called the basilar membrane. This membrane is stiff and narrow close to the oval window (called the base), while at the other end (the apex) it is wider and less stiff. In response to sine-wave stimulation a wave appears on the basilar membrane travelling from the base towards the apex, at first increasing in amplitude and then decreasing. The position of the maximum in the pattern of vibration along the basilar membrane varies with frequency; high frequencies produce peaks towards the base, and low frequencies towards the apex. Thus the basilar membrane acts as a frequency analyser, different frequencies producing activity at different places along the basilar membrane.

The information which is contained in the patterns of vibration on the basilar membrane has to be transmitted to the brain in some way in order for us to perceive sound. This transmission is achieved by an electrical 'code' carried in the auditory nerve. Each auditory nerve contains the axons or 'fibres' of

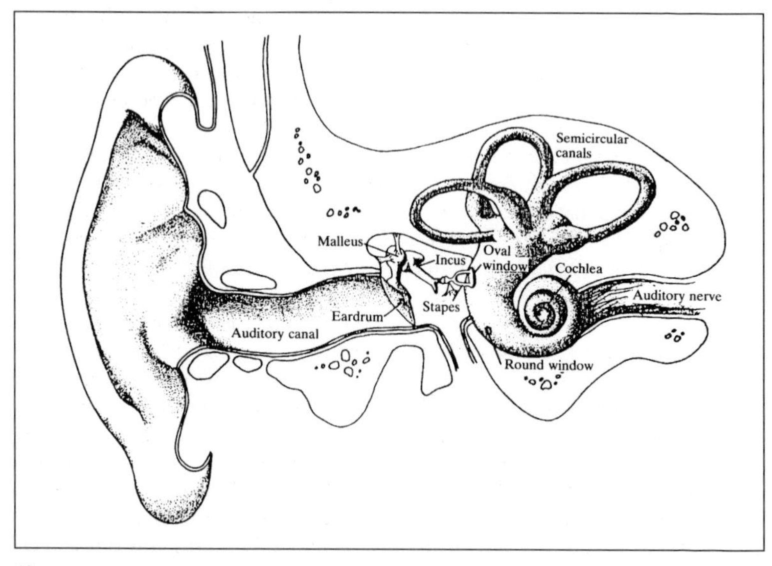

Fig. 1 The structure of the peripheral auditory system, showing the outer, middle, and inner ear.

about 30,000 individual nerves, or neurones, and information is transmitted in each of these in the form of brief electrical impulses, called spikes or action potentials. Thus transmission takes place in an all-or-none fashion; the size of the spikes does not vary, and only the presence or absence of a spike is important.

The vibrations on the basilar membrane are transformed to spikes by rows of special cells, called hair cells, which rest on the basilar membrane. The hair cells are among the most delicate structures in the cochlea, and they can be destroyed by intense sound, lack of oxygen, metabolic disturbance, infection, or drugs. They also tend to be lost with increasing age. Once lost they do not regenerate, and loss of hair cells is a common cause of hearing impairment.

The exact way in which information is 'coded' in the auditory nerve is not clear. However, we know that any single neurone is activated only by vibration on a limited part of the basilar membrane. Each neurone is 'tuned' and responds to only a limited range of frequencies. Thus information about frequency can be coded in terms of which neurones are active or 'firing' with spikes. This form of coding is called 'place' coding. Information about sound level may be carried both in the rate of firing (i.e. the number of spikes per second) and in terms of the number of neurones which are firing. Finally, information may also be carried in the exact timing of the spikes. For stimulating frequencies below about 5 kHz (1 kHz = 1,000 Hz), the time pattern of neural spikes reflects the time structure of the stimulus. Nerve spikes tend to occur at a particular point or phase of the stimulating waveform, a process called phase-locking, although a spike will not necessarily occur on every cycle.

Theories of pitch perception. The pitch of a sound is defined as that attribute of sensation in terms of which sounds may be ordered on a musical scale; variations in pitch give rise to the percept of a melody. For sine-wave stimuli the pitch is related to the frequency, and for other periodic sounds it is usually related to the overall repetition rate. Classically there have been two theories of how pitch is determined. The *place* theory suggests that pitch is related to the distribution of activity across nerve fibres. A pure tone will produce maximum activity in a small group of neurones connected to the place on the basilar membrane which is vibrating most strongly, and the 'position' of this maximum is assumed to determine pitch. The *temporal* theory suggests that pitch is determined from the time pattern of neural impulses, specifically from the time intervals between successive impulses (this used to be called the volley theory, but as discussed above, volleying is no longer considered necessary).

It is generally agreed that the place theory works best at high frequencies, where the timing information is lost, and the temporal theory works best at low frequencies, where resolution on the basilar membrane is poorest. However, the frequency at which the change from one to the other occurs is still a matter of debate. We can get some clues from studies of frequency discrimination, the ability to detect a small difference in frequency between two successive tones. For low and middle frequencies a change of about 0.3 per cent is detectable, but above about 5 kHz the smallest detectable change increases markedly. Furthermore, above 5 kHz our sense of musical pitch appears to be lost, so that a sequence of different frequencies does not produce a clear sense of melody. Since 5 kHz is the highest frequency at which phase-locking occurs, these results suggest that our sense of musical pitch and our ability to detect small changes in frequency depend upon the use of temporal information. Place information allows the detection of relatively large frequency changes, but it does not give rise to a sense of musical pitch.

The ear as a frequency analyser. We initially described how the auditory system functions as a limited-resolution frequency analyser, splitting complex sounds into their sine-wave components. Although we have argued that place information is not the most important determinant of pitch, it seems almost certain that the place analysis which takes place on the basilar membrane provides the initial basis for the ear's frequency analysing abilities.

As was described earlier, the subjective timbre of a sound depends primarily on the spectrum of the sound; the level of sound at each frequency. Presumably timbre is perceived in this way because the different frequencies excite different places on the basilar membrane. The distribution of activity as a function of place determines the timbre. Obviously, this distribution can be quite complex, but each different complex tone will produce its own distribution, and hence will have its own tone colour. This helps us to distinguish between different musical instruments, and to distinguish between the different vowel sounds in human speech.

Hearing impairments. Hearing impairments can be classified into two broad types. *Conductive* hearing loss occurs when the passage of sound through to the inner ear is impeded in some way, for example by wax in the ears, or by some problem with the bones in the middle ear. It can often be cured by simple medical treatment, or by surgery, and when this is not possible a simple hearing-aid can effectively alleviate the problem. *Sensorineural* hearing losses arise in the inner ear, or at some point 'higher up' in the auditory system. Cochlear hearing losses are often produced by damage to the hair cells and they are common in the elderly. Sensorineural hearing losses are not usually helped by surgery, and simple hearing-aids are of only limited use, since the percepts of the listener are 'distorted' in various ways.

One common problem in cochlear hearing loss is *recruitment*, an abnormally rapid growth of loudness with increasing sound level. Faint sounds may be inaudible to the sufferer, but high-level sounds are as loud to him or her as to a normal listener. A hearing-aid which amplifies all sounds will over-amplify intense sounds, and these will be uncomfortably loud. One way round this problem is to use hearing-aids which 'compress' the dynamic range of sounds, by amplifying low-level sounds more than high-level sounds. Such aids are currently being evaluated, and have met with some success.

A second common problem in cases of cochlear hearing loss is an impairment in frequency selectivity. This has a number of consequences. First, the sufferer will be more susceptible to the effects of masking. Secondly, the ability to identify the timbre of different sounds, including speech, will be impaired. These two effects mean that the sufferer will have great difficulty in understanding speech whenever there is more than one person talking at once, or when there is background noise. Present hearing-aids cannot compensate for this problem, and as a result many people with cochlear hearing losses never go to pubs or to parties.

Further research may clarify the nature of the defects in impaired ears, and suggest ways in which those problems can be alleviated. In the meantime we should remember that for most impaired people a hearing-aid does not restore normal hearing; it may make sounds louder but it does not bring them into focus.

BRIAN C. J. MOORE

ILLUSIONS are discrepancies from truth. All the senses can suffer illusions; but because we know most about *visual* perception, visual illusions are the best known and most fully understood—though even of these many remain mysterious and controversial. All perceptions are subject to errors of many kinds; but illusions pass unnoticed except when they are strikingly inconsistent with what is accepted as true, or when there are internal inconsistencies—such as contradictory sizes or shapes, ambiguities, or paradoxes—which provide wonderful opportunities for artists, as exemplified in the ambiguous and paradoxical pictures of Maurits Escher.

Illusions are an embarrassment for those philosophers who would like to hold that knowledge is based securely on perception. Such a view is part of the empiricist tradition, which is the basis of science, but it is easy to show empirically that perception is not reliable; for at least in the laboratory, and the art gallery where interesting illusions abound, it is easy to fool the senses systematically so that all observers agree on what they perceive, though all are wrong. And we can all suffer misperceptions which may be disastrous in real-life situations, such as when driving a car or playing golf, or when doctors misread X-ray pictures. For everyone, the moon appears far too near, just beyond the horizon, and only about the size of an orange (smaller when high in the sky); yet we *know* it to be a quarter of a million miles distant and far larger than any earthly object.

Illusions are 'subjective' in our experience, and they affect behaviour and skill. Distortions of appearance can be measured, much as objects are measured, by comparisons with rulers or other physical references (Fig. 2). They may also be measured by nulling—by measuring the change in size or shape of the visually distorted object or figure necessary to compensate or 'null' the distortion, though in doing so there is a danger of changing the angles, or other parameters, responsible for the distortion (Fig. 3).

So many processes contribute to perception that it is often difficult to know which is responsible for an error, or illusion, and no doubt there are some processes going on that we know nothing about. Some illusions, such as the bright or dark after-images that hover around after one looks at a bright light—owing to local loss of sensitivity of the retinas of the eyes following strong stimulation—are clearly due to physiological adaptation. Adaptation of physiological processes of visual systems in the brain is demonstrated by Fig. 4. Such illusions may be compared with errors made by instruments. Thus after-effects from prolonged stimulation by curved lines are calibration errors. They are useful for the experimental investigation of the signalling and representing of brightness, curvature, tilt, colour, movement, and so on; for these and many other characteristics are signalled by their own neural 'channels', which may be identified as they are individually adapted and so can be isolated quite simply, to find out how they work.

Cognitive illusions are different. Their physiological bases are more subtle and more difficult to determine. In explaining any illusion the problem is how to select and concentrate on the appropriate 'level' of perceptual processing, and how to discover the particular process in which the relevant action has gone wrong. We can then ignore all the other processes, however important they may be for perception. This is not so simple for cognitive illusions, as for them there may be nothing abnormal or wrong with the anatomy, the physiology, or any of the underlying eye or brain processes. For just as any working tool, or knowledge, may be misapplied, normally functioning processes may be misdirected to produce errors, without fault of physiological function. This may occur whenever inappropriate knowledge or assumptions are brought to bear in the 'reading' of sensory signals as evidence of an object's size, distance, colour, and so on. Thus physiologists and psychologists sometimes differ when accounting for particular illusions. Whereas, for example, the well-known Müller-Lyer distortion illusion is generally explained by physiologists as due to some optical effect in the eye, or to disturbance of the signals from the retina by the angles of the 'arrowheads', very different explanations lie in the domain of cognitive psychology, as we shall see.

An undoubtedly cognitive effect is the size-weight illusion: that a small object feels heavier than a larger object (for example soup tins) of the same scale weight. One anticipates a greater weight for the larger tin, because larger objects are usually heavier than similar smaller ones, and this sets up inappropriate expectations of the muscle-power required to lift them. Similarly, an empty suitcase flies up into the air (making one feel foolish!) when it is lifted, as too much force has been applied in lifting it, on the

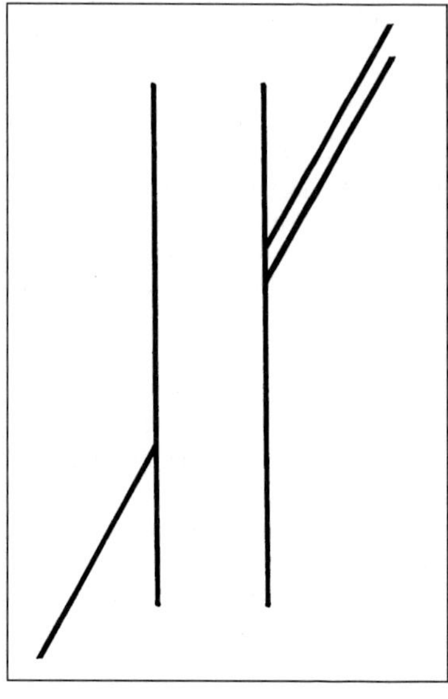

Fig. 3 Measuring a visual distortion by compensating or 'nulling' it. This can be a useful method, but it has the danger that features (such as critical angles) inducing the illusion are changed.

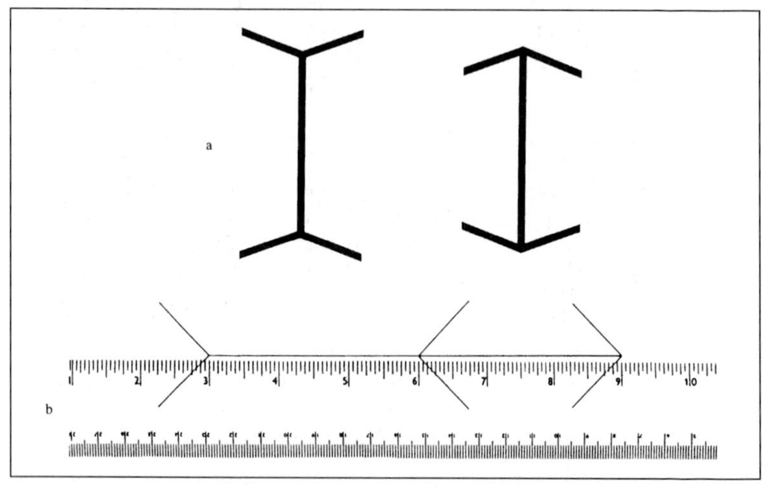

Fig. 2 **a.** Müller–Lyer illusion cancelled or 'nulled' by drawing the expanded (left) figure shorter than the shrunk (right) figure—no illusion is seen. **b.** Measuring a visual distortion by comparison with a ruler.

expectation that it will be heavy. This is a cognitive illusion because it is generated by an error of behaviour which is the result of a misleading assumption, or misleading knowledge.

For purposes of investigation, and discussion, cognitive illusions may be classified as *ambiguities*, *distortions*, *paradoxes*, and *fictions*.

Ambiguities. Some pictures, and sometimes ordinary objects, seem to change or turn into some other which may be quite different. Perception may switch between two or more alternatives (Fig. 5). What happens is that alternative hypotheses of what the object is (or where its parts lie in space) are entertained in turn. This occurs when the sensory data do not particularly favour just one possibility. A celebrated example of reversal in depth is the Necker cube (Fig. 6). A three-dimensional wire cube is a fascinating object: when it re-

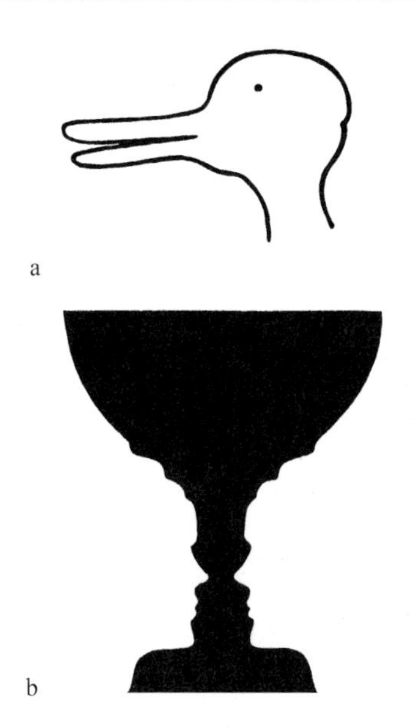

Fig. 5 Ambiguous objects. **a.** Duck–rabbit. **b.** Vase–faces. These can appear as alternative objects, according to selected rival perceptual hypothesis.

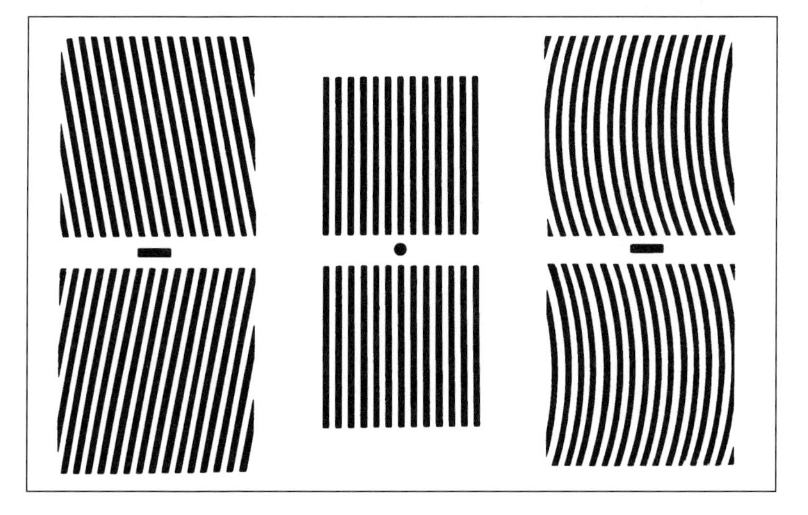

Fig. 4 Adaptation to curvature and tilt. Look at the short horizontal bar below the tilted lines for a few seconds, with the eyes moving left and right along it to avoid after-images. Then look at the vertical straight lines. Do they still look vertical? For a few seconds, they should look tilted—oppositely to the *adapting* lines. Similarly, following viewing the curved lines, the vertical lines should appear oppositely curved.

These adaptations are always opposite to the adapting stimuli—whether for shape, size, brightness, movement, or colour. It seems that specific neural channels are adapted (or fatigued), upsetting the balance of signals of position, movement, etc. The opposite colours are 'complementary' colours, such as adaptation to red producing green.

Fig. 6 Necker cube. This can be seen as switching in depth, the 'front' face reversing with the 'back' face.

verses in depth it seems to stand up on a corner, and it rotates to follow one as one moves round it. This is because the motion parallax due to the movement is 'misread', as the apparent distances of the nearer and further faces are reversed. The cube also changes in shape. Such switches in depth—or from one object to another—can occur against the evidence of other senses. Thus, holding a small wire cube in the hand while seeing it depth-reversed is remarkably interesting; for when the hand is rotated the cube is seen to rotate—impossibly—against the hand's movement. The counter information from touch does not correct the visual depth-reversal—and the wrist feels as if it is broken!

Perhaps all phenomena of ambiguity are essentially cognitive, for they depend on how sensory data are being interpreted, or 'read', in terms of objects. When there is one best bet, perception is stable; but when there are rival possibilities to be entertained, then perception becomes ambiguous, as each possibility is entertained in turn. Perception is intelligent, searching for solutions to the incredibly difficult problems of interpretation, that have to be solved hundreds of times every minute of the day.

Distortions. These are the best-known illusions: systematic distortions of size, and of length and curvature of lines or edges. Explanations remain controversial after a century of intensive investigation, by physiologists, opticians, neurologists, and psychologists—and more recently by computer programmers concerned with vision in artificial intelligence. Many distortions were discovered by optical instrument-makers placing wires in the eyepieces of measuring instruments; their aim was to improve visual accuracy, but many attempts produced disastrous errors. For example, it was found that converging lines produce distortions such as those of Fig. 7. These are large repeatable phenomena, which are easy to measure, and so are favourites for experiments. But what causes these distortions? There may be several causes, and there are certainly a score or so of (not all correct) theories.

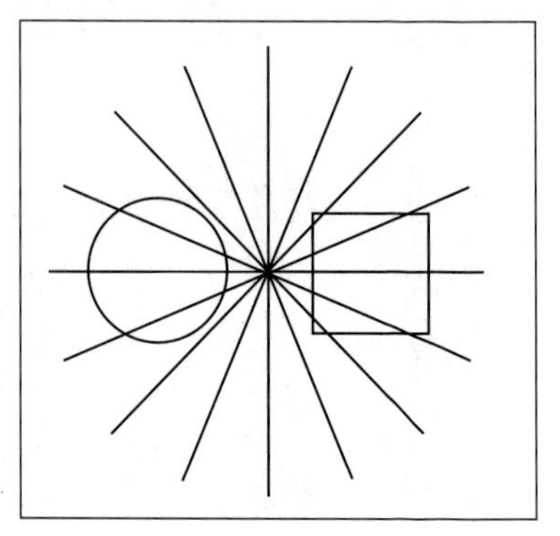

Fig. 7 Converging line distortions. One theory of why converging lines produce expansion, is that the convergence is read visually as perspective depth, or distance; this sets constancy of size for too great a distance.

Many distortions—such as adaptation to the curves, or tilted lines, of Fig. 4—are straightforwardly physiological. And there may be optical distortions such as astigmatism. A striking distortion illusion, which is almost certainly associated with physiological processes early in the visual system encoding the position of edges, is the 'café wall illusion' (Fig. 8). A reason for believing that this effect occurs early in the visual system, prior to the cognitive processes of object recognition, is that (unlike most distortion illusions) it depends on brightness differences. When the tiles are alternately coloured, for example red and green, there is no distortion, providing the colours are set to equal brightness. Also, the distortion occurs only when the brightness of the mortar, which must be narrow, lies between the brightnesses of the dark and the light tiles. Illusions due to more 'central' cognitive processes are not likely to be affected by stimulus changes which do not alter the information provided by the picture, or object. It is often very difficult, however, to be sure whether an illusion is straightforwardly physiological, or has a cognitive cause through the brain misreading the significance of information-bearing features.

Whether the distortions associated with (perspective) converging lines are straightforwardly physiological, or cognitive, remains controversial. The fact that they occur essentially unchanged for any brightness differences, for the colour-without-brightness contrast of isoluminance, and for any thickness of the lines, suggests that this is a cognitive phenomenon, which depends on certain features providing information that is misinterpreted. One theory is that depth-cues, such as perspective-convergence, set quite directly how far things appear to be, and will in some situations

Fig. 8 Café wall illusion. Named after a nineteenth-century café in Bristol which has this pattern of tiles. The long wedges are illusory. The distortion is unusual as it occurs in a figure (or object) having only right angles and parallel lines; it depends on the brightness–contrast of the 'tiles', and it only occurs when the brightness of the 'mortar' (which must be narrow) lies between the brightnesses of the tiles. There is no distortion with alternately different coloured tiles of the same brightness.

set distance or size incorrectly. An important depth-cue is perspective. The perspective shapes of retinal images are appropriate to the distances of objects only when given by objects of normal shapes, especially having parallel edges and right-angular corners. Odd shapes may be misleading: for example, the Ames room (designed by Adelbert Ames), which is not rectangular even though it gives the same image to the eye as a rectangular room, and the rotating trapezoid window which has marked perspective (as though viewed from an extreme angle), that disconcertingly persists as the window rotates.

All pictures that offer perspective challenge the eye with problems, as they present depth-cues of the objects they depict, in a space different from the picture plane. So it is hardly surprising if such pictures present problems that the visual system cannot solve without producing distortions. Pictures are essentially paradoxical, as they are flat while representing depth; so it is amazing that we see them as well as we do. These distortions obey certain rules. Features representing distance are perceptually expanded in compensation for the shrinking of the eye's images, for whereas actual objects normally look much the same size, whether near or fairly distant, their images shrink to half with each doubling of distance, just as for a camera. When the compensation for this optical shrinking is not set appropriately, it *must* produce such distortions. A test is that when depth-cues are appropriate in these illusion figures, the distortions no longer occur.

It is interesting to look at the wire cube that reverses in depth without change of the retinal image in the eye. When depth-reversed, its apparently further face looks too large, so that it seems like a truncated pyramid, expanding away from the observer. But when not reversed it looks like a true cube. Size-constancy follows the apparent distance of the faces of the cube, an example of Emmert's law. Visual size can be set in two ways—by perspective or other depth-cues, and by apparent depth—and it can be set wrongly by either. Thus there can be distortion 'bottom-up' from misleading depth-cues, or 'top-down' from inappropriate assumptions of distance.

Paradoxes. It is significant that, although we tend to see what is likely, we *can* see things that are so unlikely they appear impossible—even logically paradoxical. Striking examples are the 'impossible triangle' and 'impossible staircase' drawings of Lionel and Roger Penrose (Penrose and Penrose, 1958). But if we could see only probable objects, we would be blind to the unlikely; and this would be highly dangerous as unlikely events do sometimes occur. Indeed, if we could see only expected things there could hardly be perceptual learning. Nevertheless, it is strange that we can experience a paradox perceptually while knowing its solution conceptually, as with the 'impossible triangle' (Fig. 9). This is a simple unpainted object, made of three lengths of wood, yet from a certain point of view it looks impossible. This paradoxical perception occurs because the visual system assumes that the sides meet and touch at all three corners—though in fact at one corner they only touch *optically*, as here the sides are separated in depth. This is a cognitive effect, depending on a false assumption.

Not all perceptual paradoxes have such cognitive origins, however, for straightforward physiological errors can also produce them—as when signals arriving from one sensory channel disagree with signals from another channel, when they are differently adapted. As is well known, after one hand has been placed in hot water and the other in cold, tepid water will feel both hot and cold at the same time, when the differently adapted

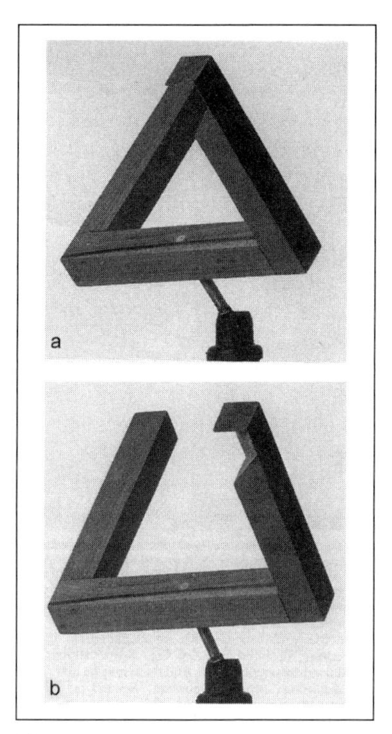

Fig. 9 Impossible Triangle. **a.** From this viewpoint it looks paradoxical. **b.** When it is rotated, one sees the answer (but returning to **a**, it still looks impossible).

hands are placed in it. Movement after-effects (from a rotating spiral) are similarly paradoxical, as they can give sensations of movement though no change of position is seen. This shows that movement and position are signalled by different neural channels, which when they disagree can produce a paradox.

Fictions. On the general account of perceptions as predictive hypotheses which is assumed here, it is not surprising that perceptions can be ambiguous, distorted, paradoxical, or even fictional. The hallucinations of schizophrenia and drug-induced hallucinations apart, some striking examples of perceptual fictions are illusory edges and ghostly surfaces, which occur in a wide variety of figures. The best examples are due to the Italian psychologist and artist Gaetano Kanizsa (Kanizsa, 1979).

Again there are several theories that attempt to account for these remarkable effects, and again there may be more than one cause. The ghostly surfaces occur in figures having surprising gaps. They are, probably, postulated by the visual system to account for the gaps, as due to occlusion or eclipsing by some nearer object or surface. In the normal course of events, parts of objects are very often hidden by nearer objects; yet we continue to recognize them as complete. The ability to recognize objects that are partly hidden is extremely useful; but to postulate a nearer object or surface on the evidence of gaps is bound to be hazardous, for sometimes gaps are surprising (Fig. 10). The tendency to postulate a surface that

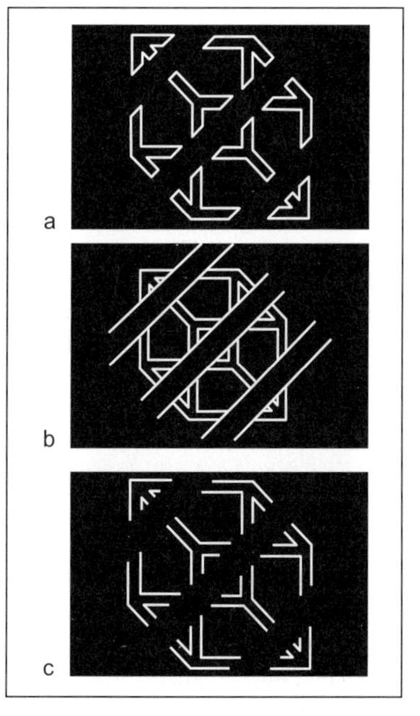

Fig. 10 Three cubes. **a.** This cube appears as separate objects. **b.** Added parallel lines reveal a cube partly hidden behind bars. **c.** Removing the parallel lines in **b** and the end blocking lines in **a** produces illusory bars—with a partly hidden cube behind them.

'should' be, but is not there, makes us see 'ghosts' in figures that have unlikely gaps with the shapes of likely objects.

The three drawings in Fig. 10 show something of the subtlety of perceptual processes, and throw light on how the world is seen as divided up into objects. This is a basic perceptual problem, as very often retinal images do not have clearly defined edges for each object. The ear has the same problem in recognizing separate words in a sentence, the sounds of speech being mainly continuous. We cannot distinguish separate words in an unfamiliar language; all we hear is an almost unbroken stream of sound. So, in order to see what is an object, and what is the space between objects, or words, perceptual learning is important.

Although one may know intellectually that one is seeing an illusion, one still *sees* the illusion. This difference between perceiving and conceiving, which applies to all robust illusions, may be because perception has to work very fast, for our survival into the next second or so. Vision, hearing, and our other senses must keep in step with external events, which are often threatening, and this requires a running prediction of what is likely to happen in the immediate future. This remarkable speed could not be achieved if perception drew upon all our knowledge. The access time would be too long. Therefore, just as the strategy of initial decision-making from a small data base is becoming necessary for large computer systems, so also is the intelligence of perception limited and subject to illusions, as sensory data are not raw, but cooked by assumptions that are often false. In many ways it is different from our total understanding—anathema though this split between perception and understanding is to philosophers expecting certainty from the senses as premises for our conceptual beliefs.

RICHARD L. GREGORY

MODELS OF MENTAL PROCESSES. The information processing tradition in cognitive psychology is constituted by attempts to specify a blueprint or circuit diagram of the functional apparatus that is assumed to underlie some aspect of intellectual performance. In this respect it has been argued that cognitive psychologists are primarily concerned with attempting to specify the mental software—the programs of the brain. Indeed in taking the software/hardware distinction further it has also been argued that cognitive psychologists can proceed without regard to any consideration of the possible neural substrate. Given such a framework for thinking about the mind, the basic aim has been to provide what have come to be called 'boxes-and-arrows accounts'. In such accounts the 'boxes' are intended to stand for a well-defined and, essentially, self-contained set of mental processes that operate upon correspondingly well-defined internal representations. The 'arrows' in such accounts merely specify the flow of information through the model. In total, the circuit diagram is assumed to specify (i) the flow of control of information from the time between when the stimulus is picked up by the senses to the execution of an overt response, together with, (ii) the manner in which the stimulus is transformed into various sorts of internal representations at different stages in the processing stream. Perhaps the most famous example of this kind of account is shown in Fig. 11.

In stark contrast to this traditional approach, connectionist accounts of mental processes begin from a quite different set of premises. Indeed by taking a connectionist view the above distinction between software and hardware is of little relevance. The starting point now is to think about how mental processes could actually be instantiated in the brain. So in order to understand the workings of the

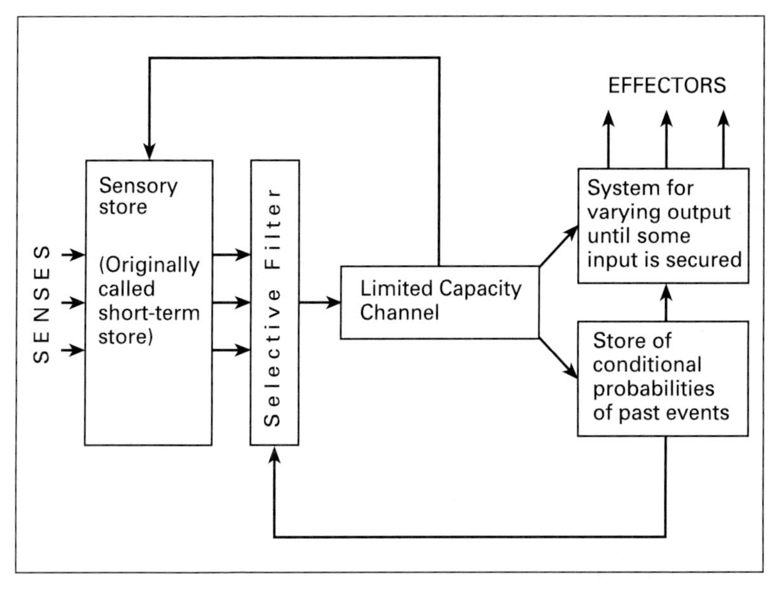

Fig. 11 A traditional 'arrows and boxes' model of human information processing. This example provides a schematic representation of Broadbent's (1958) filter theory of attention.

brain, connectionists attempted to build artificial brains. That is, connectionists have attempted to simulate mental processes by using neural-like mechanisms as specified in computer models. Fundamental is the notion that the brain is composed of independent, yet interconnected, neurons and that the behaviour of these neurons is governed by electro-chemical interactions. An aim therefore is to model, at a crude approximation, electro-chemical signal processing in simulated networks of artificial neurons. Within this framework, it is possible to discuss (i) the current state of activation across the processing units in the network—the current pattern of activation, and, (ii) the strengths of the individual connections between the units—the weights. Perhaps *the* most important insight is that learning may be characterized by adaptive changes made to the weights between the units. It is assumed that if successive and appropriate changes are made to the weights, then the network can begin to respond in a relevant manner when presented with a given stimulus.

Yet another departure from the traditional ways of thinking about cognition stems from consideration of the nature of the ways in which information is represented in a connectionist network. Typically it is possible to define a set or layer of units and to define the current pattern of activation across these units. This kind of concurrent pattern of activation constitutes what is known as a distributed representation. Different representations now correspond to different patterns of activity in the same set of units. An important contrast now is between localist and distributed representation. Whereas in traditional models of the internal representation of knowledge concepts were defined as corresponding to particular (localist) nodes in a so-called semantic network, this kind of spatial metaphor does not so readily apply to a connectionist network that utilizes distributed representations. Here different concepts correspond to different concurrent patterns of activity across the same set of units. In this sense, a particular set of units collectively represent a number of different concepts—there is no sense in which different memories reside in different parts of the machine.

One of the earliest forms of connectionist networks were known as perceptrons (Rosenblatt, 1958). Elementary perceptrons (see Fig. 12) contained a set of input (sensory) units that collectively defined the network's retina. These sensory units were connected to units known as associator units. Each of the associator units was connected to only a limited number of the sensory units. The associator units were connected to response units. Weights on the connections between the sensory and associator units were fixed, however the weights between the associator and response units were modifiable. During an initial training phase, a stimulus would be presented to the retina and activation would be propagated forward along the connections to the associator units. In the simplest case these units would, essentially, sum the product of each weighted connection and the activation as propagated along the connection. This total was compared to a threshold value and the associator unit would then take on a state of activation commensurate with pre-defined rules of activation. The pattern of activation of the associator units would then be propagated onwards to the response units. The pattern of activation across the set of response units would be computed accordingly and this would then be compared to a target pattern of activation. Any discrepancy between the actual and target output patterns—the error score—was then used in computations to change the active weights in the

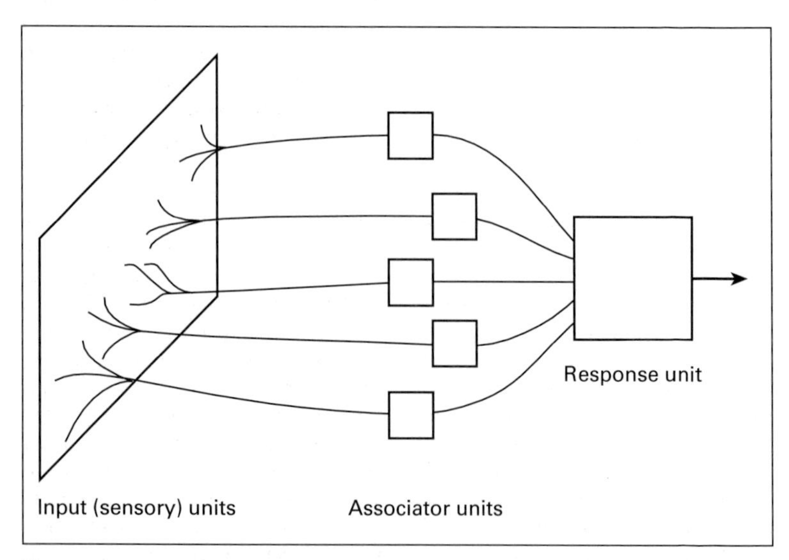

Fig. 12 A schematic representation of an elementary perceptron. Collectively the input units define the networks retina. In this example, each of the associator units is connected to three randomly chosen input units and they all also connect to a single response unit. The only modifiable weights in the network are on the connections between the associator units and the response units.

network. Although various schemes for updating the weights are feasible it was shown that certain formal methods were guaranteed to work systematically. That is, it was shown that the methods would result in the network learning to correctly classify the pattern set by making adaptive changes to its weighted connections.

Even with only a single layer of modifiable weights, elementary perceptrons were capable of mastering quite complex pattern recognition problems, for instance learning to classify the letters of the alphabet. However, these early successes were overshadowed by other work that proved in-principle limitations of these devices. For instance Minsky and Papert (1969) showed that elementary perceptrons could not learn to discriminate connected from unconnected patterns. In addition they proved that such devices could only learn to solve a very restrictive set of pattern classification problems.

Perhaps the greatest limitation however was that the networks contained only a single layer of modifiable weights. In this respect much of the more recent interest in connectionist models derives from the fact that the work has developed to a point where the behaviour of multi-layered perceptions (perceptrons with more than one layer of modifiable connections) can be explored. Landmark publications that rekindled the interest in the psychological aspects of neural network research occurred in the early eighties (Hinton and Anderson, 1981; McClelland and Rumelhart, 1986; Rumelhart and McClelland, 1986) and since then connectionist models have been developed to address most of the topics examined by traditional cognitive psychology. (See also CONNECTIONIST MODELS OF COGNITIVE DEFICITS.)

PHILIP T. QUINLAN

PERCEPTION. Our senses probe the external world. They also tell us about ourselves, as they monitor positions of the limbs and the balance of our bodies, and through pain they signal injury and illness. More subtly, there are innumerable internal signals monitoring physiological activities, and conveying and maintaining our well-being; though little of this enters our consciousness. It may surprise the non-scientist just how little of the day-by-day, second-by-second perception that allows us to survive in a threatening world is conscious. But although the processes are generally unconscious, through investigating them experimentally we can discover a great deal about the physiological basis of perception and how, as babies and later, we discover the world of objects and come to read meanings in pictures and symbols. In perception, as Sir Ernst Gombrich (1950) realized to such good effect, art and science meet.

Just how we know things through sensory experience is a question that was discussed by the Greek philosophers and has been ever since. But, perhaps curiously, planned experiments in the spirit of the physical sciences were hardly attempted much earlier than the mid-nineteenth century. Since then, the experimental study of perception has yielded fundamental knowledge for physiology and psychology, especially from the outstanding work of Hermann von Helmholtz (1867). It has revealed many surprises in the form of processes of which we are unaware, though they can often be demonstrated simply and dramatically. The study of perception, especially of vision and hearing, has allowed psychology to grow from its philosophical roots into an experimental science; yet deeply puzzling philosophical questions remain—especially over the role of consciousness. It is puzzling, both that we are aware of so *little* of perception—and that we have *any* awareness!

There is a long-standing tradition in philosophy that perception, especially touch and vision, gives undeniably true knowledge. Philosophers have generally sought certainty and have often claimed it, whereas scientists, who are used to their theories being modified and upset by new data, generally settle for today's best bet. Philosophers have a heavy investment in perception. They stake their all on the certainty of knowledge from the senses because they need secure premisses for their arguments from experience. Scientists, on the other hand, who are used to errors in measurement and observation by instruments, and have consequently found it necessary to check and compare and repeat experiments, do not so readily expect reliability from the senses. Indeed, many scientific instruments have been developed precisely because of the limitations of the senses and the unreliability of perception: for it is, after all, easy to produce and demonstrate all manner of dramatic illusions which could hardly occur if perception constituted direct reliable knowledge. Yet although illusions of object perception have been discussed by philosophers from Aristotle to Berkeley (1709), and more recently as well, philosophy generally has paid more attention to errors of logic and ambiguities of expression than to the fallibilities of perception.

Philosophers are particularly impressed by the undeniability of the 'raw experience' of sensations, such as colours and tickles and pain. The sensation of toothache may be undeniable—but are perceptions similarly as infallible? One will necessarily think so if one believes that perceptions are simply sensations; but we now regard perception as giving us knowledge, albeit surprisingly indirectly, of the causes or *sources* of sensations—such as the states of our bodies and objects in the environment—rather than of the sensations themselves. It is now clear that there are vast and still largely mysterious jumps—intelligent leaps of the mind, which may land on error—between the sensation and the perception of an object. One can indeed be wrong about the cause of toothache!

It is worth asking why we have both *perceptions* and *conceptions* of the world. Why is perception somehow separate, and in several ways different, from our conceptual understanding? Very likely it is because perception, in order to be useful, must work very quickly, whereas we may take years forming concepts, since knowledge and ideas are in a sense timeless. It would probably be impossible for perception to draw upon all of our knowledge, as it has to work so fast. Rather, it employs a rapid but not deep intelligence with a small knowledge base.

Perception is not traditionally thought of as an intelligent activity, even though the power, especially of vision, to probe distance gains the time needed for intelligent reactions to on-going events. It can be argued that the development of distance perception freed organisms from the tyranny of reflexes, and was the necessary precursor of all intelligence. The special intelligence of perception has more recently been discussed by the psychologist Irvin Rock (1984). However, an earlier account portrayed sensory perception very differently as a passive undistorting window through which the mind accepts sensations which were considered to be 'sense-data' of perception, selected and assembled somewhat like the pieces of a jigsaw puzzle. On this kind of account sense-data may be selected according to need or attention; for vision, the brain (or mind) has little to do except select and 'pick up' features of the 'ambient array' of light (Gibson, 1950, 1966).

But are sensations, such as colours and shapes and sounds, *picked up* by the senses, or are they *created* internally by the perceiver? This question about the passiveness or activeness of perception is a long-standing one which is still debated and has significant implications; for if sensations are created by the brain—a notion that receives strong support from recent physiology—they can hardly be data for perceiving the object world, whereas if they are in the world, to be 'picked up', they must exist apart from us.

This raises the question: what is 'objective' and what 'subjective'? The philosopher John Locke (1690), who was well aware of the new science of his time, suggested that there are two kinds of characteristics: *primary* characteristics, such as hardness, mass, and extension of objects in space and time—being in the world before life, and quite apart from mind—and *secondary* characteristics, which are created by mind. Thus colours are not in the world, but are created within us, though they are related in complex ways to light and the surfaces of objects.

It is generally accepted that Locke's 'primary' characteristics are present independently of mind; and it is clear that his 'secondary' characteristics are affected by states of the sensing organism—for colours change as we look through haze, or wine, and everything appears tinged with yellow if we have jaundice. It is such considerations that bring to mind the distinction between appearance and reality; even so, it is important to note that sensations do have a kind of reality, although they are created by and within us. Thus Isaac Newton, writing on sensations of colour in *Opticks* (1704), agreed with his friend Locke, saying that red light is not itself red, but is 'red-making'. Spelling this out, he said of light rays: '... there is nothing else than a certain power and disposition to stir up the sensation of this or that colour. For as sound in a bell or musical string ... is nothing but a trembling motion.' Then (in Query 23) he specifies something of the neural mechanism of vision that leads to the mysterious seat of sensation: 'Is not vision perform'd chiefly by the Vibrations of this (Eatherial) Medium, excited in the bottom of the eye by Rays of Light, and propagated through the solid, pellucid and uniform Capillamenta of the optic Nerves in the place (the "Sensorium") of Sensation?'

The empiricist school, of which in their different ways Locke and Newton were founders, rejected the notion that had been the basis of much philosophy, that minds can receive knowledge by direct intuition, quite apart from sensory experience. Mind was now regarded as essentially isolated from the physical world: linked only by tenuous threads of nerve. At the same time there were attempts to discover 'laws' of mind, corresponding in some ways to the laws of physics though seldom, if ever, seen as being in quite the same category. Newton did however write (in a letter to Henry Oldenburg, secretary of the Royal Society): 'I suppose the *Science of colours* will be granted *Mathematicall* and as certain as any part of Optiques.' Laws of colour mixture were developed later, especially following the work of Thomas Young, who made the important discovery in 1801 that all the spectral colours can be produced by mixture of various intensities of only three coloured lights. This took the sensations of colour somewhat outside the realm of physics, and yet they were seen as bound by certain laws. So evidently there could be a lawful science of sensation, and so of mind. Newton fully appreciated that colour sensations are not always given by light, as he said (*Opticks*, Query 16): 'When a Man in the dark presses either corner of his Eye with his finger, he will see a Circle of Colours like those of a Peacock's Tail.' At the same time, much like Pythagoras linking music with the physics of vibrating strings, Newton tried to describe aesthetics according to physical principles (Query 14):

> May not the harmony and disacord of Colours arise from the proportions of the Vibrations propagated through the Fibres of the optick Nerves into the Brain, as the harmony and discord of Sounds arise from the proportions of the Vibrations of the Air? For some Colours, if they are view'd together, are agreeable to one another, as those of Gold and Indigo, and others disagree.

So we find attempts to explain perceptual experience, from sensation to aesthetics, by physical principles of the natural sciences. But though, for example, colour mixture is linked to the physics of light, it is not derivable from optical principles. As the direct realism of immediate experience of the object world has been (almost universally) abandoned, we are left with having to devise bridging theories of perception, to relate mind to matter.

It is now generally accepted that perception depends on active physiologically based processes, but this notion is non-intuitive, for we know nothing of such processes or mechanisms by introspection. Moreover, perceiving objects around us seems so simple and easy! It happens so fast and so effortlessly it is hard to conceive the complexity of the processes that we now know must be involved. The notion takes us, however, to concepts familiar to engineers. It is not misleading to describe the organs of the senses—the eyes, ears, touch receptors, and so on—as 'transducers' that accept and signal patterns of energy from the external world as coded messages, which are read by the brain to infer the state-of-play of the world and of the body's own states. Another useful engineering concept is that of 'channels'. The various senses—touch, vision, hearing, and so on—are each subdivided into channels which can be discovered only by experiment. Thus, for example, although this was not at all realized before Young's (1801) colour mixture experiment, colour vision works with just three channels responding to red, green, and blue light, respectively. All the hundreds of colours we see are neurally mixtures from these three colour channels. Then there are channels representing the orientation of lines and edges, and channels for movement, as shown by direct physiological recording from the visual cortex, and demonstrated dramatically by Hubel and Wiesel (1962). By less physiologically direct methods, such as selective adaptation, it has been found that there are more or less independent channels for spatial frequency and many other visual characteristics. The ear has many frequency channels, and there is a score of channels for touch, various kinds of pain, tickle, and for monitoring the positions of the limbs and setting muscle tensions for moving them appropriately. Somehow the outputs from the many channels are combined to give consistent perceptions. Small discrepancies—such as the delay in sound between seeing a ball hit a bat and hearing the impact—are rejected, or pulled into place, to maintain a consistent world.

For signalling by the senses, as from instruments, it is important to appreciate the range of likely or possible objects that may be present. The eye receives all sorts of irrelevant stimuli which are mainly disregarded, just as unwanted data and random disturbances are rejected whenever possible by scientific instruments and in computer signal-processing. Sometimes, though, what is rejected turns out to be just what is needed! The immense difficulties encountered in current attempts to program computers to recognize objects from signals provided by television cameras indicate the incredible complexity and subtlety of animal and human perception.

David Marr (1980) suggested that object shapes are derived from images via three essential stages: (i) the 'primal sketch'(es), describing intensity changes, locations of critical features such as terminal points, and local geometrical relations; (ii) the '21/2-D sketch', giving a preliminary analysis of depth, surface discontinuities, and so on, in a frame that is centred on the viewer; (iii) the '3-D model representation', in an object-centred coordinate system, so that we see objects much as they are in 3-D space though they are presented from just one viewpoint. Marr supposed that this last stage is aided by restraints on the range of likely solutions to the problem of what is 'out there', the information-processing restraints being set by assuming typical object shapes—for example that many objects, such as human beings, are modified cylinders. Interestingly, the painter Paul Cézanne came close to this notion in 1904: 'Treat nature by the cylinder, the sphere, the cone, everything in proper perspective so that each side of an object or a plane is directed towards a central point... nature for us men is more depth than surface....'

The limited variety of typical objects may set restraints that are useful, both for the artist representing objects and for the artificial intelligence endeavour to program computers to see; but although it can be difficult to represent or see some atypical objects (or even familiar objects from atypical viewpoints) perhaps it is not clear that these difficulties reflect accepted restraints based on cylinders, spheres, and cones—for many other very different shapes can be depicted and seen without special difficulty.

Looking 'inwards' by introspection, we *seem* to know that perceptions are made of sensations, although from physiological and psychological experiment—as well as from this essentially engineering approach—it has to be denied that sensations are the data of perception. The data are neural *signals* from the transducer senses, analysed by many parallel channels to generate immediately useful predictive hypotheses, which are our perceptual reality of the object world.

It has usually been thought that perception occurs *passively* from inputs from the senses. It is now, however, fairly generally accepted that stored knowledge and assumptions *actively* affect even the simplest perceptions. The relative importance of what are called (especially in artificial intelligence) passive 'bottom-up' processes to active 'top-down' processes is a central controversy. Some evidence bearing on this is presented in the entry **illusions**. The changes of shape of wire cubes which reverse spontaneously in depth (Fig. 6, p. 18) is clear evidence of subtle 'top-down' processes affecting what used to be regarded as simple characteristics such as size and brightness. But these must be knowledge-based, 'top-down' effects because there are no changes of input from the eyes with depth-reversals of ambiguous figures. These are examples of how illusory phenomena can reveal processes of the perception we depend upon for our knowledge of the world and ourselves.

RICHARD L. GREGORY

REMEMBERING. If one asks teachers, students, or the proverbial man or woman in the street for the best available techniques for remembering something, the answers will be quite varied. However, one recurrent theme is sure to be: 'Repeat it!' A psychologist is likely to comment: 'Yes, but . . . repetition by itself, mere repetition, does not help.' Yet the history of experimental investigations of memory is to a large extent concerned with mere repetition. In fact, the father of the experimental psychology of memory, Hermann Ebbinghaus, started his investigations in Germany in the last quarter of the nineteenth century by focusing almost exclusively on the effect of repetition. How many repetitions did it take to learn a list of words (or nonsense syllables)? How many trials were saved in relearning some list as a function of its prior repetition?

Both the common lore about repetition and the influence of Ebbinghaus dictated a preoccupation with the effect of repeated rehearsals. After all, it is well known that repeating a telephone number between looking it up and dialling it protects it from disappearance. And handsome, negatively accelerated learning curves resulted from numerous experiments that studied the effect of repetition on retention. But repetitive activities do not lead to effortless retrieval. Actually, when we try to remember an address, a name, the title of a book, or the plot of a play, we seem to engage in rather complicated search operations. The success of these operations depends not so much on how often we have repeated the required information in the past as on the proper embedding (the organization) of the target information within the larger flux of our knowledges and memories. When shopping for the weekend meals, we might retrieve the meats to be bought as a single memorial 'chunk', and liquid refreshments in another. Or another shopper might organize a mental shopping list by remembering what to buy in terms of what is where in the local supermarket. Both of these schemas are kinds of organizations of the to-be-remembered things, and both require effort. Trying to recall the plot of a play, the rememberer might first recall vaguely the gist ('It was about a family who were always arguing') and then more and more details within coherent subdivisions ('Yes, there was the unhappy daughter and her pitiful suitor').

The notion that organization and structure are essential for memory retrieval is not novel. Extensive mnemonic techniques date at least to ancient Greece, where orators constructed complex spatial and temporal schemata as an aid in rehearsing and properly presenting their speeches. In modern times the associationism of British empiricism and German experimentalism was seriously questioned during the first half of the twentieth century by the Gestalt psychologists in general and by the British psychologist F. C. Bartlett in particular. Today we know in some detail what it is that repetition makes possible, what it is that is needed in addition to *mere* repetition.

A set of objects, events, or mental representations is said to be organized when consistent relations among the members of the set can be identified and specified. The result of such organization is called a structure. Structures may exist among events in the world as well as among mental events. A special kind of structure is the schema which is a mental structure, specifically an organized representation of a body of knowledge. Thus, schemata determine the expectations people have about events to be encountered, and about the spatial and temporal structure of those events.

The organization of to-be-remembered material takes time and conscious capacity. If we are told to remember a luncheon appointment while reading a book or watching our favourite television programme, conscious capacity is taken up by these primary activities and little organizational action will result. In order to remember the luncheon appointment we need to retrieve other plans (schemata) about the specific day and 'fit in' the appointment. For example, we need to store such things as 'After the dentist, go to work, but go to the luncheon an hour later'. In the temporal organization of that day's plan, dentist, work, and luncheon will form an appropriate mental schema. And thinking about these plans (repeating them) will make their proper retrieval on the appointed day more likely. But again it is not mere repetition that provides a better schema, rather it is the anchoring of the relevant events within better, richer, and more accessible events that provides the more effective schema. Thus, each repetition provides an opportunity to relate the target event (the luncheon) to other events and thoughts. We may store the fact that our best friend will be at the luncheon, that it is held at a favourite restaurant, etc. etc. Each of these additions produces a more elaborate structure, and the more elaborate the retrieval opportunities for a target event the more likely it is that it will be recalled. Repetition provides opportunities for the organization of the to-be-remembered events.

While it is the case that most events are stored in long-term memory in complex, multistructured forms, certain frequently used structures can be identified. First there is the categorical or subordinate kind of structure in which a list of instances is stored under a general concept or label. To recall all the animals we know requires the use of such subordinate structures within a hierarchy of categories. Typically we gain access to some general animal category and then generate its subcategories such as domestic animals and cat-like animals. Second there are co-ordinate structures of a few, usually less than five, events or things that are related to one another. Spatial structures, such as the directions of the compass, are one good example; another is the set of things called a table-setting. Whereas in the categorical structure the higher-order label or node retrieves the lower instances, in the co-ordinate structure the members of the set act as retrieval points for one another. The third kind of structure is a serial or pro-ordinate structure in which a string of events is organized, usually in a temporal or spatial form. An excellent example is the way we retrieve the alphabet, another is the structure that represents the route we take to work from home. Parts of the serial string act as retrieval cues for subsequent things or events.

These idealized structures usually interact within any complex memorial event. More important, they are incorporated within the more general spatio-temporal schemata mentioned earlier. Thus the understanding of a conversation involves the kinds of expectation inherent in our schemata for social conversations, story schemata tell us to look for crucial aspects and themes of a story, restaurants require that we have the proper schema for ordering from menus, talking to waiters, and so forth. The episodes of our daily lives are organized within such schemata, which in turn incorporate the three kinds of structures described above.

Up to now the description of memory systems has focused on the recall of information. Another important kind of memory feat involves the recognition of previously encountered events. We are able to determine that people, rooms, foods, tunes are events that we have previously met, seen, tasted, heard.

Not only do we know that we have encountered them before but we usually also know who or what they are. Conversely we sometimes know only that the event is familiar without knowing exactly who that person is, where we have seen that room before, what kind of food it is, what the name of a tune is. It is the latter phenomenon that has generally been studied by psychologists under the rubric of recognition.

The recognition of prior occurrence is a two stage process involving two distinct mechanisms. One of them is a judgement of familiarity, the other a retrieval process essentially identical to that discussed for the recall of information. The judgement of familiarity is an automatic process, requiring no conscious effort and occurring as an immediate response to the event. However, the familiarity of information available of the event may be inadequate to make a confident judgement of prior occurrence. In that case a search process queries the long-term memory system whether the event in question is in fact retrievable. If such an attempt is successful then the event is considered to be 'old', i.e. having been previously encountered. Thus, recognition involves a judgement of familiarity which is supplemented by a retrieval attempt. For example, we meet someone who looks vaguely familiar, but the definite judgement that we know that person is not made until we can recapture the place or context where we have previously encountered him or her.

The process of judging familiarity brings us back to the problem of repetition, because mere repetition does affect familiarity. The more frequently an event has been observed the more likely it is to be recognized on the basis of familiarity alone. Thus, repetition does have a function, but not for the retrieval of information. Repetition affects the process of integrating the representation of an event; it establishes its familiarity independent of its context or its relations to other mental contents.

Finally, errors of memory can obviously be of two kinds, retrieval errors and, less frequently, errors of familiarity judgements. Given the structural, schematic organization of memory storage, it is obvious that some events that 'fit' into the appropriate schema are likely to be retrieved even though they were not originally encountered. One might remember having witnessed an argument in a play because the structure of the play is stored under some general schema of 'family conflict', or one might 'recall' having seen a particular red armchair before, because it was stored as 'striking looking furniture'. Thus, errors of memory are often even more instructive about the nature of mental structure than the normal recovery of information.

GEORGE MANDLER

SHORT-TERM MEMORY. Memory for what happened an hour ago or a year ago fulfils an obvious function in our lives. However, our capacity to store information for periods measured in seconds is equally if not more important to our integrity as human beings. This capacity is referred to as short-term memory (STM). Descartes asserted, 'I think, therefore I am'. It is equally true to say 'I think, therefore I have short-term memory'. Indeed any mental activity extended in time, including the production and comprehension of language, must involve STM. It is certainly fortunate that STM is robust and, unlike long-term memory, is seldom affected by old age, drugs, or brain damage.

The most familiar fact about STM is the existence of the so-called span of immediate memory. A rough definition of the span is that it is the longest sequence of items that can be reproduced correctly following a single presentation. However, the same individual may manage a sequence of seven items on one occasion and make a mistake with a sequence of only five items on another. Accordingly, the span is in fact defined as that length of sequence for which the chance of correct reproduction is fifty-fifty. The span has a number of interesting properties. Two are as follows. First, for items in random order, the span is about seven, plus or minus two. This is surprising in that the amount of information per item has little effect on the span. For example, the span for binary digits (0,1) is only slightly longer than for decimal digits (the digits 0 to 9), although the latter contains over three times as much information. Second, within wide limits, the span is almost unaffected by the rate at which items are presented, and is therefore relatively independent of the time elapsing between the presentation of an item and its recall. These two facts are nicely explained by the so-called slot theory. On this theory, the span reflects the capacity of an information store in the brain with about seven 'slots'. Each slot is capable of storing a single item or unit. Once the store is full, new items can only be stored by displacing existing items. Variation in the span is attributed on this theory to the fact that a unit can sometimes comprise more than one item. For example, two or more digits can sometimes be recoded as a familiar number which can then be stored as a unit. Indeed, if an individual has an exceptional familiarity with numbers he may have a digit span of fifteen or more. However, recoding digits into familiar numbers cannot account for the digit span of eighty recently achieved by one individual after extensive practice, who reported using both recoding and a hierarchical grouping strategy. At best, therefore, the slot theory describes the mechanism which *normally* determines the span.

Two other interesting facts force another qualification to the slot theory. The span is reduced if the items of the sequence sound similar. For example, the sequence B V T C P is more difficult than the sequence S K L R N. If reproduction of the sequence involves retrieving the items from separate slots, why should this be so? Similarly, the span is smaller for long words than for short words, which is puzzling if each word is a unit and occupies a separate slot. With visual presentation, both the effect of similarity of sound and of word length vanish if the subject is asked to count aloud during presentation of the sequence. (At the same time, the counting task somewhat reduces the span.) This suggests that normally there is sub-vocal rehearsal of earlier items during presentation of later items of the sequence and that such rehearsal contributes to the span as normally measured.

Since the slot theory postulates a special store for STM, by implication there must be a different store for long-term memory (LTM). Evidence for a two-store view of memory comes from memory pathology. Amnesia due to brain damage can take one of two forms. In the common form, STM is intact but LTM, in the sense of the ability to form new permanent memories, is impaired. In a rare form, which has only been identified quite recently, the reverse is found, with LTM intact but STM impaired. Clearly independent impairment of STM and LTM is highly consonant with the two-store theory. However, recent theory tends to postulate not one but several stores for the temporary storage of information. Indeed, evidence from the study of patients with impaired STM suggests that there are separate temporary stores for auditory speech sounds and for non-verbal sounds.

Other evidence has been interpreted as showing that there are also temporary stores associated with touch and vision, although information from the latter fades in less than a second. There is also the possibility that the brain has temporary stores concerned with making responses. In the case of speech, for example, such a store might hold in readiness the codes for articulating several words and would substantially assist the smooth production of speech. Accordingly, the span of immediate memory (and STM generally) may reflect the output of one or more temporary stores, depending on circumstances. The common characteristic of these postulated stores is that each is of limited capacity and new information displaces old information. The slot theory of the span therefore seems too simple, although the facts it explains need to be accommodated in more complex accounts of the mechanisms underlying STM. If short-term memory depends on specialized stores holding information over short intervals of time, the question arises of how information reaches the store responsible for LTM. One possibility is that there is a process of information transfer from these stores to the LTM store. If so, this process is presumably successful for only a proportion of the information entering the temporary stores, since we forget more than we remember. A second possibility is that information enters the LTM store directly at the time of perception, although at a slower rate than it enters the temporary stores. On this hypothesis, STM as we observe it may depend both on information retrieved from temporary stores and on information retrieved from the LTM store. At present, there is no decisive evidence favouring either possibility. Indeed, some theorists prefer to view memory as a single complex system. For example, the different properties of STM and LTM can be held to reflect, not the operation of different stores, but factors affecting the ease of retrieving stored information. This sort of theory is not implausible in view of the fact that problems associated with the retrieval of information from a storage system often impose major constraints on efficiency. However, the detailed facts about STM do seem to favour the view that specialized temporary stores are involved. Ideally, there would be physiological evidence to show how many stores underlie memory, but at present the evidence is indirect and difficult to interpret. JOHN BROWN

SMELL. Although all living things, both plant and animal, respond selectively to at least some of the chemicals in their environments, what we ordinarily mean by smell is more limited than this. There are really two ways of deciding whether or not we are dealing with smelling rather than some other chemical sense. In the vertebrates—fishes, amphibians, reptiles, or mammals—we define smell as involving the stimulation of the first cranial nerve, the olfactory nerve. In the invertebrates, however, we refer to smell when the stimulating substance is airborne. Thus, for example, a moth finds his mate by means of smell. This inclusion of the invertebrates is important because much of the best controlled (and economically important) study has been and is being done on insects. In man, of course, both these qualifications apply and we speak of smell as involving the first cranial nerve and as having airborne molecules as its stimuli.

In man and other mammals the receptors for smell lie in the mucous membrane at the top or back of the air passages in the nose. These sensitive cells are in a constant state of decline and replacement. They are equipped with hair-like projections, the cilia, which protrude into the mucus and are the probable sites of odorant-receptor interaction. In man, the region of each nostril that they occupy is about the area of a postage-stamp—small compared with, say, that in the dog. The cells send their axons directly into the olfactory bulb, which is also relatively small. (Smell is unique among the senses in not having connections through the thalamus to the 'new cortex' or neocortex that has developed in relation to the other sense departments. In fact, the older portion of the forebrain of mammals is called the 'rhinencephalon', or 'smell brain', because of this.) There are many fewer transmission cells in the bulb than there are receptors, and this fact, in addition to the preservation of spatial distribution from receptor surface to bulb, is thought to be important in the perception of odour quality. The system is sensitive and compares well, even in man, with most laboratory methods of analysis: for example, one form of musk can be detected by a 'normal' person at a dilution of less than one ten-millionth of a milligram per litre of air.

Attempts to understand the manner in which odorous molecules affect the receptor cells have led to considerable theorizing without conspicuous success. The problem to be solved is similar to that for any of the senses: how a stimulating agent so alters a cell as to set in play the series of events that result in one or more nerve impulses being transmitted to the central nervous system. In man it is obvious that the molecules either make their way through the mucus and affect the receptor directly in some way, or act at a distance. Both means have been proposed. In explanation of action at a distance, it has been suggested that the characteristic infra-red absorption spectrum of a molecule leads it to absorb radiation from certain of the matching receptors. Unfortunately, this is thermodynamically impossible. Other absorption theories, such as the Raman spectrum and ultra violet, seem aimed more at classifying the molecules than at implying action at a distance.

Theories supposing action directly on the receptor are better supported by modern research. Many have been developed with pharmacological or immunological models in mind. The current conception of the receptor cell membrane as a lipid (fatty) double layer in which protein molecules are embedded in mosaic fashion is compatible both with the suggestion that the molecules actually dissolve in (or 'puncture') the lipid, rather like the anaesthetic action of ether, and with the notion that adsorption takes place on the proteins. Evidence of molecules that differ only in being 'right-' or 'left-handed' implies that the proteins are involved, and the theory provides a simple basis for understanding the selectivity of different cells. Precisely what energy transfer is involved is uncertain, but with modern membrane research methodology, including the use of radioactive tracers, resolution of this problem should be forthcoming.

The pervasive role of smell in everyday life is often overlooked. Many unpleasant smells, such as of garbage and offal in the city of not so long ago, have been got rid of. Highly sophisticated methods of washing, filtering, and incinerating odorous discharges have been developed, and there is a host of personal deodorants and air 'purifiers'. On the other side of the coin, the flavours of foods are pretty largely determined by odour—a fact recognized by the international flavour industry. Closely related is perfumery, with its long history.

In the fashions that have surrounded perfumery, sexual attractiveness may be involved. Certainly in many species, particularly the insects, naturally secreted odours, pheromones, play a sexual role. In mammals, pheromones also play an important role in the establishment of territories: the 'marking' activities of dogs are well known, and in other species special glands—for example, the cheek glands of the rabbit—produce marking chemicals. In the mouse the sexual and marking functions come together—the female will ovulate after smelling a male, and will, if pregnant, abort upon smelling a strange male. While some Primates—the baboon, for instance—seem to have female pheromones secreted during receptivity, it is not presently clear what role, if any, such secretions might play in man.

One function of smelling is well known: the detection of leaking gas. To non-odorous gases, a warning agent such as ethyl mercaptan is added. In mines, the ventilating system is used to carry the warning. An apparent over-representation of older people among the victims of a gas leakage in London led to useful research on the effect of age on sensitivity to smell.

For smell, unlike colour, there is no satisfactory classification scheme. One difficulty is the absence of truly abstract terms such as red or blue; rather, the terms refer to objects (for example, lavender or fruity) or condition (burnt or rotten). Possibly no simple scheme will be found, for the basic scale along which we place odours is from pleasant to unpleasant—a scale that may reflect the approach-avoidance nature of behaviour in evolutionary history. It may be the only way for the organism to classify odours.

Three other topics need mention. First, there are considerable differences between the smell sensitivity of individual persons. Some even, because of disease or trauma, cannot smell anything at all—they are anosmic—while others lack sensitivity for specific odours—they are partially anosmic. Second, adaptation (that is, temporary loss of sensitivity with exposure) proceeds fairly rapidly for smells. This is largely a matter of reduced transmission in the brain, rather than fatigue of the receptors. It makes some jobs tolerable; but sensitivity to warning agents is reduced. Finally, it may be that sensitivity declines with age. If this is in fact so, and it is not certain, then among the important consequences would be diminished stimulation from flavours (see **taste**). Possibly some of the nutritional problems of ageing are ascribable to declining sensitivity.

F. NOWELL JONES

TASTE. Flavour is usually defined as the overall sensation of taste and smell. Taste refers to sensations arising from the taste receptors in the mouth and throat while smell arises from receptors in the nose. When a person has a cold or blocks his nose, he will taste but not smell food adequately, so the flavour is reduced. It is unfortunate that in everyday language the words 'taste' and 'flavour' are used interchangeably. Taste and smell, together with texture, visual appearance, and sound will give the overall sensory percept of the food, which is important in its choice and enjoyment. People who cannot perceive the flavour of food will often not maintain an adequate diet.

There are two main groups of scientists who are interested in understanding taste. The first group consists of food scientists within the food industry, who are interested in discovering the precise mechanisms of flavour perception so as to be able to maintain and control the flavour of the products being manufactured. Furthermore, food scientists use human judges to measure the physical and chemical characteristics of foods that are important for the flavour, texture, appearance, and sound of the food. They exploit the fact that the human senses are often more sensitive than laboratory instruments, to the minute quantities of chemicals present in a food that endow it with its characteristic flavour.

The second group of scientists are more interested in the workings of the senses and the brain *per se*. Knowledge of how a taste stimulus reacts with the membrane of a taste receptor would provide information not only about mechanisms of flavour, but also about other similar chemoreceptive functions involved in drug, hormone, brain, and cell mechanisms. Changes in taste perception are beginning to be utilized as diagnostic tools in medicine, while further research is providing insights into areas ranging from genetics to the working of insect and animal attractants and repellants. For this reason, taste, along with smell, is of vital interest to a broad range of scientists.

The behavioural measurement of taste, whether for the sensory evaluation of a food flavour or for elucidating taste mechanisms, can pose problems. People do not pay as much attention to taste as they do to vision and are thus less practised at assessing the taste sensations that they experience. One consequence of this is difficulty with language, for our language is largely concerned with visual stimuli. There are many adjectives available to describe colour but few for taste. Furthermore, parents teach their children to name colours but do not do so for tastes, so that, while young children are fairly skilled at colour-naming, even adults can misname common sweet, sour, salty, and bitter stimuli. In particular, the terms 'sour' and 'bitter' are often confused, but this is merely a matter of definition. The confusion can be remedied by giving tasters citric acid and quinine to compare and informing them that the correct descriptions are 'sour' and 'bitter' respectively.

Aside from these common descriptions, there is little agreement on the use of taste adjectives and individuals usually acquire their own sets of definitions or taste concepts. For precise evaluation and communication of the taste or flavour of a foodstuff, however, a precise language has to be invented, for which the breadth of use of the taste adjectives has to be precisely controlled and agreed upon by those using the language. Usually, *ad hoc* languages are invented for a given food, so that although say, expert tea-tasters may be able to communicate amongst themselves, their language would be 'foreign' to expert wine- or mayonnaise-tasters.

The method of language invention generally adopted is to follow the way that children learn colours: words are paired with appropriate sensations. Thus, languages are invented to describe the tastes, odours, and textures of foods, using a set of physical taste standards which are always available to define the adjectives used. These methods fall under the general heading of flavour-profiling. There are problems, however, in ensuring that judges have the same breadth of use of the words in their invented language and this is still a subject of research. Without any special training, our command of vocabulary for taste is so poor that the merest suggestion of a word denoting a taste, in the instructions to a person judging a taste, will bias him to use that word. In fact, the power of suggestion is so strong that people have reported experiencing smells that they were told had been transmitted by television.

Different cultures have their own, idiosyncratic languages and confusions about taste, dependent probably on their dietary habits. Just as 'sour' and 'bitter' are confused in English, so it was reported at the beginning of this century that the islanders of the Toreros Straits confused 'sour' and 'salty'. Many tribes of North American Indians were unfamiliar with salt until they had contact with Europeans, when they described salt as 'sour'. Some inhabitants of Polynesia and New Guinea had only one word to describe sweet, sour, and bitter. Recent studies have shown a tendency among Malay speakers to qualify taste adjectives. Thus, *masin* meaning 'salty', is often qualified: *masin ayer laut* (salty like seawater), *masin garam* (salty like salt), or *masin kitchup* (salty like soy sauce). It is not clear why Malay speakers should spontaneously volunteer more detail, though it may be because mothers teach their daughters to cook by telling them to add the various ingredients until the food has a specific taste, rather than to add pre-measured amounts of ingredient according to recipes. The need for precise communication about taste would encourage the development of a precise language. Whatever the reason for such precision, it would be a useful strategy for flavour-profiling techniques.

Spanish has three words for sour and bitter: *amargo* (bitter), *acido* (sour), and *agno* (sour or bitter). Spanish dictionaries vary in their definition of *agno*, and Spanish speakers, although eager to explain the correct usage as they see it, are generally inconsistent in the use of this word. The Japanese have words for 'sweet' (*amai*), 'sour' (*suppai*), 'salty' (*shiokarai*), and 'bitter' (*nigai*), and, in addition, a commonly used taste-word that is absent from the English language: *umami*—the taste encountered in several broths that are used as a stock, in which foods are cooked and to which they give their characteristic *umami* taste. Such umami-tasting broths can be made from *komhu* (a type of seaweed: *Laminiaria japonica*), from *katsuobushi* (dried bonito flakes), or from *shiitake* (a large mushroom, *Lentinus edodus*). Nowadays, the taste principles of these foods are commercially available as *umami* seasonings such as monosodium glutamate. Although the scientific term for the taste is *umami*, many Japanese call it the 'Ajinomoto' taste, after the name of the company that first made monosodium glutamate commercially available. Although English speakers can perceive the taste, they do not have an appropriate word to describe it, unless they are specially trained, and will often call it 'salty', with the qualification that it does not taste like common salt. The situation is rather as if there were no word in English for 'orange' and people had to describe the colour as 'sort of red'.

Interestingly, the idea that there are four primary tastes, sweet, sour, salty, and bitter, is quite arbitrary. In any case, what is meant by the term 'primary taste' has not been defined. It could mean the unit of types of reaction that can take place on the membrane of the taste receptor, or of types of neural code that can communicate sensations to the brain, or even of processes that can take place in the cortex which result ultimately in the sensation of taste. Whichever of these candidates for primacy is adopted, the operative number is not known, for the idea that there are *four* primary tastes came into the taste literature by misunderstanding and accident. In spite of the absence of any firm physiological evidence, some scientists still cling to the idea. The notion is often reflected in the way that taste experiments are designed: the taste stimuli used in research studies being limited to just four, or judges being allowed to use combinations of only four words to describe their whole range of taste experience.

Measurement of taste, as with the other senses, can produce difficulties. One interesting problem is the effect of adaptation. The brain tends to protect itself from having to cope with too much information, by simply 'turning down the volume control' on stimulation that is unchanging. There is no point in paying attention to a message that is merely repeating itself. This phenomenon of sensory adaptation is often experienced with smell. Should a person enter a room that smells of sweat or perfume, the smell receptors will send corresponding smell messages to the brain. However, because the person does not leave the room, the same smell message will be repeated and the smell sensation will gradually vanish. Should the person leave the room and return, the smell sensation will reappear. Another way of envisaging this is to think of the smell mechanism as re-setting the 'zero-level' for smell—the concentration at which the smell stimulus is perceived as odourless.

Taste receptors are bathed in saliva, which is secreted from the salivary glands, and contains low concentrations of taste stimuli such as sodium chloride or potassium chloride; these can come from the blood and reflect the physiological state of the organism. The taste receptors adjust so that the zero-level for taste (or taste zero) is set at the stimulus level in the saliva. For example, the level of salt in saliva is highest in the morning, drops until the afternoon, and then rises again to the high morning value. The taste zero appears to do the same, so that these salivary changes cause no sensation of taste; rather, the taste zero changes with the slow rise and fall of secreted salivary constituents. This constant adjustment is a useful way of ensuring that tastes are registered only when sudden large changes take place, such as when foods are placed in the mouth. Salivary concentrations can vary tenfold in value and may form the basis for changes in taste sensitivity connected with various diseases; however, they are comparatively unimportant compared to the effect described next.

When, during an experiment, a taste stimulus like salt is tasted, it is sipped and then expelled from the mouth by spitting. However, spitting will not expel all the stimuli and while the person is spitting out the residual stimulus, his taste zero is rising to a higher level to render the residual tasteless. Thus, when the subject believes he has expelled all the residual stimulus, because his mouth feels tasteless, there will still be considerable amounts remaining and these will maintain a higher taste zero. The next stimulus will then be tasted with this new, higher taste zero; the taste system will not be as sensitive. This constant zero-drift has caused considerable trouble in taste measurement; the resulting changes in salivary concentration can be 100-fold and highly significant. If the residual stimulus is continually expelled from the mouth by a regime of water rinses between tastings, a lower average taste zero will be maintained. This confers a greater sensitivity, as well as ensuring that given stimuli taste more intense. Thus, the practice of rinsing between tastings, once thought to be an unimportant experimental detail, can be shown to have a major effect on taste sensitivity, and accounts for major variations in experience reported in the taste literature. One way of circumventing the problem of zero-drift in taste measurement, is to flow taste stimuli over the tongue. This prevents any residual taste stimuli from remaining in the saliva and affecting taste sensitivity. It also allows the taste receptors to be re-set to a constant zero level, between each tasting, by using a standard adapting flow. The taste receptors can adapt to tastelessness in this standard flow, thereby resetting the taste zero to the same level before tasting each new stimulus. The technique is powerful enough to allow tasters to distinguish between once- and twice-distilled water. However, little is yet known about the mechanisms of taste adaptation; even the extent to which taste receptors can 'zero-adjust' has not been explored.

Thus, a stimulus becomes tasteless to the extent that it can resemble saliva. Certainly the osmotic properties of saliva are nearer to those of tapwater than to distilled water, so distilled water has more of a taste than tapwater. The flat taste of distilled water is a sub-zero or subadapting taste; in fact, pure water can appear to have a whole range of tastes depending on the adaptation state of the taste receptors. Changes in taste zero for a range of receptors during eating or experimentation will lessen or accentuate certain aspects of the taste of other stimuli. This may form the basis for the choice of certain wines with certain foods. A sweet wine may be more suitable for drinking with a sweet dessert because adaptation to one would lessen the sweetness of the other.

MICHAEL O'MAHONEY

TOUCH. Objects in contact with the skin can arouse a variety of tactile sensations, of which introspection allows several qualities to be distinguished: for example, vibration, steady pressure, light touch. The sensations can be graded in intensity in a predictable manner in relation to the magnitude of the stimulus, as described quantitatively by the Weber-Fechner and Stevens's power law relations. The position of an applied stimulus, both absolute for a single point and relative with respect to two loci of stimulation, can be detected, with varying degrees of accuracy, in different parts of the body surface.

The physiological mechanisms underlying these perceptual properties can be analysed in a systematic manner, starting with the neural receptor elements in the skin. These are at the ends of axons connected with the spinal cord and brain stem. Neural processing occurs at the spinal, brain stem, and thalamic levels on the pathway from the skin to the cerebral cortex. Further processing in the somatosensory area of the cerebral cortex and in the adjacent association areas of the cortex leads to final elaboration of sensation, where perception is assumed to occur.

The groundwork of knowledge, as of other sensory systems, was laid in experiments on anaesthetized or conscious animals, in which very precise studies of morphology, physiology, and behaviour could be made. This knowledge has recently been extended, in a dramatic way, by electrophysiological and correlated psychophysical studies, to conscious human subjects, with a remarkable degree of concordance with the animal studies.

Cutaneous sensory tactile receptors. The skin contains several kinds of encapsulated mechanoreceptors (tactile receptors) innovated by myelinated dorsal root nerve fibres, and each kind is specialized to detect particular parameters of a mechanical stimulus. The *Pacinian corpuscle*, the first cutaneous receptor to be discovered, is relatively large, up to 2 mm long and 1 mm in diameter, and is present in the deeper layers of both hairy and hairless (glabrous) skin. It is pearl-shaped and comprises a lamellated structure, with an outer capsule, outer lamellae, inner lamellae, and in its core the specialized rod-like nerve terminal. The corpuscle is adapted to respond to vibration, with maximal sensitivity at 200–300 hertz and a range (band width) of 20 to 1,500 hertz. It is capable of detecting movements smaller than a micrometer (about one-twenty-fifth of one-thousandth of an inch). The lamellae are high-pass filters that prevent steadily maintained pressure from penetrating to the nerve terminal in the core, but allow rapidly changing pressures to do so, so that vibrations can be detected, even in the presence of maintained pressure.

Meissner's corpuscles are encapsulated and present in the glabrous skin of Primates, including man. They lie in rows just below the epidermis, in dermal papillae. The papillae correspond to the familiar surface ridges of the fingers and toes that form each individual's distinctive fingerprint. Meissner's corpuscles are innovated by myelinated axons and, like Pacinian corpuscles, also detect vibration, but at lower frequencies and with lesser sensitivity. Their maximal sensitivity is at 20–40 hertz and their frequency range from about 1 to 400 hertz. The corresponding receptors in non-Primates are the Krause end bulbs, which also detect changing stimuli.

In hairy skin, the *hair follicles* are innovated by myelinated fibres that have terminals arranged in a 'palisade' round the hair shaft. They too respond to changing stimuli, and can be subdivided into at least three sub-categories, with different band widths for maximal sensitivity to hair movement and different thresholds of movement sensitivity. All these kinds of mechanoreceptors have one feature in common—they do not respond to a steadily maintained displacement of the skin, and thus are incapable of detecting steady pressure. On the other hand, they can encode with great precision the magnitude and wavelength of vibratory stimuli of different frequencies, covering a range from less than 1 hertz to greater than 1,500 hertz.

Static or steadily maintained mechanical stimuli are detected by two other specialized cutaneous receptors. The first and more numerous are the *Merkel* cells, which occur in small clusters in the lower margin of the epidermis. In hairy skin these clusters are scattered, each innovated by a single myelinated axon, and form Iggo-Pinkus domes visible at the skin surface, especially after depilation of the skin. The receptors form *Sa I* mechanoreceptors that can sustain a discharge during static deformation, as well as during superimposed vibrations. The mechanical thresholds in hairy skin are about 1 micrometer, and the receptors can fire at rates higher than a thousand a second when the skin is stroked. The Sa I receptors are also present in glabrous skin, the Merkel cells there lying in the so-called rete pegs of the epidermis.

The other slowly-adapting receptor, the *Sa II*, has the *Ruffini ending* as its receptor. These are present in the dermis. They are spindle shaped, up to 2 mm long, with a distinct capsule, and a densely branched nerve ending in the central core of the receptor. These receptors are structurally similar to the Golgi tendon organs, and have the similar property of responding with a sustained discharge to maintained displacement of the skin. The mechanical sensitivity of the Sa II receptors is less than that of the Sa I.

Receptive fields. Each of these receptors occupies a small region of skin, from about 100–300 micrometers in diameter for the Sa I and Meissner's corpuscles in the fingertip, to several centimetres for hair follicle receptors in the arm and trunk skin. These small spots are the receptive fields from which a discharge of impulses can be evoked by an appropriate stimulus. The sizes of individual receptive fields and the density of innovation (the number of receptive fields per unit area) are important factors in determining the location of a stimulus, and for two-point discrimination, the ability to distinguish two stimuli applied simultaneously.

Central processing. This array of mechanoreceptors provides the central nervous system with a great deal of information about the characteristics of mechanical stimuli (intensity, duration, band width, location) that is further processed at spinal, brain stem, and thalamic levels before it reaches the cerebral cortex.

Direct pathways. The most direct routes go via the dorsal columns of the spinal cord to the lower end of the brain stem, where the ascending ranches of the incoming sensory nerve fibres make synaptic connections with neurones that in turn send axons to the ventro-basal thalamus. Thalamic neurones in their turn send their axons to the somatosensory region of the cerebral cortex. An important feature of this direct system is that it can preserve, to an astonishing degree, the information encoded by the cutaneous receptors—the system has the property of specificity. Individual neurones of the somatosensory cerebral cortex may have characteristics analogous to the different kinds of primary cutaneous sensory receptors, in terms of their responses to mechanical stimuli, encoding parameters such as amplitude, static/dynamic aspects, and frequency response range; but supplemented by additional properties, such as feature extraction, e.g. location of stimulated skin and direction of a moving object.

Indirect pathways. There are several other sensory pathways in addition to those via the dorsal column, medial lemniscus system. These others are more elaborate, since additional neurones are present in them, and may also be non-specific, because an admixture of inputs from different touch receptors, as well as from thermoreceptors and nociceptors, can interact. The ascending information in these pathways (such as the spinothalamic tract) may have lost, to varying degrees, some of the spatial and specific attributes of the dorsal column system. Their role in touch is still open to question, but they provide sensory pathways in parallel with the direct dorsal column routes.

Central control of sensation. A further important feature of tactile sensation, also present in other senses, is that not all the stimuli delivered to the skin surface necessarily cause excitation in the somatosensory cortex and an associated sensory awareness. There are very potent control systems, usually originating in the brain, that can modify the transmission of excitation from the skin on its way to the cerebral cortex. This is achieved through descending inhibition that interacts on neurones, at several levels in the sensory pathway, with the incoming excitatory information. This inhibition can totally or partially prevent the onflow of information, and may be used to enhance contrast between a stimulated area and adjacent regions, or to admit only certain inputs to higher levels. In this latter context it is analogous to 'attention'—a familiar capacity to attend to certain stimuli and disregard others. These interactions are based on excitatory and inhibitory synapses playing against each other on individual neurones and therefore are accessible to pharmacological manipulation, although this has been little exploited in relation to cutaneous touch.

Recent studies in man. In the past there was considerable controversy about the cutaneous sensory mechanisms, including the existence and function of cutaneous receptors. Although experimental evidence from animal studies leads to the conclusion that the general rules of specificity operate, it has only recently become possible to provide direct evidence from studies on conscious man. When a thin insulated tungsten wire electrode is inserted through the human skin and into a peripheral nerve it can, by suitable adjustment, record the impulses in a single axon coming from a cutaneous mechanoreceptor. This technique has been applied most rigorously to analyse cutaneous receptors in the hand, by recording from the median nerve in the arm. Four principal kinds of mechanoreceptor, with myelinated axons, exist in human glabrous skin, corresponding to: Pacinian corpuscles, Meissner's corpuscles, Sa I (Merkel receptors), and Sa II (Ruffini endings). The general characteristics of the receptors closely match those already well known from animal studies. The sensory function of the receptors was assessed by comparing the subject's report of his sensations with the responses of individual afferent fibres recorded at the same time. Criticism of this approach has been directed at the likelihood that a mechanical stimulus, even though controlled with great precision, could excite other receptors in addition to the one recorded from electrically, so that a one-to-one correspondence of sensation and unit receptor activity would be difficult to assert. In a refinement of the technique, electrical stimulation through the recording electrode was used as a means of precise excitation of a single, functionally identified, sensory axon. The exciting, and fundamentally important, result of this approach has been to establish in a quite convincing way, that the different kinds of receptor can indeed cause perceptually distinct sensation. Thus, the Pacinian corpuscle receptors caused a sense of tickling or vibration when stimulated at frequencies above 20–50 hertz, with a sensation of vibration related to the actual frequency of stimulation. Meissner corpuscles (Fa I) evoked a sense of tapping, flutter, buzzing, or vibration (related to the frequency of stimulation) that did not change its sensory quality if the stimulation continued for several seconds. Sa I (Merkel receptor) units did not evoke a sensation if only two or three electrically induced impulses were evoked at frequencies of 5–10 hertz, and for larger numbers of impulses at higher frequencies they evoked a sense of sustained pressure or sustained contact, lacking either the vibratory or tapping quality of the Pacinian and Meissner units. In contrast, activity in Sa II units did not give rise to any sensation, and so may be more concerned with muscle reflexes and proprioception which are not in consciousness.

These results brilliantly confirm the suggestions coming from the correlative studies in man and make possible the restatement of Muller's now ancient Law of Specific Nerve Energies. As originally stated, this asserted that excitation of a sense organ, by whatever means, always gave rise to the same modality of sensation, whether—in the case of, say, vision—the stimulus was the normal one of light acting on the retina or was an abnormal one, such as pressure on the eyeball. In late nineteenth century elaborations, the Law came to be restated as asserting that every kind of sensation required its own kind of nerve fibre, and that each kind of nerve fibre with its end organ had a 'specific energy', giving rise to a certain definite sensation and no other. The experimental results cited above give credence to Muller's original proposal—namely, that a given kind of receptor or its nerve fibre, when excited by whatever means, gives rise to a certain sensation. The sensation resulting from the simultaneous excitation of several kinds of receptor, such as mechanoreceptors and thermoreceptors, can, however, yield a sensation that arises from central interactions among the sensory inflow.

A further consequence of this new work is that the old controversy between 'specificity' and 'pattern' theories of cutaneous sensation has been resolved in favour of the 'specificity' theory.

Relation to other skin senses. This review of the 'tactile' sensory system has concentrated on the sensory receptors because it is in that area of knowledge that dramatic progress has been made in the last two decades, with the resolution of the long-standing controversy about the nature and role of the sensory receptors. Two other cutaneous sensory systems that coexist with the tactile system provide specific information about nociception (painful stimuli) and thermoreception (temperature sensation). Each is served by its own set of specific sensory receptors. The central processing of sensory information from these receptors is by the indirect route through the dorsal horn of the spinal cord. The three systems, tactile, nociceptive and thermal, do however interact. A striking example is the reduction in pain that can, in appropriate conditions, be achieved by the concurrent application of a tactile stimulus and a noxious stimulus. A familiar instance is provided by the instinctive act of rubbing a sore place on the skin. Rubbing or stroking excites sensitive tactile receptors that interact on neurones in the spinal cord with an inflow from the nociceptors and block or reduce the excitatory action of the latter. TENS (transcutaneous electrical nerve stimulation) is a method of pain relief, now in clinical use, that is based on this interaction. AINSLEY IGGO

2: THE HARDWARE OF THE MIND:
The Biological Basis of Behaviour

Emotion	Neurotransmitters
Instinct	Pain
Nervous system	Sleep

Our minds are grounded in our brains. Suggestions that minds can exist in the absence of a biological foundation are based on personal faith; while we cannot exclude the possibility that evidence will emerge of minds operating without a corporeal existence, public evidence points to a simple brain-mind relationship. When our brains are sufficiently developed then our minds become operational, and when our brains cease to function, then so do our minds. The underlying philosophy of these statements is that of emergent materialism, whereby minds are said to emerge from appropriately functioning biological systems. This means that there is no brain-mind mystery, and the question of how a physical system can produce a mental representation is no more intractable than the question of how a compact disc can produce a Beethoven symphony. In both cases a physical system, when operating in the appropriate way, yields a form that cannot be mapped directly onto the originating system the task of neuropsychology is to describe the relationships between brain systems, the emergent mental processes that we subjectively experience, and the subsequent behaviour that is observed. The analogy with a compact disc has obvious limitations, one of which is highlighted by the problem of sleep. We know something of what happens when we fall asleep, but we can only speculate as to why we should do so. And what happens to our minds while we are this state of unconsciousness?

Our ability to recognize changes in our immediate environment, and to make responses to those changes, depends upon internal communication—our **nervous system**. Sensory systems deliver information to the brain about changes detected by our receptor systems—what we can see, hear, touch, taste, and smell. The brain receives sensory information and also delivers information to the effector systems that control our actions. Transmission of information between the senses, the brain and the effectors is conducted through the circuitry of the nervous system. The neurones that form the nervous system are cells that receive signals from transmitting cells. As repeated sequences of stimuli are encountered the firing properties of particular neurones may change, so providing the foundation for learned responses. A newborn baby has a very immature nervous system, and the connections between neurones develop into a complex network as we learn to walk and talk. Brain development is regulated by the level of stimulation in an individual's environment, as well as by the demands of learning. If one area of the brain is damaged, other areas can learn to perform its function. As the network of neurones develops rich complexes of connections are formed. These inter-connected networks, which are capable of learning, are described in connectionist models of mental processes, which take the form of computer simulations of how the brain's neural network learns the relationships between stimulus and response.

Signals are received through small branching neuronal processes called dendrites and are passed, via the cell body, along the nerve fibre called an axon. The axon may be very short, or up to several feet in length—if, for example, it projects through the spinal cord. The neurone fires and transmits a signal when it is stimulated by chemical change in adjacent neurones. The electrical impulse that travels along the axon is known as the action potential. When the action potential reaches the axon terminal it stimulates the release of a chemical **neurotransmitter**. The effect is sometimes excitatory, when the signal influences other systems, and sometimes inhibitory, when the signal does not influence other systems because it would have an unwanted effect. Examples of neurotransmitters are acetylcholine (a motor neurone neurotransmitter, for muscle control) and endorphins (released to disrupt signals from **pain** receptors). The neurotransmitters operate in the synapse, a minute gap between the axon terminal of the transmitting neurone and a dendrite of the receiving neurone. The synapse has a number of receptor sites that can be influenced not only by the neurotransmitter released by the transmitting neurone, but also by other chemicals carried in the blood. These extra-neuronal chemicals are drugs; for example curare inhibits acetylcholine, resulting in paralysis, and morphine has the effect of an endorphin in relieving pain. The probability of an individual acquiring an addiction to drugs taken artificially depends upon its specific action on the nervous system; perhaps the greatest risks are associated with the opiates such as morphine and heroin, which act as neuronal depressants.

The interconnected neurones influence our behaviour by regulating the flow of signals between senses, brain, and motor effectors. The structures involved are the central nervous system, consisting of brain and spinal cord, and the peripheral nervous system, consisting of the skeletal nervous system (motor reflexes and voluntary control of our muscles) and the autonomic nervous system (hormonal systems and the involuntary muscles of our internal organs). We normally have no voluntary control over the systems that control autonomic functions such as those involving our heart rate or blood pressure, but through the use of appropriate biofeedback some level of control can be demonstrated.

Voluntary behaviour is guided by the flow of information to the brain from the senses and from the brain to the effectors. The brain itself is a mix of differentiated and homogeneous structures—some are specialized while others serve more general purposes. Among the most differentiated structures are those of the paleocortex, or limbic system, which controls the functioning of basic, primary needs such as eating and drinking. This structure sits at the boundary of the cerebral cortex and the primitive parts of the brain that are located at the top of the spinal cord. Some structures of the limbic system regulate the visceral state of the organism through the mechanism of homeostasis, whereby signals from the visceral organs indicate deficiencies (of, for example, food or liquid) and activate structures in the limbic system. This activation continues (signalling hunger or thirst) until action is taken to remedy the deficiency. Other structures in the limbic system help modify our behaviour by enabling us to learn ways of remedying the deficiencies that nearby structures have identified. Still others serve basic needs by identifying situations in which an **emotion** such as fear and anger require a 'fight or flight' reaction. Curiously, one of the structures of the limbic system appears to serve the purpose of reinforcing behaviour. When this structure is stimulated artificially with a small electric current, the experimental subject experiences pleasure. The activation of this area following a successfully adaptive response would encourage repetition and facilitate learning.

The structures of the limbic system evolved to serve adaptive functions and enabled animals to survive through altering their behaviour according to circumstances. Memories, emotions, and primary needs are regulated in this system of inter-connected neuronal bundles. The extent to which animals show a stereotypical, species-specific behaviour pattern depends more upon the functions of the limbic system than upon a highly developed cerebral cortex. William McDougall's description of an instinct closely resembles the catalogue of functions of the limbic system. Similar structures are seen in primitive and higher mammals, suggesting an early evolution. The cerebral cortex, on the other hand, is much more highly developed in humans than in other mammals, but physical differentiation is more difficult to see. More obvious are the two cerebral hemispheres, but there are also areas of the cortex within each hemisphere dedicated to sensory processing and to motor control.

The mapping of localization of brain function was initially dependent upon the identification of patients with localized brain damage associated with specific behavioural deficits. The language areas of the brain, for example, were among the first areas to receive thorough investigation, through the study of patients with different forms of aphasia resulting from strokes. If the damage caused by the stroke is highly localized, then the resulting behavioural deficit can be said to have been served by the area damaged. The language centres tend to be localized in the left cerebral hemisphere, at least for right-handed individuals. Handedness and cerebral language specialization are not linked invariably, especially for left-handed individuals. Language is a highly specialized skill and is served by highly specific cortical areas, but the localization of other cognitive functions is less straightforward. The activation of the cortex when we look at a picture or listen to music is less localized than when the language centres are operating, and when we engage in analytical thinking activation is more general still. The investigation of brain localization is proceeding through a variety of techniques that can be used with undamaged volunteers (see BRAIN IMAGING PSYCHOLOGICAL DISORDERS).

EMOTION is a topic that, more than any other, has bedevilled students of mental life. The peculiar characteristics of emotional behaviour and experience have been repeated stumbling-blocks in the attempt to see human nature as rational, intelligent, and even sublime. From the earliest philosophical speculations to the present day, emotion has been often seen as interfering with rationality, as a remnant of our pre-sapient inheritance—emotions seem to represent unbridled human nature 'in the raw'.

In modern times the single most influential contribution to the study of the emotions is Charles Darwin's work entitled *The Expression of the Emotions in Man and Animals* (1872). His general thrust represents a second major theme that has characterized the study of emotion—the notion that there are specific, fundamental emotions that find their 'expression' in the overt behaviour of humans and lower animals.

The current flux of speculations about the emotions started with a very specific event, the publication in 1884 of an article by William James in *Mind* entitled 'What is an emotion?' James turned conventional wisdom completely around. Instead of the outward signs of emotions, such as facial expressions and visceral reactions, being the *result* of some prior emotional, neural signal, he insisted that 'our feeling of the [bodily] changes as they occur *is* the emotion'. Similar points were made at about the same time by various other writers, the most important being the Danish physician C. G. Lange, whose contribution appeared in Danish in 1885 and became generally available with its German translation in 1887. Since then, the theoretical position has been known as the James-Lange theory of emotion.

The theory dominated psychological thinking well into the first half of the twentieth century. It postulated that some external event, perceived by the individual, produces bodily responses, particularly specific avoidance or approach reactions, together with responses of the autonomic nervous system. The perception of *these* events in their totality then constitutes the emotion that is experienced. Lange restricted the bodily reactions to the visceral, autonomic domain, but James stressed the total response of the organism. The obvious implication is that each specific emotional experience is generated by a specific and unique set of bodily and visceral responses.

The James-Lange theory remained dominant at least until the late 1920s, when W. B. Cannon published a detailed and trenchant critique of its position. Briefly, Cannon noted that emotional behaviour was still present when the viscera were surgically or accidentally isolated from the central nervous system; that different emotions did not seem to differ in important ways in their accompanying patterns of visceral response; that perception of visceral response tends to be diffuse and non-specific; that autonomic responses are relatively slow and that emotional experience seems to occur faster than the visceral response; and that emotional states do not follow the artificial production of visceral response as a matter of course. Cannon's major contribution to the study of emotion was this critique; the theory he offered as an alternative to James never did achieve great popularity.

In the ensuing decades speculation about emotion abounded, much research being devoted to problems of special visceral patterning; but, until the middle of the century, few new advances were made. The question seemed to remain where James and Cannon had left it: do we experience an emotion because we perceive our bodies in a particular way, or are there specific emotional neural patterns which respond to environmental events and then release bodily and visceral expressions? Do we grieve because we cry, or do we cry because we grieve?

What did happen in the decades after Cannon was the (unfortunate) American interlude known as behaviourism. With hindsight it appears that the main deleterious effect of behaviourism arose not from its insistence on dealing only with the objective and the observable as basic psychological data—in a sense all psychologists have become methodological behaviourists—but from the behaviourists' implicit dictum against complex theory, against the postulation of useful fictions to serve the explanation of behaviour. Uninhibited and expansive theorizing has generally characterized the cognitive theories, which implicate the knowledge and thought of the organism as determinants of action and experience. With the resurgence of cognitive theories particularly in social psychology, came a concern with cognitive aspects of emotion. The single most important contribution in the form of both direction-changing theory and innovative experiments was made by Stanley Schachter, a psychologist from Columbia University in New York. He postulated that only a general state of visceral arousal was necessary for the experience of emotion: i.e. that different emotional experiences arise out of the same visceral background. Next he assumed that, given a state of visceral arousal, an individual will describe his feelings in terms of the cognitions (thoughts, past experiences, environmental signals) available at the time. Schachter's contribution cut the Gordian knot in which James's theory and the Jamesian critics had been entwined. Visceral arousal was seen as a necessary condition for emotional experience, but the quality of the emotion depended on cognitive, perceptual evaluations of the external world and the internal state.

With the new insights into the possible nature of emotional experience, it was possible to raise new questions about the nature and function of emotions. If the emotional experience is a concatenation of visceral arousal and cognitive evaluation, what is the role of emotions in adaptive behaviour; what is the function of visceral, autonomic arousal?

Rather than emotion appearing as an interfering, irrelevant, and chaotic state of affairs, it seems that different kinds of situations (and cognitions) become especially marked if they occur in the 'emotional' visceral context. This notion corresponds with the common experience that emotionally tinged events occupy a special place in our memories. The visceral component of the emotion may well serve as an additional cue for the retrieval from memory of specific events, and sets them apart from the run-of-the-mill catalogue of everyday events. The 'emotional' memory of a visit to a theatre is selected from among all the plays we have seen; it is 'special'. The memory of a friend with whom one interacted in the 'visceral' mode is different from the memories of people with whom one has interacted in non-arousing contexts. But if the visceral component of emotion has this special role of selecting important events, what are the conditions that give rise to the visceral reaction?

The best candidate for the psychological conditions for visceral arousal seems to be the occurrence of some cognitive or perceptual discrepancy. The notion that emotions, both positive and negative, have as their antecedents some discrepancy or conflict between the state of the world and the expectations which the individual brings to the situation has been bruited about for at least a century. The most eminent ancestors of the suggestion are the French psychologist F. Paulhan and the American philosopher John Dewey. They implied that specific discrepancies and conflicts produce specific emotions. Current wisdom would suggest that any discrepancy, any interruption of expectations or of intended actions, produces undifferentiated visceral (autonomic) arousal. The *quale* of the subsequent emotion will then depend on the ongoing cognitive evaluation (meaning analysis, appraisal) of the current state of affairs. Thus, riding on a roller-coaster produces serious disturbances and discrepancies between our expectations and current feelings of balance and bodily support. Whether the ride is seen as joyful or dreadful depends on what we expect about the ride, who accompanies us, what we are told to expect, and whether we feel in control of the situation. Some love it, others hate it. The notion that discrepancy or interruption produces a special visceral event suggests that in addition to the homeostatic function of the autonomic nervous system there are other adaptive characteristics ascribable to it. In fact there is good evidence that, with the initiation of autonomic arousal, attentional and scanning mechanisms are directed towards important aspects of the environment. In other words, in addition to the autonomic nervous system caring for the internal balance of the energy-spending and energy-conserving functions of the body, it also serves as an alerting and marking mechanism for events that are 'important'. The concept of discrepancy or interruption provides an independent criterion for what is 'important' for the organism. When the usual, habitual actions and experiences of the individual are interrupted, when expectations of the world fail, then attention is focused on the environment, and the event itself is subsequently stored in memory as special and easily retrievable.

The modern view answers the ancient concern about emotions. They are not necessarily remnants of our pre-sapient past, but rather they are important characteristics of an active, searching, and thinking human being. Novelty, discrepancy, and interruption generate visceral responses, while our cognitive system interprets the world as threatening, elating, frightening, or joyful. The human world is full of emotions not because we are animals at heart, but rather because it is still full of signals that elate or threaten, and replete with events and people that produce discrepancies and interruptions.

GEORGE MANDLER

INSTINCT. From an early time, instinctive behaviour was regarded as the counterpart to voluntary behaviour. In everyday, though not in scientific, speech the term 'instinct' is still used to imply 'without thought'. For example, if I heard a taxi-driver say 'I instinctively stamped on the brakes', I would assume that he meant that his behaviour was reflex or involuntary, and not that he was born with an innate ability to apply the brakes in motor cars.

The irrational forces in man's nature were emphasized by Freud, but the ideas of McDougall probably had a greater influence upon the scientific development of the concept of instinct. McDougall regarded instincts as irrational and compelling motivational forces. He enumerated particular instincts, each of which was accompanied by an emotion. Examples are: pugnacity and the emotion of anger; flight and the emotion of fear; repulsion and the emotion of disgust. McDougall's views do not find favour with modern psychologists because they are derived from subjective experience and are therefore hard to verify. There is inevitable disagreement among psychologists as to the number of instincts that should be allowed.

A different line of thought was initiated by Charles Darwin. In his *Origin of Species* (1859), Darwin treated instincts as complex reflexes that were made up of inherited units and therefore subject to natural selection. Such instincts would evolve together with other aspects of the animal's morphology and behaviour. Darwin laid the foundations of the classical ethological view propounded by Konrad Lorenz and Niko Tinbergen.

Lorenz maintained that animal behaviour included a number of fixed-action patterns that were characteristic of species and largely genetically determined. He subsequently postulated that each fixed-action pattern or instinct was motivated by action-specific energy. The action-specific energy was likened to liquid in a reservoir. Each instinct corresponded to a separate reservoir, and when an appropriate releasing stimulus was presented the liquid was discharged in the form of an instinctive drive which gave rise to the appropriate behaviour. Tinbergen proposed that the reservoirs, or instinct centres, were arranged in a hierarchy so that the energy responsible for one class of activity, such as reproduction, would drive a number of subordinate activities, such as nest-building, courting, and parental care.

The concept of instinct that is identified with classical ethology does not find favour with the majority of present-day behavioural scientists, for two main reasons. The first reason is connected with the idea that there are instinctive forces, or drives, that determine certain aspects of behaviour. Although the notion of drive as an energizer has been very influential in psychology, it involves a misuse of the concept of energy. In the physical sciences, energy is not a causal agent but a descriptive term arising from mathematically formulated laws. Analogous laws can be formulated for animal behaviour, but they do not lead to a concept of energy that corresponds to the notions of drive popular with the early psychologists and ethologists. Although the idea of drive as an energizer of behaviour has intuitive appeal, this is not nowadays regarded as sufficient justification for a scientific concept. In addition there are empirical problems. Early psychologists sought to identify a drive for every aspect of behaviour: a hunger drive responsible for feeding, a thirst drive, a sex drive, etc. It proved impossible to classify animal behaviour in this way without resorting to a *reductio ad absurdum* involving drives for thumb-sucking, nail-biting, and other minutiae of behaviour. A more modern view is that animals choose from the set of alternative courses of action that is available at a particular time, in accordance with certain precisely formulated principles of decision making. This approach obviates the view that animals are driven by instinctive forces to perform particular behaviour patterns.

The second reason for abandoning the classical concepts of instinct is an objection to the implication that certain aspects of behaviour are innate in the sense that they develop independently of environmental influences. Most scientists now recognize that all behaviour is influenced both by the animal's genetic make-up and by the environmental conditions that exist during development. The extent to which the influences of nature and nurture determine behaviour varies greatly from activity to activity and from species to species. For example, the vocalizations of pigeons and doves are relatively stereotyped and characteristic of each species, and are not influenced by auditory experience after hatching. The vocalizations of other birds, however, may depend heavily upon such experience, as in the strongly imitative birds, or they may be partly influenced by experience. For example, chaffinches will learn the song they hear during a particular sensitive period of early life, provided it is similar to the normal song.

While the influence of particular genes may be necessary for the development of a behaviour pattern, it is never a sufficient condition. All types of behaviour require a suitable embryonic environment for the correct nervous connections, etc., to develop. Normally, the physiological medium provided by the parent is designed to ensure that normal embryonic development occurs. Just as the parent provides an environment suitable for the development of the embryo, so it may provide an environment suitable for the development of a juvenile. Thus a chaffinch is normally reared in an environment in which it inevitably hears the song of other chaffinches, and so it develops the song that is characteristic of its own species.

Even apparently stereotyped activities may, upon closer examination, be shown to be influenced by the environment. For example, the newly hatched chicks of herring gulls peck at the tip of the parent's bill, which bears a characteristic red spot on a yellow background. The chick's behaviour induces the parent to regurgitate food. The behaviour is typical of all newly hatched chicks, is performed in an apparently stereotyped manner, and would appear to be a classic example of instinctive behaviour. Upon closer examination, however, it can be seen that the initial behaviour of individual chicks varies considerably in force and rapidity of pecking, angle of approach, and accuracy. As the chicks gain experience their pecking accuracy improves, and the pecking movements become more stereotyped. Some of these changes are due to maturation. The chicks become more stable on their feet as their muscles develop, and their pecking co-ordination improves. Some of the changes are due to learning. Initially the chicks peck at any elongated object of a suitable size. Although the red spot on the parent's bill is attractive to them, it is not their only target. Once the chicks begin to receive food they learn to exercise greater discrimination. It is not surprising that the behaviour of different chicks develops along similar lines, because in the natural environment they are all confronted with a similar situation. Practice and experience in similar situations lead to similar results, and the behaviour of the older chick consequently becomes more and more like that of its peers.

The concept of instinct has undergone many changes over the years. Whereas, at one time, instinctive behaviour was seen as inborn, stereotyped, and driven from within, the modern approach is to treat the innate, the reflex, and the motivational aspects as separate issues. While much animal and human behaviour is innate in the sense that it inevitably appears as part of the repertoire under natural conditions, this does not mean that genetic factors are solely responsible. Maturational factors and modes of learning that are characteristic of the species may be just as important. Much of the nature-nurture controversy, particularly that associated with sexual and racial differences among humans, results from a failure to recognize the vast complexity of developmental processes.

D. J. MCFARLAND

NERVOUS SYSTEM. For the neurologist, there is no such thing as the mind. There are certain activities of the brain endowed with consciousness that it is convenient to consider as mental activities. Since one expects to find a noun adjoined to an adjective, one supposes that there must be a mind expressing itself in a mental way. But the requirements of language and of logical thought are not always the same; demands of syntax may lead to errors in thinking.

The central nervous system is the physical substance that provides its possessor with genetically determined ways of behaving and also ways of changing this behaviour. What has been inherited is structure, studied as anatomy, and the working of this structure, studied as physiology. It is often convenient, and often misleading, to categorize some parts of the functioning as mental activities. But this does not imply that behind this functioning is a structure that could be called the mind.

The life of animals consists of receiving and responding to information. In animals made up of more than a few cells, this requires a nervous system. In vertebrates, the nervous system consists of three parts: afferent nerve fibres with their receptors, efferent nerve fibres with their muscles and glands, and the central nervous system, formed by the spinal cord and the brain.

The neurone. The nervous system is made of cells, like every animal tissue. The essential cell is a nerve-cell or neurone. Neurones are the largest cells in the body. A small neurone may measure about 3 micrometres, but a large one stretches for over 1 metre, and far more than that in a whale or an elephant.

The neurone is considered to have three parts: the cell-body, the dendrites, and the axon. The dendrites are thin prolongations of the cell-body (shown in Fig. 13). Most sorts of neurone have one

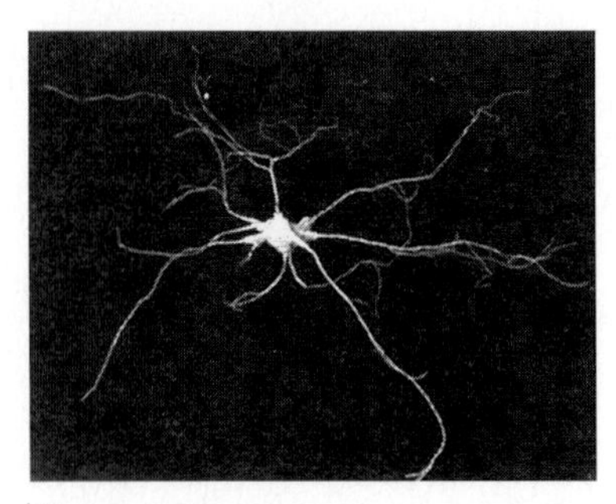

Fig. 13 Photograph of a three-dimensional model of a neurone, showing the cell-body and dendrites.

prolongation far longer than the others; this is the axon, the telegraph wire of the neurone, taking the message from one neurone to another or else to the muscle or gland that it supplies. The boundary of the neurone is a membrane, having certain properties on which the functioning of the nervous system depends. The axon with its surrounding membrane is called a nerve fibre. The ending of the nerve fibre is called, quite simply, the nerve ending or nerve terminal.

Fig. 13 is a photograph of a scale model of a neurone; it gives a better idea of the three dimensions of the cell than does a photograph taken down a microscope. The cell-body and the dendrites in actual fact would be covered with the nerve endings of other neurones.

All the neurones in the central nervous system of man are present at birth. As the baby grows, they enlarge and grow, the dendrites spread further, and the axon lengthens; but neurones, unlike most cells, do not divide and reproduce. Thus they are irreplaceable; and any neurones that we lose from accident or disease are lost for ever and we are so much the poorer.

Vertebrates have two kinds of neurones, those with myelinated and those with non-myelinated nerve fibres. Myelinated fibres have layers of a lipoprotein called myelin folded round the axon; non-myelinated fibres do not have these layers of insulating material. The myelin sheath is not continuous throughout the length of a nerve fibre; it is broken at little gaps, called the nodes of Ranvier or just nodes.

Receptors. The way into the central nervous system is through the receptors. They are connected to the central nervous system by peripheral nerves; and peripheral nerves also connect the central nervous system to the muscles, to allow the animal to stand and move. The central nervous system of vertebrates is made up of the spinal cord and the brain. The spinal cord does not fill out the length of the vertebral column, for it is only about 40 centimetres long. The brain is an immensely complex and convoluted development of the cranial end of the spinal cord.

Receptors are natural transducers, converting the kinds of energy that they can receive into electric current. They can be classified as exteroceptors, reporting events in the outside world, and interoceptors, reporting the inside world of the body itself. They include receptors in muscles, tendons, and joints, the alimentary canal, and the bladder. There are receptors recording a steady state and changes occurring in that state; these include thermoreceptors, which report warmth and cold. Other receptors are silent until something new occurs. Among these are the receptors of the skin, which take notice of pressure and touch, pulling and stretching. All over the body are nociceptors, receptors reporting events that are liable to damage the body. There are chemoreceptors. Some of these are in the alimentary canal, including the nose and tongue. They report the arrival of molecules of substances that provide us with smell and taste. Further along the alimentary canal, they work without involving our conscious awareness; they serve to adjust the correct enzymes for the digestion of food.

Some receptors are formed of special cells; others are the nerve fibres themselves, unattached to any special end-organ. In the skin many receptors are naked nerve fibres, others are nerve endings surrounded by capsules of cells, looking like the layers of an onion surrounding the growing tip. Some receptors are massed together to form a sense organ, such as the eye or the ear. Others are scattered over a large area, for instance those of the skin or the viscera. If it is desirable to know the source of distant stimuli, one needs to have two separated sense organs. They then form the base of a triangle, the apex of which is the distant stimulus. When we are uncertain where a sound is coming from, we alter the angles of the base of the triangle, by turning first one ear and then the other in the supposed direction of the sound.

Not everything that a receptor receives is sent on to the higher levels of the central nervous system. Processing of the data begins in the sense organ and continues at the entrance to the spinal cord or brain and throughout the central nervous system. The brain itself controls its own input. The manner and purpose of this control is not yet known and can only be guessed at. It may be that if a certain location of the input is important at a particular moment—say something is damaging or hurting the back of the left hand—then the input from this region might have to be facilitated and that from other regions reduced or blocked. A mechanism such as this could form the first link in the chain of mechanisms of paying attention.

All that the receptors report does not come to consciousness. Because we are occupied with what is happening around us, we tend to forget that many parts of the spinal cord and the brain are being informed about stimuli which reach no conscious level. Merely to maintain an upright posture depends on the reporting of the receptors of joints, muscles, the skin, and the organs of balance in the inner ear; this is going on all the time and none of it usually becomes conscious.

Not all of the information that the eye supplies to parts of the central nervous system makes us see something. There are visuo-motor reflexes that contribute to walking. In many birds and mammals, the cycles of life depend on the amount of light received. Lengthening periods of day light or the days drawing in have their effects on the arrival of puberty and periods for procreation. They also cause hibernation or aestivation, and tell the animal when it is time to wake up and get moving. Somehow the amount of light is recorded and appropriate behaviour is brought about.

The sense of smell is so important to many animals that it is used for communication. Odoriferous substances, put out by animals in order to signal to others, are called pheromones. Sex pheromones are very commonly used. They may play a minor role in human sexual signalling. Certainly the attraction of the female rhesus monkey for the male depends entirely on her smell, and the male monkey emits a smell attractive to the female. Man has about thirty million olfactory receptors in each nostril, and they can respond to about twenty to thirty primary odours. The other smells that we can smell are thought to be mixtures of these primary odours.

How the nervous system sends messages. The behaviour of the central nervous system consists of passing messages from one lot of neurones to another. The message itself is sent in the form of a Morse code consisting only of dots. As the dots are always grouped together, they are usually referred to as a volley of nerve impulses, or just as a volley. The nerve fibre conducts impulses in one direction only. Afferent nerves outside the central nervous system conduct impulses towards the spinal cord and brain, and efferent nerves conduct them away from the central nervous system to the muscles and glands. Within the central nervous system, each nerve fibre is a one-way street.

One can talk of taking messages, for the nerve impulse is an instruction to the cell that receives it to do something. The message or impulse is an electric current, somewhat like the current sent along a telegraph or telephone wire. In the system invented by man, the electrical events take place in metal, in long thin wires. In natural systems, the electric current is carried by a flow of ions in fluid. In the telegraph, the current is carried passively along the wire; in the natural system, the nerve fibre itself generates the current that spreads along the fibre. The nerve impulse depends on the physical characteristics of the membrane surrounding the axon. This membrane is a semi-fluid lipid, permeable to certain hydrated ions and not to others. It is very permeable to potassium ions, less permeable to chloride ions, and far less permeable to sodium ions. These differences in permeability cause a different concentration of ions on the two sides of the membrane; and the different concentration gives rise to a difference in potential between the inside and outside of the axon. This potential difference, the inside being electronegative, the outside electropositive, is called the *resting potential.* The nerve impulse is a sudden, rapid, transient change in the permeability of the membrane to sodium ions. These positively charged ions pass through the membrane of the axon from the extracellular fluid, reversing the charge on the membrane from negative to positive. In this state, the membrane is more permeable to potassium ions, and so they flow out of the axon, through the membrane into the extracellular fluid—a process that brings back the former state with the inside negative and the outside positive. If this did not occur, the membrane could not be excited again. The passage of sodium ions carrying a positive charge is referred to as depolarizing the membrane, and the return to resting conditions is called repolarizing the membrane.

What has so far been described is how a nerve fibre at rest is excited. The next question is how this minute region of excitation spreads along the nerve fibre. The transient increase in permeability is induced by a potential change coming from a receptor or from the nerve endings of another nerve fibre. The increase in permeability causes current to flow between the spot that has become more permeable and the adjacent region of membrane. This circuit of current allows positively charged ions to pass through the membrane at the adjacent region; and so the cycle of events occurs in these neighbouring regions of the membrane. By such minute steps, the current spreads along the membrane of the axon. This spreading depolarization is called the *action potential.* The process takes place in one direction only, ahead of the region that has just been activated. The reason is that the membrane cannot be depolarized until it has been repolarized: in other words these electrochemical events cannot be repeated until the previous resting state has returned. Thus it is inevitable that the spreading permeability change will pass along the membrane only in front of the region that has just been active.

Similar events occurring at the receptor are called the generator potential or *transducer potential.* They are set off by the stimuli to which that receptor is sensitive. The generator potential starts off the action potential along the afferent nerve fibre.

The most primitive and smallest animals consisted of only a few cells with nerve-nets formed of only non-myelinated fibres. The faster conduction of impulses that became necessary as animals became larger, was not achieved by making nerve fibres with greater diameters: a new step in evolution occurred, the covering of nerve fibres with myelin sheaths. The conduction of the nerve impulse in myelinated fibres is different from that in non-myelinated fibres, and the continuous spreading of the current so far described is the mode of conduction in non-myelinated fibres. Conduction in myelinated fibres is called *saltatory conduction*, as the current jumps from node to node.

In saltatory conduction the current is also due to the passage of ions through the membrane; but in this case the membrane is covered by lengths of insulating material, the myelin sheath. The nodes are little breakages in this insulation. The current spreads along these fibres by passing through the non-insulated nodes, in through one and out through the next. This is a much faster way of conducting impulses than continuous conduction.

Once the electrical events have been started in a nerve fibre, they spread along it to its end. They are self-propagating, and nothing stops them, short of damage to or cutting the nerve fibre. A nerve fibre always produces the same amount of current; for the current is related to the resistance, and the resistance is inversely related to the radius of the fibre. The rate at which the impulses are conducted is between 0.5 and 2 metres per second in the case of non-myelinated fibres and from 2 to 120 metres per second in the case of myelinated fibres.

There are two ways in which nervous systems differ in principle from telephones and cables. They consist of inhibitory as well as excitatory neurones; and they are spontaneously active. The communication systems invented by man are excitatory: either you send a message or you don't. If you were to receive an inhibitory telegram, it would just say 'Keep quiet!' In the central nervous system, excitation and inhibition tend to cancel each other out. A neurone fires off an impulse when its threshold of excitability has been exceeded. Excitatory neurones tend to fire an impulse, inhibitory ones tend to stop it firing.

The nervous system starts being spontaneously active from an early moment *in utero* and continues until death. In man-made communication systems, nothing is happening until a message is sent. Into the mass of active neurones of the central nervous system, volleys of impulses are sent. It will be seen that inhibitory neurones are needed: the spontaneous activity may need to be quietened down as well as be increased.

Between the nerve endings of one neurone and the cell-body and dendrites of the next, there is a minute gap; it is about 200 nanometres wide in most cases. This region where the message is passed from one neurone to the next is called the synapse, after the Greek word for 'clasp', and the gap is called the synaptic gap or cleft. Structures and functions are spoken of in relation to the synapse as pre-synaptic and post-synaptic. The synapse is like a diode, conducting in one direction only. Any change in a message has to be made at a synapse, for once the impulse is travelling along a nerve fibre, it generally continues to the next synapse.

Many factors have an influence on the firing of a neurone: there is its threshold of excitability, its local chemical environment, and the sum of excitatory and inhibitory impulses it receives within a brief period of time. Each nerve impulse delivers a constant amount of excitation or of inhibition. The amounts of both are increased by increasing the number of impulses sent in a brief time. Once the post-synaptic neurone has fired an impulse, its excitation has to be raised to make it fire again. The excitatory effect of an impulse arriving on a motor neurone that works a large muscle of a cat's limb lasts 5 milliseconds. In this neurone, the relation between the intensity of current supplied to the neurone and the neurone's rate of firing off impulses is linear. In some other neurones, the relation is that of an S-shaped curve. In some places in the central nervous system, arriving excitatory impulses keep the post-synaptic neurone always ready to fire; only a few more impulses arriving will then fire it off.

The cell-body, like the human body, is not equally excitable all over. Out on the ends of the dendrites, the membrane is relatively inexcitable. Excitation delivered there may never fire the neurone but it may be sufficient to increase the excitability momentarily; thus impulses continually delivered far out on dendrites may keep the membrane of the cell-body at a certain threshold of excitability.

The kinds of excitation and inhibition discussed so far are called *post-synaptic potentials*. Another kind of inhibition is pre-synaptic inhibition. It is named pre-synaptic as it stops a nerve fibre delivering its full amount of excitation just before it reaches the synapse where it ends. It is illustrated in Fig. 14. The fibre coming in from the bottom left inhibits the fibre on which it ends before that fibre delivers its quantum of excitation to the cell-body. Its effect is to cause partial or even complete blocking of the message. This blocking of the message in a fibre is an exception to the statement made above—that once the nerve impulse is travelling along a fibre, it continues to the end. As far as is known, pre-synaptic inhibition is a function only of excitatory neurones: there is no pre-synaptic inhibition of inhibitory neurones. Recent investigations lead one to conclude that dendrites of different neurones in juxtaposition can also influence each other.

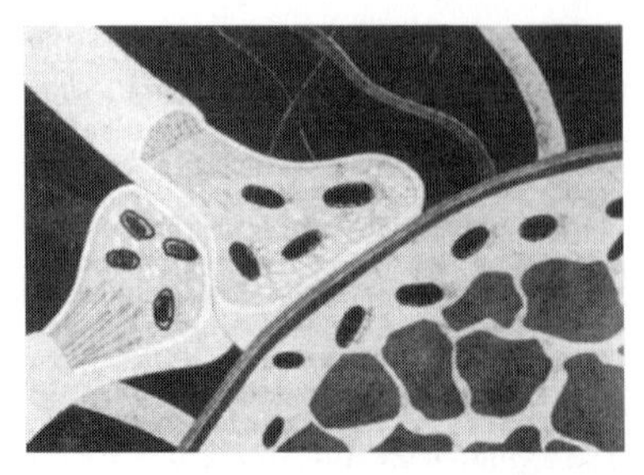

Fig. 14 A model of nerve terminals to show pre-synaptic inhibition. The nerve terminal coming from the left lower corner inhibits the nerve terminal on which it is ending before this nerve fibre can deliver its impulses to the cell-body on which it is ending.

With such a limited repertoire of interaction between neurones, it is surprising how complicated the total picture of neuronal activity can be. There are two common patterns of relations between neurones and groups of neurones. Messages can be spread far and wide from a few neurones or they can be channelled into a few pathways and sent on to only a few neurones. The first is called divergence and the second convergence. To give some idea of the figures involved, one might take as an example the large neurones known as Purkinje cells, after the anatomist who first described them early in the nineteenth century. On to each of these neurones there come 200,000 nerve endings from many other neurones: this is convergence. And a single neurone called a granule cell sends branches to 30–450 Purkinje cells: that is divergence.

There are other patterns of organization. One is surround or lateral inhibition. When a central or linearly arranged group of neurones is excited, there is concomitant inhibition of the surrounding neurones. This inhibition is strongest for the neurones immediately adjacent to those being excited and becomes weaker for the more distant neurones. The more strongly the central group of neurones is excited, the stronger will be the inhibition of the surrounding neurones. This kind of organization has the effect of emphasizing contrasts. It was first discovered in the retina, where it is probably used to accentuate the edges and boundaries of what is seen. This reciprocal organization is not static. If the source of the central excitation is, for instance, a stimulus moving along the skin, then the line of excitation and surrounding inhibition will move; the moving stimulus on the skin excites new neurones as it moves, and these excited neurones inhibit different surrounding neurones as they themselves are turned on and off.

Excitation and inhibition at the synapse are electrical occurrences similar to those in the nerve fibre. There is a sudden increase in permeability of the post-synaptic membrane, and hydrated ions pass through it. Pre-synaptic inhibition is due to the flow of ions into the pre-synaptic fibre just before the nerve ending.

The response of any neurone depends on the following factors: the region of the membrane that receives nerve impulses, the temporal scatter of arriving impulses, the previous effect of hormones and endogenous peptides, and the chemical composition of the fluid surrounding the neurone. All these factors together determine the binary response of the neurone, to send an impulse or to remain silent.

Even though inhibition and excitation of the next neurone at the synapse depends on the passage of ions through the membrane in a fashion similar to the events of transmission along the nerve fibre, there are important differences. When an impulse reaches the end of a nerve fibre, a chemical substance is put out into the synaptic gap. This substance unites with the protein of the post-synaptic membrane, and the membrane with this substance becomes permeable to some hydrated ions and not to others; according to which ions pass, depolarization or excitation, or hyperpolarization or inhibition occur. The regions of the post-synaptic membrane where these chemical substances act are known as receptor sites; and the substances are called neurotransmitters or transmitters. The transmitters are synthesized in the cell-bodies of neurones; they are then passed along the nerve fibre and stored in vesicles in the nerve endings, remaining there until a nerve impulse arrives. The impulse liberates a constant amount of neurotransmitter into the synaptic gap; this passes across the gap and unites with the receptor site of the post-synaptic membrane. Whether excitation or inhibition occurs is determined by the size and shape of the pores of the receptor site. Smaller pores allow potassium and chloride ions to pass, resulting in inhibition, and larger pores allow sodium and chloride ions to pass, resulting in excitation. Once the transmitter has reacted with the post-synaptic membrane, it is inactivated and/or taken up again into the presynaptic nerve ending.

Neurones and their nerve fibres are often named according to the transmitter substance they synthesize and emit at their endings. So, for instance, one has cholinergic neurones, releasing acetylcholine, and noradrenergic neurones, releasing noradrenaline. Acetylcholine is the transmitter that works the muscles of the body; noradrenaline works muscles of the uterus and the blood vessels. The muscles of the alimentary canal are made to contract by many transmitters, including acetylcholine, noradrenaline, and many peptides.

In vertebrates, it appears that all nerve fibres act by putting out transmitters at their endings. At the various synapses in a chain of nerve fibres in the central nervous system different transmitters will be emitted. Also, outside the central nervous system, different neurones exert their effects by putting out their transmitters, making muscle fibres contract or glands secrete. A purinergic neurone, which has a short axon about 1.5 centimetres long, may be excited by a cholineritic nerve fibre, secreting acetylcholine; and the cholinergic neurone will have been excited by noradrenaline.

Parts of the nervous system working together to carry out a certain function often use the same transmitter for all the neurones concerned. Dopamine, for instance, is secreted by neurones concerned with waking the brain from sleep. Noradrenaline is the transmitter used in the hypothalamus for controlling body temperature. Neurotransmitters are being discovered all the time, and an important research territory is that of peptides and hormones formed in the body that can act as neurotransmitters.

Moving. Plants are fixed, animals move. Here we discuss the activities of animals and the movements of various parts of their bodies.

Movement is due to the contraction of muscle fibres, and muscle fibres are caused to contract by impulses arriving in the peripheral nerves. If the nerve running to a muscle is cut, the muscle is paralysed. The nerve fibre goes to the neuromuscular junction, which is a synapse between the nerve ending and the membrane covering the muscle fibre. From this region, electrical events similar to those of the nerve impulse spread over the membrane of the muscle fibre, causing the proteins of muscle to contract.

In vertebrates, the basic patterns of movement are organized in the spinal cord. For most quadrupeds—and this includes the crawling baby—the spinal cord arranges the basic pattern of running or walking: when a forelimb flexes, the opposite hindlimb extends, the other forelimb extends, and the remaining hindlimb flexes. During a movement, the muscles around a joint work according to a pattern of reciprocal innervation; when the limb is used for standing, the muscles around the joint tend to keep contracting together. Reciprocal innervation is organized so that as one group of muscles, say the flexors, contract, the antagonist group, say the extensors, are relaxed. It is the same with the muscles used for breathing. When the muscles used for breathing in, contract, those for breathing out are relaxed.

Whether we stand, run, hop, or crawl, all the activity of the central nervous system finally ends with activating, or not activating, motor neurones. For this reason C. S. Sherrington called the motor neurone the final common path. Whatever happens to the body, impulses are sent to the central nervous system, they go round and round in the brain, and they come out there, at the final common path of motor neurones.

All animals have inherited certain ways of responding to the situations they are likely to encounter. The more simple an organism, the more inevitable the behaviour will be; and the observer would not think of the animal as choosing how to behave. A minute organism endowed with positive phototaxis must go towards a light, another species, inheriting negative phototaxis, must escape from it.

The simplest and most automatic response to stimulation is a reflex movement. The word 'reflex' was introduced early in the nineteenth century by a British neurologist, Marshall Hall. He chose this word as he thought of the muscles as reflecting the stimulus, much as a wall reflects a ball thrown against it. By 'reflex' he meant the response of a muscle or several muscles to a stimulus that excites an afferent peripheral nerve. Since that time the meaning has been enlarged. It is now used to mean an inborn, immediate response of muscles or glands to a particular stimulus, involving the central nervous system.

Even a simple reflex, with only one synapse, such as the monosynaptic stretch reflex, is not the same on every occasion. This has been realized, and often forgotten, for about a hundred years. There are many factors influencing the one synapse between the afferent and the efferent nerve. There is the local and general state of excitability, and the number of reflex responses that have preceded the one being observed. For instance, if an identical stimulus to evoke a reflex response is repeated regularly several times a second, the response either increases or decreases. If the stimulus is repeatedly applied for many minutes, the local reflex response decreases and finally stops altogether.

There are many kinds of behaviour seen in animals lower in the evolutionary scale than mammals that in fact are reflex responses, though they appear not to be. The toad, for instance, has only two kinds of behaviour in its repertoire towards any moving object that it sees: it either turns towards it to snap it up, or else it turns away to escape. These are both reflex responses; which one occurs is related to the size of the object seen. Snapping-up-food behaviour is the answer to small objects moving in the field of vision, and avoiding and fleeing is the answer to large moving objects. To the naive observer, these actions might well appear as behaviour based on choice, the animal making a decision what to do.

Most kinds of behaviour of the higher vertebrates are neither entirely reflex nor entirely subject to deliberation and decision: they have elements of both. When someone inadvertently burns you on the leg with a cigarette, a volley of impulses is sent off to the spinal cord from the skin, and nerve impulses continue to fire off for thirty minutes or so. From the local region of spinal cord, impulses are sent to many other parts of the spinal cord and brain. Some regions get the information before others, and some centres react automatically while others react only after impulses have been received from various higher parts of the brain. The sending of information to various parts of the brain is the physiological substratum for the functions classified as psychological, such as making a decision after pausing for deliberation. The first response to the burning cigarette is likely to be a flexion and withdrawal of the burnt leg with extension of the opposite limb to support the weight of the body. The lower parts of the brain are informed of the rapid movement of the lower limbs so that they adjust the posture for standing on one leg to remove the other from the damaging stimulus. A further necessary part of the reaction is to cause pain. In the brain all sensory information is integrated, the input from the eyes, the ears, the nose, the skin. The brain recognizes that the object causing the burn is a cigarette. The highest levels of the brain are needed to arrange behaviour related to the circumstances. The brain relates the new event to remembrances of things past. Memory is used. Parts of the brain compare this new event with previous experience and note whether it is new and unfamiliar or something already known.

The first reflexes develop in the womb, as the structures are formed. The very earliest reflex responses occur around the mouth; the lips are turned towards the point stimulated. After birth, other reflex responses are added to the repertoire.

The essential reflex for maintaining posture is the stretch reflex; it is a servo-mechanism used to keep the muscles contracting to the right degree. When the muscle is pulled on and stretched, receptors within the muscle are excited and send impulses to the spinal cord. The nerves from the receptors of these muscles go to the motor neurones working the muscle and make it contract. When the stretch is removed, the receptors stop firing, the stimulus to the motor neurones of the muscle has gone, the motor neurones stop firing, and the muscle relaxes. Thus stretching a muscle makes it contract, and releasing it allows it to relax. In the stretch reflex, there is only one synapse, that between the afferent nerve fibres from the muscle receptors and the motor neurones working the muscle.

A baby learns to sit up when the organs of balance in the internal ear have established reflexes with the motor neurones working the muscles of the trunk and limbs. The basic reflexes for standing, crawling, sitting, walking, and running depend on built-in circuits of neurones in the spinal cord, connected to circuits in the centre of the cerebral hemispheres and the cerebellum. The cerebellum is kept informed about the activity of all muscles, about acceleration and deceleration affecting the whole body, and about all other inputs to the central nervous system. As soon as the spinal cord starts performing a movement, impulses are sent up to the cerebellum and continue to be sent throughout the movement, so that the cerebellum is kept informed how the movement is progressing. For the cerebellum is an error-measuring device that compares the actual performance with the programme which it receives from the cerebral hemispheres.

Most movements are programmed by the brain, and they use lower-level reflex arrangements as their components. When you do touch-typing, the impulses leave the brain, programmed in time and place to hit the keys in order. Once the impulses are on their way, they cannot be interrupted. You know when you are going to type the wrong letter or the letters in the wrong order, and out they come, wrong; the knowledge comes too late to interrupt the planned movements.

The movements organized by the cerebral hemispheres depend on impulses sent down tracts of nerve fibres to the spinal cord. Some of these tracts have synapses on the way; others have no synapses until they are near the motor neurones. There is one large tract called the corticospinal tract; it is shown in Figs. 18 and 20. It is mainly a motor tract, though some of the fibres go to the posterior horn, which is an afferent part of the spinal grey matter. A recent development in evolution, it has reached its highest development in man and is used for carrying out the finest and most delicate movements of hands and feet, fingers and toes.

The spinal cord and brain. It is now necessary to describe some of the anatomical features of the spinal cord and brain. The spinal cord consists of a central region of grey matter, made up largely of the cell-bodies and dendrites of neurones, and a surrounding ring of white matter. The white matter consists of tracts of nerve fibres descending from and ascending to the brain. The input from the peripheral nerves of the body is delivered to neurones of the grey matter of the spinal cord. These data are then processed at this level, and the resultant nerve impulses are sent along the spinal tracts to various regions of the brain. The input from the organs of the special senses—as vision, hearing, smell, and taste are called—goes to the grey matter of the brain. The brain, like the spinal cord, consists of grey and white matter, but most of the grey matter is on the outside and the white matter inside;

though there are some large masses of grey matter inside the cerebral hemispheres and cerebellum as well.

The brain is really an enlargement and opening out of the cranial end of the spinal cord. The first, slightly enlarged part is called the medulla oblongata (Figs. 16 and 17); the Latin term for the spinal cord is medulla spinalis. The medulla oblongata and the pons (Fig. 17) make up the hindbrain. From the roof of the hindbrain the cerebellum developed, first becoming large and important in birds. Further forwards or, to use the anatomical term, further rostrally (towards the beak) is the midbrain, and rostral to the midbrain comes the forebrain. When you take the brain out of the skull, what you first see are the two cerebral hemispheres. Each cerebral hemisphere is divided into lobes; they are called frontal, temporal, panetal, and occipital. Many anatomists also recognize a limbic lobe, which will be referred to later. The lobes are shown in Figs. 15, 16, 17, and 20.

The most posterior ridge or gyrus of the frontal lobe is the motor strip; it is the main source of the corticospinal tract. Most of the fibres of this tract go to the opposite side of the spinal cord, for each cerebral hemisphere mainly controls the opposite limbs. Many of the fibres

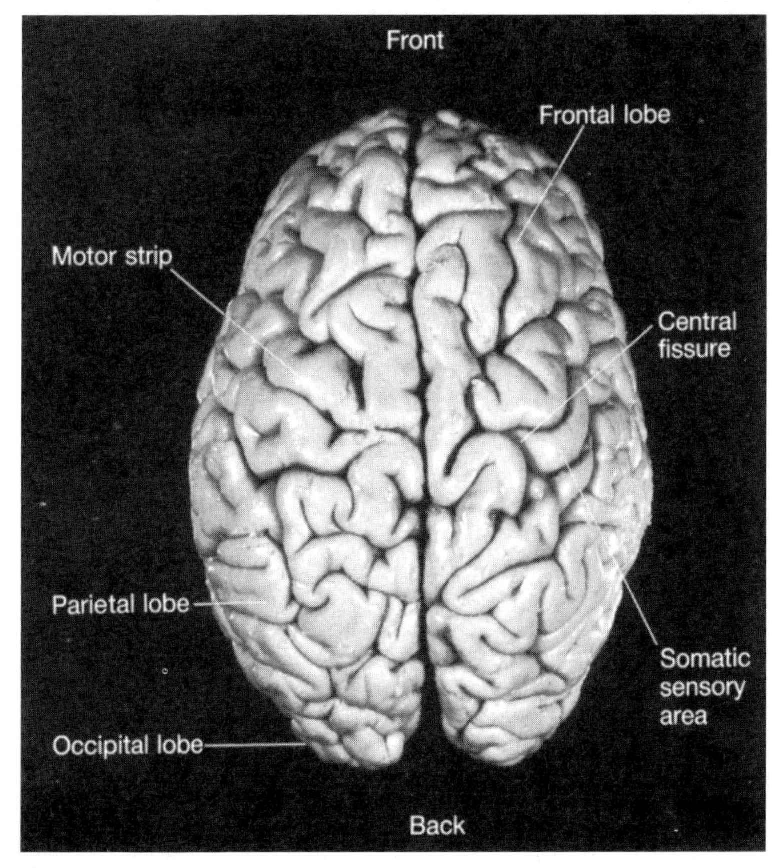

Fig. 15 Human brain seen from above.

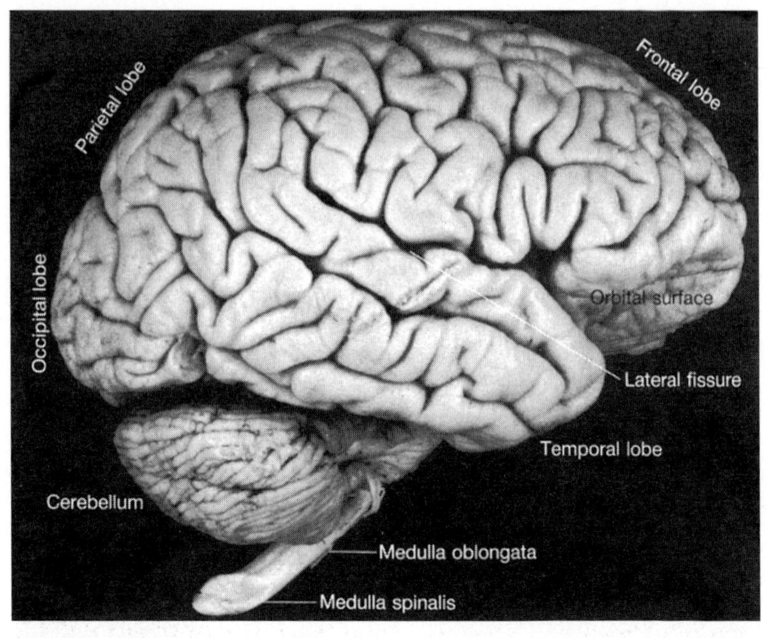

Fig. 16 Human brain seen from the right.

marked as going to and coming from the cerebral cortex in Fig. 18 would be the fibres of the corticospinal tract. As they descend through the brain, they become collected into a narrower space; most of them cross over from one side to the other as they enter the spinal cord. The gyrus from which most of these fibres come is called the pre-central gyrus; behind it is the post-central gyrus, and between the two is the central fissure (marked in Fig. 15). The post-central gyrus is the most anterior part of the parietal lobe. It is the somatic sensory area, a primary area for tactile and kinaesthetic input. There is another fissure, more prominent than the central fissure, the lateral fissure, shown in Fig. 16. It is the boundary between the temporal lobe below, and the frontal and parietal lobes above.

Once the cranium has been sawn through, the brain is easily lifted out of the skull. To remove it, one has to cut through the stalk of the pituitary (Fig. 17) and all cranial nerves, and also divide the medulla oblongata from the spinal cord. The cranial nerves were described and numbered from the front backwards by Thomas Willis in the seventeenth century. The first nerve cannot be seen in Fig. 17, as it was cut through when the brain was removed. It is the olfactory nerve, and is made up of thousands of nerve fibrils running vertically up from the cavity of the nose into the olfactory bulb (shown with most of the structures mentioned here in Fig. 17). From the olfactory bulb, impulses for smell are sent along the olfactory tract to the deeper parts of the temporal lobe. In Fig. 17, the second or optic nerve and the fifth or sensory nerve from the face can be seen. The pituitary gland is just behind the optic nerve. Tumours of the pituitary are liable to press on the optic nerve fibres and cause disturbances of vision, and, if they are not removed, blindness.

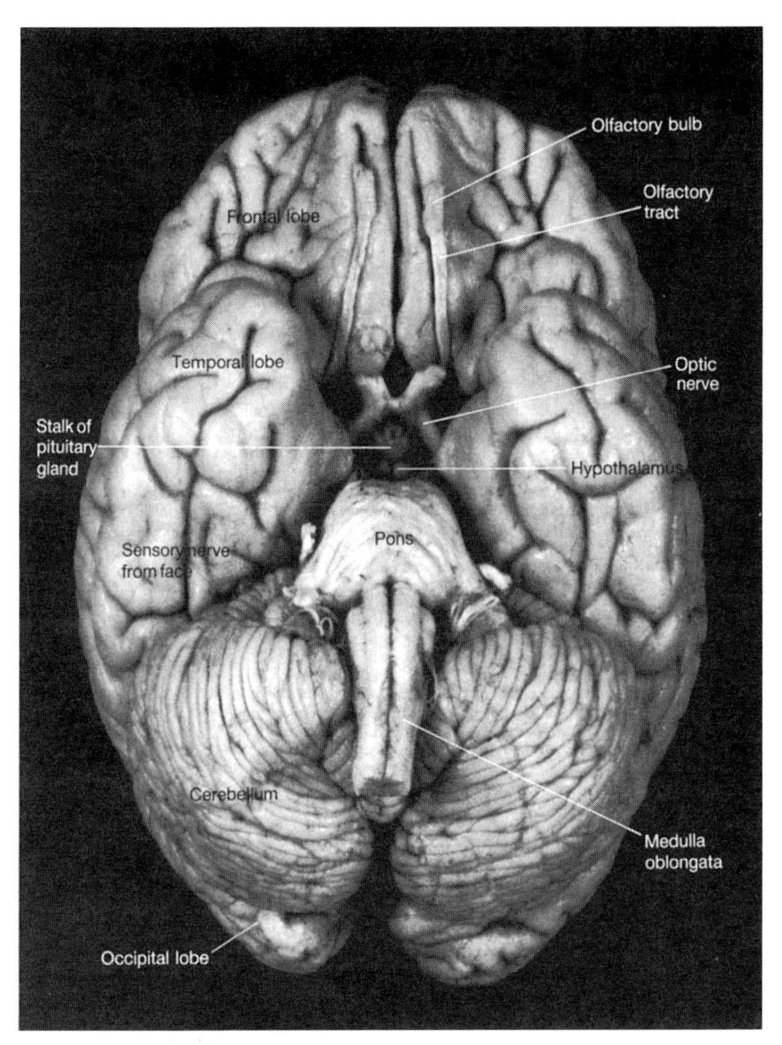

Fig. 17 Human brain seen from below.

The cortex of the cerebral hemispheres is made up of six layers, the neurones being arranged in most places in columns of six. Vast numbers of nerve fibres run into these layers, and similar vast numbers leave them. The tracts in which these bundles of nerve fibres are collected are shown in Fig. 18. This figure shows another large mass of fibres, the optic radiations, passing backwards from the midbrain to the occipital lobe, to reach the primary visual area of the cortex. The pons is cut through the midline in this dissection; it is a bridge taking fibres from one side of the hindbrain to the opposite cerebellum. The great mass of fibres going to and coming from the cerebellum is also seen in this figure, as a large white band in the centre of the cerebellum.

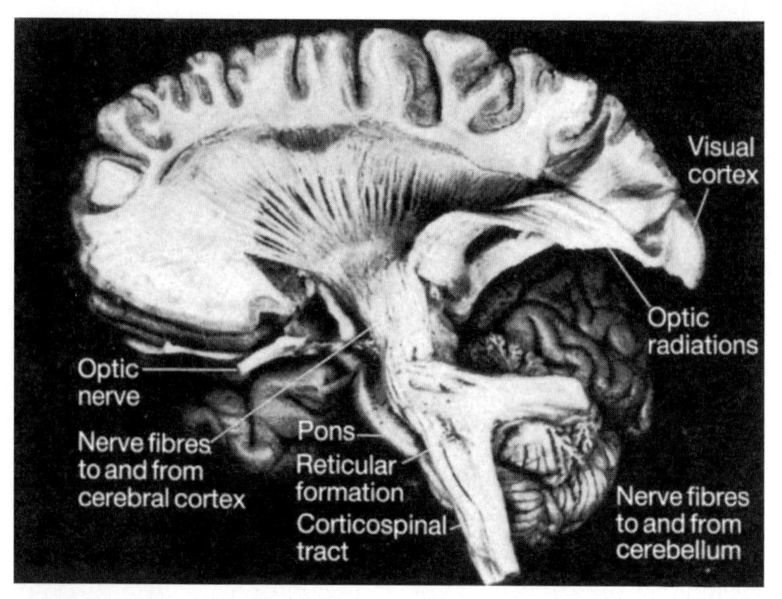

Fig. 18 The human brain dissected to show the tracts of nerve fibres going to and coming from the cerebral cortex and the cerebellum, and the optic radiations, which are fibres running from the midbrain to the visual cortex of the occipital lobe.

There is a mass of interconnecting neurones with short axons throughout the core of the brain, named the reticular formation; a part of it is shown in Fig. 18. This is a very old part of the brain, being an essential structure for working vital functions. It organizes breathing, controls the heart, blood vessels, blood-pressure; it is concerned with sleeping and waking, with relaxation, and with the opposite state-vigilance and alertness. This system stops all the input from receptors reaching the anatomical substrate of consciousness during sleep; it wakens us when the input is apparently urgent.

The two cerebral hemispheres are not equal and identical, neither morphologically nor physiologically. There is probably an inborn propensity for the two hemispheres to develop differently, and these differences are increased by experience and learning.

Each cerebral hemisphere organizes the movements of the opposite limbs, and the activity of each is co-ordinated by fibres passing across the large bridge, formed of nerve fibres, called the corpus callosum (shown in Fig. 20). The two hemispheres are not equal partners in organizing movements; the left is the leading one, just as it is for speech. It keeps the store of learned skills. It programmes most movements, and it directs the right hemisphere to control the left limbs while it controls the right ones. If the great bulk of nerve fibres through the corpus callosum is divided, the movements of the right limbs, controlled by the left hemisphere, remain normal, but programmed movements of the left limbs become abnormal in a strange way. The afflicted person cannot comb his hair when asked to do so, for instance, but makes vague movements similar to combing movements, perhaps in the air above his head. When asked how he would point the way, he may move his arm in an inadequate manner or just raise it vaguely in some direction. Although he can carry out more automatic and reflex movements, such as standing and sitting, quite normally, he cannot trace a circle on the ground with his foot nor point his toe when asked to do so. But all of these movements are performed quite normally by the right limbs. As the right hemisphere does not direct the left hemisphere, a lesion of the right hemisphere causes some paralysis of the left limbs but has no effect on the limbs controlled by the left hemisphere. (For further discussion, see SPLIT-BRAIN AND THE MIND.)

Types of muscle. The movements of the body are not only the movements of the whole body in space; there are the movements of organs of the body, movements of the heart, the intestines, the bladder, the pupils of the eyes. The muscles working these organs are different from those making up the trunk and limbs.

There are two main kinds of muscle, smooth muscle and striated muscle, the names describing their appearance under a light microscope. One may make the generalization that smooth muscles work entirely automatically, without our having much influence on them; and striated muscles are the muscles we use when we intend to do something like getting out of bed or jumping over a fence. As we have seen, muscles are made to contract by receiving impulses from nerve fibres. Striated muscles are supplied by somatic nerve fibres, and non-striated muscles by nerve fibres of the autonomic nervous system.

The autonomic nervous system. This consists of two parts, the sympathetic and parasympathetic systems, which cannot be classified as being either central or peripheral, as they are both. The autonomic system is always active, though at any time one part may be more active than the other, each being activated by emotion and behaviour depending on emotion. The sympathetic system is responsible for temperature regulation, contributes to the behaviour of threat and aggression, dilates the pupils and makes the hair stand on end, and controls the distribution of blood throughout the body by dilating or constricting blood vessels. When the person has to be active, it distributes the blood, so that the muscles of the limbs get a lot and those of the alimentary canal little. When the body is active, the sympathetic system cools it by making the sweat-glands secrete sweat, for heat is lost by evaporating sweat. The parasympathetic system organizes micturition and defecation, and it is the main controller of the alimentary canal. Sexual functioning is mainly parasympathetic, with minor, but in the male essential, contributions from the sympathetic system.

Perception. Animals are active; they are not usually sitting around waiting to be stimulated. They spend a lot of time seeking information, engaging in what ethologists call exploratory behaviour; they are curious and are trying to satisfy their curiosity. They ask the question, 'What is this?' as we can see from cursory observation of domestic pets and of cows in the field. But curiosity has to be tempered with caution, the amount of each depending on the species of animal, and mainly on whether it is a herbivore or carnivore. Some sorts of stimuli are prepotent, particularly the dangerous ones. The first question to be answered is whether the newly found object is familiar or strange, something the animal knows about or something that has to be approached with circumspection. Such perception may need knowledge, and knowledge involves memory. A rose is a rose only when compared with the memory of previous roses; but recognition usually takes place so quickly that we do not know we have put up the hypothesis—this is a rose—and have then confirmed or refuted it. Even so, just as we may need time to test a hypothesis so a cat or a dog faced with a strange object may be seen to exercise caution in determining whether it is familiar or new, related or unrelated to something already known, before reaching a decision on what to do with it.

Sometimes we behave as if we know about certain objects and situations when we have had no previous experience of them. How much of such built-in knowledge the human being has is only just being found out. In many higher vertebrates, visual patterns passing across the field of vision produce behaviour. When a young animal has never seen a shape before and yet knows what to do about it—this is the essence of knowledge. The human baby has more interest in human faces than in random lines and shapes and takes more notice of the sound of human speech than that of passing motor cars or the wind in the trees. The brain is constructed so as to receive and respond to the more significant kinds of stimulus. So, from the mass of stimuli always affecting it, the animal selects those that are important to its needs of the moment. When it is hungry, it neglects background noise and looks for food and all the signs that indicate food.

The brain can increase one sort of input and play down another. Selection starts at the receptors, continues where the nerve fibres enter the brain and spinal cord, and can operate at any synapse within the central nervous system. In order to concentrate on listening, we may find it helpful to close our eyes; to concentrate on a pain, we may want people to stop talking. One can learn to neglect an input habitually. When researchers used to use microscopes with one eyepiece, they did not close the eye that was not looking down the eyepiece, they just did not record what it was sending into the brain. Ballet-dancers learn to suppress the input from the organs of balance in the inner ear, in order to avoid vertigo when pirouetting.

All inputs to the central nervous system, gustatory, auditory, visual, and from the skin, the organs of balance, the bladder, the alimentary canal, the muscles and joints, go to the cerebellum, the reticular formation, and the thalamus (Fig. 20). Those that can eventually become conscious and cause a sensation go to certain neurones of the thalamus and thence to the cortex. In the thalamus each input has its own territory, though there is also some mixing, with different sorts of inputs going to the same region.

Each kind of sensation depends on a primary sensory area of the cortex. Next door to or surrounding the primary area is its secondary sensory area. After the secondary sensory areas, there are the association areas; and finally the motor areas. Nerve fibres of the primary areas go to the secondary surrounding areas and nowhere else. Each secondary area connects with the corresponding area of the other hemisphere, with every other secondary sensory area of its own hemisphere, and with association areas. The association areas would seem to be concerned with elaborating sensory information, and with joining the various kinds of input to make a meaningful whole. It looks like a fish, it smells like fish, it tastes like fish, and so it must be a fish. The association areas are interconnected; and finally they are connected to motor areas. The motor areas also receive other inputs—for example, to the neurones of the corticospinal tract there come fibres from the thalamus and from the somaesthetic area of the post-central gyrus, as well as fibres from other motor areas of the frontal lobe. The connections are laid down when the central nervous system is formed, according to the pattern of the species. They are then elaborated further during the experience of living.

Fig. 19 is a photograph of the brain dissected to show the optic pathways. The two optic nerves meet in the optic chiasm. There, half of the optic nerve fibres cross over to the opposite side and half remain on the same side as the retina from which they arise. The fibres then continue posteriorly, as the optic

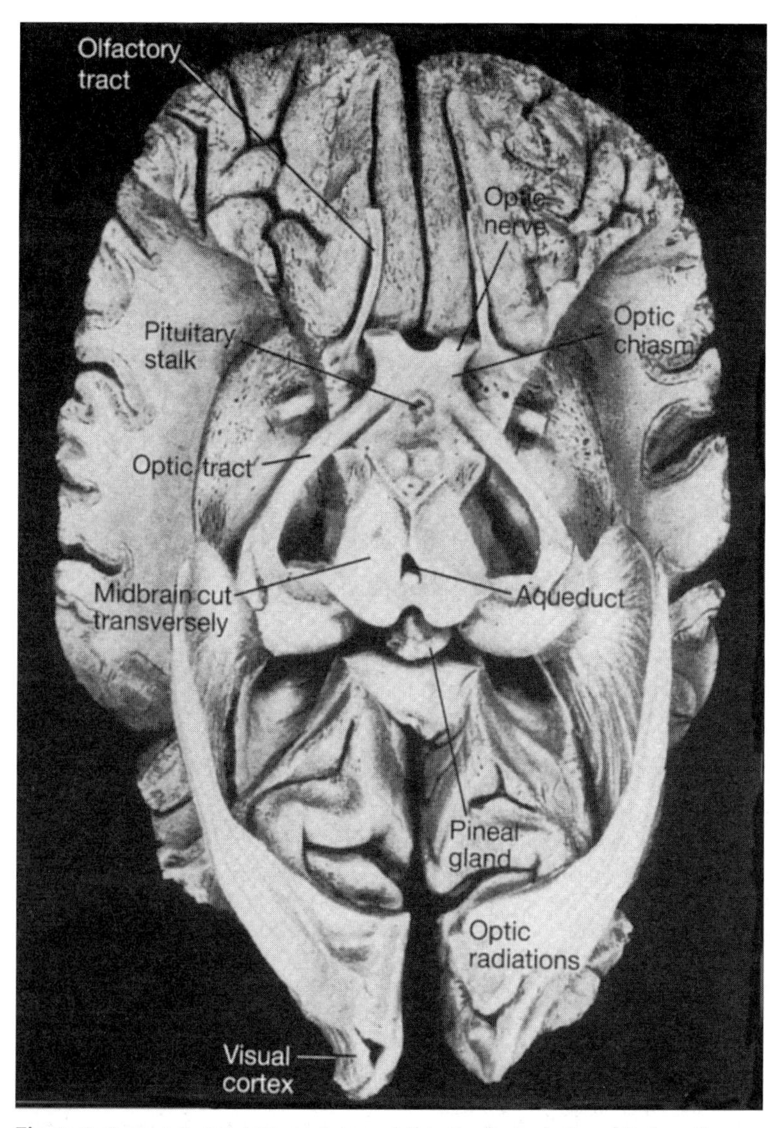

Fig. 19 The human brain dissected from below, especially to show the visual pathways. The two optic nerves fuse at the optic chiasm and then continue as the two optic tracts to the midbrain. From relays in the midbrain, fibres run posteriorly as the optic radiations to the visual area of the occipital lobes.

tract, going to a part of the midbrain. There is a relay there, and then fibres continue posteriorly to the visual areas, as the optic radiations (Figs. 18 and 19).

The primary area for hearing is in the upper part of the temporal lobe and cannot be seen until the brain is dissected. Near this region is the area for vestibular sensations, sensations which occur only under unpleasant circumstances, as when we feel giddy after spinning round and round or when we are rocked mercilessly on the sea. The area for smelling is also in the temporal lobe, and also in an older part of the forebrain, near the septal and preoptic areas (Fig. 20). The primary area for tactile feeling is in the post-central gyrus.

When a primary area is destroyed in man, the sense served by that area is not completely removed. In a few unusual cases, the primary visual cortex has been destroyed without damage to the surrounding visual parts of the cortex. The patient is blind but he can still point quite accurately to things he is shown. He knows where something is in the visual field, but he cannot say what it is. This produces the amazing situation of the patient being unable to see something but being able to put a finger on it, at the same time insisting that he sees nothing. In a sense, we may conceive of vertebrates as having two visual apparatuses, one to tell what a thing is, and another to tell where it is (see BRAIN FUNCTION AND AWARENESS).

In front of the secondary visual areas are the visual association areas. That in the right hemisphere is essential for the recognition of people's faces. In this region or in nearby regions of the cortex, the position of things in the environment in relation to ourselves is appreciated by means of connections with other parts of the hemispheres, parts concerned with knowledge of right and left, first on our own bodies and then in the world around us. If this region is badly damaged —and we know more about the effects of lesions than about how parts of the cortex normally function—then the patient cannot get any meaning out of the hands and numbers of a clock and thus cannot tell the time; neither can he understand the meaning of the points of

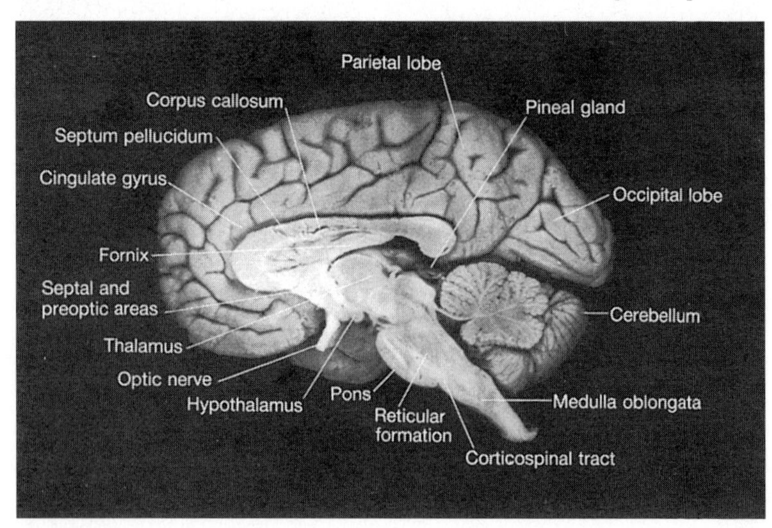

Fig. 20 Sagittal section through the human brain; it is cut through the midline and seen from the left.

the compass, or of maps, or of the plans of architects. Nor can he plan a journey, for he cannot visualize the route and has no idea which road to take whenever there is a choice. For this region of the right hemisphere of the brain is the bump of locality—and note that we still use the terms of phrenology.

Destruction of the primary area for hearing does not cause complete deafness; there is only a loss for high tones. Bats, for whom hearing is essential for life, can hear quite well with the primary auditory area destroyed.

The association areas are the important ones for all the activities we call thinking, remembering, imagining, or working things out. The ability to calculate, for instance, depends mainly on an association area of the left parietal cortex and the nerve fibres connecting to that area. This region is also essential for appreciating the relations of the fingers one to another. When this region is destroyed, the patient gets muddled in showing which of his fingers is which, and he cannot recognize, say, the index or the ring finger of the right hand of someone else. In addition, he gets confused about right and left. It is very likely that our ability to calculate is related to our knowledge of our own digits; and it is not coincidence that as we have ten fingers we use a decimal system. The cognizance of spatial relationships comes into arithmetic as well as into geometry. There are congenital defects of the cerebral cortex in which a child can learn to deal with figures up to ten but is unable to transfer a figure laterally to the next column.

Most parts of the brain are paired. For paired structures to work together, they have to be connected; the connecting links in anatomy are called commissures. The largest of the commissures connects the two cerebral hemispheres together; it is the corpus callosum, and it is made up of about 145 million nerve fibres. It is shown in Fig. 20.

From this rapid survey it will be realized that the brain is divided into separate regions with separate functions. This was first proposed by F. J. Gall, who founded phrenology on this concept in the early nineteenth century. He called the different regions of the cerebral cortex the organs of the brain.

Needs and desires. For an animal to carry out correct behaviour, it is provided with drives, desires, emotions, rewards, and punishments—functions which are a feature of the working of the brain. Correct behaviour means satisfying not only the demands of metabolism but also the demands made on the individual by other members of the group—it means correct social behaviour. Both kinds of demands, or needs, are always changing. At one moment food is required, at another drink, or shelter; at some stage a mate of the opposite sex is needed; after mating, life has to be adjusted to care for the offspring. The reward for proper behaviour is pleasure and satisfaction; the penalty for not seeking and not finding stimulation is boredom. The punishment for biologically wrong behaviour is unhappiness, and failure to satisfy essential needs is followed by discontent, which may be demonstrated in agitated activity. Thus the behaviour of human beings, like that of all other gregarious animals, is aimed at satisfying the desires that have come from the needs of both the individual and the group. Being aware, consciousness of purpose, thought, and programming and planning for the probable future are to be seen as a part of fulfilling these aims. The development of these higher cerebral mechanisms reaches its greatest extent in man.

There are many experiments showing how mammals that do not think and plan make correct choices. For instance, rats choose a correct diet when they are presented with a large variety of substances to choose from. They are placed in a sort of cafeteria where they can choose what to eat from a large variety of foodstuffs. When deprived of an essential ingredient of diet, they choose those foods that supply the missing elements. Deprived of a certain vitamin, they choose foods rich in that vitamin. Female rats take more fat when they are lactating, and return to their usual amounts when the litter has been weaned. When pregnant, they take more calcium and phosphorus, protein and fat. Human babies and young children behave similarly when they are left to their own devices. Thus, in rare cases of atrophy of the adrenal glands, in which the body cannot retain salt, the child demands salt and eats great quantities of it. That the brain can make the child choose the right food comes as a surprise, for we tend to think of it as the organ of thought; and a two-year-old cannot work out what food it requires when deprived of a necessary hormone.

The needs of individuals are not only the usual ones stressed in biology and physiology. There are the needs that one may call social: the need for companionship, the need to be part of a group with a hierarchical structure, the territorial needs of the group of which one forms a part. To satisfy these needs, the brain provides feelings and emotions, instinctual drives, and it puts energy at the disposal of these drives. Knowledge of what parts of the brain are involved in these social needs is still inadequate; our conceptions of the physiological and anatomical bases of behaviour await improvement as further knowledge is gained.

Just as some regions of the brain produce sensations and others organize movement, so parts of the temporal lobe are involved in generating emotion. The main evidence for this comes from the electrical stimulation of the brains of patients with epilepsy during operations under local anaesthesia. In some cases of epilepsy, fits are caused by scarring in the cortex of the cerebral hemisphere, and occasionally good effects come from removing the scar tissue. During the operation, the surgeon has to stimulate the brain electrically so as to know if he is operating in the right part of the hemisphere. Excitation of certain parts of the temporal lobes produces in the patient an intense fear; in other parts it causes a strong feeling of isolation, of loneliness; in other parts a feeling of disgust; and in others sorrow or strong depression. Stimulation of some parts causes a feeling of dread rather than of fear, a dread without object, the patient being unable to explain what it is he dreads. Sometimes there is intense anxiety and sometimes a feeling of guilt. Often such stimulation causes stronger and purer emotion than occurs in real life. Whereas it is the nature of the human situation that feelings of delight and joy come more rarely than feelings of misery, an ecstatic feeling that all problems are soluble can be brought about by electrical stimulation of parts of the temporal lobe.

Certain total acts of behaviour are organized by the hypothalamus. This small region (Fig. 20) organizes the metabolism of the body, heat production and the control of body temperature, the production and circulation of hormones, and the states of being awake or asleep and of aggression or timidity. It organizes mating and sexual behaviour and it controls the sympathetic and parasympathetic nervous systems.

But the hypothalamus does not initiate behaviour. The cerebral hemispheres do this—in so far as one may abstract one part from the whole and see it behaving independently. The cerebral hemispheres receive information arriving from all input channels, form a total and meaningful picture of it, the meaning including emotion, and organize a programme of behaviour. In response to such and such an occurrence, one must threaten or even attack; to a different one, be submissive or hide or flee. Stereotyped patterns of response organized by small groups of neurones in the hypothalamus can be modified or totally changed by the cerebral cortex.

The parts of the cerebral hemispheres most directly connected to the hypothalamus are regions within the temporal lobe sometimes called the limbic lobe. The limbic lobe is the most ancient part of the cerebral hemispheres and is already well developed in primitive fish. In mammals, it includes the hippocampus, the amygdala, the cingulate gyrus, the fornix, and the septal and preoptic areas (shown in Fig. 20). The amygdala is a large mass of neurones deep in the anterior part of the temporal lobe; this mass of grey matter, like other masses of archaic origin, lies within the white matter of the hemispheres. The cingulate gyrus surrounds the corpus callosum. The fornix is a connecting band of nerve fibres between the amygdala and hippocampus and the septal and preoptic areas and hypothalamus. Beneath the corpus callosum there is a septum which is almost transparent, hence its name of septum pellucidum. It separates the two ventricles of the hemispheres. Beneath the septum, the two ventricles connect through a hole to the third ventricle, which divides the hypothalamus into two. In front of the third ventricle are the septal and preoptic areas. The main centres of the autonomic nervous system are in the hypothalamus.

R. G. Heath, operating on conscious, psychotic patients in New Orleans, stimulated the septal area by means of electrodes and also by dripping in neurotransmitters. In some patients, expressions of anguish and despair changed precipitously to expressions of optimism and elaborations of pleasant experiences, past and anticipated. Patients could calculate more rapidly than before stimulation. Memory and recall were enhanced. One patient on the verge of tears described himself as somehow responsible for his father's near-fatal illness. When the septal region was stimulated, he immediately terminated this conversation and within fifteen seconds exhibited a broad grin as he discussed plans to date and seduce a girl friend. When asked why he had changed the conversation so abruptly, he replied that the plans concerning the girl had suddenly come to him.... Another patient, an epileptic, was one day agitated, violent and psychotic. The septal region was then stimulated without the patient knowing it. Almost instantly his behavioural state changed from one of disorganization, rage and persecution to one of happiness and mild euphoria. He described the beginning of a sexual motive state.

Heath's patients could not account for their changing the subject to sex; they would say that the ideas just came into their minds. Now, electrical or pharmacological excitation of the parts of the brain related to certain functions causes the subject to have the thoughts and emotions associated with those parts of the brain, and the act of copulation is organized in the front end of the hypothalamus and the nearby septal area. The neurones organizing this behaviour and accompanying emotional states do so only when they receive the right hormones in their blood supply. Somehow the hormones must change the neurones, but it is not yet known what they do or how they do it. The septal area inducing sexual thoughts, emotions, and action is either the same region or quite near the region that causes pleasure when it is excited. This region may be damaged in professional boxers, as it is vulnerable to head injuries. Some boxers become impotent and lose any interest in sex. The neurones are near those organizing micturition; and some boxers also have difficulty in controlling their bladders.

Neurones of the hypothalamus organize aggression with the accompanying emotions. When these neurones have been stimulated electrically in experiments in various kinds of animals, the animals show manifestations of rage and attack any living being in sight. A pigeon stimulated in this way and alone in a cage behaves as if it sees another bird; it circles threateningly round the hallucinatory bird, preparing to attack it.

The brain and spinal cord are not isolated within the body, encased within walls of bone though they are. They are bathed in blood; and the constituents of the blood reach all parts of the brain and have an effect. The food and drink we take soon reaches it: not only alcohol but fish and chips, and hamburgers—all contribute. The hypothalamus controls the production of hormones, which are taken by the blood to the spinal cord and to all the tissues of the body. It is a part of the brain and functions in relation to the rest of the brain. It is related closely to the parts of the cerebral hemispheres that organize emotions and total acts of behaviour such as aggression, fear, and sex. Acts such as these need hormones with their effects on neurones and other tissues of the body.

If we think of nerve fibres as like telegraph wires, we can think of hormones as like radio messages. The programme is sent out; it can be picked up by anyone who has a radio to receive it. The hormone is poured into the bloodstream and it can be picked up by any cell capable of receiving it. Most hormones are made by endocrine or ductless glands. The glands are controlled by nerve fibres from the central nervous system and also by circulating hormones of other kinds. The brain orders and controls the secretion of hormones; and the brain itself is subjected to the action of hormones.

Many factors influence the secretion of hormones. The pineal gland (Fig. 20) is affected by light. In most animals, nerve fibres connect it to the retinae. In those few species that have a third eye in the top of the skull, the nerve fibres connecting the pineal with this eye are very short: the two structures are almost touching. Light affecting the pineal gland makes it release the hormone melatonin into the bloodstream. The pineal also prevents the pituitary from secreting gonadotrophic hormones. When this control is relaxed, these hormones act on many tissues of the body, including the central nervous system, and bring about the physical and psychological characteristics of adolescence. In some birds and some small mammals, the cycle of reproduction depends on the duration of daylight. Long days allow the parents time enough to find food for the young. When autumn comes, the days draw in and the pituitary rearranges its release of hormones. With shorter days, birds fly off to a warmer climate and small mammals settle down to a quiet and boring winter of chastity and hibernation.

Some hormones act on the genes. As genes control and organize the structure and function of cells, they can change the character of the cells completely. When the gonads secrete their hormones at puberty, most of the tissues of the body are changed: the genital organs enlarge and, in the male particularly, the larynx enlarges too. These hormones also act on the neurones of the nervous system, changing the function of cells. And so one sees that the male dog, reaching puberty, cocks a leg to urinate; if he is castrated, he never does this, but passes urine in the semi-sitting position common to puppies. Hormones acting on certain neurones in the brain give us mental pictures. The amount of sexual desire is much influenced by the secretion of hormones acting on neurones of the brain.

Thinking. When one is asked what part of the brain does the thinking, one has to answer in the usual way that appears to prevaricate: it all depends on what you mean by thinking. For the word is used to mean solving problems, remembering, planning what one is expecting to do, planning what one is about to say, imagining things, considering opinions, and making judgements. Much thinking makes use of words, of internal speech. But one can have auditory thoughts, thoughts without words. The composer conceives a melody without using words. The painter pictures things without using words, seeing them in his mind's eye. One remembers faces, things one has seen, and can imagine shapes and scenes when closing the eyes. Thinking of a smell is not helped at all by speech.

The parts of the brain concerned with the activity we categorize as mental are the cerebral hemispheres. The various kinds of intellectual activities are carried out by different parts of the cerebral hemispheres. The ability to think spatially depends on a region of the right hemisphere between the occipital, parietal, and temporal lobes; and a main region for mathematical thinking is in a similar part of the left hemisphere. Neurologists imagine that the higher levels of the brain make a model of the actual world, a mental picture that parallels the world, though no doubt with distortions; it is a symbolic representation of reality. The model is made by the neurones, and the connections between the neurones, of the cerebral hemispheres. There are more than ten billion neurones in the human cerebral cortex. How connecting up regions of the cortex actually brings a memory into consciousness or allows us to imagine an event that has never occurred, we really do not know. We may conjecture that, in remembering a scene, the regions of cortex that were active when the original external stimulation occurred are brought into activity again. If this is so, and it is likely to be at least a part of the truth, there has to be some difference between the original activation of the region and the later pale image of the memory. It is obvious that a main function of the brain is to provide higher vertebrates with such mental images derived from the surrounding world. And it is customary to say that when one evokes these images, one has the picture in one's mind. Why we are unable to put all of this together is that our methods of research are apt for analysis but very poor at synthesis.

Speaking. A baby starts by listening to the sounds of speech. Endowed as he is with acute hearing for the frequencies and overtones used in speech, he comes to notice the subtle differences between these sounds. He then learns to associate meanings with the sounds; he also imitates and learns to make the sounds himself and to stop the babbling that has no meaning to those around him. Just as he moves his limbs, he makes controlled movements with the muscles of the larynx, palate, lips, and tongue.

One supposes that something like this is happening. Volleys of impulses from the inner ears reach the lower centres for hearing in the lower parts of the brain. From there, volleys are relayed to various specific parts of the brain, including the auditory regions of both temporal lobes. Surrounding each primary auditory region is a secondary auditory region in which heard phonemes are turned into sound symbols. These are sounds with meaning. The secondary auditory regions of the temporal lobes are connected to many other cortical areas that contribute to speech.

One is an area of the frontal lobes that organizes the actual movements of the respiratory muscles, larynx, and mouth to produce speech.

When a child learns to read, he organizes connections to the visual cortex, where recognition of the seen shape of letters and words occurs. Reading is associating the visual representation of the word with its auditory representation, and associating the auditory representation with the actual object. 'Associating' is a psychological term for the physiological activity of sending volleys of impulses between various cortical areas. When the child learns to write, he says the sound out loud to himself, and then draws the visual representation of that sound that has been accepted by the conventions of his society. This entails learning sequences of movements needed to draw the agreed symbols. All of it happens in milliseconds once it has been practised.

Neurologists have had to learn from observing the effects of damage to parts of the brain. When certain regions are destroyed, then such and such defects are found. From deducing what a destroyed region might have done, tentative guesses are made as to how the brain works. Learning about the brain in this way provides answers to many anatomical questions; but given the structure one still needs to understand how the rapid passage of nerve impulses results in all the activities we call thinking.

Total behaviour. The kinds of people we are depends primarily on our brains. The parts of the brain making each of us ourselves and different from everyone else are the higher levels of the brain: higher anatomically, towards the top of the head, and higher physiologically, in that their operations are least automatic and reflex, and most delayed in action and complicated. One spinal cord, one medulla, one brain-stem is much like another. But we differ in our cerebral hemispheres. They certainly start different; and they become more different on account of everything we have put into them or not put into them.

The temporal lobes are the main regions of the cerebral hemispheres for memory. The limbic lobes are the main parts for organizing the essential drives, which are kindled by emotions. They have rapid connections to both parts of the autonomic nervous system: sympathetic for activity and parasympathetic for relaxation. The hypothalamus has many functions. It organizes hormonal control of the body, total acts of behaviour, circadian rhythms, food and drink intake, and excretion and elimination among other things. It seems far too small a structure and to have far too few neurones to do all these things. Its smallness contrasts with the size of the cerebral hemispheres with their row upon row of neurones. From the whole extent of the hemispheres, one imagines, commands are sent to the limbic lobes, and from there are funnelled down to the hypothalamus. One supposes that a situation is apprehended by the cerebral hemispheres, is then related to previous experiences, probably in the hippocampus, and labelled as familiar or novel and strange. What is likely to happen next is then anticipated, and behaviour to meet it is planned. This requires not only action, but also emotions, desires, and the entire mental state that is necessary for the programme.

The more rostral parts of the frontal lobes and their connections to the thalamus, to the hypothalamus, and to the septal areas are the regions of the brain most concerned with social behaviour. Maturation of these regions takes years, and development of the anatomical connections continues until puberty. Experiments on dogs and monkeys in which connections between the frontal lobes and other parts of the brain were cut through, have demonstrated that animals losing social knowledge cannot relearn social behaviour. Animals subjected to the operation would go casually up and take food away from animals of higher rank, and would fail to learn not to do this in spite of being repeatedly punished by the other animals. Man's case is similar, though seldom extreme since lesions are not usually extensive. Large lesions in the front parts of the frontal lobes lead to lack of attention to the feelings and the behaviour of others. In 1868, Harlow of Boston reported a famous case in which a crowbar was blown through a man's frontal lobes without killing him:

> His equilibrium, or balance, so to speak, between his intellectual faculties and animal propensities, seems to have been destroyed. He is fitful, irreverent, indulging in the grossest profanity (which was not previously his custom), manifesting but little deference for his fellows, impatient of restraint or advice when it conflicts with his desires, at times pertinaciously obstinate, yet capricious and vacillating....

Early attempts at leucotomy cut many of the connections between the frontal lobes and the thalamus and resulted in apathetic beings with no energy, no interests, and no ability to concentrate on anything for long. The patients became uninhibited, their behaviour insensible to its effect on other people and unaltered by criticism. Less extensive operations resulted in less damaging effects.

The frontal lobes play an important role in determining our energy, and thus our interests, but are not primarily concerned with intellectual functions. They are concerned with mood, and with inherited and acquired behaviour in social groups, as we have seen. Connected as they are with the septal areas, it is likely that right behaviour is learned, by both man and other gregarious animals, from reward with pleasure. Conversely, wrong behaviour must be corrected, and there must therefore also be connections with aversive centres, if there are such centres in the limbic lobes. It may be that without such connections learning would not occur.

The mind? Should one think that the materialist view of the neurologist is inadequate or wrong, the best way to criticize it may be to attack it on its own ground. Such criticism would go something like this: 'Although you have explained the anatomy and physiology, you have said almost nothing. You tell me that when you hear me speaking, pressure waves reach your inner ear, and that they cause the physico-chemical events called nerve impulses in the auditory nerve. Further groups of nerve impulses finally reach the speech area of the left cerebral hemisphere, you say, and from there more impulses go to other parts of the brain, to regions where strangeness or familiarity are recognized, where memories are evoked, and where various emotions are induced. But you have chosen to leave everything out except the structure, the anatomy of the brain. *How does the activation of neurones at synapses make me feel frightened?* You answer that if during an operation the electrical stimulation of parts of the limbic lobes makes the patient feel frightened, then we may assume that fear is normally caused by the excitation of that part of the brain. But that is merely showing me a location, a bit of anatomy. Your explanation is no explanation at all.'

As we should have no preconceptions about what effects the activation of groups of neurones have, we can merely take note of what effects they do have. In one case, we have the feeling of fear; in another case, we hear a sound. These experiences are a part of the constant effort of an animal to remain alive, a station on the pathway towards activity in the world. Thus attacks on the present attempts of students of the nervous system to understand behaviour are most effective where ignorance of neural events is greatest; and they tend to fail where knowledge of neural functioning is adequate. In the example of movement, we know much of the neural events that occur, although of course gaps in our knowledge remain. Neurologists can point to the physical and chemical events that occur when we put our right foot forwards. Nerve impulses pass from the left frontal hemisphere along various circuits of neurones in the brain; and finally they come down to motor neurones working the muscles of the right lower limb, exciting some and inhibiting others. The result of this is that muscles used in putting the foot forwards are caused to contract, and opposing muscles to relax, the muscles of the trunk and upper limbs behaving similarly. There are no occurrences but physical and chemical ones, nothing but the events we study in anatomy and physiology, chemistry, and physics; and therefore, in this case, the critic cannot say that the neurologist has not shown him everything. It follows that if what happens when we move can be more or less explained, any inadequacy in the ability to account for what happens when we feel fear or remember a past event is likely to be due only to insufficient knowledge of the physiology concerned.

Put at its most superficial, it is a matter of vocabulary. In the context of neurology the adjective 'mental' is in order but the noun 'mind' is not; so it is acceptable to say that perception is a mental occurrence but bad terminology to say that perception occurs in the mind. Once one is aware of the dangers of the word 'mind', however, one may use it most acceptably.

PETER W. NATHAN

NEUROTRANSMITTERS. The soft warm living substance of the brain and nervous system stands in stark contrast to the rigid metal and plastic hardware of a modern day computer, but at the fundamental level there are clear similarities between these two apparently disparate organizational systems and, of course, one is a product of the other. Not only are the nerve cell units (neurones) self-repairing and self-wiring under the grand design built into our genes, but they can also promote, amplify, block, inhibit, or attenuate the micro-electric signals which are passed on to them, and through them, and thereby give rise to signalling patterns of myriad complexity between networks of cerebral neurones, and this provides the physical substrate of mind. Such key processes of signalling by one group, or family, of neurones to another is achieved largely by the secretion of tiny quantities of potent chemical substances by neuronal fibre terminals. These neurotransmitters stimulate selected neighbours, with whom they junction, into producing electrical responses which both qualitatively (i.e. by excitation or inhibition) and quantitatively (i.e. by frequency of neurotransmitter release) reflect the patterns of presynaptic stimulation.

In this way, the nerve impulses are passed on from cell to cell. This continuous alternation between electrical and chemical conveyance of signals on their journeys through the pathways of the brain and nervous system, provides a special opportunity for the traffic of electrical impulses to be modulated or blocked as they attempt to jump the gap between one neurone and the next at their junctions, transposed into pulses of chemical substances. This is the point where selected constellations of neurones from the vast array of neuronal populations can effectively interact, one with another, to filter, edit, integrate, and add precise direction to their interplay of communication. Thus, neurotransmitters and their functional partners, the *neuromodulators*, play a cardinal role in controlling the flow of information through the nervous system.

Neurones as information receivers and transmitters. The extensive web of branching dendrites which characterizes so many neurones in the brain (see **nervous system**) is primarily an adaptation to provide maximal surface area for receiving inputs from other nerve cells with which they make contact. *Interaction* is very much the principle theme which underlies the shape and cellular anatomy of neurones. Each pyramidal neurone in the vertebrate brain is likely to be receiving up to some 100,000 contacts from the neurones to which they are wired, and the dazzlingly complex and extensive multibranched dendritic tree of the Purkinje cells of the cerebellum, concerned with learning co-ordination tasks, probably extends to some 300,000 neuronal contacts. The axons, the single output line of the neurone, can be rather short (e.g. in so-called *interneurones*) or very long, perhaps 12 metres in cortical pyramidal cells of the giant blue whale, which course from brain to lower spinal cord. At various points along its length, the axon may branch to make contact with local neuronal communities, though most of its contacts are made towards its terminal region. Thus, it is not surprising that the cell-body region of the neurone is estimated to take up only 5 per cent or less of the cellular volume of the brain, the greater part comprising the dense fibrous feltwork of dendrites and axons (Fig. 21).

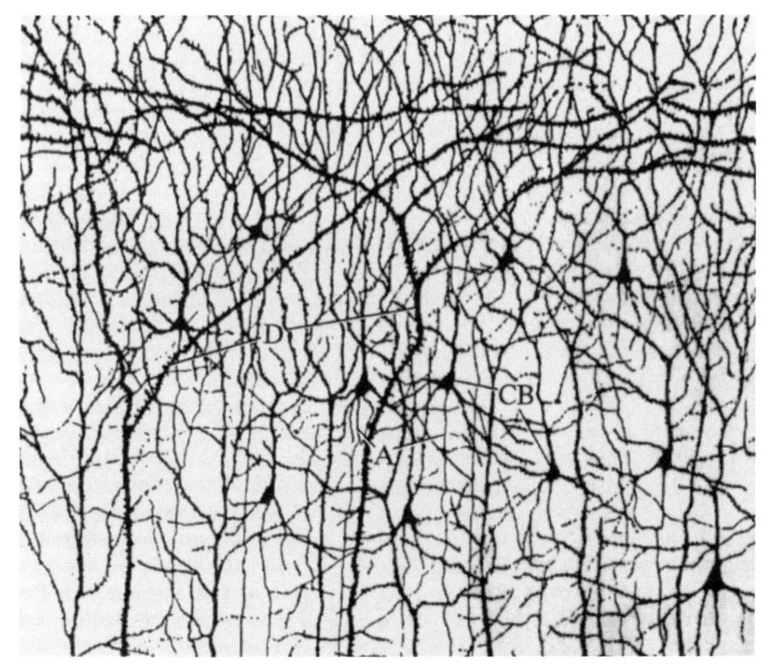

Fig. 21 Golgi preparation from the visual cortex of a human infant, showing the vertical orientation of many neuronal processes. Dendrites (D) can be identified by the spine processes which give their surface a rough, granular, appearance. In contrast axons (A) and cell bodies (CB) are smooth-surfaced.

Sometimes the neurone-to-neurone contacts or *synapses*, as they are termed, are highly organized junctions allowing an extremely close approach between the two cells so that they are separated only by a very narrow gap or *cleft* (typically 20 nanometres wide) (Figs. 22 and 23). In this case, neurotransmitters are delivered at a very precise location when their secretion is triggered by the incoming nerve-terminal. In other cases, the axon produces long chains of swellings (so-called *vancosities*) towards its terminal branching regions, and these provide multiple sites for neurotransmitter release as the nerve-impulse courses through them on its passage towards the distal regions of the neurone (Fig. 24).

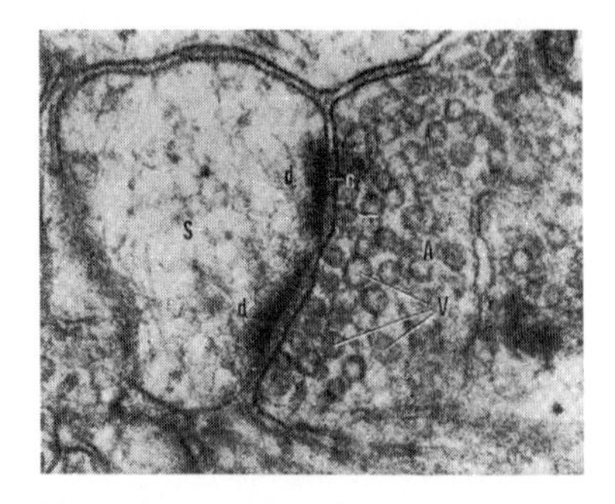

Fig. 22 Electron micrograph of nerve-ending (synapse) of the 'tight-junction' variety in rat brain. The pre-synaptic region (axon, A) synapses onto the post-synaptic region (dendrite spine, S). Note the synaptic cleft (C), synaptic vesicles (V), and post-synaptic densities (d). The latter are double because the density forms a 'doughnut-like' ring and is seen as a cross section through this ring. This arrangement of the density, is not uncommon. Note synaptic vesicles exocytosing (*arrow*). Compare with Figure 23.

These varicosities, whilst containing synaptic vesicles and granules of the

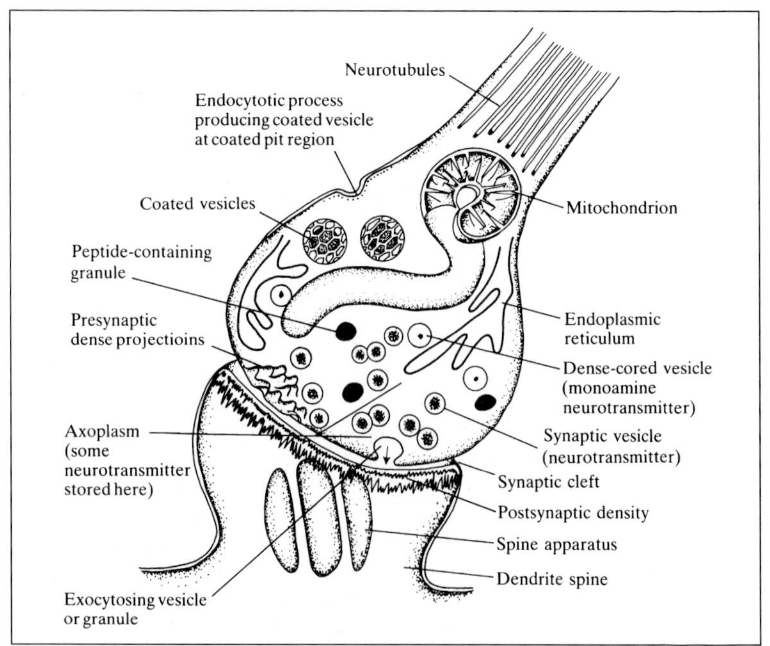

Fig. 23 Diagrammatic version of an axon terminal forming a synapse on a spine apparatus of a dendrite. The structures shown are not to scale. Endocytosis produces complex vesicles consisting of a hexagonal basketwork of fibres (cytonet), which form part of the inner surface of the nerve terminal membrane at regions called 'coated pits'. In this diagram, vesicles containing monoamines, neuropeptides, and other neurotransmitters are shown. A vesicle is shown expelling neurotransmitter into the synaptic cleft by exocytosis.

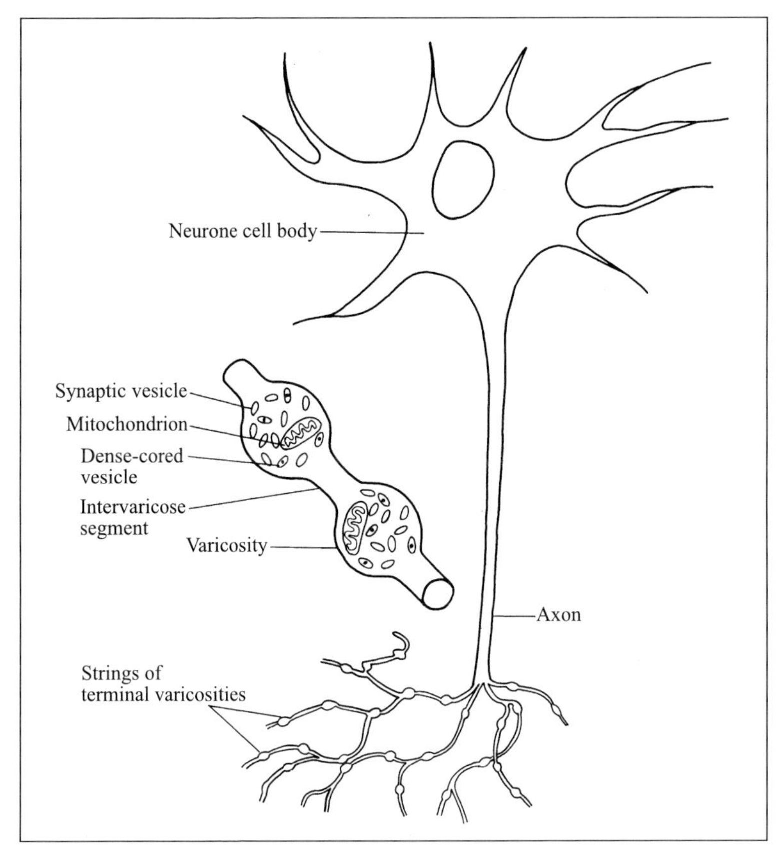

Fig. 24 Diagram of a neurone with terminal varicosities.

type characteristic of the 'tight-junction' synapses described above, do not exist in highly organized apposition to other neurones, and the highly structured synaptic cleft (gap between neurones) or post-synaptic thickenings typical of 'tight-junction' synapses are rarely present (compare Figs. 23 and 24). The neurotransmitter is probably released from the whole bulbous surface of the varicosity as a miniature cloud which will diffuse away, diminishing in concentration, until it encounters the appropriate neurotransmitter neuroreceptors at which it can bind and act. These varicose modifications of nerve axons were first discovered in the peripheral nervous system, but in the past decade they have become established as a common feature of the synaptic organization of the brain itself, and provide a semi-localized form of neurotransmitter release called *paracrine* neurosecretion.

How many neurotransmitters are there? The search for chemical agents which could transmit the activity of peripheral nerves onto their target organs began early in the twentieth century. In the 1920s and early 1930s, after a long trail of research *acetylcholine* was unequivocally demonstrated to be mediating the inhibitory influence of the vagus nerve on the heart, as well as the excitatory action of motor nerve terminals on voluntary muscle. At that point, acetylcholine became the first chemically identified neurotransmitter substance. *Adrenaline*, too, was an early candidate as neurotransmitter in the peripheral nervous system at ganglionic sites, but after long accumulation of evidence its unmethylated derivative, *noradrenaline*, was finally shown in the mid 1940s to be the actual agent responsible. *Dopamine*, a closely related amine (monoamines), followed a similar history, with doubt and then certainty following its progress to acceptance as a neurotransmitter in the 1950s. In the 1940s another neuroactive monoamine, *serotonin*, first isolated from blood was accepted as a neurotransmitter in the brain and peripheral nervous system.

Thus, in the 1950s only four compounds, together with a few other unlikely candidates, including a peptide (*substance P*), were the full armoury of agents known to be acting as neurotransmitters. They were found to be localized to the neurones from which they were released. These substances seemed to be specialized for their task as neurotransmitters and were not involved in other biochemical activities. At that time, it seemed likely that, together, they provided the principal means of chemical neurotransmission throughout the nervous system. However, it was also in the 1950s and later in the 1960s that four amino acids (*glutamate*, *aspartate* as excitatory agents, and *GABA* and *glycine* as inhibitory agents), also amines (but carrying an acidic group as well), were being considered as new and important contenders as neurotransmitters in the brain and spinal chord. They were most unlikely candidates, being found ubiquitously in all cells and organs in high concentrations, and being involved in a wide range of metabolic pathways and biosyntheses in the general biochemical economy of the cell.

The first members of yet another entirely different biochemical category of neurotransmitters became serious contenders in the 1970s, namely the *neuropeptides* (2 to 50 residue oligo-peptides). Unlike the amino acids, the neuropeptides are mostly present in extremely small quantities in localized regions of the nervous system. The earliest candidates proved to be already operating in the brain as local *neurohormones* in the hypothalamus and anterior pituitary gland. One example is thyrotropin-releasing-hormone (*TRH*, a tripeptide). During the 1970s and 1980s many or most of the peptides known to be serving an endocrine or neurotransmitter role in the gastrointestinal system were found to be also serving as neurotransmitters in the brain. The significance of the dual existence and bioactivity of these peptides is not clear, but specific neuroreceptors for them exist in both brain and gastrointestinal systems, allowing the possibility of brain-gut interactions at the neurohormone level, and giving rise to the concept of the '*brain-gut axis*'.

Some of these neuropeptides seem to evoke rather more complex responses than simple synaptic excitation or inhibition (both of which they also mediate). For example, very small quantities of TRH can induce euphoric states, and it can act as an antidepressant drug for the treatment of affective disorders. Another neuropeptide, *β-endorphin*, causes muscular rigidity and immobility (catatonia), whilst *luteinizing-hormone-releasing-hormone* (*LHRH*) is reputed to stimulate the libido, and has been used to cure oligospermy. *Cholecystokinin* (*CCK*) promotes feelings of appetitive satiety and causes cessation of feeding in animals. *Bombesin* dramatically lowers body temperatures, controls many aspects of gastric secretion, and stimulates appetite by actions at sites within the brain. The endorphins and *encephalins* not only produce fairly complex and sophisticated behavioural effects, they also induce analgaesia, behaving like endogenous 'morphine-like compounds'. Unfortunately, they (and their active synthetic derivatives) are also addictive when given in quantity as analgesic drugs. The endorphins seem to serve a neurohumoral role as well as that of neurotransmitter .

Peptide-releasing neurones show certain special features in their organization. Thus, cholinergic (i.e. 'worked' by acetylcholine), monoaminergic, and amino acidergic neurones synthesize neurotransmitter principally in their nerve terminals, by simple enzymatic processes. Peptidergic cells in contrast, synthesize their peptide neurotransmitters as sub-components of large 'mother' proteins by protein synthesis processes occurring in the cell body. These are then loaded into large granules and transported down the length of the axon to the terminal regions of the neurone. During this journey, the active neuropeptides are 'snipped' off the mother protein by specific enzymes (proteases), and the peptide neurotransmitters are then ready for release on arrival (Fig. 25). Inactivation of the released peptide neurotransmitter is by enzymatic hydrolysis, as for acetylcholine, and unlike most other neurotransmitters—which are rapidly reabsorbed back into the terminals, and into surrounding glial cells.

When one surveys the currently known neurotransmitters, it can be seen that apart from the simple amines and amino acids discovered during the first seventy years of this century, some fifty neuropeptides must be included. The latter serve in hybrid capacities as neurotransmitters-neurohormones-neuromodulators, and in this way trigger off complex patterns of behaviour. In order to be accepted as a neurotransmitter, the substance must satisfy some seven key criteria. Until they satisfy all criteria, they are called *putative* neurotransmitters. **How do neurotransmitters work?** These highly potent substances are released

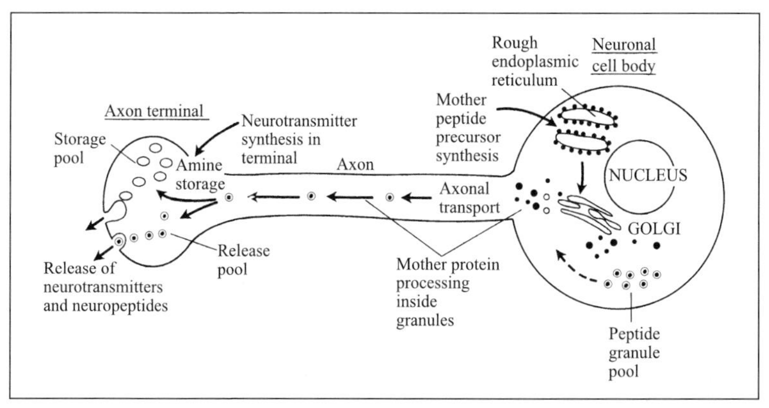

Fig. 25 Diagram illustrating the biosynthesis, packaging, and release of peptides and other neurotransmitters in neurones. The peptides are generated from large precursor molecules (pre-proproteins) produced in the rough endoplasmic reticulum (RER) of the neuronal cell body. These are packaged into secretory granules or vesicles in the Golgi membrane stacks. The granules are then transported out of the cell body (*axonal transport*) to the terminals, where upon stimulation they release their contents by exocytosis. Other neurotransmitters are produced in the cytosol of the cell body, axon, and principally in the nerve terminal, and they are packaged by uptake into preformed granules or vesicles.

from their storage sites in the close apposition synapses, or in terminal varicosities (or dendrites), and diffuse shorter or longer distances until they encounter neurotransmitter receptors with which they are designed to specifically interact. Once bound to the neurotransmitter in question, the neuroreceptor, which is a large glycoprotein molecule, spanning the membrane thickness (10 nanometres), undergoes conformational or other structural change, and this results in one of two known categories of response. The first of these is called an *ionotropic* response, and results in the appearance of a 'hole' or 'passage' right through the neuroreceptor protein molecule from outside to inside the membrane, through which only a particular charged ion can pass (Na^+, K^+, or Cl). The specific ion in question proceeds to move through the neuroreceptor molecule either into or out of the cell interior, driven down its concentration gradient, and attracted or repulsed by the prevailing electric field across the membrane, according to the nature of its own net charge (Fig. 26). Each neuroreceptor channel may be open for only a very brief period (e.g. 1 microsecond) as the neurotransmitter rapidly dissociates and is inactivated, or may remain open for much longer periods (e.g. 1 sec.) depending on the ion channel concerned. As the post-synaptic membrane is densely packed with these structures, the net effect is a substantial movement of charged ions across the membrane. This movement generates excitatory or inhibitory synaptic potentials and, from this pattern of impingement of electrical signals (information) onto its dendrites and cell body (inhibitory inputs), the target neurone will be triggered to fire its own action potential, or remain quiescent, as appropriate according to the intensity of the excitatory, and inhibitory signals received. Individual

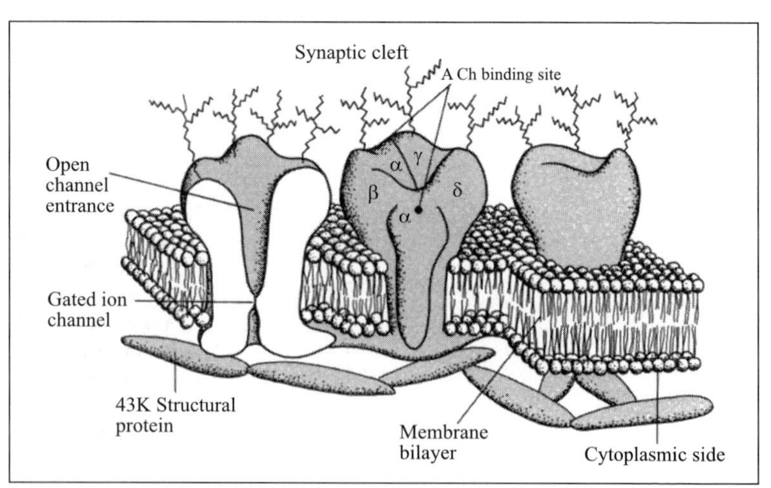

Fig. 26 Three-dimensional models of the nicotinic acetylcholine receptor from the electric ray fish *Torpedo californica* depicted as membrane proteins in the post-synaptic membrane of the synapse between the nerve and the electric organ which works essentially like a neuromuscular junction and employs acetylcholine as neurotransmitter. The sub-unit arrangement around the central channel is tentative. The sites on the two α subunits that bind acetylcholine and other related substances are shown as dark patches. The proposed shape of the central channel can be seen in the vertical section. Also shown is the membrane structural protein of mol wt 43,000 often found in association with the receptor in *Torpedo*.

neuroreceptor channel-opening and -closing events can now be distinguished by so-called 'single channel recordings' by 'patch clamping' electrophysiological recording techniques where neurotransmitter is perfused onto the post-synaptic membrane and the properties of small patches of membrane are studied.

The second category of neuroreceptor response is known as *metabotropic* because enzymes are involved. These enzymes are buried in the lipid membrane close to, and linked permanently or temporarily (depending on the cellular location) to, the neuroreceptor protein molecule. Following neurotransmitter-receptor activation there are conformational changes in the neuroreceptor-enzyme complex, which cause activation of the enzyme. The latter consequently acts upon its substrate, which is situated on the inner surface of the membrane, to produce a soluble product which diffuses into the neuronal cytoplasm and evokes responses which mostly lead on to produce a change in local membrane potential, usually resulting in the generation of a synaptic potential. These soluble enzyme products are called *second messengers*, as they produce actions which are secondary to the primary action of the neurotransmitter.

How are neurotransmitters released? Calcium ions are the critical factors in triggering neurotransmitter release. Normally these ions are at almost undetectable levels in neuronal cytoplasm (10^{-9}M), but rapidly flood into the terminals from the surrounding fluid through special channels during nerve-terminal depolarization caused by the action potential. Equally rapidly, the raised cytosolic levels of calcium are cleared by transport into mitochondria and endoplasmic reticulum within the terminal.

It has been demonstrated that neurotransmitters can also be released from the *dendritic tree* of the neurone as well as from nerve *terminals* as classically conceived. Indeed, the dendrites show localized accumulations of synaptic vesicles which are characteristic of all neurotransmitter release sites (e.g. synapses, terminal varicosities). Such release has been unequivocally demonstrated to occur in the dopaminergic neurones of the substantia nigra of the brain and also by the mitral cells and GABAergic axonless granule cells of the olfactory bulb. It may be that neurotransmitters can be released from other regions of the neuronal cell surface, including the unmyelinated regions of axons, and from the cell bodies themselves, though the greater proportion of neurotransmitter is localized to the nerve terminals.

Whether neurotransmitter is actually released from these various sites by a single process remains unclear. Certainly the traditional view envisages an exocytotic process involving the fusion of neurotransmitter-filled synaptic vesicles with the nerve terminal wall, resulting in the expulsion of about 1,000 molecules (one quantum) of neurotransmitter into the synaptic cleft from each vesicle. Many multiples of such quanta are released as the nerve impulse invades the nerve terminal, and this involves fusion and exocytosis by equivalent multiples of vesicles. However, the synaptic vesicles involved must already be in contact with the terminal membrane and ready to release their content as there is less than 200 microseconds between first entry of calcium and first detectable appearance of neurotransmitter in the cleft. It is likely that the vesicles which release neurotransmitters are positioned on, or close to, the calcium channels.

An alternative view is that neurotransmitter is released not from synaptic vesicles, but directly from the cytoplasm through membrane pores or membrane 'shuttle' devices which require calcium to open or operate. By opening for a predetermined short period (microseconds) a quantum of neurotransmitter could be expelled into the synaptic cleft via these 'vesigates' or 'operators' as they have been called. The dispute is far from resolved, but the balance of evidence is in favour of the vesicular release hypothesis, though this may not be exclusive, and both or either process could be occurring according to the neurotransmitter in question.

Why are there so many neurotransmitters? The answer to this question is far from resolved. Certainly, sub-groups of the fifty or so neurotransmitters produce different categories of effect in both qualitative and quantitative respects, and many will co-exist in different neuronal populations. First, there is the differential speed of response following receptor activation, with ionotropic being some 10- to 30-fold faster than metabotropic responses. Another dimension is provided in the *variety* of second-messenger activation of *different* cascades of biochemical sequelae, with particular metabotropic neurotransmitter actions being mediated by one or other second messenger system. Further possibilities for adding to the qualitative features of the response could come through the range of distances through which the neuroactive compounds exert their influence once released. This may be 20 nanometres within the synaptic cleft but several millimetres from varicosities or unstructured release points, and of course the concentration of neurotransmitter diminishes rapidly with the distance travelled. Actions ranging over a greater volume of tissue would activate specific neuroreceptors sited on a larger variety of neurone types, producing complex sequences of neuronal triggering, and therefore a greater spectrum of overall responses (so-called *trophic* actions). Continuous (*tonic*) release of neurotransmitter, as opposed to discrete and occasional release, would also provide a basis for variation in the patterns of activation of targeted neurones due to changes in sensitivity, accommodation, and desensitization of neuroreceptors which ensues during continuous neuroreceptor stimulation.

Thus, the large number and the chemical variety of neurotransmitters, together with their tendency to activate anatomically distinct neuronal pathways, often in pairs, and the evidence that they provide many palpable possibilities for variation in response, can be seen to provide a chorus of informational voices, each adding tonal colour or timbre to the final output of the brain and nervous system. H. F. BRADFORD

PAIN. Pain research and therapy have long been dominated by specificity theory which proposes that pain is a specific sensation subserved by a straight-through transmission system, and that the intensity of pain is proportional to the extent of tissue damage. Recent evidence, however, shows that pain is not simply a function of the amount of bodily damage alone, but is influenced by attention, anxiety, suggestion, prior experience, and other psychological variables. Moreover, the natural outcome of the specificity concept of pain has been the development of neurosurgical techniques to cut the so-called pain pathway, and the results of such operations have been disappointing, particularly for chronic pain syndromes. Not only does the pain tend to return in a substantial proportion of patients, but new pains may appear. The psychological and neurological data, then, force us to reject the concept of a single straight-through sensory transmission system.

In recent years the evidence on pain has moved in the direction of recognizing the plasticity and modifiability of events in the central nervous system.

Pain is a complex perceptual and affective experience determined by the unique past history of the individual, by the meaning to him of the injurious agent or situation, and by his 'state of mind' at the moment, as well as by the sensory nerve patterns evoked by physical stimulation.

In the light of this understanding of pain processes, Melzack and Wall (1965) proposed the gate control theory of pain. Basically, the theory states that neural mechanisms in the dorsal horn of the spinal cord act like a gate which can increase or decrease the flow of nerve impulses from peripheral fibres to the spinal cord cells that project to the brain. Somatic input is therefore subjected to the modulating influence of the gate *before* it evokes pain perception and response. The theory suggests that large-fibre inputs (such as gentle rubbing) tend to close the gate while small-fibre inputs (such as pinching) generally open it, and that the gate is also profoundly influenced by descending influences from the brain. It further proposes that the sensory input is modulated at successive synapses throughout its projection from the spinal cord to the brain areas responsible for pain experience and response. Pain occurs when the number of nerve impulses that arrives at these areas exceeds a critical level.

The subjective experience of pain clearly has sensory qualities, such as are described by the words throbbing, burning, or sharp. In addition, it has distinctly unpleasant, affective qualities which are described by words such as exhausting, wretched, and punishing. Pain becomes overwhelming, demands immediate attention, and disrupts ongoing behaviour and thought. It motivates or drives the organism into activity aimed at stopping the pain as quickly as possible. On the basis of these considerations, Melzack and Casey (1968) have proposed that there are three major psychological dimensions of pain experience: sensory-discriminative, motivational-affective, and cognitive-evaluative. Psychophysiological evidence suggests that each is subserved by specialized systems in the brain which interact to produce the multidimensional qualities of pain experience.

Drugs, especially opium and its derivatives, are among the oldest methods for controlling pain. Thomas Sydenham in 1680 wrote: 'Among the remedies which it has pleased Almighty God to give to man to relieve his sufferings, none is so universal and efficacious as opium.' Since then, more effective derivatives of opium, notably morphine and heroin, have been discovered. The invention of the hypodermic needle and syringe not only stimulated the search for pure, injectable analgesics but also, unfortunately, increased the risk of drug dependence. The quest for preparations free from addictive properties has proved to be fruitless, but withholding such pain-relieving drugs from the terminally ill lest they become 'addicted' is as ridiculous as it is inhumane. Other drugs said to have analgesic properties include the antidepressants, but it does not appear that relief of depression is their mode of action. Possibly this may be by blocking the re-uptake of serotonin and so potentiating the effect of encephalins in the brain.

Many new methods to control pain have been developed in recent years. Sensory modulation techniques such as transcutaneous electrical nerve stimulation (TENS) and ice massage are widely used in the attempt to activate inhibitory neural mechanisms to suppress pain. These techniques have a long history but were not understood until recently. Acupuncture, for example, is an ancient Chinese medical procedure in which long needles are inserted into specific points at the skin. The traditional Chinese explanation is that the needles bring Yin and Yang (which flow through hypothetical tubules called meridians) into harmony with each other. It has been discovered, however, that the sites of insertion correspond to myofascial 'trigger points' which are well known in Western medicine. It has also been found that acupuncture and electrical stimulation through electrodes placed on the skin (TENS) are equally effective in relieving low-back pain and several other forms of pain, including pains due to peripheral nerve injury. The neural mechanisms which underlie the relief produced by these forms of stimulation are not entirely understood, but evidence suggests that the intense stimulation produced by acupuncture or TENS activates an area in the brain which exerts a powerful inhibitory control over pathways which transmit pain signals.

Psychological techniques that allow patients to achieve some degree of control over their pain have also been developed. These techniques include biofeedback, hypnosis, distraction, and the use of imagery and other cognitive activities to modulate the transmission of the nerve-impulse patterns that subserve pain. Psychological techniques are being used increasingly and provide relatively simple, safe approaches to pain control. They represent a significant advance over the earlier tendency to treat pain by neurosurgical operations intended to cut the 'pain pathway' and which so frequently ended in failure.

The techniques of sensory modulation and psychological control work well in conjunction with each other. A large body of research demonstrates that several of these procedures employed at the same time—'multiple convergent therapy'—are often highly effective for the control of chronic pain states, particularly those such as low-back pain which have prominent elements of tension, depression, and anxiety.

While great strides have been made in the control of pain, there are still many pain syndromes which are beyond our comprehension and our control. Back pains, especially of the lower back, are the most common kind of pain, and literally millions of sufferers are continually seeking help. Sometimes they obtain temporary relief, but most continue to suffer. Migraine and tension headaches similarly plague millions of people. Perhaps the most terrible of all pains are those suffered by some cancer patients in the terminal phases of the disease. In recent years, specialized medical units have been developed to cope with these problems. Their major feature is that physicians and other health professionals from many different disciplines work together in the attempt to alleviate the pain of each individual patient. Pain clinics have been set up in every major Western city to cope with benign chronic pain, and hospices or palliative care units in hospitals have been developed to control pain (and other miseries) of patients who are terminally ill with cancer.

The development of pain clinics and hospices represent a breakthrough of the highest importance in the clinical control of pain. They are radical, new approaches to old problems. Chronic pain and terminal pain are major challenges to the scientist and clinician. But the giant step has been the recognition that they are special problems. The challenges ahead are clear: to conquer pain and suffering in all their forms.

RONALD MELZACK

SLEEP. A third of our lives is spent in sleep. Of the remainder, some is spent in wishing that our small children would sleep longer, and, during our later years, some is spent wishing that our sleep was less broken. What is sleep? It is a healthy state of inertia and unresponsiveness that is recurrently imposed by unknown mechanisms within the nervous system. In most animals the sleep–wakefulness rhythm is coupled to the twenty-four-hour light-dark environment, as are the rest-activity cycles of lower life forms; there is no sharp demarcation between creatures which can be said simply to have rest phases and animals which certainly sleep. In animals possessing developed brains there are electrical rhythms that differ in sleep and in wakefulness, being generally slower during sleep.

The biological clock that makes us sleepy every twenty-four hours means that shift workers and those who have just flown to different time zones are often tired and inefficient while they are trying to be alert. If it is a long time since we last slept then that too makes us sleepy. Monotony, warmth, restricted movement, and a sense of waiting for something that cannot happen yet—all of these make us sleepy. A sleep-like state of 'animal hypnosis' can also follow extreme stimulation.

The amount of sleep each species takes is proportional to the need for restoration, i.e. to the waking metabolic rate, but is in part also determined by predator status: those animals who sleep safely sleep longer. Among human beings there are wide variations. A few are happy and healthy with under three hours' sleep a night; a minority of others will take as many as ten hours. In general those who habitually sleep longer have shorter reaction times and higher body temperatures by day. Infants sleep a lot, but the sleep of ageing people becomes more and more broken with the years. A person sleeps less if he gets thin and sleeps longer if he gets fat.

There are two kinds of sleep that in man alternate with each other about every 100 minutes. Orthodox sleep (non-rapid eye movement, or NREM sleep) occupies 80 per cent of the night, and paradoxical sleep (rapid eye movement, or REM sleep) about 20 per cent. The amount of paradoxical sleep is greater in the new-born, but in adults is proportional to body weight, and among mental defectives to intelligence. It is diminished by anxiety and by many drugs.

Neither of the two kinds of sleep should be thought of as deeper than the other: they are different. Mental life continues in both, but whereas awakenings from orthodox sleep and questions about preceding mental life, generally lead to reports of 'thinking', awakenings from paradoxical sleep are generally followed by detailed descriptions of 'dreaming'. However, the recall of dreams is much diminished if as little as five minutes of orthodox sleep intervenes prior to awakening. In paradoxical sleep most body muscles are profoundly relaxed and many reflexes are lost, the blood flows faster through the brain than during wakeful rest, and in men the penis is erect.

Talking may also occur in both kinds of sleep, and reports made after prompt awakenings show concordance between the words and what was being thought or dreamt about. Sleep-walking and 'night terrors' arise from orthodox sleep early in the night, as do most episodes of bed-wetting. The shriekings of a night terror often occur with sleep-walking, and liability to them runs in families. They are never remembered in the morning.

Indeed, memory of the events of sleep is always very poor. 'Sleep learning' by means of a tape-recorder playing lessons all night is ineffective: although what has been heard while still awake may be remembered, nothing of what was played during sleep will be recalled; to remember we must have paid attention, and in sleep we do not pay attention. Even so, sleep is important for memory. If a list of nonsense words is learned, and memory of them is tested eight hours or twenty-four hours later, more of the list will be remembered after twenty-four hours, given an intervening period of sleep, than after eight hours without sleep. It seems that memory-traces are strengthened during sleep, maybe especially by paradoxical sleep; and since they presumably depend upon the durable molecules of brain protein, this can be understood.

Protein synthesis is favoured by sleep and so sleep enhances growth and restoration. Tissues such as the skin are restored by growth of new cells, and this growth proceeds faster during sleep. Throughout the body's tissues there are protein molecules being broken down and being synthesized all the time. There is a twenty-four-hour variation in the rate of synthesis, the rate being fastest during the period of rest and sleep. In the cerebral cortex, and the retina, protein synthesis is faster during sleep, and in the anterior pituitary there are more cell divisions. The fact that the balance shifts away from degradation towards greater net protein synthesis is a consequence of a lower rate of cellular work during sleep.

In higher animals there are hormones that reinforce the more fundamental effect of the lower rate of cellular work. In man, growth hormone is specifically released by orthodox sleep with the largest continuous slow electrical brain rhythms ('slow-wave sleep'). Growth hormone promotes protein synthesis. On the other hand, adrenaline and corticosteroids are hormones which are plentiful during wakefulness and which increase protein breakdown. In the blood during sleep, these latter hormones are diminished, and that means that the growth hormone is even more effective. Slow-wave sleep is not merely the time of growth-hormone release, it is the time when responsiveness to meaningful sounds or to an itchy skin is minimal, when the body's oxygen consumption is lowest, and cellular work is lowest, and therefore slow-wave sleep is 'worth more' than lighter (more responsive) stages of orthodox sleep. If there is a greater need for restoration, as after sleep-deprivation, or after an athlete has trained hard, then the next night there is a higher proportion of slow-wave sleep and extra growth hormone.

Sleep-deprivation causes sleepiness. It is difficult to keep awake anyone who has been deprived of sleep for 60 hours. Such a person has frequent 'microsleeps' and recurrently fails to notice things he ought to notice, being unable to sustain a high level of attention. Sometimes visual illusions or hallucinations are experienced or the individual becomes paranoid. After about 240 hours there are signs of adaptation to a more uniform but inert and dulled state.

People who complain of lack of sleep (insomnia) actually sleep more than they suppose. Indeed, the most distinguishing feature of their sleep is the degree to which it exceeds their own estimates—but we cannot yet measure its relative restorative value. Complaints are commonest among women, among those of nervous temperament, and among older folk; and it is they who account for most of the sleeping pills consumed. Although most sleeping pills today belong to the benzodiazepine class and are safe and effective, prolonged use leads to dependence, and attempts to stop them are accompanied by heightened anxiety, nightmares, and poor sleep for a week or two. Regular physical exercise; a good-quality firm mattress; a warm but ventilated room; a malted milk drink, and sexual satisfaction at bedtime—all these promote good sleep; but they will not cure everyone's complaints. It has to be accepted that broken sleep is as normal a part of growing older as are grey hairs or wrinkles, though insomnia of sudden onset can be the result of mental depression, an illness amenable to treatment.

Finally, let it be emphasized that sleep is not a slothful habit. Its study as a necessity encompasses the whole functioning of the body and, with the study of dreams, some of the mind's most intriguing qualities. IAN OSWALD

3: BRAIN, MIND, AND CONSCIOUSNESS

When physical structures like brains generate mental processes like perceiving, remembering and thinking, we have some explaining to do. But the artificial brains of desktop computers can perform these kinds of activities, and the only problem that this presents is the similarity between human intelligence and artificial intelligence. The programs running in these machines can solve problems, play games, and comment on a writer's use of different grammatical structures. They perform activities that, if performed by a human, would be declared as intelligent. They are simulations, of course, but they are the equivalent of activities that we know as mental processes. In the view of the school of emergent materialism that is implicitly held in current theories of human cognition, the **mind and body** are aspects of a single system. When the brain is operational in a particular intact electrochemical configuration then a mind will emerge. This is one of many stances that have been taken of course, and while philosophical descriptions of this mind–body problem continue to be debated, the phenomena observable in a psychology laboratory are consistent with the idea that our minds become available as a function of our brains. If we build electronic circuits in a particular way, then they solve problems etc, and human brains similarly have mental processes. This is no longer the greatest problem, and the real mystery is where **consciousness** comes from. If this model of the relationship between the brain and the mind is too simplistic, then one of the causes of concern that it will have to take into account is that of influences of the mind on the body. In the case of **psychosomatic disease**, for example, mental states such as stress can be seen to have unwanted effects upon the well-being of the physical structures that support those mental states. These effects present a problem for the simple, linear model that proposes that mental states emerge from the brain in the way that music emerges from a CD player. The influence of mind over matter is further illustrated in the role of mechanistic accounts of determinism and free will.

The distinction here is between mind and consciousness, with consciousness meaning awareness of mental processes. When we are aware of ourselves and of the immediate environment and of our effects upon the environment, then we can be said to be conscious. Mental processes then take on an additional quality, and are described in terms of qualia, whereby we refer to our phenomenological experiences comparatively. We can describe a perceptual experience of a sunset by talking about the intensity and redness of the light, but these are qualitative, subjective statements, intended to convey something of our personal awareness. The property of intentionality helps describe this quality. Mental processes, as distinct from objects in the world (bricks, baseball bats, blackbirds, brains, etc) are *about* things, and this can be said to mean that our mental states are differentiated on the basis that we have beliefs about things, or we can remember things, or that we perceive things or that we think about things. We do not simply believe, remember, perceive, or think in the abstract.

The challenge to be faced by the materialistic view of the originals of mental life comes from reports of phenomena such as the out-of-the-body-experience, in which the mind is experienced as separating from the body to the extent that the world is seen from a physically new perspective. Although personal reports of these subjective experiences are detailed and committed, attempts to investigate them have not been illuminating. They possibly arise, under unusual sensory circumstance, when a strong representation of the environment is available to replace current sensory input. The difficulty of establishing the existence of these experiences is similar to that of investigating paranormal phenomena such as precognition, telepathy and telekinesis—phenomena that do not seem to lend themselves to laboratory investigation. One difference is with the intensity of subjective reports associated with out-of-the-body-experiences, and this might suggest that it is a real and natural phenomenon that does require a scientific explanation. This does not mean that minds can detach from brains, of course, but it does mean that we need to explain how we can gain the impression that we can perceive the world from an unvisited perspective.

Mental processes can lead to awareness, but do not necessarily do so. Actions can be performed without awareness, as when extensive practice results in automatized everyday behaviour such as tying shoelaces, changing gear while driving, or switching on a light when entering a familiar room. Mental actions are also performed without awareness, as when we walk a route while engaged in conversation or distracted by our thoughts

—we have registered the visual world without having a conscious record of our perceptions. The memories that we collect over a lifetime influence our behaviour continuously, in that our attitudes and prejudices are based in our memories, and whereas we are guided by our previous experiences we are not continuously aware of them. It would be impossible to be so. Our conscious minds are severely limited in scope relative to our extensive experiences, and only a small part of those experiences can be available for conscious recollection at any one moment. At such a point our other memories are accessible, but not consciously active. Our unconscious minds are much more extensive than our conscious minds, of course, but the actions that can be controlled unconsciously are most probably restricted to those that are stereotyped through extensive practice and familiarity with the immediate surroundings.

When we lose consciousness altogether our minds can generate forms of mental activity that are the subject of current investigation. The extent to which we have mental life during concussion or **anaesthesia** is limited but uncertain, but most of recognize that when we SLEEP we experience a vivid and paradoxical mental life during **dreaming**. These experiences are paradoxical because they are phenomenologically rich processes that occur while we are deeply unconscious. We experience a detailed mental life and yet appear to have no awareness of events in the immediate environment. Mental life continues when we are not dreaming, but in the absence of phenomenological vividness. When in a state of falling asleep particularly vivid images are sometimes reported as being experienced—hypnagogic hallucinations—and these images are thought to differ from dreams not only in their intensity but also in the extent to which they can be controlled at will.

Investigations of consciousness are taking to the procedure of observing the differences that occur in mental processes when consciousness is and is not available. There is now a catalogue of observations linking **brain function and awareness** from case studies of patients with well-defined damage. Concussion and anaesthesia can eliminate awareness completely, but when only part of the brain is functional, then awareness may also be incomplete. For example, damage to the visual cortex of the brain may result in an individual being unable to give a report on part of the visual scene. By this measure they are said to be unable to see, but with laboratory procedures it is possible to establish that they can indeed distinguish between different objects upon which they cannot comment. These 'blindsight' patients have the ability of perceptual discrimination in the absence of awareness of their perceptions, and it is non-cortical perceptual pathways that are considered to be helping with discrimination in these cases. Similarly, some amnesics cannot intentionally remember information given to them, and cannot say whether test material has been presented previously or not, but they do show knowledge of the material when presented with new tasks in which the old material could be useful. These are examples of implicit perceptions and implicit memories, in which mental states can once again be seen to influence behaviour without awareness of those states or of that influence. The most compelling demonstration of the relationship between brain and mind comes from the loss of mind in absence of normal brain function, or with hallucinations resulting from modifying agents such as psychoactive drugs. Changed states of awareness can also result from an unusual experience during extreme **arousal**. In these cases changes in brain function are correlated with changes in conscious experiences, but in other, challenging, cases, there are no readily observable physiological changes. In the case of **hypnosis**, for example, an altered state of awareness is induced by suggestion, resulting in idiosyncratic perceptions such as selective deafness, attenuation of pain, and hallucinations. The sensory inputs generating these perceptions are the suggestions of the hypnotist, and evidence of physiological change is proving elusive.

Perhaps the most dramatic demonstration comes from investigations of the **split-brain and the mind**. The cerebral cortex of the brain has a central main divide, separating the left and right hemispheres. In the normal brain the hemispheres are connected by the corpus callosum, which is principally the means by which information is passed between them. When the corpus callosum is cut, as it is to alleviate the effects of epilepsy in severe cases, then the two halves of the brain appear to generate their own mental processes. Awareness is no longer whole, and objects perceived with one hemisphere are unavailable for description by the other hemisphere. At least in the restricted world of the laboratory, where sensations can be delivered to one and only one hemisphere, it appears that each hemisphere has its own isolated experiences and separate awareness.

ANAESTHESIA may be described as a reversible loss of consciousness produced by a drug, from which arousal does not take place even with painful stimuli such as setting a fracture or surgical operation. In this latter respect it differs from sleep or the change in consciousness following sensory deprivation; and it is this that made it so revolutionary a discovery, opening the gateway to modern surgery and safer childbirth. The name is not quite exact, since loss of consciousness is not the same as loss of feeling; and a good anaesthetic in clinical practice should exert other actions, such as some analgesia (to diminish reflex responses to what would be very painful stimuli) and muscular relaxation (to facilitate the surgeon's work). When an anaesthetic such as ether or chloroform is given, there is a characteristic progression of effects, first described by Guedel in 1937: first analgesia, some loss of memory, and perhaps euphoria; then consciousness is lost, but the patient may struggle, breathes irregularly, is sweating and flushed; in the third stage, the patient becomes quieter with regular breathing, but the eyeballs move rhythmically and a good many reflexes are still present. As anaesthesia deepens, and the patient passes through the successive planes of the third stage, various reflexes progressively fall away, the breathing becomes shallower, and eventually death may ensue (the fourth stage). In modern practice anaesthesia is induced with a suitable barbiturate (such as thiopentone) injected intravenously: the patient then passes through the early stages within seconds; once 'under', anaesthesia is usually maintained by some other substance.

How do anaesthetics work? It is paradoxical that more is known at the molecular level than at any other. A remarkable feature is the astonishing range of substances that can produce anaesthesia: in addition to the classical anaesthetics and the barbiturates, nitrogen in the air (if given at high pressure) and many other gases, alcohols, dry cleaning fluids (such as trichloroethene), industrial solvents, and certain steroids can all produce typical anaesthesia. There is no common chemical structure such as would suggest a specific action on some particular part of the brain. Instead, as two pharmacologists, Overton and Meyer, pointed out over eighty years ago, anaesthetics all share the property of dissolving in fat; and it is remarkable that one can predict the potency of an anaesthetic quite accurately by measuring the pressure of a gas or the concentration of a vapour which will produce a given concentration (about 0.05 moles per litre) of the substance concerned in olive oil. Modern work has revealed the significance of this: the cell membrane, which defines the cell's limits, and across which an electric potential is maintained, consists of an ordered array of fatty molecules (mostly phospholipids and cholesterol); the anaesthetic dissolves in it, and slightly expands and disorders the membrane. Since the membrane also carries large protein molecules (enzymes, ion channels, receptors, transport mechanisms) which mediate its 'traffic' with its environment and with other cells, disturbance of their normal function becomes possible. A fascinating aspect is that very high pressures (which compress and reorder the membrane) cause recovery from anaesthesia. Conversely, a suitable amount of an anaesthetic can be used to neutralize the adverse effects of high pressure. The 'high pressure nervous syndrome', which includes tremor, bursts of 'micro-sleep', and convulsions, threatened to limit the depth to which divers could go; but the addition of nitrogen (using it as a small dose of anaesthetic) to the diver's helium-oxygen mixture has extended that limit.

But if one asks, 'On what synapses, or on what cell groups of the brain, is this molecular action particularly exerted?', no satisfactory answer exists. The simple fact of surgical anaesthesia shows that higher brain functions are particularly sensitive, while respiration and simple reflexes, as well as other bodily processes like the heartbeat, are relatively resistant. Detailed analysis yields a bewildering variety of effects, with actions both pre- and post-synaptically, varying with the synapse and with the anaesthetic. A simple view is that the anaesthetic picks out any delicately poised nervous activity, and that the pattern of anaesthetic activity is simply that of reduced activity in the most vulnerable nervous pathways—particularly complex nervous functions rather than (for example) simple reflex movement. Theories include the idea of a specific effect on the 'ascending reticular activating system', in the absence of whose activity the cerebral cortex is believed to relapse into a sleeping state, or on cortical cells generally. Some recent drugs (such as ketamine), which produce the so-called 'dissociative anaesthesia', may help to throw light on the problem; these differ, both in having a specific chemical structure, and in producing a rather different pattern of anaesthesia.

There is an abundant literature on the effects of anaesthetics on mental function, short of anaesthesia, and Humphry Davy's description (in 1800) of the effect of nitrous oxide (laughing gas) on himself and his friends (including Southey, Coleridge, Roget, and Wedgwood) reveals the salient features recorded many times subsequently: considerable variation with the individual; excitement; euphoria or sometimes dysphoria; compulsive movements or laughter; 'thrilling' sensations in the limbs; feelings of deep significance; rush of ideas; synaesthesiae; drowsiness; warmth, rapid breathing, palpitations, giddiness; and often a strong desire to repeat the performance. This last characteristic brings the risk of addiction in its train, particularly for those (such as anaesthetists and nurses) with easy access to the drugs; and it shows itself again in 'glue-sniffing' in children, or with workers using some solvents in industry.

An important feature with all these volatile substances is the speed with which effects are produced by inhalation, by which the vapour passes very quickly into the circulation. More familiar to most people will be the effect of anaesthetics such as alcohol or barbiturates taken orally, with an onset delayed by circulatory absorption; and the fact that by this route some of the more dramatic effects are lacking (although euphoria and the risk of addiction remain) suggests that these effects are largely due to especially rapid access to, and uptake by, particular parts of the brain, producing a selective action which fades as distribution of the drug becomes general. With sustained exposure to any anaesthetic, the adaptation known as 'tolerance' develops, by which an increasing dose is required to produce the effect. 'Cross-tolerance' occurs between different anaesthetics—hence the difficulty often encountered of anaesthetizing an alcoholic when exposure stops and the drug is withdrawn, characteristic symptoms appear: for example, insomnia after a short course of any sleeping pill, or delirium tremens (d.t.'s) after prolonged high exposure to alcohol, or convulsions after chronic barbiturate use. While some of the adaptive changes may be biochemical, some of them certainly represent a change in nerve cell function, and there are interesting indications that the composition of the cell membrane changes so as to reduce the effect of the anaesthetic.

One would like to think that experience with anaesthetics would deepen our understanding of consciousness, mood, sensation, pain, memory. Yet it is still impossible to move convincingly from the subjective phenomena to physiological understanding. Perhaps it is unreasonable to expect to do so until our knowledge of normal neurophysiology is more satisfactory, or perhaps pharmacology and physiology need to proceed, collaboratively, in parallel. Some areas may be picked out as potentially fruitful.

1. The effect on *sense of time*. There is a puzzle here: nitrous oxide and alcohol appear to reduce 'felt' time compared

with 'clock' time, whereas ketamine (like cannabis) prolongs it. With the latter drugs, one can readily suggest, as William James suggested, that 'disinhibition' in the brain, allowing a greater than normal sensory input, could give rise to an experience of more numerous mental impressions than usual per unit of 'clock' time, and hence a greater 'felt' time. But why should other anaesthetics differ?

2. The effect on *pain sense*. There is some evidence that enkephalins or endorphins may play a part in analgesia produced by anaesthetics. But there remain remarkable differences between anaesthetics, some with pronounced analgesic action, some potentiating the response to a painful stimulus. Bearing in mind its practical relevance, as well as the recent advances in our knowledge of the neuroanatomy and neurochemistry of the nociceptive pathways, and the successful application of decision theory to the study of pain, a systematic study of the action of a range of anaesthetics on pain discrimination and pain report seems well worth while.

3. The effect on *sensation generally*. An intriguing but neglected observation is that anaesthetics facilitate the generation of impulses in the vagal nerve fibres registering the inflation of the lung, which accounts for the ability of many anaesthetics to produce what is known as 'rapid shallow breathing'. It is an intriguing action, and exerted peripherally on the proprioceptive endings in muscles might account for the 'thrilling' sensation described by Davy. But more generally there might also be an important effect both on the pattern of sensory input to the brain, and on subsequent processing.

4. Effect on *memory*. With the recent advances in our knowledge of registration, consolidation, and retrieval, systematic study of the effect of a range of anaesthetics on memory is overdue, although the problem is complicated by 'state dependence'. An old method of anaesthesia for childbirth, 'twilight sleep', exploited the effect of the drug hyoscine on memory, so that even if pain was felt, it was not remembered. The method has been abandoned because of the effect on the baby, but the approach is still interesting.

5. The concept of *disinhibition* is constantly, and plausibly, invoked to account for phenomena such as the rush of ideas, synaesthesia, and electroencephalographic synchronization. The underlying idea is that the great complexity of mental activity does not merely need some neurones to be active, but also needs others to be actively 'switched off' (inhibited): if the latter process were interfered with (disinhibition), then differential activity and 'gating' of information transfer could become progressively impaired. Simple model systems exist, illustrating how depression of an inhibitory pathway can lead to release phenomena; but no serious attempt has been made to extend the idea to more complex systems. Yet if certain inhibitory mechanisms are particularly vulnerable, it should be possible, by careful choice of systems sharing common elements, to identify them more closely.

6. A tedious but necessary development is that of knowledge about the kinetics of *anaesthetic distribution* in the brain. Some knowledge exists of the rise and fall of the concentration of an anaesthetic during and after an exposure, for samples of brain containing thousands or millions of neurones. But this is merely a gross average, telling us nothing of local concentration in synaptic detail. Equilibrium with an anaesthetic is virtually never reached in clinical practice, and rarely in experimental work, so that (as mentioned earlier) there is ample scope for differential effects arising, not from the properties of the drug itself, but from varying access and uptake. For in-

stance, evidence is accumulating that if any part of the brain becomes particularly active it consumes more energy, with a corresponding increase in blood-flow; that would at once open the way to differential access by an anaesthetic.

7. Finally one must recall that, despite all the advances in neuroanatomy, it is only a tiny minority of nervous pathways that can be precisely and completely described in anatomical and neurochemical detail, with the specific neurones and their connections specified. But some beautiful techniques now exist for mapping out these pathways, for recording the activity of single or groups of neurones, and for neurochemical analysis: the new methods of anaesthesia that a deeper understanding will provide are not far away. W. D. M. PATON

AROUSAL. Arousal differs from attention in that it involves a general rather than a particular increase (or decrease) in perceptual or motor activity. There can, however, be quite specific 'arousal', such as sexual arousal. General arousal is mediated by a diffuse neural system, centred in the brain-stem, which not only sets a level from sleep to wakefulness (and sometimes over-arousal) but also provides moment-to-moment changes of arousal which are usually appropriate to the prevailing situation, or task in hand. A great deal is known of the neurology of arousal.

Subtle moment-to-moment changes of arousal are experienced, for example, while driving a car; arousal immediately increasing with any small unexpected event or situation. It has been suggested that fatigue results from over-arousal; the blurring of perception perhaps being due to raised 'neural noise', or increased randomness of neural signals (which may also occur in ageing) in over-arousal. Experiments conducted on vigilance during the 1939–45 war found that radar operators and others looking out for infrequent signals or events rapidly became inefficient as their level of arousal dropped—errors or misses increasing in as short a time as half an hour. This loss of arousal in repetitive or boring situations (though it also occurs in the stress and danger of battle) can be distinguished experimentally from fatigue.

Arousal has been related to stress; indeed stress may be over-arousal. There is an optimal level of arousal, which has been thought of as following an inverted 'U', for performing a task. But the performance of skills at low arousal differs from that when arousal is 'over the top' of optimal arousal; this suggests that the arousal-function is not truly U-shaped. Errors under conditions of under-arousal tend to be omissions while over-arousal tends to lead to errors of commission or over-correction.

Learning is improved with increase of arousal—again up to an optimum level, when over-arousal becomes associated with distractions of various kinds. There is considerable evidence that long-term but not short-term recall is improved with increased arousal. This is presumably because the laying-down of memory traces is more efficient, perhaps with more cross-associations for future reference, for learning while arousal is high. Many people learn to control and optimize their arousal level when working or studying, by varying the task, or perhaps with the aid of music, or (not to be recommended!) smoking. There is little point in working when arousal falls close to the level of sleep.

RICHARD L. GREGORY

BRAIN FUNCTION AND AWARENESS. It is something of a paradox that the most exacting studies of brain function are apt to come from research on animals, whose behaviour we can study with increasing sophistication, but who cannot communicate with us very fluently. In contrast, studies of human brain function derived from the clinic are apt to depend on just those methods of communication that we are precluded from using with animals. That is, most clinical tests of psychological capacity of human patients involve considerable verbal interchange between the patient and the examiner, often expressed in a form intended directly to reveal the patient's disorders. So, in a classical and routine examination of visual capacity, the patient is asked, 'Tell me what you see', 'How many spots do you see?', 'What letter is it?', and so forth. Or the patient with a memory disorder is asked, 'Tell me what you can remember from this morning', 'Do you recognize me?', 'What words can you recall from the list you just read?'

In studying animals' vision or memory, it is often assumed that we are simply transforming the questions we usually ask of human patients into an equivalent form, albeit one that is rather more cumbersome to transmit. Examined more closely, however, the resemblance is less than close. The animal reveals his capacity by displaying a discrimination between stimuli or events, which he has usually been trained to demonstrate by following some particular rule, and for which he is rewarded. The human subject also discriminates between stimuli or events, of course; but often the clinician does not study the discrimination as such, but rather the subject's commentary upon it, such as 'Yes, now I see the flash', or 'I can see the letter A in the bottom line'. Even when the verbal response appears to be just an embellishment on, or a short cut to, the discriminative response, serious problems can arise if the subject is unable to render a commentary but nevertheless is capable of making the relevant discrimination—i.e. if he is restricted in the way that an animal is restricted when we study its visual capacity. We refer here not to the relatively trivial difficulty when a subject has, say, an impairment in the mechanics or the organization of speech. Even if a human subject is able to communicate freely and efficiently he may nevertheless be unaware of his own discriminative capacity and hence have nothing to communicate as a commentary.

It is only recently that this distinction, between a capacity and a subject's commentary upon it, has been recognized, and it has thrown light on some persistent puzzles in the comparative study of brain function in human and animal subjects. Two examples can be given. In both instances the differences between the results of research on humans and on other animals appeared to be so great that it was argued that the brains of animals must be organized in a qualitatively different way from human brains, despite the very close anatomical similarity between them.

First, if the region of cerebral cortex to which nerve fibres from the eye ultimately project is removed, animals (unlike humans) can still discriminate visual events, although not as well as normally. This in itself is not surprising, because the eye sends information not only to the so-called 'visual cortex' but also directly to a variety of other structures in the midbrain and elsewhere. Indeed, the way in which vision is altered after blockage of one of the targets helps one to infer the type of capacity that the remaining targets must have. This residual visual capacity of animals has been studied over several decades, and techniques have been developed for yielding a good description of it. The paradox is that the human brain, while organized anatomically in a way that appears closely similar to the brains of other Primates, is said nevertheless to yield a state of blindness after removal of the 'visual cortex'. (Because the visual field projects upon the visual cortex in a well-known retinotopic manner, most blindness is in fact commonly restricted to just a certain portion of the visual field, depending upon which part of the visual cortex is damaged, it being rare for the entire visual cortex in both cerebral hemispheres to be damaged.) For example, when a light is flashed in the blind field of a human patient and he is asked whether he sees it, he will say no. A monkey, in contrast, if appropriately trained will reach out to touch a brief visual stimulus, can locate it accurately in space, and can discriminate between lines of different orientation and between simple shapes. He will pick up even quite minute specks of food if they contrast well with the background.

This difference in outcome puzzled investigators as long ago as the end of the nineteenth century. They appealed to a doctrine of 'encephalization of function' to account for it. This doctrine asserted that, in evolution, visual and other functions some how migrated to higher and new structures in the brain, so that in man visual function had reached the highest level, namely the visual cortex, whereas in lower animals a greater degree of visual capacity was subserved by lower midbrain or even brain-stem structures. It was a somewhat curious doctrine, because the lower structures do not wither away in man, and therefore one wonders just what role they would have after they had been deprived of their earlier role. Be that as it may, it is only very recently that investigators have actually started to ask their human patients the questions in a form in which one is perforce obliged to ask them of animals. That is, the subject is asked to discriminate between stimuli, using a forced choice method—whether or not he says he can 'see' the stimulus. He is asked to guess, say, whether or not a stimulus occurred, whether it was located at position A or B, whether it was a cross or a circle, and so on. Using this approach it has been found that some human subjects with damage to the visual cortex can perform about as well as animals in the absence of such cortex. The subjects themselves may be quite unaware that they are able to perform so well, and indeed surprised to learn that they can, because they say they did not actually 'see' the stimuli. This residual capacity is called 'blindsight'. Of course, pathology in man is varied, and more often than not when visual cortex is damaged, the surrounding tissue is also damaged. Therefore, not all patients with blind fields associated with brain damage show blindsight.

There is an additional aspect to this discovery. The residual capacity in the monkey actually increases as the animal continues to use it; significantly, this improvement does not occur spontaneously, but with practice the region of only partial vision actually contracts. Recently, some human patients with field defects have been shown to have the same benefit: their regions of blindness (if caused by damage to the visual cortex but not, of course, if caused by damage to the eyes themselves) also contract with specialized practice designed to make them give forced-choice responses to visual stimuli in their 'blind' fields. It is not clear how much of this recovery is mediated by the surrounding intact visual cortex, and how much by one of the parallel pathways from the eye to the midbrain, probably both are involved.

A second example implying differences in the organization of primates' brains comes from the field of memory defects. Damage to certain midline structures in the human brain can yield a persistent state of profound memory failure. Patients apparently cannot remember fresh experiences for more than a few seconds. Paradoxically, in animals it seemed for a long time that these same midline structures—apparently anatomically identical to those in man—could be dispensed with almost with impunity. No obvious losses of memory or learning capacity appeared to result. The story is similar in some respects to that of blindsight. It has emerged that the sorts of tasks that animals were traditionally taught to test their learning capacity, and which they succeeded in learning and retaining, can also be learned quite well by amnesic patients. Indeed, there is now a large catalogue of tasks that such patients are known to succeed in learning and retaining. They all share one property: in none of them is it necessary actually to ask the patient, 'Do you recognize this?' or 'What do you remember of the task we just saw?'. Indeed a patient may acknowledge no memory for the task, even though he succeeded in it. For example, if shown a list of words, and later asked what the words were, he may well say he cannot remember even seeing a list of words. But if shown the first few letters of each of the words and asked to guess what words they stand for, he is likely to produce the very words for which he says he has no memory. Or, to take another example, a patient will show a benefit of having solved a particular jigsaw puzzle by solving it faster the next day (but only the jigsaw he solved before). Amnesic patients can learn such tasks and show good retention over quite long periods—weeks or even months, in fact—although, again, as with blindsight, the capacity is distinct from an acknowledgement of it by the subject. It remains to be seen whether methods of retraining such patients, whose lives are severely crippled by memory impairment, can also be developed. There are at least serious efforts being made along these lines.

Examples taken from human clinical research go beyond anything that can be drawn from comparative research with animals. (Although, of course, corresponding regions of the brain can be studied, how can one ask an animal not only to discriminate or select a stimulus from an array but to reveal to us whether or not he can 'recognize' it or 'characterize' it?) Even so, some progress along these lines can be seen. Animal investigators in recent years, spurred on in part by the paradoxical discrepancies between their findings and those from the human clinic, have been able to evolve new methods of testing recognition memory in animals. It appears that recognition can be altered independently of an animal's capacity to discriminate stimuli and form simple associations between visual events and reward. But work has scarcely begun on the more fundamental problem of how to allow an animal not only to discriminate or learn and to retain but to acknowledge these acts. And, therefore, while the paradoxical gap between the results of animal and human brain research may have been reduced, we are left with the even more difficult problems: how would one know whether an animal possesses blindsight and when is an animal aware that he can discriminate? Is a frog or an insect ever aware of such a capacity? That question was raised in the nineteenth century by some of the pioneers of research on the visual cortex, but then afterwards largely ignored. For a long time it appeared that it could be ignored safely—that it might even be a pseudo-problem. But it is difficult to accept that animals, especially advanced primates, differ so fundamentally from humans that they do not demonstrate the same division between automatic unmonitored acts and those acts that are so effectively monitored as to enable further action to be based upon the knowledge of them. To ask such a question of an animal would appear to require not only the standard methods used to study its discriminative and mnemonic capacities, powerful as they are, but the introduction of a parallel response which could serve as a 'commentary' response, by which the animal could signal its acknowledgement that it has indeed 'seen' the signals, and ultimately might even offer a confidence level. Perhaps the important contribution that animal research has made towards uncovering unsuspected capacities in human patients will be repaid by the development of techniques that will allow us to ask much deeper questions of our animal relations. L. WEISKRANTZ

CONSCIOUSNESS is both the most obvious and the most mysterious feature of our minds. On the one hand, what could be more certain or manifest to each of us than that he or she is a subject of experience, an enjoyer of perceptions and sensations, a sufferer of pain, an entertainer of ideas, and a conscious deliberator? On the other hand, what in the world can consciousness be? How can physical bodies in the physical world contain such a phenomenon? Science has revealed the secrets of many initially mysterious natural phenomena—magnetism, photosynthesis, digestion, even reproduction—but consciousness seems utterly unlike these. For one thing, particular cases of magnetism or photosynthesis or digestion are in principle equally accessible to any observer with the right apparatus, but any particular case of consciousness seems to have a favoured or privileged observer, whose access to the phenomenon is entirely unlike, and better than, anyone else's, no matter what apparatus they may have. For this reason and others, not only have we so far no good theory of consciousness, we lack even a clear and uncontroversial pre-theoretical description of the presumed phenomenon. Some have gone so far as to deny that there is anything for the term to name.

The mere fact that such a familiar feature of our lives has resisted for so long all attempts to characterize it suggests that our conception of it is at fault. What is needed is not just more evidence, more experimental and clinical data, but a careful rethinking of the assumptions that lead us to suppose there is a single and familiar phenomenon, consciousness, answering to all the descriptions licensed by our everyday sense of the term. Consider the baffling questions that are inevitably raised whenever one turns one's attention to consciousness. Are other animals conscious? Are they conscious in the same way we are? Could a computer or robot be conscious? Can a person have unconscious thoughts, or unconscious pains or sensations or perceptions? Is a baby conscious at or before birth? Are we conscious when we dream? Might a human being harbour more than one conscious subject or ego or agent within one brain? Certainly good answers to these questions will depend heavily on empirical discoveries about the behavioural capacities and internal circumstances of the various problematic candidates for consciousness, but about every such empirical finding we can ask: what is its bearing on the question of consciousness, and why? These are not directly empirical but conceptual questions, and answering them is not an alternative or competitor to answering the empirical questions, but an essential preliminary—or at least accompaniment.

Our ordinary concept of consciousness seems to be anchored to two separable sets of considerations that can be captured roughly by the phrases 'from the inside' and 'from the outside'. *From the inside*, our own consciousness seems obvious and pervasive: we know that much goes on around us and even inside our own bodies of which we are entirely unaware or unconscious, but nothing could be more intimately known to us than those things of which we are, individually, conscious. Those things of which I am conscious, and the ways in which I am conscious of them, determine *what it is like to be me*. I know in a way no other could know what it is like to be me. From the inside, consciousness seems to be an all-or-nothing phenomenon—an inner light that is either on or off. We grant that we are sometimes drowsy or inattentive, or asleep and on occasion we even enjoy abnormally heightened consciousness, but when we are conscious, *that* we are conscious is not a fact that admits of degrees. There is a perspective, then, from which consciousness seems to be a feature that sunders the universe into two strikingly different kinds of things: those that have it and those that do not. Those that have it are *subjects*, beings to whom things can be one way or another, beings it is like something to be. It is not like anything at all to be a brick or a pocket-calculator or an apple. These things have insides, but not the right sort of insides—no inner life, no point of view. It is certainly like something to be me (something I know 'from the inside') and almost certainly like something to be you (for you have told me, most convincingly, that it is the same with you), and probably like something to be a dog or a dolphin (if only they could tell us!), and maybe even like something to be a spider.

When one considers these others (other folk and other creatures), one considers them perforce from *the outside*, and then various of their observable or determinable features strike us as relevant to the question of their consciousness. Creatures react discriminatively to events within the scope of their senses: they recognize things, avoid painful circumstances, learn, plan, and solve problems. They exhibit intelligence. But putting matters this way might be held to prejudge the issue. Talking of their 'senses' or of 'painful' circumstances, for instance, suggests that we have already settled the issue of consciousness—for note that if I had described a robot in those terms, the polemical intent of my choice of words would have been obvious (and resisted by many). How do creatures differ from robots, real or imagined? They are organically and biologically similar to *us*, and we are the paradigmatic conscious creatures. This similarity admits of degrees, of course, and one's intuitions about which sorts of similarity count are probably untrustworthy. Dolphins' fishiness subtracts from our conviction, but no doubt should not. Were chimpanzees as dull as sea-slugs their facial similarity to us would no doubt nevertheless favour their inclusion in the charmed circle. If house-flies were about our size, or warm-blooded, we'd be much more confident that when we plucked off their wings they felt pain (*our* sort of pain, the kind that matters). What makes us think that some such considerations ought to count and not others?

The obvious presumption is that the various 'outside' indicators are more or less reliable signs or symptoms of the presence of that whatever-it-is each conscious subject knows from the inside. But how could this be confirmed? This is the notorious 'problem of other minds'. In one's own case, it seems, one can directly observe the coincidence of one's inner life with one's outwardly observable talents for perceptual discrimination, introspective avowal, intelligent action, and the like. But if each of us is to advance rigorously beyond solipsism, we must be able to do something apparently impossible: confirm the coincidence of inner and outer in others. Their *telling us* of the coincidence in their own cases will not do, officially, for that gives us just more coincidence of outer with outer: perceptual capacities and so forth normally go hand in hand with capacities for 'introspective' avowal. If a cleverly designed robot could (seem to) tell us of its inner life (could utter all the appropriate noises in the appropriate contexts), would we be right to admit it to the charmed circle? We might be, but how could we ever tell we were not being fooled? Here the question seems to be: is that special inner light really turned on, or is there nothing but darkness inside? And this question looks unanswerable. So perhaps we have taken a mis-step already.

My use of 'we' and 'our' in the last paragraph, and your unworried acquiescence in it, reveals that *we* don't take the problem of other minds seriously—at least for ourselves and the human beings with whom we normally associate. The temptation then is to decide that, in so far as there is a serious, coherent question yet to be answered about the imagined robot (or about some problematic creature), it will turn out to be answerable by straightforward empirical means once we have better theories of the organization of our brains and their role in controlling our behaviour. This is to suppose that somehow or other the facts we individually get 'from the inside' reduce to facts publicly obtainable from the outside. That is to say, enough of the right sort of outside facts will *settle* the question of whether or not some creature is conscious.

Determining that this internal process occurs in a particular organism is presumably a difficult but clearly empirical task. Suppose that with regard to some creature it were completed successfully: the creature is, by this account, conscious. If we have understood the proposal correctly, we will not find any room to wonder further. Reserving judgement here would be like being shown in detail the operations of a car engine and then asking, 'But is it *really* an internal combustion engine? Might we not be deluded in thinking it was?'

Any proper scientific account of the phenomenon of consciousness must inevitably take this somewhat doctrinaire step of demanding that the phenomenon be viewed as objectively accessible, but one may still wonder if, once the step is taken, the truly mysterious phenomenon will be left behind. Before dismissing this sceptical hunch as the fancy of romantics, it would be wise to consider a striking revolution in the recent history of thinking about the mind, a revolution with unsettling consequences.

For John Locke and many subsequent thinkers, nothing was more essential to the mind than consciousness, and more particularly self-consciousness. The mind in all its activities and processes was viewed as transparent to itself; nothing was hidden from its inner view. To discern what went on in one's mind, one just 'looked'—one 'introspected'—and the limits of what one thereby found were the very boundaries of the mind. The notion of *unconscious* thinking or perceiving was not entertained, or, if it was, it was dismissed as incoherent, self-contradictory nonsense. For Locke, indeed, there was a serious problem of how to describe all one's memories as being continuously in one's mind, when yet they were not continuously 'present to consciousness'. The influence of this view has been so great that when Sigmund Freud initially hypothesized the existence of unconscious mental processes, his proposal met widely with stark denial and incomprehension. It was not just an outrage to common sense, but even self-contradictory, to assert that there could be unconscious beliefs and desires, unconscious feelings of hatred, unconscious schemes of self-defence and retaliation. But Freud won converts. This 'conceptual impossibility' became respectably thinkable by theorists once it was seen that this way of thinking permitted one to explain otherwise inexplicable patterns of psychopathology. The new way of thinking was also supported by a crutch: one could cling to at least a pale version of the Lockian creed by imagining that these 'unconscious' thoughts, desires, and schemes *belonged to other selves* within the psyche. Just as I can keep my schemes secret from you, my id can keep secrets from my ego. By splitting the subject into many subjects, one could preserve the axiom that every mental state must be someone's conscious mental state, and explain the inaccessibility of some of these states to their putative owners by postulating other interior owners for those states. This move was usefully obscured in the mists of jargon so that the weird question of whether it was like anything to be a super-ego, for instance, could be kept at bay.

It is easy to speculate, but hard to confirm, that Freud's expansion of the bounds of the thinkable was a major pre-condition for a much more pervasive, and much less controversial, style of theorizing in experimental, and especially cognitive, psychology in recent years. We have come to accept without the slightest twinge of incomprehension a host of claims to the effect that sophisticated hypothesis-testing memory-searching inference—in short, information processing—occurs within us even though it is entirely inaccessible to introspection. It is not repressed unconscious activity of the sort Freud uncovered, activity driven out of the 'sight' of consciousness, but just mental activity that is somehow beneath or beyond the ken of consciousness altogether. Freud claimed that his theories and clinical observations gave him the authority to overrule the sincere denials of his patients about what was going on in their minds. Similarly the cognitive psychologist marshals experimental evidence, models, and theories to show that people are engaged in surprisingly sophisticated reasoning processes of which they can give no introspective account at all. Not only are minds accessible to outsiders: some mental activities are more accessible to outsiders than to the very 'owners' of those minds!

In the new theorizing, however, the crutch has been thrown away. Although the new theories abound with deliberately fanciful homuncular metaphors—with subsystems sending messages back and forth, asking for help, obeying, and volunteering—the actual subsystems are deemed to be unproblematically non-conscious bits of organic machinery, as utterly lacking in a point of view or inner life as a kidney or kneecap. (Certainly the advent of 'mindless' but 'intelligent' computers played a major role in this further dissolution of the Lockian view.)

But now Locke's extremism has been turned on its head; if, before, the very idea of unconscious mentality seemed incomprehensible, now we are losing our grip on the very idea of *conscious* mentality. What is consciousness *for*, if perfectly unconscious, indeed subject-less, information processing is in principle capable of achieving all the ends for which conscious minds were supposed to exist? If theories of cognitive psychology can be true of us, they could also be true of zombies, or robots, and the theories seem to have no way of distinguishing us. How could any amount of mere subject-less information processing (of the sort we have recently discovered to go on in us) add up to or create that special feature with which it is so vividly contrasted? For the contrast has not disappeared. Karl Lashley once provocatively suggested that 'no activity of the mind is ever conscious', by which he meant to draw our attention to the inaccessibility of the processing that we know must go on when we think. He gave an example: if asked to think a thought in dactylic hexameter, most of us can readily oblige; but how we do it, what goes on in us to produce the thought, is something quite inaccessible to us. Lashley's remark might seem at first to herald the demise of consciousness as a phenomenon for psychological study, but its true effect is just the opposite. It draws our attention unmistakably to the *difference* between all the unconscious information processing—without which, no doubt, there could be no conscious experience—and the conscious thought itself, which *is* somehow directly accessible. Accessible to what or to whom? To say that it is accessible to some subsystem of the brain is not yet to distinguish it from the unconscious activities and events which are also accessible to various subsystems of the brain. If some particular and special subsystem deserves to be called the *self*, this is far from obvious. What feature of its particular traffic with the rest of the nervous system would make it a thing it was like something to be?

Strangely enough, this problem is the old chestnut, the problem of other minds, resurrected as a serious problem now that psychology has begun to analyse the human mind into its functional components. This comes out most graphically in the famous split-brain cases. (For details, see **split-brain and the mind**.) There is nothing very problematic in granting that the people who have undergone severing of the corpus callosum have two somewhat independent minds. It is not problematic because we have grown used to thinking of a person's mind as an organization of communicating sub-minds. Here the lines of communication have simply been cut, rendering the mind-likeness of the individual parts particularly salient. But what remains entirely problematic is whether both sub-minds 'have an inner life'. One view is that there is no reason to grant (full, 'inner-life') consciousness to the non-dominant hemisphere, since all that has been shown is that hemisphere, like many other unconscious cognitive subsystems, can process a lot of information and intelligently control some behaviour. But then we may ask what reason there then is to grant consciousness to the dominant hemisphere, or even to the whole intact system in a normal person. We had thought that question was frivolous and not worth discussing, but this avenue forces us to take it seriously again. If, on the other hand, we grant full, 'inner-life' consciousness to the non-dominant hemisphere (or, more properly, to the newly discovered person whose brain is the non-dominant hemisphere), what will be said about all the other information-processing subsystems posited by current theory? Is the Lockian crutch to be taken up again, at the expense of populating, quite literally, our heads with hosts of subjects of experience?

Consider, for example, the striking discovery by J. R. Lackner and M. Garrett of what might be called an unconscious channel of sentence comprehension. In dichotic listening tests, subjects listen through earphones to two different channels, and are instructed to *attend* to just one channel. Typically they can report with great accuracy what they have heard through the attended channel, but can say little about what was going on concomitantly in the unattended channel. Thus, if the unattended channel carries a spoken sentence, the subjects typically report that they heard a voice, and even a male or female voice. Perhaps they even have a conviction about whether the voice was speaking in their native tongue, but they cannot report what was said. In Lackner and Garrett's experiments, subjects heard ambiguous sentences in the attended channel, such as 'He put out the lantern to signal the attack'. In the unattended channel one group of subjects received disambiguating input (e.g. 'He extinguished the lantern'), while another group had neutral or irrelevant input. The former group could not report what was presented through the unattended channel, but they favoured the suggested reading of the ambiguous sentences significantly more than the control group did. The influence of the unattended channel on the interpretation of the attended signal can be explained only on the hypothesis that the unattended signal is processed all the way to a semantic level—that is, the unattended signal is comprehended—but this is apparently unconscious sentence comprehension! Or should we say it is evidence of the presence in the subjects of at least two different and only partially communicating consciousness? If we ask the subjects what it was like to comprehend the unattended channel, they will reply, sincerely, that it was not like anything to them—they were quite unaware of that sentence. But perhaps, as is often suggested about the split-brain patients, there is in effect someone else to whom our question ought to be addressed: the subject who consciously comprehended the sentence and has relayed a hint of its meaning to the subject who answers our questions.

Which should we say, and why? We seem to be back to our unanswerable question, which suggests we should find a different way of looking at the situation. Let us then entertain the hypothesis that what we had taken to be one phenomenon is actually two quite different phenomena: the sort of consciousness that is intrinsically connected to the capacity to say in one's natural language what is going on; and the sort of consciousness that is just a matter of intelligent information processing. On this proposal, adding the capacity to make 'introspective reports' *changes the phenomenon*, so when we wonder what a dolphin or dog could tell us, or what a non-dominant hemisphere could tell us, if only they could talk, we are wondering about a radically different phenomenon from the phenomenon that exists in the absence of such a linguistic capacity.

It is a familiar theme in discussions of consciousness that human consciousness is somehow tied to our capacity for language, and is quite different from animal consciousness. Developing this idea in a cognitivistic model of linguistic production and comprehension should clarify the conditions of this dependence of human consciousness on language. Of course many perplexities must be confronted along the way. How should we conceive of the gradual acquisition of language by children (or chimpanzees, perhaps!), and what should we say about the 'experience' (conscious or unconscious) of the pre-verbal Helen Keller? A theory of consciousness that does justice to the variety of complications will almost certainly demand of us a revolution in our habits of thought about these issues, but we have already partially absorbed the first shocks of that revolution in the overthrow of the Lockian vision of the transparent mind.

DANIEL C. DENNETT

DREAMING. In our sleep we all intermittently experience insanity. Some of our dreams differ so from normal awareness that they have often been attributed to the departure of the soul to another world, or to the visitation of alien beings, such as angels. Since earliest history, dreams have been interpreted in order to give guidance for the future, up to the dream books of the nineteenth century and punters' guides of the twentieth. In the 1950s Nathaniel Kleitman of Chicago, with E. Aserinsky and W. Dement, opened an era of laboratory techniques for studying dreams.

Dreams are often misleadingly defined as successions of visual images, but these are merely common accompaniments. A dream is an experience of living in a fantasy world in which things happen, emotions are felt, actions are carried out, people are present, with all the waking sensations coming and going. The congenitally blind have dreams that are no less vivid even though they see nothing. Visual images in dreams are as often in colour as in real life.

Dement and Kleitman introduced the technique of awakening and questioning volunteers about possible dreams at critically sensitive moments during sleep, and found that during periods of sleep accompanied by rapid eye movements (REMs) detailed dream reports could usually he elicited, whereas recall from other times during sleep was meagre. Dement wakened some further volunteers repeatedly as soon as their REMs began, and later found a compensatory increase of sleep with REMs. He proposed that he had deprived them of dreams, that they needed to dream, and that if they did not they might become insane. This notion achieved wide circulation but has not since been supported. We may need to dream, but no one has yet devised an experiment to see whether we have such psychological needs at night.

There are two kinds of sleep; they came to be called non-rapid eye movement (NREM or orthodox) and rapid eye movement (REM or paradoxical) sleep. In 1962 David Foulkes of Chicago asked of his subjects not the leading question, 'Have you been dreaming?' but instead, 'What was passing through your mind?' He found that NREM sleep allowed recall almost as often as REM sleep, but its less colourful content was more often characterized as 'thinking' and, despite considerable overlap, it was possible to distinguish between the 'dream' reports from REM sleep and those from NREM sleep. Typical dreams can be elicited especially easily from NREM sleep at the end of the night and when first falling asleep. The brief dreamlets that come as we drowsily drift to sleep are known as hypnagogic hallucinations or images.

In subsequent research Molinari and Foulkes made awakenings from REM sleep both just after one of the intermittent bursts of REMs and when over thirty seconds of ocular quiescence had elapsed during REM sleep, and sought details of mental life just prior to waking. The first type of awakenings elicited many 'primary' visual and other experiences (for example, a little brother suddenly vomiting 'on my shoulder'), the second elicited secondary cognitive elaborations resembling the thinking characteristic of NREM sleep. Jerky eye movements, limb twitches, face twitches, middle-ear muscle twitches, and sudden respiratory changes are all *phasic* components of REM sleep, whereas muscle relaxation and penile erections are *tonic* features. It seems that the special 'dream' elements are injected intermittently in company with the phasic components of REM sleep.

As the night progresses, the REM periods contain a higher rate of phasic components, and dreams are more active and less passive in quality. Sleeping-pills diminish the phasic elements and dreams become more passive. There has been a lot of controversy about such relations between bodily events and the contents of a dream. While the majority of the REMs certainly cannot be ascribed to scanning the visual field of a dream-world, there are occasional large eye movements that do seem to bear a relation to described dream content. Closer correspondence has been found for movements of the limbs: Jouvet made lesions in the lower brains of cats so that they were no longer paralysed during REM sleep, and they rose up and appeared to the observer to be acting out their dreams. There is certainly a strong correlation between dream emotionality and heart-rate fluctuations or skin potential fluctuations, while in anxiety-ridden dreams there is loss of the usual penile erections.

The intensified dreaming qualities to the mental life that accompanies each REM sleep period about every 90–100 minutes led to findings that, while awake and in unchanging environments, people engage in intensified oral activity and have more day-dreaming qualities to their thoughts according to a daytime cycle of 90–100 minutes. Day-dreaming and night-dreaming are both associated with a 90–100 minute rhythm.

The term 'nightmare' is today used for dreams that occur during REM sleep, usually in the later night, and in which a series of events is associated with anxiety. As the sleeper awakens from his nightmare, he is often aware of the inability to move that characterizes REM sleep. On the other hand, night terrors arise in the early night, from NREM sleep with large slow electrical brain waves. They involve brief and less elaborately detailed experiences of entrapment, of being choked or attacked, often with shrieking, sitting-up, or sleep-walking, and tremendous acceleration of the heart. Both nightmares and night terrors occur unpredictably in even the most emotionally stable people, but become more frequent when there is greater daytime anxiety; they are frequent among wartime battle evacuees and night terrors are commonly experienced by children aged 10–14. Likewise, those who are depressed by day have dreams by night that contain themes of failure and loss.

Environmental circumstances influence dream content. Dreams reported after awakenings by investigators in the home have more aggressive, friendly, sexual, or success-and-failure elements than those reported in the laboratory, but in both cases most are duller than would be supposed. Anxiety-provoking films seen prior to sleep can lead to dreams containing related themes. Events occurring around the sleeper during dreams are often incorporated, so that, for example, the words 'Robert, Robert, Robert' spoken to a sleeper led to his reporting a dream about a 'distorted rabbit'.

Dream reports from successive periods of REM sleep in a single night can be distinguished from those of other nights, and the dreams of one individual are different from those of another: dreams thus reflect both day-to-day psychological variations and enduring individual traits. Sigmund Freud, C. G. Jung, and many others since, have sought hidden features of personality and understanding of an individual's emotional conflicts, through examination of, or free association from, dreams described by day. Whatever the clinical value of such dream recollections, they hardly compare with the rich reports that can be elicited by awakenings at night. Despite the symbolism and fascinating condensation of ideas to be found in dreams,there is no evidence that a more useful understanding of personality can be gained from them than can be divined from the realities of waking behaviour.

IAN OSWALD

HYPNOSIS. In the course of the twentieth century, interest in hypnosis has largely passed from the physician to the experimental psychologist, whose concern is with its nature and mechanisms rather than with its therapeutic efficacy. While a few scattered experiments, such as those of D. R. L. Delboeuf, were reported towards the end of the nineteenth century, the modern era in the study of hypnotism may be said to have been ushered in by the work of Clark L. Hull and his co-workers at Yale University in the early 1930s. While militantly disowning hypnotism's murky past, Hull insisted that hypnosis is an essentially normal phenomenon that can be studied in precisely the same way as any other mental capacity which varies from one individual to another. His book published in 1933 represents the first systematic attempt to apply the experimental and statistical methods of modern psychology to the study of hypnosis and suggestibility.

Hull's work was to a considerable extent designed to cast doubt on the extravagant claims current in some quarters that individual capacity in the hypnotic state might transcend the limits of the normal. Thus it has been argued that exceptional feats of sensory discrimination, of muscular strength, or of memory might be performed in the hypnotic state, suggesting that hypnosis *per se* enhanced many aspects of human capacity. Hull and his co-workers were able to show that whereas hypnosis as such does not appear to confer any obvious advantages, it is none the less possible to influence human performance, sometimes dramatically, by hypnotic suggestion. For example, he produced evidence of some increase in muscular capacity, more especially in sustained resistance to fatigue, and alterations in threshold of a variety of sensory stimuli, whereby the lower limits of intensity of stimulation necessary to produce a conscious sensation were appreciably raised. As regards memory, whereas no improvement in the reproduction of recently memorized material under hypnosis could be demonstrated, there was some evidence that memories of childhood might become more readily accessible. Hull's work, while producing no real evidence of the transcendence of normal capacity in hypnosis, did undoubtedly demonstrate the reality of many classical hypnotic phenomena (for example, hypnotic anaesthesia or analgesia and posthypnotic amnesia) under reasonably well-controlled experimental conditions. His work also served to bring out the essential continuity between the effects of suggestion in the waking and the hypnotic states.

Experimental hypnosis rapidly expanded in the 1950s and 1960s, some of its foremost representatives being F. X. Barber, E. R. Hilgard, M. T. Orne, and T. R. Sarbin. One of the main preoccupations at this period was the construction of standardized scales of hypnotic susceptibility, of which the best known and most widely used were the Stanford scales devised by A. M. Weitzenhoffer and E. R. Hilgard in 1961. The rationale of their construction and use was well described by Hilgard (1965) and one need only comment here on some of the more interesting findings. In the first place, contrary to traditional belief, there is no real evidence that women are more readily hypnotizable than men, or are capable of greater depth of hypnosis. In the second place, a critical period seems to exist as regards hypnotic susceptibility. While it has long been known that children are in general more easily hypnotized than adults, it has been found that children between the ages of 8 and 12 are more easily hypnotized than either older or younger children. The advantage may lie in part in the fact that whereas children of 8 and below find sustained concentration difficult and are readily distracted, children above the age of 12 or so have developed greater powers of self-criticism and are consequently less suggestible. Although changes in hypnotic susceptibility over the adult life span do not appear to be striking, the natural history of hypnosis is certainly deserving of closer study.

From Hull onwards, experimental methods have been widely used to study such classical phenomena of hypnosis as hypnotic anaesthesia or analgesia (Hilgard and Hilgard, 1975) and sensory deceptions or hallucinations. In some ingenious experiments, Hilgard has shown that it is not difficult to induce selective deafness for sounds of weak intensity—for example, the ticking of a watch—without interfering with the subject's perception of the experimenter's voice. In susceptible subjects, it may even prove possible to effect profound attenuation of sensation within a particular sensory modality, such as touch or pain. Experiments by A. M. Halliday and A. A. Mason (1964) have, however, shown that, in such cases, the nervous messages from the sense organs do in fact reach the relevant areas of the cerebral cortex, where they give rise to electrical responses ('evoked potentials') of normal amplitude. It therefore seems that the conscious sensory responses with which these electrical activities are ordinarily correlated must undergo some form of suppression or dissociation. That this is so is strongly indicated by a dramatic experiment of Hilgard's, in which he showed that a hypnotized subject in whom a profound loss of pain sense had been induced by suggestion, and who entirely denied feeling pain when appropriately stimulated, did in fact admit to doing so when tested by automatic writing, the content of which was ostensibly unknown to him. This is a classical example of hypnotic dissociation of the kind much discussed by Pierre Janet and other early expositors of the relations between hypnosis and hysteria. It strongly suggests that hypnotic anaesthesia and analgesia are true dissociative phenomena rather than mere exaggerations of ordinary suggestibility.

Sensory deceptions (illusions) and even hallucinations induced by suggestion have also been demonstrated on occasion, using healthy, volunteer subjects in an experimental situation, but only in those whose susceptibility to hypnosis is unusually high (Hilgard, 1965; Weitzenhoffer, 1947). In such cases, a distinction should be made between the generation of behaviour appropriate to an imagined object, which is not difficult to induce, and the production of what is described by the subject as a true perceptual experience (hallucination proper). For example, Hilgard has shown that many subjects will react positively to the suggestion that a fly has alighted, say, on their face, by grimacing or brushing it off. This might almost be regarded as play-acting in the sense of T. R. Sarbin and others who stress the 'role-playing' element in hypnosis. Even so, a few such subjects will say when asked that the experience was very real and lifelike, suggesting a true positive hallucination. Further experiments, in which it is suggested that the subject will perceive two dim lights, when only one is shown, likewise on occasion elicit surprisingly convincing reports of a hallucinated experience. It is possible in such cases that suggestion in alliance with the artificial hypnotic state has produced a condition akin to dreaming, in which a visual image can assume the vividness and reality of an actual external object. At all events, such phenomena seem to magnify, if not transcend, the effects of suggestion in the ordinary waking state.

Similar considerations also arise in

connection with so-called age-regression, in which a subject aged perhaps 20 is told that he will experience himself as he was when, say, 10 years old (Hilgard, 1965, pp.167–75; Gill and Brenman, 1966). He will thereupon comport himself, superficially at least, in accordance with his suggested age. Without further or more specific suggestions being given, he will commonly write or draw in a strikingly more juvenile manner and may even develop an apparent disorientation, stating, for example, that he is in the school he attended at the age of 10 and that the experimenter is a schoolmaster at that time known to him. In such cases it is often difficult to decide whether the patient is an accomplished, if unintentional, actor or whether there is a genuine reactivation of long superseded attitudes and modes of behaviour, i.e. a true regression to an earlier state of the person and genuine re-enaction of the past. One simple test might be to suggest to him that he should progress rather than regress in age, and see to what extent he can duplicate the presumed behaviour of a very much older person. It is also entirely conjectural whether regression, as some believe, can be pursued into earliest infancy.

As might be expected, experimentalists have given much attention to the relationship between hypnosis and ordinary sleep (see Hull, 1933, pp. 193–243). Although subjects often refer to lethargy, drowsiness, and diminished contact with reality as characteristic of hypnosis, it seems clear that this state, whatever its nature, differs categorically from normal sleep, with or without dreaming. As James Braid observed in the nineteenth century, the muscles do not relax as in ordinary sleep and the subject does not drop an object held in the hand as he becomes hypnotized. Further, reflexes which disappear in sleep can be elicited normally in the hypnotic state. Finally, study of the electrical rhythms of the brain (electroencephalography) shows that the electroencephalogram (EEC) in hypnosis in no way resembles that in any of the recognized states of sleep but is essentially identical with that of ordinary wakefulness. From the electrophysiological point of view, therefore, the hypnotized person is awake.

Let us now turn briefly to theories of hypnosis. William James wrote in 1890 that the suggestion theory of hypnosis may be approved, provided that we regard the trance state as its essential prerequisite. Although the term 'hypnotic trance' is seldom used today, most people regard the hypnotic state as something *sui generis* with its own peculiar properties. In addition to greatly enhanced suggestibility, these are commonly said to consist in voluntary suspension of initiative, restriction of attention to a narrow field, and marked reduction in self-consciousness and critical appraisal. Some would add that the hypnotized person, much like the dreamer, is not fully in contact with reality and exhibits a facile mode of reasoning ('trance logic') in some respects characteristic of childhood. Although the state of hypnosis lacks definite physiological or biochemical criteria of an altered state of consciousness, it does not of course necessarily follow that no such criteria will ever be discovered. Indeed, it is only in comparatively recent years that firm physiological correlates of ordinary dreaming have been securely established.

None the less, this lack of physiological criteria of the hypnotic state, together with its resemblances to many phenomena in ordinary waking life involving the effects of suggestion, has induced some recent workers, in particular F. X. Barber, who has published much useful work in experimental hypnosis, to argue that the concept of a trance state is an unnecessary assumption (Barber, 1969). As he sees it, hypnosis is to be viewed as an essentially normal state of waking consciousness in which a voluntary compact between experimenter and subject enables each to exercise his respective role, which is, so to speak, enshrined in traditional expectation. Although such a view has the merits of parsimony, it fails to account for many features of the hypnotic state, such as spontaneous posthypnotic amnesia in highly susceptible subjects, loss or diminution of pain sense, and the operation of posthypnotic suggestion. Further, the production of sense deceptions and hallucinations is more reminiscent of the effects brought about in indisputably altered states of consciousness, such as may be produced by drugs or toxic agencies, than the ordinary operations of waking suggestibility.

To say this is not of course to deny that there are important psychogenic factors in hypnosis which are closely related to suggestion and fantasy in daily life. Josephine Hilgard, in particular, has emphasized the links between susceptibility to hypnosis and the propensity to become immersed in novels, plays, and films and to participate in the fictional existence of the characters. She likewise stresses the element of identification with parents or other emotionally significant features in early life, and indeed calls attention to many aspects of hypnosis, among them the blurring of fantasy and reality, the ready involvement in games of pretence, and the tendency to believe uncritically in the pronouncement of others, which may be viewed as 'part and parcel of childhood' (Hilgard, 1965, pp.343–74). But just as dreaming, in itself essentially psychogenic, presupposes the altered state of consciousness characteristic of a certain stage of sleep, so it may be argued that hypnosis, likewise essentially psychogenic, presupposes the less dramatic alteration of consciousness formerly known as the hypnotic trance.

In conclusion, one may ask whether experimental hypnosis presents any hazards. By and large, the procedure seems harmless enough, though medical men rightly warn that it can be dangerous if the subjects should happen to include emotionally disturbed individuals or those with a history of psychiatric illness. In such cases, the experimenter may well lack both the knowledge and the experience to handle the emotional relationships, positive or negative, which may unwittingly be generated in the process. A related question is whether experimental hypnosis calls for ethical guidelines. We know, for example, that certain types of psychological experiment involve calculated deceit, as in the work of Stanley Milgram on obedience. Milgram explained to his subjects that it was necessary for the purposes of his experiment to deliver shocks of potentially lethal intensity to other human beings, and he found, somewhat to his surprise, that many subjects were prepared to undertake this in spite of their ignorance of the deceit which was being practised upon them. If such an experiment were repeated under conditions of hypnosis, it is entirely possible that even greater conformity with the instructions of the experimenter would be forthcoming. While it remains true that, in general, hypnotized subjects cannot be induced to perform actions that are morally repugnant to them, and that the danger of crimes being committed as a result of hypnotic suggestion appears to be extremely small, there is no doubt that any form of experiment on the effects of suggestion, with or without hypnosis, must be regarded as open to potential abuse. It is to be hoped that the psychological fraternity will take due notice of these hazards and introduce appropriate ethical guidelines for the conduct of human experiments, in particular those making use of hypnosis.

O. L. ZANGWILL

MIND AND BODY. Until quite recently most philosophers have held a dualistic view of the relation between mind and body. This dualism has, however, taken several different forms. There have been those, like Descartes, who ascribe mental attributes to spiritual substances which are supposed to be logically independent of anything physical but to inhabit particular bodies in a way which it has not proved easy to define. Others, like Hobbes, have admitted only a duality of properties, ascribing both mental and physical attributes to human bodies. Others again have recognized an ultimate category of persons, differentiating them from physical objects just on the ground that they possess mental as well as physical attributes. Exactly what constitutes a mental attribute is itself not easy to define, but it can perhaps be sufficiently illustrated by examples, which may be chosen so as to cover the different varieties of sensation, perception, imagination, feeling, and thought.

For the most part, those who have subscribed to one or other form of dualism have also held that there is causal interaction between mental and physical events. The main opposition to this view has come from those who conceive of the physical world as a closed system, in the sense that every physical event must be explicable in purely physical terms, if it is explicable at all. If they also accept the existence of irreducibly mental occurrences, they regard them as accompanying and perhaps being causally dependent on physical events, but as not themselves making any causal intrusion into the physical world.

This refusal to admit psychophysical interaction does not seem justified, especially if one takes a Humean view of causation as consisting basically in nothing more than regular concomitance. Even if there were a physical explanation for every physical event, this would not preclude there being alternative forms of explanation which relied at least in part on mental factors. It is, however, unlikely that such psychophysical correlations would be nearly so stringent as the laws of physics, and the same would apply to any generalizations that were couched in purely mental terms.

The difference in the type of causal laws to which they are subject is one of the ways in which mental and physical events are distinguished in the theory of neutral monism, which was advanced by William James and subsequently by Bertrand Russell. According to this theory, the elements of our experience consisted of actual or possible sense-data out of which the physical world was supposed to be constructible. These elements were also regarded as entering into the constitution of minds so that one and the same sense-datum might as a member of one group be a constituent of some physical object and as a member of another group be a constituent of a mind in whose biography a perception of the object occurred. Apart from the fact that there were also images and feelings, which entered only into the constitution of minds, the difference between mind and matter was represented not as a difference of substance, or content, but as a difference in the arrangement of common elements, involving their participation in different forms of causality. This was in many ways an attractive theory, but it met with serious difficulties. Though there may be a sense in which physical objects can be generated out of the immediate data of perception, an outright reduction of one to the other seems not to be feasible. Neither did the exponents of the theory succeed in giving a satisfactory account of personal identity or of the special relation in which the elements that make up a person's mind stand to the particular physical object which is that person's body.

Similar difficulties beset the attempt made by Berkeley to eliminate matter in favour of mind, by representing physical objects as collections of sensible qualities, which he termed ideas. In Berkeley's case, the want of a criterion of personal identity is especially flagrant, since he followed Descartes in treating minds as spiritual substances. It is, indeed, one of the principal objections to this view of the mind that it is incapable of furnishing any such criterion.

In recent times, monistic theories have mainly taken the other direction. They have gone beyond the older forms of materialism in that they not only ascribe mental attributes to certain physical objects, but also treat these attributes themselves as physical. The strongest theory of this type is that in which it is maintained that propositions which would ordinarily be construed as referring to mental states or processes are logically equivalent to propositions which refer only to people's overt behaviour. This theory may be allied to a verificational theory of meaning. Since the only way in which we can test the truth of the propositions in which we attribute experiences to others is through observation of the ways in which these other persons behave, it is deduced that this is all that such propositions can legitimately be taken to refer to. Then, since it can be shown that one cannot consistently combine a behaviouristic treatment of propositions about the experiences of others with a mentalistic treatment of propositions about one's own experiences, the conclusion is drawn that all references to one's own experiences are to be construed behaviouristically, even when they are made by oneself.

This argument can, however, be turned on its head. One can start with the premise that the knowledge which one has of one's own experiences cannot be fully set out in any series of propositions which refer only to one's overt behaviour and then use the fact that the analysis of propositions about a person's experiences must be the same, whoever asserts them, as a ground for rejecting a purely behavioural account of propositions which refer to the experiences of others. And, indeed, unless one is prepared to feign anaesthesia, it would seem undeniable that this premise is true. The advocates of logical behaviourism were indeed able to show that references to behaviour are often comprised in the use of what are classified as mentalistic terms. They were even justified in claiming that intelligent thought and action do not necessarily require the occurrence of inner processes. Nevertheless we do very often have thoughts that we keep to ourselves, and the existence of such thoughts cannot be logically equated with any disposition to report them. Neither, on the face of it, is there any logical equivalence between a person's having such and such sensations or perceptions and his dispositions to engage in any form of overt action.

In recent years logical behaviourism has given way to the less radical theory in which mental occurrences are held to be not logically but only factually identical with states of the central nervous system. On this view, for a person to have such and such an experience is for his brain to be in such and such a state, in the way in which lightning is an electrical discharge or temperature is the mean kinetic energy of molecules. As in those other cases, the suggested identity is supposed to be established not through the analysis of concepts but on the basis of empirical research. It rests on the assumption that there is a perfect correlation between a person's experiences and events which take place in his brain. In fact, this assumption goes further than the evidence yet warrants. There is, indeed, very strong evidence of a general dependence of mental occurrences on the functioning of the brain, but it has still to be shown that the correspondence is so exact that from observation of a person's brain one could arrive at a knowledge of his experiences in every detail.

Even if we make this assumption, it is not clear that it justifies the postulation of identity. If events which appear from their descriptions to belong to different categories are capable of being empirically correlated, the implication is rather that they are distinct. It is only on the basis of some theory that we can proceed to identify them. In this case the theory seems to be linguistic. It is thought that a general acceptance of the hypothesis that mental events are causally dependent upon events in the brain will lead to the denial of their separate existence. It has even been suggested that the use of psychological terms will be given up altogether.

This does not seem probable. Even if we were aware of what was going on in people's central nervous systems, it is unlikely that we should cease to find a use for explaining their behaviour in terms of their conscious thoughts and feelings. Nor is it likely, in a case in which an inference drawn from one's physical condition conflicted with one's awareness of one's own experience, that one should not continue to treat this awareness as the better authority.

If we have to adhere to dualism, the most defensible form of it would seem to be that in which we admit only a duality of properties. Unhappily, the problem of showing how these predicates combine to characterize one and the same subject has not yet been adequately solved.

A.J. AYER

PSYCHOSOMATIC DISEASE. Diseases are designated as psychosomatic if two conditions are fulfilled: if (i) the symptoms are accompanied by demonstrable physiological disturbances of function and (ii) the illness as a whole can be interpreted as a manifestation or function of the patient's personality, conflicts, life history, etc. The first condition distinguishes psychosomatic illness from psychoneurosis, particularly conversion hysteria, in which, by definition, the physical symptoms are not accompanied by demonstrable physiological disturbances. The second condition distinguishes psychosomatic illness from physical diseases pure and simple, which are explicable solely in terms of bodily dysfunction without reference to the psyche of the patient.

Although the word 'psychosomatic' was used by Coleridge, and its reversed form 'somapsyche' occurs in the original Greek of the New Testament, the concept of psychosomatic disease dates properly from the first half of the twentieth century, when it became necessary to have a concept that cut across the division of diseases into physical (somatic) and mental (psychical) which had been established by Freud and Breuer's demonstration that the psychoneuroses were not functional disturbances of the central nervous system but symbolic expressions of psychical conflict. Given the resulting tendency to assume that illnesses were either physical and all in the body, or mental and all in the mind, the term 'psychosomatic disease' became necessary to categorize illnesses resembling psychoneuroses in being expressions of psychical conflict but yet had solid, demonstrable physical signs and symptoms.

As the preceding two paragraphs perhaps reveal, psychosomatic disease is logically and philosophically speaking a most tricky concept. Since its meaning and precise implications necessarily depend on each particular user's basic assumptions about the relationship between body and mind. Presumably a materialist must hold that all diseases, including so-called mental ones, are ultimately somatic, and an idealist must hold that all physical illnesses are ultimately mental, while those who hold that physical and mental events belong to different causal sequences have to explain, if they believe in the possibility of psychosomatic disease, how the leap from one to the other is effected. However, in actual practice, the term is only used to categorize illnesses which present with physical signs and symptoms but none the less require the clinician to explore the patient's biography and state of mind. It is never used to refer to illnesses which present with mental symptoms but are none the less due to physical causes as, for example, depression caused by a brain tumour.

Georg Groddeck (1866–1934), the maverick German psychoanalyst, is often regarded as the father of psychosomatic medicine. His way of formulating the relationship of body and mind was to assume that both are the creations of a third, impersonal force, *das Es*, the It:

> the body and mind are a joint thing which harbours an It, a power by which we are lived, while we think we live . . . The It, which is mysteriously connected with sexuality, Eros, or whatever you choose to call it, shapes the nose as well as the hand of the human, just as it shapes his thoughts and emotions . . . And just as the symptomatic activity of the It in hysteria and neurosis calls for psychoanalytical treatment, so does heart trouble and cancer.

However, psychosomatic disease remains an elusive concept. Many, perhaps most, clinicians feel that there is something in it, but the problem of formulating correctly the nature of the relationship between body and mind implicit in it has proved recalcitrant.

CHARLES RYCROFT

SPLIT-BRAIN AND THE MIND. The problem of how the mind relates to the brain stands as the greatest challenge to a scientific age which seeks an objective explanation for all nature. Our physicalist world view and our pragmatic approach to social problems may both be transformed by significant discoveries concerning the way human experience and human social consciousness arise in cerebral activity.

Much has been learned by observing how physical damage to the brain in different locations causes losses or distortions of motives, wishes, skills, feelings, and conscious experiences. Perhaps the most striking results have come from a brain operation that segregates the highest brain functions into two unlike sets: by cutting some 800 million nerve fibres that connect one half of the cerebral cortex with the other it is possible effectively to divide the mind.

It is a principal characteristic of the mind to exhibit a harmonious unity and a coherent command—to make the consciousness of an individual person. Ever since nerve conduction was understood it has been speculated that the great interhemispheric bridge, the corpus callosum (meaning 'thick-skinned body'), is essential for mental unity. When it and other smaller interhemispheric connections are cut, communication between the two sides must pass by the stem of the brain, which is normally considered unconscious, or through external relations of the body with the world of stimuli and the effects of actions.

Famous psychologists, including G. T. Fechner and William McDougall, have wondered what would happen to consciousness if the brain were divided in this way. McDougall, it is said, even tried to persuade the physiologist C. S. Sherrington to undertake to divide his, McDougall's, corpus callosum if he became incurably ill. Nerve connectionists tended to think conscious experience would be destroyed or divided, but McDougall, a mentalist, believed consciousness would remain unified. It was frustrating that, for a long time, studies of animals, and a few human cases, with corpus callosum sectioned gave no interesting evidence. Consciousness appeared to be slightly depressed and there were transitory lapses in voluntary co-ordination, but that was all. In irony, Karl Lashley suggested that the corpus callosum might serve simply to hold the hemispheres together. Warren McCulloch said its only known function was to spread epilepsy.

Cerebral commissurotomy, the split-brain operation, has been performed with varying completeness on a small number of human beings since the mid-1940s, always in hopes of checking crippling epilepsy, to stop the non-functional neural discharges reverberating between the hemispheres and severely damaging the cortical tissues. The breakthrough in estimation of the mental effects of this operation came from investigations in Roger Sperry's laboratory at the California Institute of Technology, following the first effective experiments on the consequences of commissurotomy in cats and monkeys. The animal studies had established new methods. They revealed simple explanations for why all previous research had observed only trivial and uninformative consequences of so great a change in brain structure. With control for orienting, and of information exchange between the hemispheres through transactions with the external world, the split-brain animals were found to have totally divided perception and learning. When free, their movements, alertness, and general motivation were entirely normal.

In Los Angeles, the neurosurgeons Philip Vogel and Joseph Bogen concluded that selected epileptic patients would benefit from the surgery and suffer no serious mental loss. Between 1962 and 1968, nine complete operations were performed with success in reducing fits. Psychological tests performed by Michael Gazzaniga, Sperry, and Bogen at the California Institute soon revealed that, while the general psychological state and behaviour was, in most cases, little affected, there was a profound change in mental activities. Other studies with commissurotomy patients carried out since, in the U.S., France, and Australia, have produced similar findings.

For the commissurotomy subject, direct awareness is no longer whole. An object felt in the left hand out of sight cannot be matched to the same kind of object felt separately and unseen in the right hand. As long as the eyes are stationary, something seen just to the left of the fixation point cannot be compared to something seen on the right side. Comparable divisions in olfactory and auditory awareness may be demonstrated. Furthermore, although sight and touch communicate normally on each side, left visual field to left hand or right visual field to right hand, the crossed twohemisphere combinations fail, as if experiences of eye and hand were obtained by separate persons. There is no evidence that perceptual information needed to identify an object can cross the mid-line of the visual field, or between the hands, to unify the patient's awareness. While the division of sight for detail is extremely sharp at the centre of the field, as long as the patient keeps his eyes still, with freedom to look to left and right and to see in both halves of vision what both hands are holding, the division of awareness ceases to be apparent. Indeed, the subject himself seems unaware of anything amiss, except when evidence is presented to him of an inconsistency in his conscious judgement. Then it would appear he feels some lapse of concentration, or absent-mindedness.

With stimuli on arms, legs, face, or trunk, there is some transfer of feeling between the sides. These less discriminatory parts of the body are represented in duplicate, with both sides in each hemisphere of the brain, and their functions, sensory and motor, are cross-integrated at levels of the brain below the hemispheres. Interesting results have been obtained with large, long-lasting stimuli moving in the periphery of vision. Seeing the spatial layout in surroundings at large, called 'ambient vision', is vital in steering on a confined or irregular route or in a cluttered environment, and even in maintaining the balance of standing or walking. It also functions to give approximate location to off-centre targets of attention before the eyes move to fixate. Evidently the semi-conscious appreciation of the location and orientation of major features in outside space, mainly picked up from dynamic transformations of the visual image, is not divided by commissurotomy. Indeed, the general background or context of body coordination and orienting must be intact for commissurotomy subjects to retain the freedom of action and coherence of awareness they ordinarily exhibit. To this degree the operation does not divide the agency of the subject, or the experience of whole-body action. The two halves of the neocortex are kept in functional relationship, coordinated through ascending and descending links with the sub-hemispheric regions of the brain stem.

By far the most dramatic finding of the early tests was the total failure of the right cerebral cortex on its own to express itself in speech. It could not utter words to explain its awareness or knowledge. In contrast, when stimuli were given to the left cortex the subject could say perfectly normally what the experience had been like. Objects were named, compared, and described, and the occurrence or non-occurrence of stimulus events was correctly reported. Yet similar tests of the right half of the brain, with stimuli in the left visual field or left hand, totally failed. The subjects often gave no response. If urged to reply, they said that there might have been some weak and ill-defined event, or else they confabulated experiences, as if unable to apply a test of truth or falsity to spontaneously imagined answers to questions.

These events not only confirm a division of awareness, but they raise important questions which have been debated in clinical neurology since the discovery, over a century ago, that muteness or disturbance of language comprehension can result from brain injury confined to the left hemisphere. Could the right hemisphere comprehend spoken or written language at all? Could it express itself to any degree in signs, by writing, or by gesture? Could it make any utterance? Could it reason and think? Was it really conscious? The commissurotomy patients offered a wonderfully direct approach to these questions, and ingenious experiments were designed by Sperry and his students to interrogate the unspeaking right hemisphere.

Some comprehension of spoken and written language was certainly present in the mute side of the brain. Information about how the right hemisphere should perform a test could be conveyed by telling it what to do, and if the name of a common object was projected to the right cortex only, the patient could retrieve a correct example by hand, or identify a picture of it by pointing. The right hemisphere could solve very simple arithmetic problems, giving its answer by arranging plastic digits out of sight with the left hand. Nevertheless, it was clear that both the vocabulary as understood and the powers of calculation of the right hemisphere were distinctly inferior to these abilities in the left hemisphere of the same patient. Rarely, a patient was able to start an utterance or begin to write a word with the right hemisphere, but, in these tests, the vigilance of the more competent left hemisphere blocked all such initiatives after the first syllable or letter. In general only the left hemisphere could speak, write, or calculate.

When Levy applied non-verbal tests, the results indicated that there were some functions for which the left hemisphere did not dominate: for some modes of thinking the right hemisphere was superior. All these right brain tasks involved visual or touch perception of difficult configurations, judgements involving exploration of shapes by hand or manipulative construction of geometric assemblies or patterns. It appeared that the right hemisphere was able to notice the shape of things more completely than the left. Taken with evidence that systematic calculation and forming logical propositions with words were better performed by the left hemisphere, these results favoured the idea that the right hemisphere is better at taking in the structure of things synthetically, without analysis, assimilating all components at once in an ensemble, figure, or Gestalt. Nebes discovered that the right hemisphere may have a clearer memory of the appearance of things, in the sense that it was better able to recognize familiar objects with incomplete pictorial data, and better able to perceive whole shapes from parts seen or felt in the hand.

The way hands are normally used hints at differences in awareness of the hemispheres. In normal manipulation, a right-hander supports and orients an object in the grasp of the left hand, to facilitate discrete moves of the right fingers that are more finely controlled. Consider such a simple act as taking the last drop of soup from a bowl with a spoon. To grasp, support, and orient objects, the left hand must understand the dimensions and distribution of matter in an object, and usually this kind of judgement does not need visual inspection. In contrast, the discrete and precise acts of the right hand require a succession of decisions that are aimed or guided by a sequence of brief visual fixations. Writing is a cultivated skill that uses the right-hand endowment for rapid repeated cycles of action in the service of language. It may be a learned adaptation of the brain mechanism for gestural communication, the right hand of most persons being dominant for expressive gesticulation. In many tests, the left hand of the commissurotomy patients was more efficient than the right at feeling shapes that resist analysis into highly familiar elements. The left hand palpated complex raised patterns as wholes, as if sensing shape directly. In contrast, the right hand tended to feel the contours, corners, etc., one-by-one, as if trying to build up an inventory of discrete experiences along a line in time. Recently, experiments with the same subjects have demonstrated that the right hemisphere tends to be superior at metaphorical rather than literal perceptions, and that it perceives the emotions or moods in facial expressions or vocalizations better than the left.

To further explore the processes that direct awareness in the hemispheres, Levy, Trevarthen, and Sperry gave split-brain subjects a free choice of which hemisphere to use to control responses in tests. Halves of two different pictures were joined together down the vertical midline to make a double picture called a stimulus chimera. When this is presented to the split-brain patient with the join on the fixation point, information about each half is received in a different hemisphere. The tasks are designed so that in every trial the correct choice may be obtained by using the experience of either the left or right hemisphere. Preference for one half of the chimera depends on one-sided mental strategies that arise in response to the test instructions. With this kind of test, preferred modes of understanding of the hemispheres can be sensitively determined, as well as the cerebral functions that allocate attention between the two hemispheres.

The choices of the commissurotomy patients with chimeric stimuli confirm that thought in words favours the left hemisphere. Single words can be read by the right hemisphere, but the left is always preferred if the meaning of the words must be understood and not just their visual appearance or pattern. Further tests show that the right hemisphere is virtually unable to imagine the sound of a word for an object seen, even a very common one like an 'eye', so it cannot solve a test requiring silent rhyming 'in the head' (for example, 'eye' matches 'pie', 'key' matches 'bee'). It seems as if the habitual, and inherently favoured, dominance of the left hemisphere for speaking is tied in with a one-sided ability to predict how words will sound. The right hemisphere can know the meaning of a word from its sound, but it cannot make a sound image for itself from sight of the word, or from sight of the object the word stands for.

Preference for the right hemisphere in matching things by their appearance becomes strong when meaningless or unanalysable shapes are used, especially if these are not representing familiar objects, with a simple name. An extraordinary superiority of the right hemisphere for knowing a face, especially when it lacks bold distinctive features such as glasses, moustache, hat, or birthmark, relates to a rare consequence of damage to the posterior part of this hemisphere. This inability to recognize even the most familiar faces, called prosopagnosia, can greatly embarrass social life. With split-brain persons and stimuli restricted to the left hemisphere, face recognition is poor and identification is achieved by a laborious check-list of distinctive semantic elements to be memorized and searched for. There is obviously a stark contrast in hemisphere cognitive style, reminiscent of differences described in the way the two hands go about knowing or using objects. In addition to these apparently fixed differences in the organization of hemispheric cognitive structures, commissurotomy patients show a varying activation of the hemispheres under brain-stem control that can favour one or other side independently of task requirements. Sometimes the 'wrong' hemisphere is active in doing a task, and performance suffers. This 'metacontrol' may cause differences in the way normal individuals process cognitive problems; i.e. it may determine differences in mental abilities—for example, making one person skilled at visuo-constructive tasks while another is gifted at verbal rationalizations.

There are still many questions concerning the complementary styles of intelligence and conscious awareness revealed by commissurotomy and about how hemispheric functional states are coordinated. Some of the findings blur classical distinctions. Not all linguistic or propositional functions are confined to the left hemisphere, and though the right hemisphere is better at perceiving resemblances between complex forms, the left can perceive and recognize. In neither case is the monopoly of cognitive style complete, and cerebral asymmetry of function is now regarded as a matter of degree. However, as the chimera studies showed, there are some factors, not necessarily simple in their relationship to conventional psychological tests, but more involved in the strategy by which the brain as a whole allocates mental operations or motivates consciousness, for which left and right hemispheres do have markedly different capacities and preferences. Since the hemispheres of commissurotomy patients become progressively more alike, or less differentiated, by post-surgical learning or other changes compensating for their separation, they probably can reveal to us only weakened forms of hemisphere specialization.

Eran Zaidel has developed a method for blocking off half of the visual field of one eye of a commissurotomy patient. He attaches to the eye a contact lens which carries a small optical system and a screen. The patient can cast his eye over a test array in a normal way while picking up visual information by only one hemisphere. The subject has to interpret a story or picture or solve puzzles, many involving choice of the one picture from a group that will identify a concept to which he or she has been cued by a preceding stimulus. These tests prove that both hemispheres have elaborate awareness of the meanings of words and pictures. Metaphorical relationships form an important component of consciousness of meaning in both of them. Objects may be linked in awareness by their abstract properties or customary usefulness and social importance as well as by more obvious features. The usual names, colours, temperatures, and many other properties of things may be correctly identified when each thing is represented by a simple black and white picture. The tests of Zaidel and Sperry have shown that both hemispheres of commissurotomy patients have awareness of themselves as persons and a strong sense of the social and political value, or meaning, of pictures or objects.

Comprehension of words, spoken or written, is surprisingly rich in the right hemisphere, and all grammatical classes of words may be comprehended; but its consciousness does fail with relatively difficult, abstract, or rare words. When words are combined in a proposition, the comprehension of the right hemisphere falls drastically. When simplified items of no particular identity, such as plastic chips of differing size, form, and colour, are used as tokens for arbitrary grouping defined by short descriptions (for example, 'Point to a small red circle and a large yellow triangle'), this too proves difficult for the right hemisphere. A token test of this description was discovered by the Italian neuropsychologists Di Renzi and Vignolo to be extremely sensitive to left hemisphere lesions. The linguistic abilities of the right hemisphere thus resemble those of a nursery school child who understands language best when it is fitted into the world of objects, interpersonal acts, and events, all of which sustain the meaning of what is said. Disembedded or context-free propositions lacking interpersonal force require concentration of the mind on categories, critical formulae, or rules for action. These processes of thought may be developed by transformation of inherent human skills for establishing precise identity or harmony of purpose between thinking agents. Such propositions are difficult alike for young children and the disconnected right hemisphere of an adult.

Commissurotomy patients have helped us understand how consciousness, intention, and feelings are generated in activity at different levels of the brain. Thus separated cortices may experience and learn separately, but each may command coherent activity of the whole body. Feelings of dismay, embarrassment, or amusement, generated in one hemisphere by perceptions of threat, or risk, or teasing, invade the brain-stem to cause expressions and emotions of the whole person, in spite of the operation. Levels of attentiveness and the shifting aim of orientation and purpose are also patterned within brain-stem regions, which can transmit no detailed evidence of experience. The precautions needed to reveal divided awareness after brain bisection emphasize how, in normal active life, information about the world is constantly reflected to all parts of the brain as it and the body engage in changing relations with the external world. It does not appear necessary to imagine that the 'self', which has to maintain a unity, is destroyed when the forebrain commissures are cut, although some of its activities and memories are depleted after the operation.

The evidence on hemispherical differences reveals inherited motive structures for speech and rational thought that have evolved to establish intentional and experiential communion between persons. The brain is adapted to create and maintain human society and culture by two complementary conscious systems. Specialized motives in the two hemispheres generate a dynamic partnership between the intuitive, on the one side, and the analytical or rational, on the other, in the mind of each person. This difference appears to have evolved in connection with the human skills of intermental co-operation and symbolic communication.

Research with normal subjects stimulated by the commissurotomy studies shows that individuals vary greatly in the development of asymmetrical functions in their brains and in the ways the hemispheres are habitually activated. Such diverse factors as sex, age, handedness, education, and special training correlate with psychological and physiological measures of cerebral lateralization and hemispheric activation. The evidence is that human kind is not only very diverse in outside appearance: minds in any race, even in a single family, are inherently different in cognitive bent. It is not hard to perceive advantages of such psychological diversity in the most highly co-operative of beings, in whom mind and the experiences of society and culture become inseparable.

COLWYN TREVARTHEN

4: WHEN MINDS ARE DAMAGED

Amnesia
Aphasia
Cognitive deficits
Connectionist models of cognitive deficits
Dementia
Dyslexia
Epilepsy
Mental handicap

The complexity of the brain is such that it really should be a surprise that so many brains operate so well for so long. Our brains are vulnerable to damage from many sources. The most common acquired **cognitive deficits** affect speech, reading and spoken language comprehension, object and face recognition, and memory. Damage to the system can be physical (such as a blow to the head in a road traffic accident, or a stroke), or electrical (as in **epilepsy**), or chemical (through ingestion of a drug). The damage can occur at any time during the life cycle, of course, and the timing of the onset of damage will have implications for the severity of the effect and for chances of recovery. Early damage may be compensated for by plasticity in the nervous system, or recovery may be more difficult, as in some cases of **mental handicap** associated with genetic damage. Generalized organic damage occurring late in life is known as **dementia**, and is associated with neuronal degeneration. Damage in these cases is widespread, and has effects on any number of psychological functions, but **aphasia** and **amnesia** are commonly observed.

The effects of the damage will vary according to the function of the system concerned. The action of drugs may result in mood changes, or depression or stimulation of the central nervous system, depending upon the neuronal pathway being blocked or enhanced. Psychedelic drugs such as LSD and mescaline act upon the user's mind to produce changes to sensory perceptions, and can deliver a heightened state of awareness and self-awareness. Although the primary effects of these drugs are localized, neuronal transmission provides a generalized effect. The damaging effects of drugs depend upon dosage, and the effects of other damaging agents such as an epileptic seizure or a stroke also vary in extent. An epileptic seizure may be so mild as to result in a brief altered state of consciousness, or so extensive that surgery is required to restrict the damaging electrical activity to one part of the brain.

Neuropsychologists are particularly interested in the damage experienced by stroke patients who show localized effects upon mental processes. When the blood supply to a part of the brain is impeded, either through a haemorrhage or through arterial blockage, psychological systems become dysfunctional. This simple relationship is of psychological interest because when damage is highly localized and a specific function is then lost, we have evidence of the purpose of the cortical area that has been damaged. Relationships between damaged brain structures and damaged psychological functions also give evidence of the independence of component sub-functions. In the case of reading, for example, a number of acquired deficits have been identified, each suggesting routes by which the undamaged reader is able to extract visual information from a page, identify a particular word, generate the associated speech sound, and integrate the word with the rest of the sentence. These are the component sub-functions, and when specific parts of the brain are damaged, then specific sub-functions may be lost. Currently available brain imaging techniques give clear information about the localization and extent of stroke damage in surviving patients. Structural damage caused by the arterial blockage can now be related to active function without waiting for a post-mortem autopsy, as was necessary in the original investigations of aphasia by Paul Broca and Carl Wernicke. In the case of aphasia damage is almost always localized in the left temporal lobe of the brain and is often accompanied by apraxia. A number of centres and pathways in the left hemisphere have been identified as having specific speech functions. Damage can be seen in a number of psychological functions, and three in particular are attracting the attention of neuropsychologists. Hemianopia is the phenomenon of visual neglect, whereby part of the visual field disappears; acquired dyslexia following a stroke is the selective inability to read, or the selective dysfunction of part of the reading process; and prosopagnosia is the selective inability to recognize the faces of familiar people. **Connectionist models of cognitive deficits** have been used to help us understand acquired dysfunctions such as aphasia and dyslexia, using computer programs that can be 'damaged' with the same effect as that observed in some stroke patients.

AMNESIA. The popular conception of amnesia is probably typified by the occasional newspaper report of the appearance of someone who has mysteriously lost his memory. The person has no idea what his name is, where he comes from, or indeed about any of his past. Such cases usually recover their memory within a day or two, and typically turn out to be people attempting to escape from some socially stressful situation by simply opting out through the mechanism of dissociation. The precise nature of their memory defect is variable and seems to depend very much on their own views about how the human memory system works. In this respect they resemble hysterical patients suffering from glove anaesthesia, numbness in the hand which extends up to the wrist but not beyond and bears no relationship to the underlying pattern of innervation of the hand, indicating that it is of psychogenic origin rather than based on a physiological defect. The extent to which psychogenic amnesia represents genuine inability to recall, as opposed to conscious refusal to remember, is hard to ascertain. For further details see Pratt (in Whitty and Zangwill, 1977).

The most extensively studied form of amnesia is that resulting from damage to the limbic system of the brain, typically involving the temporal lobes, hippocampus, and mamillary bodies. Such damage may occur in people suffering from Korsakoff's syndrome, which results from a prolonged period of drinking too much alcohol and eating too little food, leading to a vitamin deficiency of thiamine (vitamin B1). Such patients often go through a delirious confused state, before stabilizing. They may then show a range of symptoms extending from considerable general intellectual impairment with relatively little memory decrement to occasional cases in which a relatively pure memory defect occurs. A broadly comparable memory defect occasionally occurs following encephalitis, and may also be produced by other kinds of brain damage such as stroke, tumour, or coal gas poisoning. There is some controversy over whether such a wide range of patients have a common memory defect, or whether subtle differences occur but the broad pattern of symptoms is similar.

Such patients have no difficulty in knowing where they grew up or telling you about their job or family background. In the case of relatively pure amnesics at least, their ability to use language is unimpaired, as is their general knowledge of the world. Their short-term memory also appears to be intact, at least in many cases. Their ability to repeat back a telephone number is just as good as would be the case in a normal person, and if you present them with a list of words, they show the normal tendency for the last few words presented to be well recalled. Their retention of the earlier words in a list is, however, likely to be very poor indeed.

The amnesic defect in the case of these patients appears to be one of episodic memory. They would be quite unable to tell you what they had for breakfast, and would very probably have no idea where they were or how long they had been there. If you had spent the morning testing them, by the afternoon they would probably fail to recognize you, and if asked for items of current information such as the name of the Prime Minister, would be likely to come up with a totally inappropriate response, naming a figure from twenty or thirty years ago. They have great difficulty in learning lists of words, whether you test them by recall or recognition, and have similar problems in remembering non-verbal material such as pictures of faces or objects.

There are, however, aspects of long-term memory which seem to be relatively unimpaired. Amnesic patients can learn motor skills, and one case, a pianist who was taught a tune on one day, had no difficulty in reproducing it on another. But characteristically such patients have no idea how or when they acquired the relevant information. A classic example is that cited by the Swiss psychologist Claparede, who on one occasion secreted a pin in his hand before shaking hands with an amnesic patient. On a subsequent day when he extended his hand the patient withdrew hers. When asked why, she could give no justification other than the general comment that sometimes things were hidden in people's hands. As one would expect from this demonstration, amnesics appear to be quite capable of classical avoidance conditioning. They are also quite capable of learning verbal materials under certain conditions. For example, Warrington and Weiskrantz used a learning procedure whereby subjects were presented with a series of words, and recall was tested by presenting the first three letters of each word and requiring the subject to produce the whole word. When tested in this way, amnesics were virtually normal.

What characterizes the long-term learning tasks that amnesics can do? This is still a controversial issue, but broadly speaking the tasks seem to be ones in which the patient simply has to use the information available in his memory store, without needing to worry about how it was acquired. The case where he is cued by being presented with the initial letters may be interpreted as simply a problem-solving task where he must find a word that fits these particular constraints. Having recently been presented with the relevant word will in fact make it more available, but he does not need to know this in order to take advantage of such an effect.

While classic amnesics like those just described are theoretically extremely interesting, patients having such a dense amnesia unaccompanied by more general intellectual deterioration are relatively rare. It is much more common for memory disturbance to stem from the after-effects of a blow on the head, as is often the case in road traffic accidents. Consider, for example, a motorcyclist who is involved in an accident involving a severe head injury. He is likely to lose consciousness for a period which may range from a few seconds to several months; if and when he regains consciousness he is likely to show a range of memory problems. It is usual to distinguish three separate types or aspects of such traumatic amnesia, namely retrograde amnesia, post-traumatic amnesia, and anterograde amnesia.

On recovery there will be evidence of loss of memory extending over the period between the injury and full return of consciousness. Following a head injury there will be a period of confusion characterized by the patient's inability to orient himself in time and place. The duration of post-traumatic amnesia, which will comprise the duration of total and partial loss of consciousness, provides a useful measure of the severity of the patient's injury and so permits some estimate of the extent of probable recovery to be made. On emerging from post-traumatic amnesia the patient is still likely to show considerable retrograde amnesia. This is indicated by an inability to remember events before the accident. In the case of a severe blow the amnesia may extend over a period of several years. Typically this blank period becomes less and less, with earlier memories being recovered first, although the process is far from systematic, with 'islands' of memory cropping up in periods that are otherwise still blank. Typically the retrograde amnesia shrinks up to a point within a few minutes of the accident. These final few moments are seldom ever recovered, possibly because the memory trace was never adequately consolidated. This point was illustrated rather neatly in a study of American football players who had been 'dinged' (concussed) during a game. As they were led off the field they were asked the code name of the play in which they had been engaged when concussed (e.g. 'Thirty-two pop'). Typically they were able to supply this information immediately on leaving the field, but when retested 20 to 30 minutes later they were quite unable to provide it. A subsequent study showed that this was not simply due to normal forgetting, nor to the mnemonic limitations of American football players, but suggests that failure of memory traces to consolidate during the concussed state may be an important factor.

The third memory disturbance associated with head injury concerns difficulty in learning and retaining new information. During the process of recovery from a closed head injury, memory problems are commonly reported, together with difficulties in concentrating and a tendency to become fatigued much more rapidly than was previously the case. While the memory problems of patients with head injuries have been rather less extensively investigated than those of the classic amnesic syndrome, we do know that they show some of the same characteristics. Typically short-term memory is not greatly affected, and if one presents an amnesic head-injured patient with a list of words, he is likely to do reasonably well on the last few presented, but relatively poorly on the earlier items in the list. Although not much work has been done in directly comparing such patients with other types of amnesics, it seems likely that the pattern will be somewhat different, since closed head injury appears to cause neuronal and vascular damage in large areas of the brain as opposed to specific subcortical damage in the classic amnesic syndrome. Furthermore, whereas the classic amnesic patient does not completely recover, head-injured patients typically do improve quite substantially from the time when they emerge from their initial period of post-traumatic amnesia. In many cases they return to performing at what appears to be their level before injury.

Amnesia is an important component in senile and pre-senile dementia. In both these cases intellectual deterioration probably results from a substantial loss of cortical neurones, and in addition to showing memory problems such patients usually show a more general intellectual deterioration. This in turn increases the memory problem, since they seem unable or unwilling to use effective learning strategies.

We have so far discussed patients who have long-term learning problems but normal short-term memory. However, the reverse has also been reported. Shallice and Warrington (1970) describe a patient who had great difficulty in repeating back sequences of numbers, the longest sequence he could repeat back reliably being two digits. He was, however, quite unimpaired in his long-term memory as measured both by his ability to learn word sequences and by his memory for faces and for the events of everyday life. As is suggested in its entry, short-term memory is almost certainly not a single unitary function, and there is some evidence to suggest that there are other patients who have different defects of the short-term memory system.

Theoretical interpretation of the various ways in which memory can break down obviously depends crucially on one's interpretation of normal memory. As such, amnesia presents a theoretically important though difficult question. We have in recent years made progress in exploring and defining more precisely the amnesic syndrome, but are as yet some way from constructing a completely adequate interpretation at a psychological, neurological, or biochemical level.

ALAN D. BADDELEY

APHASIA. The ability to talk may not, as was once thought, be the crucial factor that distinguishes humans from the animals, but loss of the power of speech is one of the most distressing things that can happen to a human being. Aphasia (the disruption of speech) commonly follows a stroke—especially if the stroke also impairs movement of the right arm or leg. The loss of articulated language is not always or necessarily accompanied by loss of other linguistic functions, like reading and writing. Least of all is it necessarily accompanied by loss of comprehension: a sufferer often knows that the words he is uttering are wrong, but he cannot correct or alter them ('Pass me the bread—no not the bread the *bread*—no!') However where one of the linguistic skills is seriously disturbed, one or more of the others tends to be somewhat reduced as well. Neither does the disruption of speech mean that all aspects of it are disrupted, nor, even if it is seriously reduced in the early stages after the disrupting incident, that it can never be regained. But the recovery of abilities by an aphasic person does not follow the same principles of learning as the acquisition of learning a language by a normal, healthy child or adult. Asking the patient to repeat a word or phrase over and over again is not necessarily going to help him to say it later on; it is more likely to make him angry and depressed. Impairment of language does not necessarily imply loss of other faculties, such as intelligence or memory.

The three aspects of aphasia which have been studied most intensively are the manner in which speech breaks down, the causes of the breakdown, and treatment of and recovery from it.

The manner of breakdown. The different forms of breakdown can be classified in different ways, but most people nowadays consider just two major groups: non-fluent (or Broca's aphasia) and fluent (or Wernicke's aphasia).

In non-fluent aphasia the sufferer has difficulty finding words, particularly uncommon ones. He has difficulty naming objects, and his syntax is often faulty. He tends to talk hesitantly and gropingly, although he is often acutely aware of how stupid he sounds. The fluent aphasic, on the other hand, emits a stream of words the intonation of which is perfectly normal. Heard from a distance they sound obscure or clever, but close listening reveals meaningless jargon. Unlike the non-fluent aphasic, the fluent one seems undisturbed by, and even unaware of his poor communication. In each of these conditions, concomitant disorders of reading, writing, and comprehension may be present in some degree but are usually more severe in fluent than in non-fluent disorders.

The causes of breakdown. Aphasia is caused by damage to tissue within the brain. But whether injuries to different areas of the brain cause different types of disorder, and whether the same patterns of disorder occur in all individuals, is less certain. Each hemisphere of the brain not only controls movement and sensation of the opposite side of the body (the left hemisphere controls the right side, and the right hemisphere controls the left side), but seems to specialize in particular mental functions. It is the left hemisphere that seems to be most closely concerned with language, although in left-handed people and those with a family history of left-handedness the association is not so strong. Moreover it is not inevitable. People whose left hemispheres are damaged in early infancy or childhood can 'learn to speak' perfectly and adequately with their right. By and large however, it is damage to the left hemisphere that most commonly causes aphasia; that to the anterior part causing non-fluent disorders, and that to the posterior part causing those of the fluent type. It is sometimes held, though, that in fluent aphasia there is also usually some damage to the right non-dominant hemisphere as well as to the left.

An important factor relating to breakdown is the degree to which a person made use of language before his injury. Although after breakdown the words and phrases previously used most commonly can usually be found more easily than others, this does not necessarily mean that the first language of a bilingual or polyglot is the one best preserved: it is frequency of usage rather than recency that is important. Even so there is a tendency for sufferers of non-fluent aphasia to emit swear-words and taboo-words when searching for those they cannot find. Here it is the words which have not been uttered in the past that appear before those which have. The reason for this is probably that inhibition or repression of an act gives it particularly strong emotional force; and the emotional aspects of mental behaviour are not controlled by the same areas of the brain as language. Indeed they tend to be released when intellectual control is removed.

Recovery. The vast majority of aphasic people, especially in the younger age-groups, recover a good deal of speech as time goes on; and a few of the more literary ones have written accounts of their experiences. Unfortunately these seldom contain information about how the faculties were regained, probably because such processes—like many other forms of learning and remembering—occur at a level which is not available to normal consciousness. Psychologists who have been able to watch and study these people have, however, identified several factors which seem to be involved, especially in non-fluent aphasia.

1. Arousal of previous or common contexts. In most languages there are words that have different meanings in different contexts. In English, the word *hand* can be applied to a part of the human body, parts of a clock-face, a unit for the measurement of horses, a style of penmanship, a pledge of fidelity, a member of a ship's crew. The first usage here is undoubtedly the commonest and aphasics can often name the body part when asked to do so, even when they cannot find the word 'hand' in its other contexts. However, once a word has been found in its most common context, it can often be found in others too ('Of course, those are called "hands", aren't they?').

2. Narrowing of syntactical constraints. In most languages, words are uttered and understood in sequences rather than individually, and are controlled by those preceding them. For instance, in a sentence starting 'The man was bitten by—', there is a limit to the choice of words that can follow. Narrowing the field of possibilities by such means seems to be very helpful to the aphasic patient, who can often find words if they form parts of familiar sentences (or song phrases) when not able to do so otherwise.

3. The hesitancy seen in non-fluent aphasia is usually due to the patient's knowledge that the first words which occur to him are wrong and must be corrected. Yet if these words are uttered they are usually far from random. Indeed, they tend to be closely related to the word being sought. They arise from the same semantic field or consist of functional descriptions of the object to

be named ('They're the things that point to the time—the fingers—no the pointers—no!')

Summing up, it seems that in non-fluent aphasia the difficulty is one of having lost not the ability to speak, but only the ability to find the right words at the right moment. Any stimulus which gives a 'lead in' to the general semantic field helps. After this, it is a matter of sifting through the various items until the target is found. (How one recognizes the target is a different problem, and although this ability seems to be intact in the non-fluent aphasic, it seems to be at fault in the fluent one, who does not try to inhibit or correct his 'near misses'.)

Experiments with normal healthy humans indicate that the processes whereby they find and utter words are very similar to those seen in aphasia, but that the processes take place more quickly and efficiently. But rare words take longer to find than the common one; and if the sorting/sifting/correcting process is impeded by external factors (such as distraction) or internal ones (such as intoxication), 'near misses' of much the same sort as those given by the aphasic may be emitted.

MOYRA WILLIAMS

COGNITIVE DEFICITS. Deficits in cognition can be distinguished according to whether they are acquired or developmental in nature; acquired deficits result from organic damage to a normally developed cognitive system whilst developmental deficits affect how cognitive processes are established in childhood and need not be associated with known organic damage. The study of cognitive deficits contributes in at least two important ways to our understanding of the normal mind. First, it provides strong constraints on how the cognitive system must be functionally organized; second, it provides one source of evidence (along with functional imaging and physiological studies) on the localization of cognitive processes in the brain. Evidence on the functional organization of the cognitive system comes particularly from demonstrations of double dissociations in which one ability is affected selectively in one patient whilst leaving other abilities intact, whilst, in a contrasting patient, the opposite pattern of deficit is found (ability one being intact and ability two affected). Such double dissociations are consistent with forms of modular organization in which different (dissociable) abilities are served by independent cognitive processes. The dissociative approach to understand cognition can be based on either single case analyses or on groups linked by common lesion site or common functional impairment. Study of the localization of cognitive function more typically involves groups of patients with the analysis focusing on location(s) where lesions overlap across patients.

Acquired deficits have been documented in nearly all aspects of human cognition, though only the major disorders affecting spoken and written language, object recognition, action, and memory will be considered here. The origins of the study of cognitive disorders were case studies made by neurologists such as Paul Broca and Carl Wernicke at the end of the 19th century. These initial studies involved the assessment of disorders of spoken language comprehension and production, known as *dysphasia* (in general, the prefix *a*— is used to refer to the abolition of a cognitive ability, and the prefix *dys*—refers to a disorder of this ability). Broca documented a form of non-fluent dysphasia characterized by slow, halting, and often agrammatical speech; Wernicke documented a form of dysphasia in which speech is fluent and grammatical but often meaningless and there is poor comprehension. These early studies illustrate that aspects of grammatical construction are functionally independent of word meaning, so that the retrieval of either aspect of language can be impaired according to the site of damage. Subsequent work has shown that there can be finer gradations in each form of dysphasia. For example, poor word comprehension can result from a range of deficits starting from those that affect early perceptual processing of speech through to those in which speech perception is normal and there is even access to stored representations for spoken words, but these words then fail to contact their associated meanings (in *word meaning deafness*). Access to some form of stored knowledge can be demonstrated by patients being able to write to dictation words with irregular spellings for which they show no aural comprehension. Similarly, there can be selective deficits for particular forms of grammatical construction.

In the early 1970s, the field moved forward again with the study of, respectively, disorders of short-term memory and reading. These studies were now linked to explicit models of normal cognitive function, a linkage that characterizes the discipline of *cognitive neuropsychology*. Studies of patients with impaired short-term verbal memory helped to redefine contemporary theories of memory since they showed that, despite having a short-term span on only a few items, such patients could often commit new meaningful material to long-term memory—refuting the idea that short-term memory was necessary in order for long-term memories to be formed. More recent studies, however, have shown that short-term verbal memory is important for learning novel verbal sequences (as when we learn words from a foreign language), suggesting that what is critical is the type of information being learned.

Studies of reading helped to define several sub-types of *dyslexia*, two of which illustrate how double dissociations can constrain normative theories. *Surface dyslexics* are able to read aloud words that follow the spelling-to-sound rules of the language (regular words) and they can also pronounce non-words; however they are impaired at reading irregular words that break spelling-sound rules. *Phonological dyslexics*, in contrast, are able to read both regular and irregular words but are poor at pronouncing non-words. There is a double dissociation between the reading of irregular words and non-words in these patients. This is consistent with so-called 'dual route' theories which maintain that there are parallel lexical and non-lexical routes (using, respectively, memories for known words and spelling-sound rules) for reading. Surface dyslexics may have an impaired lexical route and phonological dyslexics an impaired non-lexical route. Similar distinctions have also been made in studying breakdowns in spelling. Here *surface dysgraphics* have difficulty in spelling irregular words and *phonological dysgraphics* have difficulty in spelling non-words given to them in dictation. Again, these disorders may be accounted for in terms of the existence of independent lexical and non-lexical processes in spelling. Though interactive accounts of lexical and non-lexical processes can be offered for both reading and spelling, it remains the case that these processes need to show different patterns of breakdown to accommodate the cognitive neuropsychological data.

Disorders of object recognition are known as *agnosia*, and different forms of agnosia have been demonstrated both according to the modality of stimulus input and (as with dysphasia) according to the particular process affected. Lissauer (1890) first distinguished between *apperceptive* and *associative* agnosia. Apperceptive agnosia reflects an inability to establish normal perceptual representations of stimuli, although basic sensation should be intact. Associative agnosia follows from an impairment in linking normal percepts to stored memories. These distinctions have been applied most often to patients with *visual agnosia*. Clinically, patients labelled as having associative visual agnosia can copy objects they fail to recognize and they may also pass other tests of perception (e.g. a patient may to able to judge whether an object is the same when seen from different viewpoints whilst still being unable to recognize what it is). More recent accounts make further categorizations, according to the particular process disrupted. For example, disorders affecting the coding of basic features of objects are separated from disorders affecting the integration of those features, from those affecting the ability to judge that objects remain the same across viewpoint shifts, and from those affecting access to different forms of stored knowledge (e.g. stored perceptual knowledge and stored associative knowledge, of the relations between objects). A particular form of agnosia, affecting the recognition of faces over and above other objects, is known as *prosopagnosia*. Prosopagnosia is not simply a mild form of agnosia (affecting faces but not other objects) since patients can be agnosic for objects without being prosopagnosic for faces. On one view, face recognition depends on using visual information that is configural in form whilst objects can be recognized non-wholistically, from their parts. Accordingly, whether faces or objects are the more affected depends upon whether a lesion disrupts the coding of configural or parts-based visual information. Even so, forms of associative agnosia which seem to stem from poor access to stored memories rather than from poor perceptual encoding, still need to be accounted for. Also disorders of recognition are distinguishable from disorders of naming, where recognition seems to be generally intact but patients cannot find the name for the object (or face). Name retrieval is separable from the process of recognition.

Though visual agnosic patients may be severely impaired at recognizing seen objects they typically remain able to reach objects to pick them up. In contrast, disorders of space perception and action can disrupt reaching and picking up whilst leaving recognition intact. This contrast indicates that visual information may be used in distinct ways, respectively for recognition and for action. In one disorder of spatial processing, the syndrome of *unilateral neglect*, patients with a unilateral brain lesion can fail to react to stimuli presented on the side of space contralateral to their lesion site. This is not merely due to loss of perception in the affected field; performance can be improved when patients are cued to attend to the neglected region and, in cases of *extinction*, the deficit on the affected side arises only when another competing stimulus is presented on the 'better' side of space. In some cases, the area neglected seems related to the position stimuli occupy with respect to the midline of the patient's body, in other cases patients neglect one part of an object. Spatial information seems to be coded in a variety of ways (in terms of the position of objects to the observer's body, in terms of the positions of parts with respect to an object, etc.), which can be selectively affected by different brain lesions.

Disorders affecting the retrieval of learned actions are known as *apraxia*. Patients can be impaired at accessing information about how to use objects, even when they can name them (*ideational apraxia*), indicating that knowledge of learned actions is represented separately from other forms of stored knowledge about objects. In other cases, some knowledge about the correct action is retrieved but the action is executed in a clumsy or spatially inaccurate manner (*ideomotor apraxia*). Here there is disruption to the processes involved in co-ordinating the parameters for action, and these are distinct from the apparently more abstract processes that represent stored knowledge of the action and that allow the action to be expressed across different contexts.

Many everyday tasks not only require that actions are carried out to single objects, but also that sequences of actions are effected, with these sequences being organized in an orderly way (e.g. to wrap a present, or to make a cup of tea). In some cases, brain lesions can affect this ability to plan and effect action sequences, even when actions can be executed correctly to single objects. This results in disorganized behaviour, in which component actions are omitted or sometimes repeated inappropriately. Information about the sequential orders of actions can be distinguished from representations of single actions. This form of behavioural disorder on complex tasks is often associated with lesions to the frontal lobes, and lesions to the frontal lobes also frequently disrupt behaviour when tasks are relatively novel or when we have to switch from one task to another. Patients may perform a learned behaviour but one which is inappropriate in the context of a novel task, or they may fail to switch between tasks. Such disorders provide a means of analysing how complex behaviour sequences are represented and retrieved, and how we are able to modulate action so that it is governed by specific task goals and not simply by previously learned information.

Although patients may have disruption to the processes involved in recognizing objects and words, or in effecting appropriate actions to objects, they can nevertheless lay down new memories of the events that take place around them. In contrast, patients with *amnesia* can have severe difficulties in establishing new memories (*anterograde amnesia*) or in retrieving old memories of events in their past (*retrograde amnesia*). The process of forming new memories is distinct from the processes that put information, once learned, into effect (e.g. for recognizing learned objects or actions). Studies have also shown that amnesiacs can establish some forms of sensory or procedural memory (for specific stimuli or for the performance of specific tasks), but still fail to recollect that they have encountered the stimulus or task before. This work indicates that there are several memory systems, with different learning and storage characteristics. Each of these different cognitive disorders is also associated with contrasting brain lesions. Fluent and non-fluent dysphasias are linked to lesions affecting the left temporal and inferior frontal lobes respectively. Similar lesions also disrupt reading and spelling. Modality-specific agnosia are found after damage to the sensory and associative cortex for the specific modality, so that, for visual disorders, damage affects posterior brain regions close to the sites of visual projections from the eyes. Disorders of spatial processing and action are most frequently correlated with damage to posterior and frontal brain regions, whilst amnesia is found after damage to regions of the forebrain (the hippocampus and amygdala) which connect to, and may be involved in laying down memories within, areas of cortex involved in stimulus recognition and action. Hence the study of patients with these disorders is informative about the brain regions within which cognitive processes take place as well as about the nature of the processes themselves.

For many of the acquired cognitive deficits found after brain lesions to adults there are equivalent forms of developmental disorder, most notably as concerns disorders of reading and spelling where it is possible to distinguish surface and phonological dyslexias and dysgraphias amongst children. Nevertheless, it is unclear whether models of adult disorder represent the best way to conceptualize disorders in children, which are found in the context of an adapting brain and cognitive system, and are likely to be subject to considerable re-organization.

GLYN W. HUMPHREYS

CONNECTIONIST MODELS OF COGNITIVE DEFICITS. Some of the very earliest work with connectionist systems explored two of their properties that appear to be shared with the brain: namely (i) resistance to noise, and (ii) graceful degradation (see also MODELS OF MENTAL PROCESSES). An early examination of resistance to noise (Block, 1962) concerned the ability of a connectionist network to learn to classify a set of patterns correctly when the patterns themselves were corrupted. It was found that although performance was impaired relative to the 'noise-free' case the network did, nevertheless, learn the classification scheme. Graceful degradation refers to the breakdown in the network's ability to keep functioning effectively when processing units and/or their connections are damaged. The early work clearly demonstrated that the decline in classificatory performance was gradual rather than sudden and that it varied directly with the amount of damage to the system. In the more recent literature much has been made of the claim that graceful degradation bears some degree of resemblance to what happens in the human case when some form of neurological damage occurs.

There are now many examples of connectionist models of various psychological deficits, ranging from those concerned with attentional deficits in schizophrenia to those dealing with memory problems in old age. Nevertheless, two general methodologies have emerged. In the first, a hand-sculptured network is configured and is shown to behave in a way that corresponds to some normal human ability. This network is then damaged and its performance is examined relative to that of humans with a given psychological deficit. A second method is to train a network to behave in a particular way and then inflict the damage. Damage can be inflicted in a number of different ways. For instance, by removing connections and/or units, by adding random noise to the weighted connections, by adding noise to the stimulus patterns themselves, etc. Both the amount and type of damage can be varied and studied systematically and the behaviour of the network can be examined accordingly.

An example of inflicting damage to a hand-sculptured network can be found in the work of Burton, Young, Bruce, Johnston, and Ellis (1991) in their study of the putative mechanisms that underlie the recognition of human faces. In their model different pools of units were defined such that each pool's units were identified with a particular type of knowledge store. Within each pool the units competed with each other via inhibitory connections. Across the different pools, though, units could mutually activate one another. With this kind of model Burton et al. were able to, essentially, attenuate the strength of the weighted connections between two distinct pools of units and show how this kind of damage might account for problems associated with prosopagnosia—a brain disorder that renders the person unable to recognize faces.

Many examples of systems which are both trained and damaged can be found in Plaut and Shallice (1994). They were predominantly concerned with modelling various aspects of human word recognition and its associated disorders. For example in extending the work of Hinton and Shallice (1989), Plaut and Shallice examined several different connectionist networks that captured various intuitions about the mapping between a system that deals with the encoding of the written form of English (or orthographic units in the model) and that between a system that codes meaning (semantic units). In one such model an intermediate set of units were inserted between the orthographic and semantic units and a further set of so-called clean-up units were connected up with the semantic units. The clean-up units provided an additional teaching signal that allowed the network to essentially develop the same sorts of semantic representations to highly dissimilar words. For instance a MAMMAL kind of semantic representation had to be learnt for both 'cat' and 'pig'. Without such clean-up units the network defaulted to its more normal mode of operation in which similar inputs gave rise to similar ouputs e.g., 'cat' and 'cot' would (incorrectly) give rise to similar kinds of semantic representations. Part of the aim of this research was to attempt to better understand certain forms of dyslexia in which written words with similar meanings are confused. For instance in deep dyslexia a patient might read the word 'peach' as 'apricot'. However as Hinton and Shallice point out such a patient is also likely to produce various other sorts of errors in which visually similar words are confused, e. g., 'cat' is read as 'cot', or, both semantic and visual attributes are confused, e. g., 'cat' is read as 'rat'. In the simulations, and following an initial training period, the network was damaged and its semantic responses to input words was then re-assessed. Both the amount of damage and the site of the 'lesion' were examined systematically. Of the many important demonstrations contained in this work were those that showed that the whole range of error-types observed in patients occurred with a single lesion and that this was irrespective of the site of the lesion. Indeed, the work has provided a new and important way of thinking about psychological deficits and has provided a useful set of tools for exploring what the consequences of certain types of brain damage may be. PHILIP T. QUINLAN

DEMENTIA is defined by W. A. Lishman (1978) as 'an acquired global impairment of intellect, memory, and personality but without impairment of consciousness'. Although often considered to be an irreversible condition, recent studies have shown that about 10 per cent of patients with dementia have conditions for which treatment can reverse the otherwise inexorable decline of mental function. The progressive dementias are most often diagnosed in the elderly under the headings of senile dementia of the Alzheimer type and multi-infarct dementia. The former is caused by widespread degeneration of nerve-cells in the brain and their replacement by elements known as plaques and neurofibrillary tangles. Post-mortem studies of the brains of patients who have died from senile dementia have enabled correlation of the numbers of these elements with the degree of mental impairment shown by psychometric testing during life. Multi-infarct dementia, which is less common than senile dementia, is caused by loss of brain substance following repeated closure of small or large blood vessels, incidents which cause minor or major strokes. The older term arteriosclerotic dementia, has now been superseded.

These areas of degeneration may be widespread and scattered, or concentrated in certain areas of the brain. If the latter, the mental changes will be much more severe in some functions than in others. For instance, the person may lose his speech (developing aphasia) but not his memory, or vice versa. One of the last things usually to be affected is his basic personality, and some of the last skills to be lost are the social ones. Hence some demented persons will retain the major features of personality, remaining well-mannered, considerate, and responsive if these were the former characteristics. On the other hand, blunting of emotion and loss of control of social behaviour may lead to episodes of petulant and irritable behaviour or tactless and inappropriate remarks which would not have been uttered before the onset of the illness.

The difference between dementia and the more limited losses of mental ability due to focal injuries is that the demented person can seldom make compensations for his disabilities in the way the others do; and, indeed, very often seems to be unaware of them. He tends to live his life entirely for the present moment, although the present for him may be an era from his own distant past.

Although it is characteristic of the truly demented person that he has little insight into his defects, inability to cope with his environment may make him severely perplexed, or trigger off a condition described by Kurt Goldstein and called by him the 'catastrophic reaction'. The individual becomes tearful and angry; he may repeat non-adaptive stereotyped movements in a repetitive manner, or start sweating and becoming restless. The 'emotional lability' that accompanies dementia is one of its outstanding characteristics and helps to differentiate it from true depression, in which the individual remains sad and retarded no matter how his circumstances alter. Dementia must also be differentiated from another, much less common form of emotional disorder: that accompanying bulbar palsy, in which the individual may respond to any sudden stimulus or strong effort by screwing up his face and bursting into tears, without any of the unhappiness which usually causes such outbursts. 'I just can't help crying', he may be able to tell you between spasms. 'Don't pay any attention to me.' In contrast to both of these, the emotional state of the demented person seems to reflect exactly the situation of the moment. If he is faced with a problem too difficult for him to solve, he shows all the signs of distress, but if this is removed and he is presented with a simpler one, the next moment he will be laughing and cheerful. It follows that even severe dementia may not necessarily cause its sufferer any personal pain, depending on where and how he is cared for. If his environment is simple, cheerful, and constant (i.e. unchanging) he may to all outward appearances (and on his own admission) be perfectly cheerful and contented.

It is important to distinguish dementia from the other disorders which commonly affect the elderly, as although there is, as yet, no known method of retarding or reversing dementia, many of the other conditions are fully treatable. In the speech disorders of dementia, comprehension is usually just as badly affected as expression, whereas in the aphasia due to focal lesions this is very rare. Moreover, the errors made when trying to name objects are rather different. The aphasic person usually manages to indicate that he knows perfectly well what the object is even though he cannot find its name, but the demented person often seems to fail to recognize the object too. If asked to name different parts of his body, the aphasic person can usually name those parts which are commonly mentioned (such as feet, hands, and arms) but not those less frequently so (knuckles, eyebrows, ankles); in the demented there is seldom any difference.

The failure of memory seen in senile dementia is also different from that seen in normal old age or in the organic amnesic conditions. In the latter, cues or prompts very often help, but in the demented they seem rather to do the opposite. If one considers recall as being like searching for an item in a vast territory, a cue for the amnesic narrows the field of search and directs his attention to a specific area; for the demented, it seems to direct him to a new part of the field. For instance, if the target is the word 'cart', a useful cue for an amnesic would be the words 'Horse and——'. A case of senile dementia might respond by saying, 'Horse? Yes, I remember we had many horses when I was a child, one particular one . . .'.

The ability to handle and manipulate objects is usually little impaired in dementia. Those motor skills which were learned in the past are well retained, but since he is inclined to forget what he is aiming to achieve before he has half done it, the demented person gets himself into difficulties. At first appearance he may seem to be suffering from apraxia (the loss of such skills due to focal lesions), but closer study will reveal differences. For example, both apraxic and demented individuals often have difficulty dressing themselves, but in the case of the apraxic the difficulty is due to 'forgetting' how to tie knots, do up buttons, or put an arm into a sleeve; in the demented it is due to forgetting whether he is supposed to be getting dressed or undressed at the time. When preparing meals—even such a simple task as making a pot of tea—the apraxic forgets how to put tea into the pot or stir it with a spoon; the demented can do all these things, if reminded constantly of the task in hand, but if distracted at all is liable to lose track of how far he has got and start from the beginning again.

Finally, there are two conditions which may be easily mistaken for dementia. The first is a severe depressive illness which may produce the condition sometimes called pseudodementia which only a skilled psychiatrist can distinguish from true dementia, but which responds to appropriate antidepressant treatment. The second is a delirious state, triggered off in an old person by physical disorder such as pneumonia, a heart attack, or hypothermia. Unlike dementia, which usually comes on slowly over a long period, delirious states are likely to appear suddenly and will be accompanied by severe disorientation and even hallucinations. These symptoms, however, clear up completely once the underlying physical disorder is rectified, and in former days it was quite common for an old person to 'wake up' after such an illness and find himself in a mental hospital labelled, to his great consternation, a case of senile dementia.

MOYRA WILLIAMS

EPILEPSY. A person is said to suffer from epilepsy if he is prone to recurrent epileptic seizures. The epileptic seizure is a transient episode of altered consciousness and/or perception, and/or loss of control of the muscles, which arises because of abnormal electrical discharges generated by groups of brain cells. Many varieties of seizures are recognized. They differ according to the nature of their symptom content. Most last for no more than a few minutes, but occasionally they are prolonged beyond 30 minutes or else recur so rapidly that full recovery is not achieved between successive attacks—these conditions are labelled *status epilepticus*.

It has been estimated that 6–7 per cent of the population suffer at least one epileptic seizure at some time in their lives and that 4 per cent have a phase when they are prone to recurrent seizures (i.e. can be said to suffer from epilepsy). Between 0.05 and 0.1% of the population suffer from 'active epilepsy'—that is, they have had a recurrent seizure within the previous five years or are taking regular medication to prevent the occurrence of seizures. Seizures are particularly liable to occur in early childhood, during adolescence, and in old age.

The history of epilepsy is probably as long as that of the human race. The definition of the condition as a clinical entity is generally attributed to Hippocrates. He recognized that it arises from physical disease of the brain. He also took the first step towards unravelling the intracacies of cerebral localization of function with his realization that damage on one side of the brain can cause convulsions which commence on the opposite side of the body. Further significant advances in this direction, based on observations of seizures, were delayed more than 2,000 years until the nineteenth century, and in particular until the observations and deductions of Hughlings Jackson.

William Gowers, writing towards the end of the nineteenth century in the same era as Hughlings Jackson, proposed a dichotomy with his suggestion that some people have epileptic seizures because of overt cerebral pathology whereas others have them because of some factor in their brains' innate constitution unaccompanied by any detectable abnormality of structure. To some extent this is reflected in the current classification which divides epileptic seizures into the two main categories: 'primary generalized' and 'focal' (or 'partial' in the current terminology). However, further advance lay beyond simple clinical observation and was delayed until the technique for recording the electrical activity of the human brain (the electroencephalogram or EEG) was developed, first in the 1920s by the German psychiatrist Hans Berger and then in the 1930s by the Cambridge physiologists E. D. Adrian and B. H. C. Matthews. The technique was rapidly applied to the analysis of epilepsy especially by E. L. and F. A. Gibbs, W. C. Lennox, H. Jasper, and H. Gastaut. Their findings, and the findings of those who followed them, have supported the view that seizures can be broadly divided into the two main categories mentioned above. Primary generalized seizures are those in which the symptoms of the seizure, and the EEG if it is being recorded at the onset, indicate that the whole of the brain becomes electrically abnormal synchronously at the moment when the seizure commences. In contrast, focal (partial) seizures are those in which the symptoms, and the EEG if it is being recorded at the onset, suggest that the electrical abnormality commences in a restricted area, usually a part of the cerebral cortex, even though the electrical abnormality may then spread more or less widely.

The commonest forms of primary generalized seizure are the tonic-clonic convulsion without aura (the *grand-mal* convulsion), the *petit-mal* absence, and the myoclonic jerk. The convulsion commences with the tonic phase in which the muscles stiffen symmetrically on both sides of the body and this is followed by the clonic phase of muscle jerking. Consciousness is lost from the outset and the person falls to the ground if he was standing. There may be an epileptic cry at the outset, a blue coloration may develop around the lips (cyanosis) and the facial skin especially in the tonic phase when breathing is interrupted, the bladder and/or the bowels may be emptied and the tongue may be bitten. When consciousness is regained the person may be confused and may act in an automatic fashion; a period of sleep may follow. The *petit-mal* absence lasts only a few seconds. There is loss of awareness but the person does not fall to the ground; he stares blankly and any movement is confined to flickering of the eyelids and/or very slight twitching of the facial and/or arm muscles. There are a number of varieties of absence seizure, but the true *petit-mal* absence is characterized by an EEG pattern consisting of spike-wave activity occurring at the rate of 3 cycles per second. The myoclonic jerk consists of a very rapid symmetrical upward jerk of the arms accompanied by a nod of the head and a forward bend of the trunk.

The true *petit-mal* seizure occurs very predominantly in childhood and adolescence. It is almost invariably a manifestation of constitutional epilepsy rather than due to cerebral pathology, and it is strongly associated with a hereditary factor. Children who are prone to *petit-mal* seizures may also have myoclonic jerks and tonic-clonic convulsions. *Petit-mal* absence seizures and myoclonic jerks tend to become much less frequent after adolescence but convulsions may continue. Primary generalized convulsions and myoclonic jerks are most often seen in childhood and adolescence when the epilepsy is usually due to a constitutional predisposition—idiopathic epilepsy—but they can be due to diffuse cerebral pathology.

Focal (partial) seizures commence with electrical discharges in a restricted area of the brain. The initial symptom of the attack depends upon the location of the focal discharges. Thus, when the focus is in the motor cortex the seizure usually begins with jerking in a restricted group of muscles on the opposite side of the body, especially those of the face, hand or foot, since these are represented by the largest areas within the motor cortex. As the electrical discharges spread to other parts of the motor cortex, so more and more muscles on the opposite side of the body are incorporated into the convulsion. This spread in a pattern corresponding to the homunculus mapped on the motor cortex is known as the Jacksonian seizure and indeed enabled Hughlings Jackson to predict such a map. When the electrical discharges extend beyond the motor cortex, and especially when they pass through the corpus callosum to the opposite cerebral hemisphere, consciousness is lost and the convulsion may become generalized involving both sides of the body.

A particularly common variety of focal seizure originates from discharges in the structures of one or other temporal lobe—temporal lobe epilepsy. The demonstration, particularly by the Montreal school under the leadership of Wilder Penfield, that some cases of temporal lobe epilepsy can be cured by surgery has been an enormous stimulus to detailed study of many of its facets. The seizures often commence with a visceral sensation or an alteration of thought processes and perception which can be remembered afterwards. This is the aura. Those who experience an aura often find the content very difficult to describe, partly because their awareness and memory systems are distorted by the seizure and partly because the appropriate words to convey the quality of these abnormal sensations do not exist. Common visceral sensations include a feeling of nausea in the stomach or chest which may rise to the throat or head, nausea felt elsewhere in the body, hallucinations of smell or taste, giddiness, and palpitations. The alterations of thought process and perception often have an emotional content and frequently involve a distortion of memory. Brief feelings of extreme fear, anxiety, or depression are common. Feelings of elation are much less so. The aura may contain a feeling of familiarity as if everything has happened before (déjà vu), there may be a feeling of intense unreality, sensations of perceptual illusion such as macropsia or micropsia may occur, and occasionally a complex visual or auditory hallucination is experienced. The aura may be followed by an automatism (referred to as a complex partial seizure in the current terminology). That is a period of altered behaviour for which the person is subsequently amnesic and during which he appears to have only limited awareness of his environment, if any at all. The behaviour in an automatism is usually primitive and stereotyped consisting of, for instance, lip smacking, chewing, grimacing, and gesturing, but sometimes much more complex behavioural acts are performed. Very occasionally an automatism continues for a prolonged period—a state known as an epileptic fugue.

Whereas primary generalized seizures are characteristic of epilepsy due to a constitutional predisposition (idiopathic epilepsy) focal seizures are attributed to a focus of pathology. It is usually impossible to define the precise nature of this pathology, but occasionally it is a tumour or an area of brain damage due to head injury. Some cases of the most severe temporal lobe epilepsy are due to loss of neurones in the hippocampus (a structure situated in the medial part of the temporal lobe) caused by a prolonged convulsion occurring in early childhood, and when this abnormality is restricted to one side of the brain there is a good chance that surgery will effect a cure. Regular medication can suppress the seizures of many people prone to epilepsy but unfortunately by no means all.

Lastly, mention must be made of the concept of an epileptic personality. It has been claimed that a particular personality type is associated with epilepsy. The matter is complicated because epilepsy is associated with many factors which themselves may affect not only personality but many other aspects of mental function. These include cerebral pathology, anti-epileptic medication, the depression to which many people with epilepsy are prone, and the restrictions which society imposes on them. It is difficult to find any evidence that a particular personality is associated with epilepsy *per se* after due allowance has been made for these factors.

JUNE CROWN

MENTAL HANDICAP. It is estimated that about one in every thousand children in the United Kingdom and the United States of America is mentally handicapped. It is not easy to judge the total number because of the various definitions of mental handicap. The American Association on Mental Deficiency (AAMD) describes retardation as 'subaverage general intellectual functioning which originates during the developmental period and is associated with impaired adaptive behaviour'. 'Subaverage' means more than one standard deviation below the normal average level of intelligence commonly accepted (in the UK, 100; in the USA, 90–100); 'developmental period' means from birth to about 16 years of age; and 'impaired adaptive behaviour' means failure to mature, to learn, or to adjust socially.

This definition has been challenged because it does not take account of environmental and social factors, both of which may have an important influence on retardation. The lack of a clear definition has significance, for failure to diagnose may lead to failure to treat.

The problem of mental retardation emerged in the nineteenth century.

Before that time, the retarded were assimilated into the general background of rural societies or they did not survive at all. The percentage of children who were mildly mentally retarded increased with the growth of towns, because of poor housing, lack of care before, during, and after birth, malnutrition, poverty, and poor working conditions for mothers. These causes remain, but, with the improvement of general standards of living and literacy, children retarded in this way are now among the 'ablest' of the mentally handicapped. As societies become more complex and technologically oriented, the number of people unable to cope with life increases, and the burden on the working population is correspondingly increased.

In the nineteenth century many schemes to train and educate the mentally retarded were begun and found to be successful. Possibly the first attempts at education were made by Jean-Marc-Gaspard Itard, who described his work with a wild boy found in the woods of Aveyron. Truffaut's film *L'Enfant sauvage* is an account of Itard's attempts to socialize and educate the boy Victor, who was, however, probably already retarded when he was found.

Since the success of treatment depends very much on the cause of the illness, improved skills in diagnosing mental retardation have also meant improved chances of rehabilitation. The aetiology of mental retardation is divided into two parts: intrinsic and extrinsic causes.

Intrinsic causes. These are biological, mainly genetic. One of the commonest is Down's syndrome, which results from a chromosome abnormality. One birth in 250 will have a chromosome abnormality, which can be diagnosed by counting the chromosomes taken in smears. Unfortunately the cause of the damage to the chromosome structure that produces Down's syndrome has not yet been identified, although a connection with infective hepatitis has been suggested. Genetic counselling may reduce the incidence of one type of Down's syndrome, for if one or both parents has an abnormal chromosome structure there is a greater likelihood that their child will have an abnormality. The chances of an abnormal birth increase with the age of the mother, and after the age of 35 special attention should be paid to the chromosomal compatibility of the parents.

Other intrinsic causes are metabolic. In phenylketonuria (PKU), which occurs in one in 10,000 births, failure to metabolize the amino acid phenylalanine results in a toxic condition which affects the brain and causes retardation unless a phenylalanine-free diet is given to the child. In the United Kingdom, every new-born baby is now tested for PKU, and so a dangerous condition is prevented by early intervention. Osteogenesis imperfecta ('brittle bones'), Tay-Sachs disease, and Duchenne's muscular dystrophy (both degenerative killing diseases) are other intrinsic causes of mental retardation. The causes of many intrinsic diseases are not yet known. The American Association on Mental Deficiency and the American Psychiatric Association maintain lists of most of the categories of intrinsic causes of retardation, and these lists are updated as knowledge extends.

Extrinsic causes. These are mental handicaps that result from infections, accidents, poisoning, or other brain damage. Difficult or premature births may cause brain damage because of anoxia (shortage of oxygen supply to the brain). Babies may be born blind and/or mentally retarded if the mother is infected with rubella (German measles) before the fourth month of pregnancy. Congenital syphilis can also damage the child. (It used to be thought that this disease was the cause of Down's syndrome. The misery and anxiety such a mistaken belief must have caused parents whose children suffered from Down's syndrome can hardly be imagined.) Smoking, excessive use of alcoholic drinks, poor prenatal care, malnutrition, infection, or poisoning from environmental pollution (such as mercury or lead) may lead to immature or damaged babies.

During the neonatal period, factors such as high fever, jaundice, failure to breathe properly, or inadequate or unsuitable nutrition may cause retardation. The child's brain may be damaged by poisoning from sucking toys painted with paint containing lead monoxide or cadmium, or by baby battering, or by falls. One category in the AAMD list should be looked at with particular attention: diseases and conditions due to unknown or uncertain factors with structural reaction alone manifest—a category into which the 'wild boy' of Aveyron might well fit. It is known that a child deprived of tender loving care will grow up with deficient sensory and social ability. If the impoverishment and lack of stimulus in a child's upbringing are not remedied early, he will grow up with reduced social and intellectual capacity and may be diagnosed as a case of 'mild' (category I) retardation. Autism is a condition which may fit into any of the categories of retardation, from I to V, and which causes great distress—particularly, perhaps, as at first sight the child may seem to be quite normal. There continues to be much debate about the nature and causes of autism.

Treatment and provisions. The amount of retardation in individual cases varies as much as intelligence does among 'normal' people, and this range makes management and discussion complex and difficult. Diseases caused by poisoning (intoxication) may be halted or even cured by removing the source of the poison, and eliminating the poison already in the child, before there is irreversible brain damage. Diseases caused by social factors—such as malnutrition, lack of care before, during, or after birth, poor stimulus, or infection of the mother—would be eliminated or at least reduced by social welfare programmes (for example, inoculation against measles and rubella) and by the education of parents to help counter retardation of this kind.

Treatment of intrinsic causes is more difficult because the damage is irreversible. However, prevention is beginning to be possible. Amniocentesis can be used to detect chromosome abnormalities while the child is still in the womb. The technique cannot be used until the fourth month of pregnancy, and, as the fluid has to be taken out of the uterus, there is the possibility of damage to a normal foetus and the risk of natural abortion; also it must be practicable to offer induced abortion as an alternative. Once a child is born with irreversible brain damage, drugs can help to prevent fits and special programmes can help to develop existing intelligence and mobility. The Doman-Delacato course of treatment may improve the abilities of some children, although it demands tremendous dedication and energy on the part of the parents, while the cost to the family as a whole should not be disregarded. More usually, brain-damaged children go to nursery schools and then to special schools where attention is paid to individual differences and needs. If this sort of help is given from birth onwards it may be possible to educate the child and support the family who look after it.

In some parts of the world there are excellent provisions, while in others they are sadly lacking or even non-existent. At best the mentally handicapped may be helped to lead relatively normal lives, to do some sort of work, and to live in sheltered housing with some support. Whether the work is in workshops or on the land, it will give the moderately handicapped a sense of individual dignity and purpose. The severely handicapped will have to spend their lives in hospitals and will need dedicated nursing as well as support from all the other social services. It is important to distinguish here between the mentally handicapped and the mentally ill. In the popular mind these two conditions are often confused, leading to much ill-informed fear and prejudice. None the less, there is good evidence that the mentally handicapped do have a higher incidence of neurotic and psychotic disorders.

Wherever adequate provision is made for the mentally handicapped, it will be found that the cost is great. Against this cost must be set the cost of *not* providing. The incidence of broken marriages is ten times higher where there is a mentally handicapped child. There are risks to physical and mental health—mothers typically suffer more than fathers, while the normal children in the family are also under pressure. Widows and deserted wives figure prominently in surveys.

In the past the mentally handicapped often died at birth or in early childhood. They survive into mature adulthood with the help of care before and after birth and the widespread use of antibiotics. Should doctors perhaps not strive 'officiously to keep alive' if spina bifida has been diagnosed and the child, and later the adult, is condemned to a crippled and handicapped life after operations which may relieve the symptoms but cannot cure the condition? How can we balance, for instance, the cost of keeping a mentally handicapped child against the cost of a kidney machine for a working man who supports a family? In a sensitive and civilized society, euthanasia is an emotive and difficult subject. Doctors need guidelines and support to avoid accusations of murder when they must make decisions which affect not only the individual family but society as a whole.

PAM HANNAM

5: DISTURBED MINDS

When we think, feel or act in characteristic ways we are said to be displaying our 'personality'. Individuals can be described as shy, gregarious, anxious, placid, ruthless, helpful, and so on. These are terms to describe a personality, and we label people as having one kind of personality or another on the basis of observing them over time. We tend to respond consistently to events around us, and we can see similar consistencies in the people that we know well. For example, individuals who respond with **terror**, or **stress** and **anxiety** to a physical threat in one situation are likely to respond in the same way when aggression is shown in another situation. These consistencies are expressions of our individuality, and enable those around us to anticipate our reactions. The consistencies that we think of as the dimensions of personality are present in us all and are to some extent a product of our previous experiences. We have learnt that a particular kind of response gains us some satisfaction and we continue to use that response. However, these characteristic patterns of behaviour can be disrupted by a number of environmental and organic factors. When more than one set of learned responses is displayed by an individual we describe that person as being inconsistent, and in the extreme form, described as a dissociation of the personality or multiple personality, it appears that two or more sets of personality characteristics exist. There is some doubt, however, as to whether such a phenomenon is anything more than a construction in the minds of the psychiatrists who describe it.

Although some individuals may be described as 'having personality' or 'being a personality' these are misuses of the term, in much the same way as some moderately well-known people are described as 'TV personalities' (usually by publicity agents or journalists). To describe someone as having a personality is akin to saying that they have an appetite. What is actually meant is that the individual lies at a positive extreme of a personality characteristic—for example, they are very gregarious (but not very shy) or very helpful (but not very ruthless). Most people, by definition, have personalities in the mid-range between any pairs of extremes that can be found, and are thereby said to be in good mental health and able to respond consistently rationally. When personality characteristics become very extreme and socially undesirable, then the individual may be classified as suffering from **mental illness**. In these cases, social or organic changes may cause abnormal behaviour, with either inconsistent or irrational behaviour replacing the predictable and normal. Not all abnormal behaviour is attributable to a change from mental health to mental illness, of course, and in cases of personality disorder such as a **psychopathic personality**, extreme deviation from society's average may be the norm for a particular individual. Such an individual may behave perfectly predictably throughout their lifetime, consistently showing asocial **obsessions and compulsions** which, for that individual at least, can be viewed as normal behaviour.

Based on the work of Sigmund Freud, the psychoanalytic description of personality suggests that consistent patterns of behaviour arise in part from unconscious conflicts between supervisory social restraints ('superego') and pleasure-seeking instincts ('id'). Although this approach has had huge influence on Western culture, it employs procedures that are beyond validation and is theoretically unsubstantiated. A related approach that does not rely upon speculative structures such as the superego and the id is the humanistic perspective of Abraham Maslow and Carl Rogers. The central concept in this perspective is that of self. Consistent patterns of observable behaviour are said to develop around our self-concept. Questionnaires form the basis of an assessment procedure that aims to evaluate what individuals think of themselves both actually and ideally. This approach, inherent in much pop-psychology, lends itself to person-centred counselling that aims to help individuals adapt to their social environments.

Notorious use of questionnaires is made by 'trait' approaches to the description of personality. These approaches attempt to describe dispositions towards specific patterns of behaviour in terms of objective, statistical averages. An ongoing argument among trait theorists centres around the number of dimensions of personality that must be taken into account in order to capture the full range of human behaviour with the fewest dimensions. Perhaps the best known of these dimensions is the extraversion-introversion distinction, between individuals who are gregarious, thrill-seeking, and socially outgoing party animals, and those who are reserved, sober, and socially cautious bookworms (to parody somewhat). We all show behaviour that lies somewhere along this scale, and the task for trait theorists is to establish how many scales are necessary, and then to establish that an individual's responses to questionnaire items are indicative of a consistent tendency to behave in a particular way. The search for the minimal number of dimensions that accounts for the greatest amount of individual variation has resulted in a list of the so-called 'big five' personality traits—emotional stability, extraversion, openness, agreeableness, and conscientiousness. For some theorists these characteristics are genetically determined, in the way that earlier theorists had proposed a link between body build and personality. For example, 'mesomorphs' with a compact, muscular build were seen as self-assertive, and 'endomorphs' with a soft, round build were seen as sociable.

Mental disorders can become apparent in behaviour through any number of organic and social causes, with the further possibility of an interaction between the two, in the form of a genetic predisposition to react in certain ways in certain environments. In the case of the eating disorders **anorexia and bulimia**, for example, a genetic susceptibility is indicated by co-occurrence in identical but not fraternal twins. Perhaps the commonest form of disorder is an extreme mood change that is manifest as **depression**, resulting in a changed disposition to respond in a new, maladaptive but consistent pattern. The mood change itself may be quite rational, as in the case of bereavement, and is only described as a disorder if it persists abnormally, or if it prompts **suicidal behaviour** in an otherwise healthy individual. In contrast, our minds can become disorganized to the extent that we lose contact with reality and experience the distorted perceptions, delusions such as **paranoia**, and hallucinations that characterize **schizophrenia**, the common functional psychosis. Recent technological developments in brain imaging allow us not only to observe normal mental activities, but also to provide descriptions of organic changes associated with disorders (see **brain imaging psychological disorders**).

The treatment of mental disorder depends in part upon the disorder itself, and partly upon the theory of personality favoured by those administering the treatment. Psychoanalysis and humanistic therapies such as Gestalt therapy attempt to reconcile the patient's difficulties through dialogue and interaction, and in so doing they recognize the essentially psychological nature of the disorder. An underlying assumption of treatments such as these is that psychological problems can be diminished by having the patient recognize them. An alternative psychotherapy known as behaviour therapy makes use of the principles of learning to help patients overcome disorders such as **phobias**. Rather than changing the patient's way of thinking by discussion or re-learning, biomedical therapies rely upon external intervention to prompt physical changes in the brain. Drug therapies using anti-psychotic agents such as chlorpromazine and anti-depressants such as fluoxetine ('Prozac') are in widespread use, but more extreme and more controversial interventions involve electro-convulsive therapy in cases of severe depression, and **psychosurgery** to treat a range of disorders from depression to aggressive behaviour and deviant sexual behaviour. Not least of the difficulties with removal or disconnection of part of the cortex is the irreversibility of the treatment.

ADDICTION. For most people the concept of drug addiction is dominated by images of physical and mental degradation brought about by the use of chemicals such as heroin and cocaine. It is generally forgotten that the most widely used drugs are caffeine (in tea and coffee), nicotine, and alcohol; and that the most successful drug 'pushers' are tobacconists and publicans. Of course the great majority of those who enjoy these drugs are not necessarily addicted, if addiction means a tendency to excessive use of the drug, a craving for it when it is not available, and the development of a variety of physical and psychological symptoms when it is suddenly withdrawn.

Addiction is a difficult word to define, and a WHO expert committee in 1970 substituted the words 'drug dependence'. This is characterized by psychological symptoms such as craving and a compulsion to take the drug on a continuous or periodic basis, and physical effects developing when the drug is withheld or is unavailable. Although many drugs will meet these criteria, those of overriding concern are the opiates, alcohol, and the sedatives, particularly barbiturates, all of which cause both physical and psychological symptoms of dependence. Other drugs of significance are stimulants such as cocaine and the amphetamines, the hallucinogens, of which mescaline and lysergic acid diethylamide (LSD) are examples, and cannabis. Most of these drugs do not induce the symptoms of physical dependence associated with abrupt discontinuance, and it is their psychological effects which are the main driving forces behind their continued use. Glue sniffing and the inhalation of volatile solvents by children are probably increased by publicity. None of these substances can be regarded as addictive; apart from the risk of liver damage from the solvents, the chief danger is from asphyxia, should the user place the glue in a plastic bag and pull it over his head. Glue sniffing is a form of behaviour which usually ceases with adolescence—and possibly with legal access to alcoholic drinks.

Although government concern centres principally on the illegal use of heroin, the number of known 'addicts' is relatively small in comparison with the very large number of people who have become dependent on alcohol. Precise figures are impossible to obtain but, as the purchase of alcoholic drinks has increased considerably over the past few decades, so has the number of alcoholics. A well-known formula has related the estimated number of alcoholics in a community to the annual consumption of liquor calculated as pure ethanol per head of population. In Great Britain the overall consumption of alcohol between 1950 and 1976 increased by 87 per cent, and it was estimated that in 1979 there were at least 300,000 alcoholics in the country. Whereas in the past alcoholism and excessive drinking were mainly male attributes, over the past few decades there has been a sharp increase in the number of women damaged by intemperance, a phenomenon which is probably related to the ease of purchase of liquor from supermarkets and other retail outlets, and of its concealment.

The problem of addiction to alcohol is not peculiar to the twentieth century. The Romans passed laws to control drunken charioteers and Victorian philanthropy was well acquainted with the evils of drink. Now as then, excessive drinking results in medical and social damage. Research in Great Britain and Australia has shown that 15–20 per cent of hospital beds are occupied by patients suffering from diseases or injuries directly or indirectly brought about by excessive indulgence in alcohol. As its consumption has increased, so have deaths from cirrhosis of the liver and the other diseases it causes, while psychiatric hospitals are familiar with the acute and chronic psychoses due to it. The social damage is not always recognized or acknowledged. In Great Britain, Australia, and the USA, for example, some 50 per cent of deaths and injuries from car crashes and 20–40 per cent of other accidental deaths such as falls, drowning, and incineration can be attributed to the effects of alcohol. It is impossible to obtain accurate figures on the role of alcohol in occupational accidents but there is a striking correlation between the numbers of patients admitted to hospital with alcoholism and those of patients undergoing treatment for injuries sustained at work. The contribution of alcohol to antisocial behaviour is well known: violence in the streets, at football matches, and in the home; the battering of wives and of babies are all familiar examples of the phenomenon. Criminal behaviour such as rape and homicide can often be attributed to intoxication of the aggressor and, in some cases, of the victim as well. Yet in the West it continues to be a widely advertised drug; from it in 1983–4 the British government reaped tax of £3,900 million. As to nicotine, in recent years much publicity has been given to the contribution of tobacco to diseases of the heart and lungs to whose aetiology heavy smoking is an important contributor. Following the introduction of tobacco into England in 1565, James I wrote his trenchant 'Counterblaste to Tobacco' (1604). Wiser than some other rulers, however, he did not attempt to ban its use but placed a tax on it; and governments ever since have found it a singularly lucrative source of revenue.

The reputation of heroin with its addictive properties may mislead some people into thinking that other drugs are relatively trouble-free. But in the case of sedative drugs, the widespread use of barbiturates—predominantly by middle-aged women—in the 1960s was an epidemic which caused considerable ill health and an increase in the rates of suicide and attempted suicide. For therapeutic use they have been largely superseded by the safer benzodiazepines (Valium, Mogadon, etc), though these are not so free from addictive potential as was believed initially. Sudden cessation of their regular use by an individual accustomed to them can cause a drug withdrawal syndrome with both physical and psychological symptoms (Ashton, 1984). While their popularity for the control of anxiety, insomnia, and a variety of psychosomatic symptoms is testified to by Tyrer's estimate (1980) that some 40 billion doses were being consumed each day throughout the world, the publicity given to benzodiazepine dependence in recent years has probably influenced doctors towards greater caution in prescribing them for long periods of time. The greater the dose and duration of consumption, the greater is the risk of dependence developing.

Cannabis (also known as marijuana, pot, and hashish) grows wild as hemp in many parts of the world. It was used medicinally in China as long ago as 2737 BC, Herodotus (*c*.484–425 BC) mentions its being inhaled by Scythians as part of a funeral ritual, and the physician Galen says that it was customary to give hemp to guests at feasts to promote hilarity and happiness. In recent times every kind of evil has been attributed to smokers of marijuana, but the evidence for these baneful effects is far from satisfactory and there are singularly few dangers to health that can be attributed to cannabis alone—though anyone driving while affected by cannabis is at risk and even more so if alcohol has also been consumed. Few addicts confine their intake to a single substance, and interactions are often more hazardous than the effects of single substances; even so, the cultivation and possession of hemp products are generally prohibited by law. Whether such laws should continue has become a matter for continued debate.

The control of drug trafficking and misuse is based on the United Nations Single Convention on Narcotic Drugs (1961) to which most countries are signatories. This instrument wholly restricts the use of a wide range of substances and requires governments to enforce by punishment its regulations on the cultivation, manufacture, and sale of the drugs listed. Unfortunately, total prohibition of the recreational use of drugs which users are determined to obtain appears to be a singularly unsuccessful policy, as the USA discovered when alcoholic drinks were forbidden for nearly fourteen years from 1919. Attempts by governments to prevent their citizens from smoking tobacco have been equally futile: suppliers were liable to decapitation in ancient China; smokers were tortured to death or exiled to Siberia in Tsarist Russia, and had molten lead poured down their throats in Persia; and the popes from time to time threatened excommunication. Similarly, with suppliers and users of opiates and cannabis, the draconian laws of some countries seem not to inhibit those who are prepared to risk apprehension.

In the United Kingdom great emphasis is placed on the control of opiates. In many cities heroin addicts can be treated in special centres, where the main task of the therapist is to wean the addict off the heroin by reducing his daily intake or else to substitute a long-acting opiate, such as methadone, that will block the action of heroin if this continues to be used. In addition, much attention is paid to the addict's life circumstances, with counselling offered by social workers, psychologists, and other members of the centre's staff. Whereas withdrawal of the drug is comparatively easy, the task of ensuring continued abstinence is decidedly difficult, and relapses are commonplace. It is questionable whether young addicts mature out of dependence on reaching an age even of 30–35, yet it is possible that a change in circumstances coupled with a desire to be free from the constant need for opiates and money for their purchase may persuade a sufferer to find other satisfactions in life.

The treatment of alcoholism is scarcely easier, largely because of the ready availability of alcoholic drink: a person persuaded to give up the drink habit in the clinic may suffer immediate relapse on returning to former surroundings. Yet there is evidence to show that some alcoholics can abstain sufficiently to permit a return to 'normal social drinking', an elastic-sided term that depends on the attitudes of a society to drinking behaviour. F. A. WHITLOCK

ANOREXIA NERVOSA AND BULIMIA NERVOSA. Many people are now familiar with the disorder of anorexia nervosa, which is diagnosed by the criteria of self-induced weight loss (which may be so severe as to result in amenorrhoea in female patients) coupled with a morbid fear of becoming fat and a relentless pursuit of thinness. Other distinguishing features of the condition include a denial of the subjective feelings of hunger, a distortion of body image, and a desire to increase energy expenditure by elevated physical activity. It is potentially a fatal disorder, with mortality rates ranging from 5 to 15 per cent, mainly from suicide.

Anorexia nervosa most commonly occurs in middle-class females, although it has also been reported in males. The disorder appears generally during adolescence, though it has been known to begin prior to this period, or even during adulthood. In Britain, the incidence in young women has been estimated to range between 1 and 4 per cent. Many believe that it is a disorder of very recent origin; however, patients with such a disorder have been described by physicians practising from the seventeenth century onwards.

The related disorder, bulimia nervosa, is far less well known, perhaps partly because of its antisocial and somewhat shocking symptoms, which may have retarded its identification. Bulimia was not differentiated from anorexia and was not described as a distinct disorder until very recently. Like anorectics, bulimics have a distorted body image, are obsessed with their body weight, and have a tremendous fear of becoming fat. However, bulimics have an overwhelming desire to eat large quantities of food at a single sitting (termed 'compulsive' or 'binge' eating); they then immediately self-induce vomiting, abuse laxatives, or use both these forms of purging before the food has had time to be digested and absorbed. The majority of bulimics induce vomiting by pushing their fingers into the throat, thus producing the gagging reflex. Use of this method frequently results in calluses over the dorsum of the hand caused by its rubbing against the upper teeth. But some bulimics have developed their purging techniques to such a degree that they simply need to stoop over the toilet to vomit.

Thoughts about food and body weight are obsessional, and the behaviour related to food becomes compulsive. For example, some bulimics have as many as twenty or thirty episodes of bingeing and vomiting in a 24-hour period. The energy value of food consumed during frequent binges has been measured, and it was found that a bulimic subject may be eating food with an energy value of at least 26 megajoules (about 6,214 kilocalories) per day. Obviously, much of this energy would never be absorbed, because the partly digested food would be expelled by vomiting immediately following the binge. By contrast, women with no history of eating disorders and with comparable indices of body weight were eating food with an energy value of under 15 megajoules (approximately 2,585 kilocalories) per day.

Many bulimics have never been treated for their disorder, since many retain normal or slightly below normal weight through the use of these bizarre purging methods. Hence, unlike the painfully thin anorectic, whose illness is obvious to both her doctor and others around her, the bulimic may be ill for years without anyone discovering her secret disorder, not even her husband, parents, or friends.

The causes of these two disorders are not known; there is no convincing evidence for either inherited or biologically determining factors. Anorexia nervosa has been viewed in the psychodynamic sense as a struggle towards a self-respecting identity, as a 'defensive, biologically-regressed' attitude taken in response to pressures (especially sexual ones) experienced in puberty, and as an attempt to realize society's current view of the ideal feminine figure as sylphlike. Similarly, evidence has been provided that the development of bulimia is related to the struggle to attain a perfect stereotyped female image of beauty, helplessness, and dependence.

BARBARA SAHAKIAN

ANXIETY. The characteristics of anxiety as an emotion are that it is distressing, and that its sources are indefinite. In the latter respect it is unlike fear, which has reference to a specific aspect of the outside world. Fear with a more or less specific reference but out of proportion to the real danger is a phobia. Agoraphobia, for instance, is a morbid fear of public places. An anxious person is in suspense, waiting for information to clarify his situation. He is watchful and alert, often excessively alert and over-reacting to noise or other stimuli. He may feel helpless in the face of a danger which, although felt to be imminent, cannot be identified or communicated. Hope and despair tend to alternate, whereas depression describes a prevailing mood of pessimism and discouragement.

With the emotion of anxiety may be associated such bodily symptoms as feelings in the chest of tightness or uneasiness which tend to move upwards into the throat, sinking feelings in the epigastrium, or light feelings in the head which may be described as dizziness. The patient tends to be pale or, less often, flushed. His pulse is rapid, and his heart overacting. He shows effort intolerance, mild exertion producing an undue increase in pulse and respiration rate; he tires rapidly. His posture is tense, his tendon reflexes brisk. Sexual interest tends to be in abeyance. The function of every organ in the body is affected in some degree. Numerous studies have examined physiological changes associated with the experience of anxiety. Among the better known is the change in skin conductivity, the galvanic skin reflex (GSR), the basis of action of the so-called 'lie detector'. Increased anxiety causes sweating and a sharp drop in the resistance between the two electrodes attached to the subject's finger. In an anxious person, however, spontaneous fluctuations of the GSR will be recorded. Such an individual, when tested by a lie-detector, would show even greater fluctuations in the tracing, sufficient, probably, to make an interpretation of the results invalid.

Freud's psychoanalytic theory offers explanations of anxiety, which occurs in greater or lesser degree in almost every form of mental disorder. In his earliest formulation, Freud argued that anxiety is a vicarious manifestation or transformation of sexual tension (libido) not discharged through normal sexual activity. It might sometimes be a repetition of the experience of being born. In his later work he wrote of it as reflecting motives which, although excluded from consciousness by repression, threaten the dissolution of the ego. The contemporary explanation, although similar, is expressed in different terms.

Anxiety has also been used in a

broader sense as a term for the drive aroused by a danger signal, i.e. a conditioned stimulus associated in previous experience with pain, physical or psychological. To a danger signal a response is made which has proved effective in avoiding the pain. The pain is not experienced again, but the response is reinforced every time it reduces the anxiety aroused by the danger signal. Responding by avoidance has other consequences. It precludes further exploration of the danger situation, and, not being explored, the sources of the danger remain ill-defined, and other ways of coping with them are not learnt. Avoidance responses tend, therefore, to become firmly established.

The emotion of anxiety is felt whenever responses made to a danger signal appear to be ineffective. Because it is frustrated, the behaviour associated with anxiety tends to become vacillating and disorganized; also, destructive impulses occur. The anxiety is then mixed with anger. To these effects are due some of the special qualities of anxiety as an emotion.

The agoraphobic patient does not feel anxious while he succeeds in avoiding whatever dangers public places contain for him; otherwise he would feel helpless in the face of whatever demands being in a public place might make. These demands might represent threats to his conception of himself or to the assumptions he makes about the world. Akin to agoraphobia is 'separation anxiety', which arises when a person faces demands while being denied, as a result of separation, the reassurance and support of a parent or other significant person. Existentialist theory equates anxiety with the dread of being alone or of being nothing; without the reassurance given through a relationship with another person, the sense of self is threatened.

DEREK RUSSELL DAVIS

BRAIN IMAGING PSYCHOLOGICAL DISORDERS. At present the diagnosis of a psychotic illness such as schizophrenia is based largely on subjective reports. The patient describes the voices he or she is hearing (hallucinations) or claims to be a rock star and a Russian chess grand master while being unable to play the guitar or speak Russian (delusions). There is considerable evidence that these disorders have a biological basis, most notably the fact that dopamine blocking drugs can, in most cases, reduce the severity of hallucinations and delusions. However, as yet no one has found reliable 'biological markers' of psychosis analogous to the characteristic brain abnormalities associated with Alzheimer's disease or Creutzfeld-Jacob disease.

The existence of hallucinations (false perceptions) and delusions (false beliefs) has major implications for our understanding of the mind. How can I be sure of my mental ground if my perceptions and beliefs can be false? Brain imaging allows us to start looking directly for the biological basis of false perceptions and false beliefs.

Imaging techniques. A high proportion of the energy needed by the human body is consumed by the brain in order to support neural activity. Although the brain is only 2% of the weight of the body it accounts for 20% of the total oxygen consumption. The energy is supplied by blood flowing through microvessels which are immediately adjacent to the neurons. However, not all the millions of neurons in the human brain are active simultaneously. For example, neurons concerned with visual signals will show little activity when our eyes are shut and there are no visual signals to be processed. By mechanisms as yet little understood localized variations in blood flow occur so that energy is supplied to just those brain areas where it is most needed. Over 100 years ago it was recognized that by detecting these changes in blood flow, it should be possible to identify those regions of the brain that were currently most active.

Since the 1980s two methods have become widely used for detecting regional changes in human brain activity on the basis of blood flow measurements. Positron Emission Tomography (PET) requires trace amounts of radioactivity (usually water containing oxygen 15 which emits positrons) to be injected into the blood stream. More positrons will be emitted in those brain regions where the blood is flowing faster due to greater neural activity. The density of positron emission can be measured by suitable detectors and a 3D picture of the brain can be constructed indicating the regions of highest activity. Magnetic Resonance Imaging (MRI) supplies a detailed picture of brain structure by placing the brain in a powerful magnetic field. Increases in blood flow due to neural activity can also be detected using this technique. This is because these blood flow changes actually overcompensate for the energy lost and lead to an excess of oxyhaemoglobin. Since this substance is less paramagnetic than deoxy-haemoglobin the change can be detected through functional magnetic resonance imaging (fMRI) providing an indirect measure of brain function known as blood oxygenation level dependent contrast (BOLD). PET has a spatial resolution of about 7mm and a temporal resolution of about 30 seconds. fMRI has a spatial resolution of 2mm and a temporal resolution which is determined by the speed of blood flow changes which are in the order of 10 seconds. In both cases the basic experimental paradigm involves the comparison of at least different states determined by what the volunteer was doing during the scan. For example, in one series of scans the volunteer hears words being spoken while in the comparison series he or she hears only the background noise of the scanner. Comparison of these two conditions shows increased signal in the auditory cortex on both sides of the brain. This result is typically displayed as a set of coloured patches indicating where the activity occurred superimposed on a black and white image of brain structure.

Both PET and fMRI have revealed patterns of brain activity which are entirely consistent with results from direct studies of neural activity in animals and from the effects of localized brain lesions in humans; the location of changes in blood flow are determined by the exact nature of the sensory stimulus being perceived, or the motor response being produced. This concordance is most striking in the visual areas of the brain since these areas have been intensively investigated in animals. For example, it is well known that the primary visual cortex at the back of the brain is topographically organized: items in the left visual field are represented in the right hemisphere, while items in the lower part of the visual field are represented in the upper part of the visual cortex. This relationship can be shown using PET, or even better with fMRI, by stimulating appropriate parts of the visual field and observing the location of the associated increases in blood flow. It is also known that the visual system of the monkey brain is functionally segregated. Beyond the primary visual cortex (V1) there are a series of adjacent regions which are specialized for different visual attributes: V3 for shape, V4 for colour, and V5 for movement. When a volunteer passively views a moving stimulus, there is activity in an area at the junction of temporal, parietal, and occipital cortex which is not present for stationary stimuli. Likewise, there is an area activated by colour nearer to the middle of the brain in the fusiform gyrus.

These regions, revealed by brain imaging, are the human homologues of V4 and V5 in the monkey brain. Regions associated with higher cognitive functions can also be revealed. For example, it is well known that short-term memory for verbal material such as telephone numbers is aided by the strategy of saying the numbers 'in one's head'. Studies of neurological patients with impairments of verbal short-term memory suggest that left sided language areas of the brain (in particular the inferior frontal gyrus or Broca's area and the inferior parietal lobe) play a crucial role in this form of inner speech. Volunteers have been scanned while they tried to remember strings of letters presented visually for a few seconds. There was clear activation in traditional language areas on the left side of the brain, including Broca's area and inferior parietal lobe even though no overt speech had occurred in the experiment.

A major limitation of both PET and fMRI results from the restrictions on what a volunteer can actually do while he or she is being scanned. The volunteer lies supine for an hour or more and, just as with old-fashioned long exposure photography, the head must remain as still as possible. With fMRI in particular, the possibilities for presenting visual and auditory stimuli are limited and movement is severely restricted (see figure 28). Great care is needed to ensure that speech or even limb movements do not produce unwanted head movements. As a consequence the ideal paradigm is one in which the volunteer simply lies in the scanner and 'thinks'. An ironic consequence of these limitations is that the advanced technology associated with brain scanning has encouraged experiments which depend upon subjective reports rather than measures of behaviour. In the past, psychologists have been wary of subjective report in the absence of behaviour since no external validation was available. Brain imaging provides a measure of neural activity which can be related to subjective report in the absence of behaviour. In the rest of this entry I shall briefly describe some studies which have been specifically concerned to measure patterns of brain activity associated with different kinds of subjective report.

Pain is an extreme example of a subjective experience which cannot be validated on the basis of external criteria such as behaviour or the nature of the stimulus inducing the pain. It seems reasonable that pain should be associated with, for example, extremely hot or extremely cold stimuli since such stimuli can cause damage. However, a strong experience of pain can also be induced by stimulating the skin with an array of copper wires in which alternate wires are either mildly hot or mildly cold. In isolation neither temperature would feel painful, but the combination produces an 'illusion' of pain. An imaging study has shown that the feeling of pain, whether real or 'illusory', is associated with activity in the anterior cingulate cortex. The experience of pain can also be modulated by hypnosis even though the stimulus inducing the pain remains constant. An imaging study of the effects of hypnosis on pain also showed that the experience of pain was related to activity in the anterior cingulate cortex. Thus activity in a particular brain region is associated with the experience of pain rather than physical stimulation.

A small proportion of the population who are otherwise completely normal report the experience of synaesthesia. Synaesthesia occurs when stimulation in one modality induces an experience in another modality and can take many forms. Composers such as Liszt and Scriabin experienced colours in association with particular chords. In the most

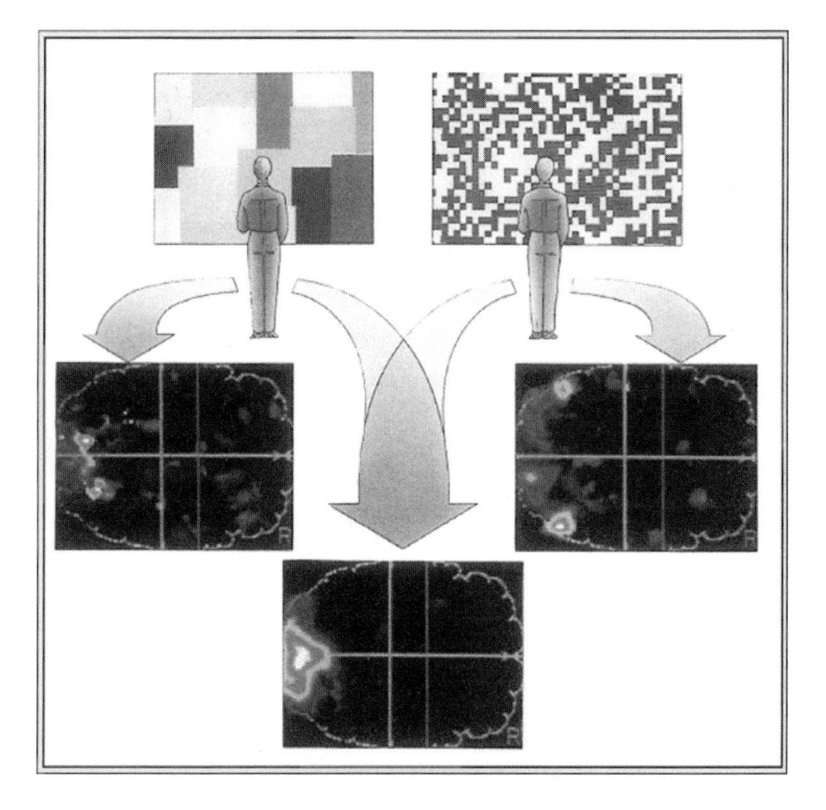

Fig. 27 Functional segregation in the human brain. Both colour and movement activate the primary visual cortex (centre panel). However, in higher visual areas activity elicited by viewing colour (left panel) is in a distinctly different location from that elicited by viewing movement (right panel). These are the human analogues of areas V4 and V5 in the monkey. (Image supplied by Professor S. Zeki)

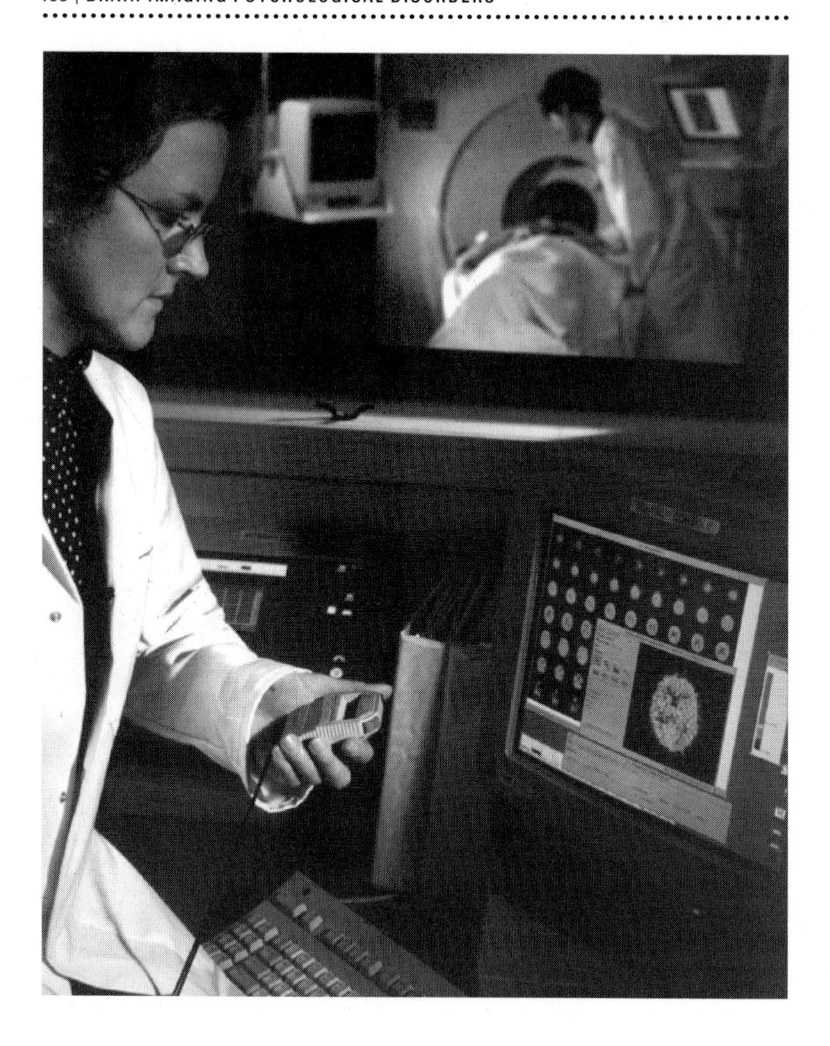

Fig. 28 A view of a positron emission tomographic (PET) scanner from the control room. A volunteer can be seen lying in the bed of the scanner with his head inside the ring of detectors through which the image of brain function is obtained. Examples of the raw images obtained by the scanner can be seen on the right. The screens by the scanner can be used to present visual stimuli to the volunteer. (Image supplied by the Wellcome Trust)

frequent form of synaesthesia colours are experienced in association with hearing words. Synaesthetes claim that this is an involuntary experience which is perceptual in quality and not simply a form of imagery. Brain imaging studies have shown that, in comparison to normal controls, people with colour-word synaesthesia do indeed show activity in 'visual' areas of the brain. By delineating the function of these visual areas more precisely we shall gain an understanding of the nature of this purely experiential phenomenon in physiological terms.

It has long been known that there is no pleasure in tickling oneself. However, the same tactile stimulus is felt much more intensely when applied by someone else. An imaging study has identified a number of brain regions where activity reflects these differences in tactile sensation including primary and secondary somatosensory areas. It is assumed that, when a tactile stimulus is self-produced, activity in these somatosensory areas is modulated by signals arising in the regions where the movement is being generated. Future experiments which further elucidate this mechanism will have direct relevance to our understanding of how the brain enables the mind to perceive itself to be an agent.

I have given here a very few examples from the hundreds of imaging studies that are now being reported every year. While there have been speculations about the relationship between the mind and the brain for centuries, it is only with the new brain imaging techniques that we are able to collect so much data relevant to this topic.

Psychopathology. By scanning patients while they are hallucinating it is possible to see which brain areas are active during such experiences. The cortical regions activated reflect the content of the hallucination, i.e. whether it is auditory or visual. However, it is secondary rather than primary sensory areas that are activated. In the case of auditory hallucinations the pattern of activity seems to resemble that associated with imagining a voice rather than actually hearing one. Even when symptom free, patients who are prone to hallucinate during acute episodes of their illness show an abnormal pattern of activity when imagining the sound of another's voice. Currently the speculation is that, when these abnormalities become sufficiently extreme, the patient experiences his or her own imagining as coming from the outside world. This might occur because the areas concerned with initiating thoughts and images are no longer in proper contact with the high-level sensory areas where these images are represented. Brain scanning studies are beginning to provide direct evidence for such disconnections. As yet there are no imaging studies which examine the neural basis of beliefs or false beliefs.

There have been a number of studies examining the pattern of brain activity associated with severely depressed mood. The pattern can vary depending on the precise form of the depression. Retarded depression in which the abnormal mood is associated with a general reduction of speech and action is associated with reduced activity in the frontal areas of the brain. However, the same pattern is also seen in schizophrenic patients with the so-called negative features of social withdrawal and poverty of action, but in whom there is no evidence of depression.

CHRISTOPHER D. FRITH

DEPRESSION. Psychiatry shares with general medicine a tendency to adopt words with commonly understood meanings and give them specialized, unfamiliar interpretations. Obsession, conversion, pervert, and depression are psychiatric examples of such words. In everyday language we speak of feeling depressed, thereby indicating a transitory downturn in mood whose origin can usually be traced to some set-back, even to the prospect of returning to routine living after too convivial a weekend. On the other hand, depression as an illness signifies a severe emotional disturbance whose source may or may not be traceable to external causes—misfortunes, bereavements, financial loss, illness, etc. Emil Kraepelin distinguished two major psychotic illnesses under the headings of *dementia praecox* (schizophrenia) and manic-depressive psychosis. The latter condition takes the form of alternating periods of extreme melancholia and equally extreme periods of elation and excitement. But as time has gone by, this relatively clear description has been complicated by the inclusion of persons suffering from recurrent bouts of severe depression without any periods of mania or for that matter major psychotic symptoms—the so-called endogenous depression. In addition, there are individuals who experience less intense attacks with less clearly demarcated changes in mood, whose depression appears to be an understandable response in a vulnerable personality to lesser or greater degrees of adversity—a reactive or neurotic depression.

This simple dichotomy is unfortunately beset with difficulties. Indeed, the very terminology invites—and gets —criticism. To say that somebody has sunk into the depressive phase of a manic-depressive psychosis overlooks the obvious fact that many such cases do not develop psychotic symptoms. Delusions, hallucinations, and bizarre hypochondriacal beliefs about one's bodily functions may be, but often are not, present. More frequently the sufferer will manifest a state of deep despondency and hopelessness coupled, in some instances, with self-accusations and guilt over trivial misdemeanours previously ignored. The term *endogenous* depression seems to imply that the victim has some innate predisposition to this variety of mood disturbance; and there may be genetic evidence for such a predisposition, adding emphasis to the aetiological significance of the word 'endogenous'. On the other hand, speaking of neurotic (reactive) depression is probably saying as much about the quality of the symptoms as about their origin. To use more than one base for a classification hardly makes for clarity, and the word 'reactive' signifies that some external event is responsible for the onset of the individual's state of gloom. However, as some indubitable cases of endogenous depression and the depressive phase of manic-depressive psychosis can be preceded by psychological stresses such as bereavement and serious ill health, the distinction between endogenous and reactive depressions becomes distinctly blurred; and it would be erroneous to assume that in all persons with reactive depressions one can delineate external events determining the quality and time of onset of the illness.

For at least fifty years there has been controversy over whether endogenous and neurotic depressions are distinct and separate illnesses or merely alternative terms for severe and milder forms of mood change lying at the ends of what is essentially a continuum of affective disorder. Numerous attempts have been made to settle this dispute, with powerful statistical techniques being employed in the hope that mathematics will decide once and for all a debate which, some might think, has taken up more research time than the facts warrant. In the end the question of whether a person is suffering from a reactive or an endogenous depression will be decided on clinical grounds without recourse to statistics;

and treatment will be given according to the judgement made at the time.

Numerous typologies aiming at a better classification of depression have been devised, but possibly a dimensional rather than a categorical approach to the problem is the most appropriate way of overcoming the difficulty of finding clearcut natural boundaries between one type of depression and another. It is a fact that between patients with endogenous and reactive depressions lies a group with atypical symptoms who fail to fit neatly into one category or the other. This seems to presuppose a continuum of depressive disorders rather than a set of distinct classes of illness. But, as Kendell has written (1976):

> The attempt to resolve our classification problems by the statistical analysis of clinical data has failed up to now and may continue to do so. We may have to live with our uncertainties and disagreements until we understand enough about the physiological or psychological basis of depression to construct a new classification on that basis.

Does it matter? Yes, but in all probability not so much as the protagonists in this debate might wish us to believe. The diagnosis of depression rests on consideration of the patient's symptoms, his previous history, and the course of his illness. Simple rating scales can be used, if required, to permit a fairly accurate diagnosis to be made. Treatment will depend on this clinical decision, for what may be appropriate in one type of depression may be ineffective in another. Electroconvulsive therapy (ECT) may be life-saving for patients with severe endogenous depression, when the risk of suicide can be high. But ECT rarely benefits those with neurotic depression, for whom drugs and psychological treatments are usually more effective. In recent years prominence has been given to a form of behaviour therapy, cognitive therapy; but it is clear that although this may be beneficial for neurotic depression, its impact on the symptoms of endogenous depression will be slight.

There is another complication introduced into the classification of depression that has a bearing on treatment. Persons with recurrent attacks of mania and depression (bipolar affective disorder) are more responsive to treatment with lithium salts than are those with recurrent attacks of depression only (unipolar affective disorder). Opinions differ on this point, but for the most part those with repeated attacks of endogenous-type depression appear to react best either to ECT or to tricyclic antidepressants, or to a combination of both. Neurotic (reactive) depression, on the other hand, is probably best treated with other types of drugs in conjunction with psychological methods designed to help the patient take a more realistic view of his situation.

In the end, in spite of many refined arguments, it appears that there are individuals who become severely depressed, sometimes losing touch with reality to a degree that warrants the label 'psychotic'; and there are those whose depressions are of a milder nature but, none the less, are sufficiently troublesome to interfere with enjoyment of life. One can for convenience designate the former as 'endogenous' and the latter as 'reactive' or 'neurotic'; but such labelling does not say as much about the origins of these mood disturbances as the terms themselves suggest. In both cases we are faced by illnesses requiring far more help than will be derived from the admonition 'pull yourself together and snap out of it'. Although such advice may be beneficial for individuals with mild degrees of cyclothymia and an overdeveloped sense of self-pity, it is worse than useless for those whose depressed mood has gone beyond the limits of normal human variation.

Finally, one point of singular importance must be mentioned. All persons suffering from depression should be adequately assessed for the risk of suicide. Relatives, and some physicians, sometimes hesitate to enquire directly about suicidal thoughts lest such questions prompt the actions they are most anxious to prevent. This is not so. Most depressed patients answer truthfully to enquiries of this kind, and may even be relieved by the opportunity to discuss their innermost feelings of despair and dread of the future. It is sometimes believed, however, that those who mention suicidal thoughts never put them into practice. This is quite incorrect, and all mention of suicide by a depressed person must be taken with the utmost seriousness so that prompt admission to hospital for treatment can be arranged.

F. A. WHITLOCK

MENTAL ILLNESS. Most people think of mental illnesses as strange and frightening conditions which can affect other people but not themselves or their families. But in the average family doctor's surgery psychological symptoms are surpassed in frequency only by common colds, bronchitis, and rheumatism. In the course of a year, about one in every eight people in Britain consult their general practitioners for problems which are predominantly or completely psychological in nature. General practitioners refer about 10 per cent of such patients to a psychiatrist; most of these will be treated as out-patients but some will need admission to hospital, which in Britain is nearly always on a voluntary basis. Thus, out of all those who seek medical help with psychological problems, only a small minority become psychiatric in-patients. It is then a striking indicator of the extent of such problems that psychiatric patients occupy nearly half of all the hospital beds in Britain and in most other industrialized nations.

Arguments continually rage over the exact limits of mental illness. Some authorities regard the concept of mental illness as a myth while others, by contrast, consider that the majority of seemingly normal people suffer, often unknowingly, from psychiatric abnormalities amenable to treatment. Furthermore, some believe that psychiatric disorders are simply mental equivalents of physical diseases, while others argue that there are as many sorts of psychological problems as there are individuals who suffer from them.

In practice it is possible to discern certain recurring patterns of complaints and disabilities which can be regarded as reasonably discrete entities. These disorders can be divided into two broad groups: organic disorders, in which some demonstrable physical illness including brain disease underlies the psychological symptoms, and functional disorders, where no definite physical abnormality has yet been replicably demonstrated. Since most forms of mental illness fall into the latter category, the classification of psychiatric disorders is generally based on the clinical distinction between different clusters of symptoms each with a characteristic outcome. In general medicine, advances in classification occurred when technological progress allowed the elucidation of the underlying causes of illnesses. Unlike their colleagues practising general medicine or surgery, however, psychiatrists are unable to rely on laboratory or other tests to refute or confirm their clinical diagnoses, but the search for laboratory tests to aid with the diagnosis of affective disorders and other conditions continues.

In the meantime it is useful to distinguish between the neuroses and the psychoses. Neurotic symptoms correspond to what is commonly called 'nerves' and comprise feelings and thoughts which most normal people have experienced at some time or other, albeit in a relatively minor form. However, if they become persistent and severe, such symptoms can become markedly disabling, and result in a frank neurotic illness or 'nervous breakdown'. Psychotic symptoms, on the other hand, are not part of normal experience and are almost invariably severe. The picture of psychotic illness is quite distinct from normality and corresponds to what in popular usage is called 'madness' or 'insanity'. Women outnumber men among neurotics by about two to one, but psychosis is equally frequent in the two sexes.

Neurotic problems account for about two-thirds of those consulting family doctors because of psychological symptoms, the remainder being made up by a variety of conditions including psychosomatic complaints, abnormalities of personality, alcoholism, and the psychoses. Most neurotics are treated by their general practitioners, but individuals with psychotic illnesses are almost always referred on to psychiatrists. Thus, while those with psychoses form only about 4 per cent of patients consulting GPs because of psychological problems, 25 per cent of psychiatric out-patients and more than half of all psychiatric in-patients suffer from psychotic illnesses.

Neuroses.
Anxiety states are among the most common of all psychiatric disorders and are characterized by persistent apprehension and fear, at times amounting to panic. They are often accompanied by sensations caused by over-activity of the autonomic nervous system: these include excessive sweating, tremor, faintness, choking or breathlessness, and 'butterflies' in the stomach. (See **anxiety** for further discussion.)

Phobic neuroses have much in common with anxiety states in that the predominant symptoms are again of fear or panic together with autonomic over-activity. But in phobic neuroses the symptoms are provoked by certain specific stimuli, such as dogs, spiders, the sight of blood, or having to talk to strangers. The most common variety is agoraphobia, which literally means fear of open spaces. The agoraphobic is afraid of leaving home and subject to panic attacks in crowded public places such as supermarkets. He or she often dreads travelling on public transport, especially underground trains, and has great difficulty in tolerating lifts or rooms from which there is no ready exit. Since these symptoms considerably limit normal life, agoraphobic patients may become totally house-bound. (See **phobias** for further discussion.)

Obsessive-compulsive neurosis is much rarer, but nevertheless the symptoms which form its core are phenomena with which, in milder form, most people will be familiar. There can be few people who have not at some time been unable to stop a song going round in their head, or had an irrational urge to avoid stepping on cracks in the pavement, or re-checked windows and doors which they know they have already secured. In obsessive-compulsive neurosis, such thoughts or practices become pathologically exaggerated. Fears of having been contaminated by dirt, or of having harmed someone, may preoccupy the sufferer for most of the day even though he recognizes that they are silly. Similarly, he may wash his hands or check taps a hundred times a day, while all the time trying to convince himself that his behaviour is ridiculous. Such repetitive thoughts and compulsive acts become so intrusive that productive activity becomes impossible. (See **obsessions and compulsions** for further discussion.)

The predominant features of depressive neurosis are gloom and despondency. Bouts of weeping are common, as are edginess, irritability, and a tendency to tire easily. There is a general loss of ability to concentrate and in particular a lack of interest in things which were previously enjoyed. The symptoms tend to vary in intensity, but often cause difficulty in getting off to sleep. (See **depression** for further discussion.)

A variety of neurosis which was formerly common but is now much less so is hysteria, which in its classical forms beguiled nineteenth-century physicians such as J. M. Charcot and Sigmund Freud. Indeed, it was while studying a hysterical patient, the celebrated 'Anna O.', that Freud and Breuer developed many of the concepts upon which psychoanalysis came to be based. The essence of hysteria is that, in the face of intolerable stress, symptoms develop which provide a defence against the stressful circumstances. Characteristic symptoms include a paralysed limb, loss of speech, convulsions, or blindness, and are often called conversion hysteria because the psychological trauma has figuratively been 'converted' into a bodily form. Some forms of hysteria involve a different mechanism called dissociation, in which an individual may forget even his own identity. He may wander off in a 'fugue state' which carries him many miles from home, or he may take on some new identity or switch from one identity to another—the 'split personality' of popular films, such as *The Three Faces of Eve*. Although hysterical mechanisms are usually unconscious, many psychiatrists doubt the genuineness of some of the more theatrical forms. Indeed one of the problems confronting psychiatrists in legal work is where to draw the dividing line between hysteria and conscious simulation or malingering. Fortunately, hysterical symptoms are becoming less common due to improved education and awareness of psychological matters; this allows the expression of emotional difficulties for what they are, and renders the communication of suffering via hysterical symbolism redundant. None the less, it is important to remember that conversion hysteria can develop against a background of serious organic brain disease, either pre-existing or unsuspected, in a considerable percentage of cases.

In contrast to hysteria, anorexia nervosa appears to be on the increase, particularly among adolescent girls and young women. The central feature is self-imposed starvation, which frequently starts with a slimming diet and occasionally ends with complete inanition and death. Weight loss, physical over-activity, cessation of menstrual periods, and the growth of downy hair on the face and back are the cardinal symptoms. Surprisingly, most patients shun treatment and instead show considerable ingenuity in avoiding weight gain. Thus they hide food or secretly throw it away, and abuse laxatives. Like the obsessive-compulsive, the anorexic often recognizes the pointless irrationality of her behaviour but nevertheless feels bound to continue. Psychoanalysts have suggested that anorexia is a desperate unconscious attempt to stave off imminent sexual maturity, but a simpler explanation is that the anorexic has a distorted perception of her body which causes her consistently to overestimate her own size. The rise in anorexia has been attributed to increasing pressure on women to diet, as over the past thirty years or so the ideal female shape has become thinner and less buxom. All anorexics can be shown to have abnormalities of function of the hypothalamus, a part of the brain which controls appetite and many hormonal responses, but it is unknown whether this is cause or effect of the illness.

Causes and treatment of neurosis. Everyone is probably capable of experiencing neurotic symptoms in some form or degree, but individuals differ in their susceptibility to stress. Some neurotic patients develop their symptoms without obvious precipitating factors, whereas others only become ill after major tragedies, such as the loss of a husband or child. Vulnerability to anxiety states and to phobic and obsessional neuroses appears to be partly influenced by hereditary traits such as introversion, general nervousness, and the reactivity of the autonomic nervous system. But it is generally agreed that life experiences play a major role. What is not generally agreed is which life events are crucial, and how they produce their effects. According to psychoanalytical theory, neurosis is an outward manifestation of deep-seated intrapsychic conflicts which were set up in early life. Treatment, which is necessarily prolonged and intensive, aims to make this unconscious material accessible to consciousness, and the resultant insight is expected to produce resolution and relief. The behaviourists, however, think that the symptom is the neurosis and that it is the result of faulty learning processes. Theoretical assumptions concerning unconscious mechanisms and insight are regarded as irrelevant. Instead the aberrant behaviour is examined closely and broken down into its component parts, and the goal is then to persuade or educate the patient into adopting more appropriate and adaptive patterns of behaviour. This approach is particularly useful with phobias and obsessive-compulsive neurosis.

Psychoanalytically-based psychotherapy, behaviour therapy, or an eclectic mixture of the two are the approaches favoured by psychiatrists. However, in practice most patients with milder neuroses never see a psychiatrist, but are instead treated by their general practitioner with a combination of simple support and minor tranquillizers of the benzodiazepine group (such as Valium® and Librium®). These drugs are very useful in allaying anxiety over a few weeks, but their effectiveness tends to diminish over longer periods. Unfortunately, they are often prescribed for inappropriate reasons, with the result that their consumption is increasing at a rate alarming to all —bar the manufacturers. Antidepressant drugs like Tryptizol® and Tofranil®, which are effective against discrete episodes of depression, are less likely to be misused, although they can be very dangerous when taken in overdosage by someone with suicidal intent.

Organic psychoses.

Acute. A variety of physical illnesses may produce an acute reversible mental disorder called delirium; the causes include fever or disturbance in body chemistry as well as infections of the brain. Delirium may also follow intoxication with drugs or withdrawal from barbiturates or alcohol ('DTs'). The most striking feature is the rapid onset of confusion. The patient has no idea where he is or what day it is, and only the most tenuous grasp of what is going on around him. He may see or hear things which are not really there (hallucinations), or experience distorted perception of things which are there (illusions). He is often very fearful and may believe he is being attacked or persecuted. Evelyn Waugh's *The Ordeal of Gilbert Pinfold* is an excellent, presumably first-hand, account of an acute organic psychosis which could possibly have been an example of alcoholic hallucinosis complicated by the taking of other drugs. Most delirious patients recover completely when the cause of the insult to the brain is corrected.

Chronic. By contrast, dementia refers to chronic insidious organic psychoses which are usually progressive. Loss of memory for recent events is often the first symptom. Thus, an elderly woman may be able to describe vividly the days of her childhood, but be unable to recall what she has just eaten for breakfast. She then begins to forget the faces of friends and relatives, and may be unaware of where she is or what year it is. Deterioration in intellect and personality may show itself as a lack of propriety, lack of attention to personal appearance, and loss of normal social niceties and inhibitions. In about 10 per cent of cases dementia in later life is caused by remediable conditions such as benign brain tumours and hypothyroidism, but the great majority of cases are due to degenerative disease of the brain or its blood vessels. The ageing of Britain's population has rendered these disorders, senile and so-called multi-infarct dementia, so common that the increase has been called 'the quiet epidemic'. Sadly, there are at present no effective cures.

Functional psychoses.

Schizophrenia. In 1898 Emil Kraepelin made the now classical distinction between the two major types of functional psychosis. He contrasted manic-depressive psychosis with its recurrent gross swings in mood with a more severe and progressive illness starting in young adulthood which he termed *dementia praecox*. This distinction still holds, although *dementia praecox* is now termed schizophrenia because this better describes the characteristic disintegration of mental life. Most schizophrenics suffer at some point from hallucinations which usually take the form of voices talking to or about them. Occasionally these voices are friendly but in the main they are disparaging and abusive. The schizophrenic is beset with strange beliefs (delusions). He may think, for example, that he is the victim of a plot, that everyone can read his thoughts, or that alien forces are inserting or removing thoughts from his head or controlling his body.

Schizophrenia is only correctly diagnosed when these beliefs are unshakeable and totally out of keeping with the ideas and philosophies of the sufferer's own class and culture. Thus, a West Indian who believes he is a victim of a voodoo spell, or a spiritualist receiving instructions from the dead, is unlikely to be schizophrenic. But an Englishwoman who is absolutely convinced that her every action is personally controlled by a famous pop singer through a radio receiver he has installed in her mind may well be.

About 80 per cent of schizophrenic patients make a good recovery from their first attack. Unfortunately, many patients later relapse and require further admission to hospital, and in the long term only about 50 per cent remain quite free of any disability. More severely affected people become so preoccupied with their delusions and hallucinations that they tend to withdraw from social contact, and lose touch with reality. As a result their social and occupational functioning deteriorates, and about 10 per cent of all those initially affected become long-term hospital in-patients. In spite of the disorganized and irrelevant speech and disintegration of personality of such severe schizophrenics, their basic intelligence is usually unaffected and improvement can still occur after many years of hospitalization.

If, as some claim, schizophrenia is a myth, then it is a myth with a strong hereditary component! The risk of the identical twin of a schizophrenic also developing the disorder is about 50 per cent, whereas the risk for a non-identical twin is less than 15 per cent; this difference presumably reflects the greater genetic similarity of identical twins. Similarly, children of schizophrenic parents who were adopted and raised by normal families still have an increased risk of schizophrenia, whereas children born to normal parents and by mischance raised by a schizophrenic do not. The precise way in which liability to schizophrenia is transmitted is not known, but biochemical factors may be important. Some drugs, such as amphetamines, can in excess produce a mental state mimicking schizophrenia; this has led to the suggestion that schizophrenics could be endogenously producing some aberrant chemical.

The once fashionable theories that abnormal childhood experiences could by themselves induce schizophrenia can now be discounted, but environment is undoubtedly important. Traumatic life experiences or intense intrafamilial pressures can precipitate breakdown in the susceptible individual. For example, in many recovered schizophrenics, prolonged contact with excessively critical and over-involved relatives can cause relapse into florid psychosis.

In treating schizophrenia, the two essential elements are antipsychotic drugs and social rehabilitation. Intrusive therapies such as psychoanalysis are harmful, but a long-term supportive relationship with a concerned psychiatrist or social worker can be invaluable. Phenothiazine drugs are effective against florid symptoms such as delusions and hallucinations, and are needed to induce an initial remission and in some cases to retain it. Thereafter, a variety of social measures are used to provide a social and work environment to suit each patient's individual need. Rehabilitation may involve occupational therapy, attendance at a day hospital, or residence in a halfway hostel. The aim of such measures is, of course, to help the patient to find a satisfying role in the community and to stop him becoming institutionalized in hospital. Voluntary organizations such as the Schizophrenia Fellowship often play a major role in this. (See also **schizophrenia**.)

Manic-depressive psychosis. In its full-blown form, this is a cyclical disorder in which opposite extremes of mood are successively shown. Mania is characterized by an extraordinary sense of well-being, over-activity, and elation and is usually accompanied by a conviction of great self-importance which causes the individual affected to make grandiose pronouncements—for example, that he is the most talented and intelligent person in the world. He may consequently enter into wild and ruinous business ventures, or indulge in other unaccustomed excesses of spending, eating, drinking, or sex. His talk is profuse and prolix, flitting from topic to topic with an unstoppable stream of ideas interspersed with puns and feeble witticisms. His jollity may initially be infectious, but before long he becomes overbearing and tiresome. Not surprisingly most manics eventually dissipate their energy and return to normal, but an unfortunate minority descend straight into depression with no intermediate period of normality.

Mania is much less common than depressive psychosis, the predominant symptoms of which are profound gloom and despair. Life appears futile and hopeless and suicidal ideas are usually entertained, and, not infrequently, successfully acted upon. Depression produces a marked depletion in self-confidence and self-regard and the depressive may see himself as the most evil and wicked individual who ever lived. Racked with guilt, the previously blameless character becomes convinced that he has committed some grave infamy or that he is to blame for all the sin and misery which exists in the world. Less commonly he may believe that he has been stripped of all his possessions, or that his body has become hideously diseased and is rotting and decayed. Real bodily disturbance of a less bizarre nature does usually occur. Appetite is poor, weight loss ensues, and there is often constipation and loss of sex drive. Some depressives physically slow down, and their talk may decrease or altogether cease, a condition known as psychomotor retardation: occasionally such a patient develops a state of mute, immobile stupor. In others restlessness and edginess may culminate in severe agitation.

Manic-depressive illness, like schizophrenia, is partly determined by genetic factors. Again there is evidence that biochemical factors are important: for example, drugs which deplete the brain of chemical messenger substances called monoamines can induce depression, while drugs which raise the level of monoamines relieve depression and can precipitate mania. Despite the importance of these biological components, the part played by psychological factors can in no way be discounted. Adverse life circumstances or bereavement or other forms of loss are known to result frequently in depression, and psychoanalytical theory considers that it is the turning-in on the self of the consequent feelings of hostility and annoyance which produces the illness. Some behaviourists on the other hand have stressed the importance of learning experiences, such as exposure to inescapable mental trauma which produces a feeling of helplessness. This, they believe, forms the basis of the depressed state.

Manic-depressive illness is a serious condition, not just because of the misery and the disruption it causes, but because about 15 per cent of sufferers eventually die by suicide. Fortunately, treatment is effective. Antidepressant drugs are of proven efficacy in the majority of typical cases, and although the manner in which it works remains obscure, electroconvulsive therapy can often relieve depression which has proved resistant to other treatments. Hospital admission, which is the general rule for cases of mania, provides a temporary sanctuary for many depressives, and is essential when the risk of suicide seems great. Psychotherapeutic help is invaluable and, in people who have recurrent episodes of illness, the chemical element lithium may be used on a long-term basis to prevent further relapses.

PETER MCGUFFIN AND
ROBIN M. MURRAY

OBSESSIONS AND COMPULSIONS. To say that an individual is obsessed with an idea, a pursuit, or a particular person usually implies, often with more than a hint of disapproval, that he is thus wholly preoccupied. But such obsessions may not necessarily he unhealthy or neurotic, even though, as Kräupl-Taylor (1979) comments, they have an element of compulsion attached to them. They have to be distinguished from obsessive-compulsive neuroses, or the psychotic's absorption with his delusions. A person may say that because of his beliefs, religious, political, or philosophical, he has to act in a certain manner: he is compelled by convictions which, if ignored, would cause him unease or anxiety. Such a person is not necessarily obsessional. The term obsessional personality is rather applied to one who is conventional, conscientious, reliable, scrupulous, or punctual well beyond average. He may find it necessary to check and re-check his work to assure himself that no errors have been committed; he may adhere rigorously to a routine which, if disrupted, will cause him considerable unease; and he will probably be singularly competent at clerical work, proof-reading, typesetting, or other tasks requiring attention to detail. The characteristics of the obsessional personality are not to be despised: they could be essential qualities for anyone engaged in precision work, and much scientific research could not be carried out without them.

In comparison, the individual who suffers from an obsessional-compulsive neurosis is a sick person. The late Sir Aubrey Lewis (1967) appraised the subject. With some reservations he adopted Carl Schneider's definition of obsession as 'contents of consciousness which, when they occur, are accompanied by the experience of subjective compulsion, and which cannot be got rid of, though on quiet reflection they are recognized as senseless'. Usually 'the contents of consciousness which preoccupy the obsessional neurotic are concerned with ideas of harm, contamination, sex, and sin, although repetitive ruminations about abstract problems and manipulation of words and numbers are not infrequent'. These may be obsessional *symptoms* which can occur independently of the neurosis proper. Fortunately the neurosis is rare, affecting about 0.05 per cent of the general population in Britain and the USA, for example, although obsessional symptoms crop up from time to time in the lives of otherwise perfectly normal individuals. (The symptoms can also complicate other psychiatric disorders, particularly severe depression.) Children, as is well known, engage in repetitive games and rituals such as avoiding treading on the cracks between paving stones; and, as any parent knows when reading a familiar story, an attempt to vary or skip a part of it may be resisted by the child. Many minor compulsions can be discerned in adult superstitions: failure to touch wood or avoid walking under a ladder for instance; and a sense of mild anxiety may briefly follow the breaking of such rituals. Anxiety is indeed a main driving force in the life of the obsessional neurotic. Resisting a compulsion may arouse acute distress, which can he assuaged only by bowing to the inner need and going back to complete a ritual.

Lewis divides obsessions into primary and secondary. 'An example of the first,' he wrote, 'would be the insistent feeling that one is dirty and then there is the impulse to wash—the secondary phenomenon, developed in order to obtain relief from the primary disturbance. The secondary phenomenon can be regarded as defensive and aimed at preventing or relieving tension.'

Standard textbooks of psychiatry give detailed accounts of the many varieties of symptoms which can cripple performance of the everyday activities of the obsessional neurotic. For example, the patient who fears contamination may wash his hands repeatedly only to find himself having to restart the whole process on account of a fear that chance contact with the tap may have again soiled his fingers. Such compulsions can occupy a large part of his waking day, as can the checking rituals of those who fear that they might inadvertently harm somebody close to them. A sufferer may spend hours checking and re-checking gas taps, electric switches, and the contents of kitchen drawers to ensure that sharp objects such as knives have not been left lying where they could injure another person. Mothers of young children are sometimes tortured with the idea that some carelessness on their part could seriously injure a recently born infant.

There are many examples of well-known persons who have found it necessary to engage in compulsive rituals. Boswell described such a ritual performed by Samuel Johnson:

> He had another particularity, of which none of his friends even ventured to ask an explanation. . . . This

> was his anxious care to go out or in at a door or passage, by a certain number of steps from a certain point, or at least so as that either his right or his left foot . . . should constantly make the first actual movement when he came close to the door or passage. Thus I conjecture: for I have, upon innumerable occasions, observed him suddenly stop and then seem to count his steps with a deep earnestness; and when he had neglected or gone wrong in this sort of magical movement, I have seen him go back again, put himself in a proper posture to begin the ceremony, and, having gone through it, break from his abstraction, walk briskly on, and join his companion. (*Life of Johnson*, Aetat. 55.)

John Bunyan in *Grace Abounding* gave a good example of an obsessional phobia: 'Sometimes again, when I have been preaching, I have been violently assaulted with thoughts of blasphemy and strongly tempted to speak the words with my mouth before the congregation.' But there is no reason for thinking that either Johnson or Bunyan suffered from obsessional neuroses, though clearly they did have troublesome symptoms; for fortunately the symptoms did not detract from their competence and genius. Obsessional doubts about religious observance are phenomena well known to confessors and theologians. Such scruples certainly tormented Bunyan as they did Martin Luther.

Successful treatment of patients suffering from obsessional neurosis is far from easy; and this despite the fairly obvious psychopathology—in psychoanalytic terms—of the neurosis. The frequent association of depression with the neurosis implies that appropriate treatment of the affective disorder might well mitigate the full impact of the patient's disabilities. In many cases supportive psychotherapy and behaviour therapy as well as the passage of time seem to ensure that the patients will come to terms with their symptoms sufficiently well to enable them to lead relatively normal lives. In about 60 per cent of the cases of patients who are severely afflicted, one of the modern forms of psychosurgery will bring relief. It may not entirely eliminate the symptoms, but they become less obtrusive and no longer dominate the patient's life.

F. A. WHITLOCK

PARANOIA. Although paranoia today is a diagnosis used to describe patients who exhibit systematized delusions of grandeur and persecution, its original meaning, as the etymology of the word indicates, was 'being out of one's mind'. Heinroth in 1818 appears to have equated paranoia with *verrüchtheit* (madness); Kahlbaum in 1863 was the first psychiatrist to give it its modern meaning, and although he regarded paranoia as a persistent, chronic condition, he believed that paranoid patients suffered from a disorder of intellect. The term survives as the name given to one type of functional psychosis, viz. that in which the patient holds a coherent, internally consistent, delusional system of beliefs, centring round the conviction that he (or, more rarely, she) is a person of great importance and is on that account being persecuted, despised, and rejected. As Henderson and Gillespie's *Textbook of Psychiatry* (9th edn., 1962) puts it: 'A person so affected believes that he is right, that he is justified in his beliefs, and that anyone who opposes his point of view is behaving maliciously or at least non-understandingly towards him.' Such a person does not subscribe to the view that he is ill, does not accept treatment, does not enter hospital voluntarily, and may do great harm to himself and others: to himself by coming into active collision with a world that does not subscribe to his own exalted view of himself, and to others by attacking those he conceives to be persecuting him. Paranoiacs on occasion commit murders, not infrequently engage in futile litigation, and generally make an infernal nuisance of themselves, quarrelling incessantly with their neighbours and falsely accusing people of trespass or their spouses of infidelity.

True paranoia is, fortunately rare; it has a bad prognosis and is not amenable to any known treatment. However, despite its rarity, it is for a variety of reasons of considerable interest and importance.

First, incoherent, internally consistent delusions of grandeur and persecution occur in other psychoses, notably in schizophrenia, where they form part of a clinical picture that includes hallucinations, emotional withdrawal, and autistic thinking (in which syntax is disrupted). These are three classes of symptom which are conspicuous by their absence in true paranoia. Most but not all textbooks of psychiatry list 'paranoid schizophrenia' as one of three varieties of schizophrenia, the other two being hebephrenic schizophrenia, which is characterized by withdrawal, bizarre mannerisms, and neglect of the person, and catatonic schizophrenia, characterized by periods of excitement and stupor.

Secondly, many people who are not regarded as mentally ill, and who do not come under the care of psychiatrists, display a cluster of personality traits which can be, and nowadays often are, described as paranoid. These people are opinionated, touchy, and have an idea of their own importance which the rest of the world does not endorse. Such people patently suffer from a disorder of self-esteem, not of intellect—their opinions must be correct because they hold them; their families, their careers, their lives must be especially important because they are *their* families, *their* careers, *their* lives—and the same must presumably be so for true paranoia. According to classical psychoanalytical theory, paranoia and paranoid traits generally are narcissistic disorders, the implication being that they indicate fixation at some infantile stage of development during which the self is its own love object; but many contemporary analysts hold that narcissistic self-overestimation is a compensatory reaction to humiliation in infancy and childhood. Later research has shown that Daniel Paul Sebreber (1842–1911), the subject of Freud's classic paper 'Psycho-analytical Notes on an Autobiographical Account of Paranoia (Dementia Paranoides)' (1911), was from birth subject to gross mechanical restraints by his father, who was determined to nip in the bud all signs of self-will and 'innate barbarity' in his infant son. Freud, however, made no enquiries into his subject's childhood, took his expressed devotion to his father at its face value, and interpreted his delusions of being persecuted by God as a reversal and projection of repressed homosexual longings for his father.

Thirdly, paranoiac delusions bear a disconcerting, embarrassing resemblance to the beliefs held and propagated by founders of religions, by political leaders, and by some artists. Such people often make claims on behalf of themselves, their religious ideas, their country, their art, which would be regarded as grandiose and delusional if their ideas did not harmonize with the needs of their contemporaries and thereby achieve recognition and endorsement. Nowadays anyone who claimed to be the Messiah, who addressed God as his personal father, and asserted that 'he who is not for me is against me' would be at risk of being referred to a psychiatrist and diagnosed a paranoiac. But presumably in the first century AD His Word spoke to many—as indeed it continues to this day to do. Similarly, any politician who asserted the innate superiority of his own race and claimed that his country was the victim of an international conspiracy would today raise doubts as to his sanity, but in Germany in the 1930s Hitler found all too many people prepared to agree with him. There must, it seems, be some as yet unformulated relationship between the psychology of paranoia and that of prophets and leaders.

Fourthly, the adjective 'paranoid' is sometimes used by psychoanalysts to describe anxiety and ideas that are inferred to be projections of the subject's own impulses, so that, for instance, a person who is unaware of his own hostility may suffer 'paranoid anxiety', imagining that everyone else is hostile towards him, or a person who is unaware of his own homosexual tendencies may have the 'paranoid idea' that other men are always about to make a pass at him. This usage derives historically from Freud's idea that the psychology of paranoia hinges on reversal and projection of unconscious homosexual impulses.

Finally, it must be mentioned that the word 'paranoid' has slipped into general use to refer to enhanced suspiciousness, and often with the implication that such suspiciousness is evidence of unusual sensitivity and perceptiveness. Hence the catch-phrases 'Paranoia is total awareness' and 'The fact that you're paranoid doesn't mean that you aren't being followed'.

CHARLES RYCROFT

PHOBIAS. Persons to whom the label 'phobic' is applied fall into two main groups: (i) those who respond with unusually intense fear to a specified situation, for example to animals of a certain species, but who show no other symptoms; and (ii) those who exhibit unusually intense fear in a number of situations, often difficult to specify. Whereas those in the first group are in general emotionally stable, those in the second are not; they are prone to bouts of fairly acute anxiety and depression which may last weeks or months. They are often reluctant to leave home, and are described as agoraphobic if adult or as school phobic if children.

Attempts to explain the origin of phobias have been of two main kinds. One, the learning theory approach, holds that when a person is intensely afraid of something that others do not particularly fear, it is because the object or situation in question has become associated in his mind with a childhood fear, as of loud noises or falling. The other, the psychoanalytic approach, holds that the feared object or situation has become symbolic of something feared unconsciously. In the case of the 5-year-old boy, Little Hans, who was afraid to go out of the house for fear that a horse would bite him, the explanation offered by Sigmund Freud was that Little Hans's fear resulted from the repression and subsequent projection of his aggressive impulses, comprising hostility directed towards his father and sadism towards his mother, and that 'the motive force of the repression was fear of castration'. Empirical studies have given little support to either of these theories.

Research shows that specific and limited phobias have usually been present from early childhood but are normally diminished during adolescence. Since the fear is specified, treatment by means of desensitization is often appropriate.

The states of mind labelled agoraphobic, or school phobic, are much more complex than the specific phobias. These two conditions are closely related and are probably due to the same causes. Children who are school phobic, and nowadays referred to as school refusers, generally express much anxiety when pressed to attend school, their non-attendance being well known to their parents. Not infrequently their truancy is accompanied by, or masked by, psychosomatic symptoms of one kind or another; anorexia, nausea, abdominal pain, or feeling faint, for example. Fears of many kinds are expressed—of animals, of the dark, of being bullied, of mother coming to harm, of being deserted. Occasionally a child seems to panic, and anxiety, tearfulness, and general misery are common. As a rule, the children are inhibited and well behaved. Most come from intact families, have not experienced long or frequent separations from home, and have parents who express great concern for them and their refusal to attend school. Relations between child and parents may be close, sometimes to the point of suffocation.

There is now general agreement that the refusal is much more to do with anxiety about leaving home than fear of what might happen at school. Why do they have this fear of leaving home? Among the many explanations suggested, those best supported by evidence point to trouble within the family. For example, in some cases one or the other parent, most often the mother, is a sufferer from chronic anxiety and is glad to have the child at home as a companion. In others a child becomes alarmed about what might happen at home during his absence and stays there to prevent it. In some cases both these influences are active. We examine each further.

A mother (or father) who retains a child at home may do so deliberately and consciously or may be completely unaware of what she is doing—and why. In either case she is commonly found to have had a difficult childhood and to be seeking from her child the affection and security she herself had lacked. In doing this she is inverting the normal parent-child relationship—requiring the child to act as parent whilst she becomes the child. To someone unaware of what is going on, it may appear that the child is being spoiled, but a closer look shows the reverse: the mother is in fact placing a heavy burden on her child. It is sometimes found moreover, that a parent who is treating her child in this way swings abruptly from a genuine concern for his welfare to hostility and threats. Thus, if the child is to be helped, the parent must be helped to change. How best to do this is considered later.

In cases of a child staying at home for fear of what might happen while he is away—for example, he may be afraid of some harm coming to his mother—the problem is one of explaining why a child should think like that. Among psychoanalysts it has been usual to attribute the trouble to the child's harbouring unconscious hostile wishes towards his parent and being afraid lest his wishes come true. An alternative explanation is that the fear arises from actual events to which the child is being exposed: for example, (i) an illness of his mother's which the child is afraid may prove serious or even fatal; (ii) the death of a close relative or neighbour that leads the child to fear his mother might die also; (iii) threats or even attempts by the mother to commit suicide (which occur far more frequently than is usually realized); (iv) threats by a parent to abandon him, used as a disciplinary measure. (Little Hans's mother is reported to have used various threats to discipline him, including threats that she would go away and never return.)

A first task in helping a child who remains at home is to get his parents to recognize any part they may be playing and to change their ways. Depending on the part played and on the nature of their own problems, this may be easy or difficult. A mother prone to invert her relationship with her child can often be helped to release him if she is treated with sympathy. When encouraged to talk about her own childhood, she is likely to tell of unhappy experiences of certain specific kinds: for example, the loss of her mother by death or desertion; long absences from home in an institution, hospital, or foster home; having been an unwanted child; being threatened with abandonment; or witnessing a parent threatening or attempting suicide. She has grown up anxious not to lose anyone to whom she becomes attached and tends therefore to cling tightly to them. A person who has developed in this way is often called 'over-dependent' or 'immature' but is far more appropriately described as anxiously attached (in contrast to securely attached). Similarly, in cases of mistaken disciplinary measures, a parent may be helped to stop threatening the child when he or she appreciates the ill effects this has.

Most of the research on adults who are diagnosed as agoraphobic has neglected systematic study of what is happening in their families. In such study as has been undertaken, it is commonly found that the sufferer, usually a woman, is being subjected to the same sorts of pressure as the school-refusing child, and usually from the same source, namely her mother (though sometimes it is from the father or husband). Once established, the condition may persist even after the pressures that led to it have ceased.

One variety of adult agoraphobia was described by M. Roth in 1960 under the title of the phobic-anxiety depersonalization syndrome. The majority of victims were middle-aged housewives who, often after a sudden traumatic experience, developed intense anxiety associated with feelings of unreality and depersonalization. Thereafter their ability to go shopping alone was severely curtailed, especially if they were required to travel by public transport. Once inside a large store or supermarket they would become assailed with intense panic requiring their immediate departure from the shop. Their fears of travel and situational phobias could to some extent be allayed if accompanied by another person, even one of their children. The term 'housebound housewife syndrome' has come to be used for this variety of phobic-anxiety. Further study of the family experiences, past and present, of these women is called for.

JOHN BOWLBY

PSYCHOPATHIC PERSONALITY. Strictly speaking, this term should be applied to all varieties of abnormal personality. Schneider (1958) defined the psychopathic personality as an abnormal personality who either suffers because of his abnormality or makes the community suffer because of it. In the UK and the USA greater emphasis has been placed on the second part of this definition, mainly because of the frequent involvement of such persons in breaches of the law. American authors prefer the terms 'sociopath' and 'antisocial psychopath' which more clearly define the individual by virtue of his criminal propensities. In the UK, before the Mental Health Act of 1959 the psychopath was an entity unrecognized by law, but the Act defined psychopathic disorder as a 'persistent disorder or disability of mind (whether or not including subnormality of intelligence) which results in abnormally aggressive or seriously irresponsible conduct on the part of the patient, and requires or is susceptible to medical treatment'. Although a good deal of controversy surrounds the last seven words of this definition, quite clearly the Act considered psychopathic disorder to be a form of mental illness. If such a person is 'ill'—and he would be the last person so to regard himself—it is up to the medical profession to treat him. The Mental Health Act of 1983 apparently recognizes the questionable value of medical treatment, as the phrase is omitted from its definition of psychopathic disorder. None the less, the term stays under the general heading of mental disorder.

Numerous attempts have been made to identify the principal characteristics of the psychopath. The term in a general sense is often applied to adolescent or young adult males who appear unable to conform to the rules of society. The qualities of this sort of person's psychological make-up include an inability to tolerate minor frustrations, an incapacity for forming stable human relationships, a failure to learn from past experiences, however unpleasant they might have been, and a tendency to act impulsively or recklessly. Henderson (1939), in a well-known essay on the subject, divided psychopathic personalities into three categories: the predominantly inadequate, the predominantly aggressive, and the creative. They are by no means mutually exclusive but, whereas the first two have gained general acceptance and receive more psychiatric attention, far less has been heard about the creative psychopath, whose sometimes erratic behaviour may seem less significant than the creations of his fertile imagination. He is less likely to come before the courts or to the attention of the mental health services, for his eccentricities are not usually regarded as indicative of mental disorder.

The question of whether, in the long run, psychopaths do learn from experience was considered in a follow-up study of children who showed persistent antisocial behaviour in St Louis (Robins, 1966). Of those who survived—there was a high mortality from accidents, suicide, and alcoholism—a significant number appeared to be keeping out of trouble by middle life, finding that relative conformity was preferable to constant conflict with society and the law. Whether maturation or learning from experience was the more responsible for this beneficial change is uncertain, but it does appear that some so-called antisocial psychopaths do ultimately learn to mend their ways. There was little evidence that medical treatment had made much contribution to this outcome.

It is often said—erroneously as it happens—that our present-day concept of psychopathic personality originates from the introduction of the diagnosis of moral insanity into English medical and legal theory and practice by J. C. Prichard, a Bristol physician, in 1835. At the time, Prichard and many others were considerably influenced by Gall's writings on phrenology which localized human propensities to specific parts of the brain. Among these propensities was included the moral faculty, and it was widely assumed that moral insanity was caused by a derangement of that part of the brain concerned with making a choice between good and evil. Prichard, however, was using the term moral insanity to denote emotional disturbances —delusions and hallucinations—that were devoid of the usual hallmarks of insanity. None of his cases bore the remotest resemblance to the present-day psychopath, but because he used the word 'moral' it was widely believed that this form of insanity was responsible for the actions of individuals who exhibited a persistent tendency to indulge in criminal behaviour. Hence the plea of moral insanity in the courts in attempting to exculpate the offender from the full penalties of the law. Understandably, it was not an excuse which found much favour with the judges of the day. As they reasonably pointed out—and it has continued to be pointed out—it was impossible to decide whether a crime had been caused by the innate wickedness of the offender, or whether it resulted from a fit of moral insanity.

The Mental Deficiency Act of 1927 softened the term 'moral imbecile'—incorporated in the earlier Act of 1913—to 'moral defective', but retained in its definition the words 'mental defectiveness coupled with strongly vicious or criminal propensities', and added, and 'who require care, supervision and control for the protection of others'. This was the forerunner of the psychopathic disorder definition in the Mental Health Act of 1959. Because many of those so constrained were not devoid of normal intelligence, placing them in hospitals for the mentally defective was neither appropriate nor beneficial.

Why *psychopathic* personality? As already mentioned, Schneider used the term to denote all varieties of abnormal personality, but his subgroups of explosive, affectionless, and weak-willed come close to Henderson's categories of aggressive and inadequate psychopaths. Koch in Germany in 1891 introduced the term 'psychopathic inferiority' as a catch-all phrase implying a constitutional predisposition not only to neurosis but also to abnormalities and eccentricities of behaviour. At the time of his writing, psychiatric thought was dominated by concepts of degeneration and the hereditary transmission of 'the taint of insanity'. As such degeneration was often attributed to parental excesses, particularly alcoholism and sexual profligacy, it is understandable that what at first sight appeared to be persistent immoral or criminal behaviour became linked with the prevailing notions about psychopathic inferiority and moral insanity. Although in Britain the Royal Commission on the Law relating to Mental Illness, 1954–7, repeatedly used the word 'psychopath', it avoided making any precise definition of what the word meant. Baroness Wootton (1959) considered that the modern psychopath is the linguistic descendant of the moral defective, which takes us back to nineteenth-century writings on moral insanity. Whatever word is used, it has to be admitted that making clear distinction between the mentally healthy offender and the presumably mentally abnormal one is not an easy task.

The question thus arises whether psychopathic personality should be classed as a form of mental disorder. Opinions differ widely, but as the psychopath now has legal status the existence of such a condition has understandably been put forward in criminal proceedings as a plea for mitigation of sentence. In some cases of homicide, the verdict has been reduced from murder to manslaughter on the basis of diminished responsibility as defined in the Homicide Act of 1959. But many psychiatrists would have reservations about claims that psychopathic disorder is a mental illness on a par with neurosis or psychosis. While it could be argued that it amounts to an abnormality of mind which could seriously impair the responsibility of an offender for his alleged homicidal act, what is 'abnormality of mind' in this context? The subject was clarified by Lord Chief Justice Parker, who said that it meant 'a state of mind so different from that of ordinary human beings that the reasonable man would term it abnormal'. He went on to indicate that such an opinion applied to a person's acts, his ability to decide whether they were right or wrong, and his capacity for exercising will-power to control such behaviour in accordance with rational judgement. None the less, as Nigel Walker (1965) comments, 'It is clear . . . that while a diagnosis of psychopathy is now recognized by English courts as an acceptable basis for a defence of diminished responsibility, the psychopath's chances of succeeding in this defence are by no means high'.

The causes and treatment of psychopathic disorder are as contentious as its legal implications. Theories of aetiology have included brain damage in childhood, late maturation of the central nervous system, and adverse circumstances of upbringing, particularly difficult relationships with parents and those in authority. As far as treatment is concerned, there is little evidence that a purely psychiatric approach to the problem has been successful. Controlled studies are hard to come by, but one such investigation found that firm but sympathetic handling in a disciplined environment was better than a more permissive approach based on group therapy and a self-governing type of regime. As the psychopath appears to lack the inner controls normally developed during childhood and adolescence, this result is hardly surprising. Time, however, seems to be a significant factor in treatment, an observation which could be interpreted as favouring the late maturation theory of psychopathic disorder. But in all probability learning over a period of years may also play a part in this process of maturation. F. A. WHITLOCK

PSYCHOSIS. The word 'psychosis' seems to have been coined in the mid-nineteenth century and to have meant originally any kind of mental disturbance arising from whatever cause. But after the turn of the century its meaning was restricted by excluding both the mental consequences of familiar physical illnesses (such as delirium associated with fever) and the neuroses. In contemporary psychiatric terminology, 'psychosis' is a classificatory and descriptive term, referring to a specific range of illnesses and symptoms, the illnesses being those in which the patient's basic competence as a person is called in question, the symptoms being those which seem to indicate some gross disorder of perception and thought (such as hallucinations and delusions). A psychosis is, therefore, any mental illness which is liable to render its victim *non compos mentis*, and unfit to plead in a court of law; and a symptom is 'psychotic' if it betrays misapprehension and misinterpretation of the nature of reality.

If, for instance, someone asserts that he is Napoleon, or emperor of Canada, or has had sexual intercourse with God, he is psychotic, since such assertions are by common consent untrue and anyone making them seriously must be misapprehending the nature of reality and failing to distinguish between his fantasies and the facts of the case. In contrast, if someone asserts that he spends time imagining that he is Napoleon, or daydreaming that he has established an empire in Canada, or that he has dreamt he was emperor of Canada or has had intercourse with God, he is not psychotic, for he has correctly distinguished between his own imaginings and the nature of the external world. Similarly, if someone asserts that he has committed terrible crimes (when he hasn't) and deserves lifelong imprisonment for having done so, he is psychotic, but someone who complains of feeling irrationally guilty is not; nor is a religious person who has a lively sense of original sin.

The International Classification of Diseases 1955, published by the World Health Organization and used by the National Health Service in Britain, lists eight specific psychoses. Four of these, the so-called organic psychoses (senile, pre-senile, arteriosclerotic, and alcoholic), are generally agreed to be the result of degenerative changes in the brain. They excite little interest within the psychiatric profession and practically none at all with the general public. The other four, the so-called functional psychoses—schizophrenia, manic-depressive psychosis (see **depression**), involutional melancholia, and paranoia

—arouse considerable controversy within the profession and great interest with the general public, partly because their symptoms are dramatic, but more importantly because research has (as yet) failed to discover any convincing, as opposed to plausible, causes for them—and in the absence of any specifiable physical causes it is possible and legitimate to question even whether the medical model is the appropriate one to apply to psychosis.

However, the majority of psychiatrists do seem to believe that the functional psychoses are true medical diseases and that, one day, physical causes will be found for them—and that as a result, rational, effective treatments will become available. If they are right, not only will an enormous amount of suffering be relieved, but the claims of the medical profession to be the appropriate people to care for and treat the mentally disturbed will finally be vindicated. In fact, the advent of effective drugs for the treatment of schizophrenia and manic depressive psychoses has given considerable support to the possibility that biochemical rather than structural changes in the brain could be causes of these diseases. The medical model therefore gains some plausibility from these discoveries.

But, it must be stressed, at least two non-organic, non-medical conceptions of psychosis are also in circulation. One, held by some but not all psychoanalysts, argues that the functional psychoses are not in principle all that different from the neuroses; it is merely that the fixation points are earlier, the regressions deeper, the infantile traumas more massive, the defence mechanisms more primitive. If the analysts who hold this view are right, the functional psychoses are psychogenic, not organic, illnesses, and their symptoms require interpretation in terms of their concealed meanings, not explanations in terms of cerebral dysfunction.

The other, non-organic conception, held by anti-psychiatrists, 'family process' therapists, and the post-Laingian counter-culture generally, explains the functional psychosis of any single individual as the end-result of complex and skew interactions within his family that have driven him into bizarre and incomprehensible behaviour, which is then 'disauthenticated' by being labelled 'mad' or 'psychotic'. This theory exists in more than one form. In one the psychotic patient is the victim of a villainous schizophrenogenic parent, usually the mother; in another he is the overt casualty of a deeply concealed family tragedy. This last is a socio-political theory which locates pathology not in the body or the mind of the individual patient but in the power politics of society and the family. CHARLES RYCROFT

PSYCHOSURGERY. This term is used to denote operative procedures on the brain specifically designed to relieve severe mental symptoms that have been unresponsive to other forms of treatment. Although surgery for mental illness had been attempted sporadically—mostly in the form of trephining—since early times, it was not until 1935 that the Portuguese neurologist Egas Nioniz, in association with the surgeon Almeida Lima, performed the first systematic series of operations known as prefrontal leucotomy, severing the connections between the prefrontal cortex and the rest of the brain. Although the operation was crude, of the first twenty cases seven recovered and seven improved. The best results were obtained in cases of agitated depression, a finding which has been repeatedly confirmed by later workers. Unfortunately, some patients developed adverse personality changes, an effect which could have been predicted from the case of Phineas Gage, a competent worker in the USA who, in 1847 had the misfortune during a rock-blasting operation to have an iron bar blown through the front part of his head. He survived this extremely violent form of prefrontal leucotomy but, on recovery, was found to have undergone a profound change in personality. He swore in the grossest manner, behaviour not previously indulged in, and his overall qualities as a likeable individual were severely impaired. Despite these changes to his character he did not show any decline in intelligence or memory. Although patients treated by prefrontal leucotomy did not usually show such severe impairment of personality as Gage did, it is undeniable that adverse alterations in behaviour occurred sufficiently often to arouse opposition to the operation.

None the less, it was taken up enthusiastically in the USA by Freeman and Watts (1942) and with rather less vigour in the UK, where it was carried out on 10,365 patients suffering from mental illnesses between 1942 and 1954 (Tooth and Newton, 1961). It was stated that only 3 per cent showed undesirable side-effects and that more than 40 per cent had been ill for at least six years. The operation was performed in only a few centres, a fact which seems to imply that, regardless of its alleged usefulness, attitudes opposing it were strongly held by medical staff in many hospitals. By 1961 the annual frequency of leucotomy had fallen substantially.

As time has gone by there have been many modifications of the original operation, and today it has been almost entirely replaced by exact stereotactic procedures which allow very small lesions to be placed in certain key areas of the brain. Such methods are designed to alleviate symptoms without causing undesirable changes in personality. Comparatively few patients are treated each year by psychosurgery, largely because of the development of more effective drugs and behavioural methods for the treatment of mental illness.

What kinds of symptoms are most susceptible to surgical intervention? The phrase 'tortured self-concern' is often quoted to indicate the degree of distress which has failed to respond to less drastic treatments. The best results have been obtained from patients suffering from severe chronic anxiety, agitated depression carrying a high risk of suicide, and those afflicted with incapacitating obsessive-compulsive disorders.

Although there is every indication that, with careful selection and post-operative management, many patients with these apparently intractable symptoms have benefited from the more precise forms of psychosurgery, very strong opposition has been mobilized in some quarters against any form of surgery for the relief of psychiatric symptoms. Such opposition has been most vigorously expressed in the USA, where in some states these operations are forbidden by law. Peter Breggin, a psychiatrist in Washington, has claimed that there is no scientific justification for the operation and that the price paid in terms of blunted emotions and other personality changes is too high. Furthermore he has argued that psychosurgery could be used as a means for controlling antisocial behaviour and the activities of political dissidents. While there may be too few skilled in stereotactic surgery to permit its extensive use for political and social reasons, in India and Japan operations on the amygdaloid nucleus of the brain have been performed to control 'hyperactivity' in children. Although there is no doubt that outbursts of unbridled violence can be caused by diseases of the limbic brain, there is very little evidence that psychosurgery has been systematically applied to control such symptoms in the UK. And at present the requirements of Section 57 of the Mental Health Act of 1983 would almost certainly prevent any form of brain surgery being carried out expressly for the purpose of controlling antisocial, aggressive, or politically dissident behaviour.

Others have been concerned not only about the irreversible nature of the operation and permanent alteration of the personality, but also that in some way the patient's immortal soul would be damaged. Perhaps such considerations are best left to the theologians and the Almighty. A charitable view might be taken of man's efforts to relieve his fellow creatures of suffering. Be that as it may, given the safeguards that limit psychosurgery to the alleviation of distress, there seems to be a place for it as one form of effective treatment.

Although psychosurgery has been used for the treatment of deviant sexual behaviour, drug dependence, and alcoholism such methods can only be condemned partly because they are unlikely to be effective but also because of uncertainty over whether such kinds of behaviour fall within the ambit of psychiatric illness. In any case they are unlikely to cause 'tortured self-concern' to those who are so afflicted although the disturbing effects of these behaviours upon relatives can not be denied. But psychosurgery to allay the anxieties of relatives has not yet achieved whole-hearted support even from its most enthusiastic practitioners. F. A. WHITLOCK

SCHIZOPHRENIA. Towards the end of the nineteenth century Emil Kraepelin suggested that most of the variegated forms of insanity familiar to his contemporaries were manifestations of two major disorders, which he named *dementia praecox* and manic-depressive insanity. His claim was based on a meticulous study of large numbers of patients followed for many years and it had a profound effect on the subsequent development of psychiatry. *Dementia praecox* was a progressive illness which started in adolescence or early adult life and followed an inexorable downhill course; recovery, if it occurred at all, was always incomplete. Manic-depressive insanity, on the other hand, was a phasic illness. Although in the course of a lifetime a patient might have several episodes, and spend many years in hospital, individual episodes always ended in recovery and full restoration of the previous personality. The term schizophrenia, meaning 'split mind', was coined by Eugen Bleuler, the medical director of the Burgholzli Hospital in Zurich, during the period of ferment that followed this seminal innovation. Bleuler's schizophrenia was an expansion and elaboration of Kraepelin's *dementia praecox* and he believed that its protean manifestations were due to a 'splitting', or loss of co-ordination, between different psychic functions, particularly between the cognitive (intellectual) and conative (emotional) aspects of the personality. The monograph he published in 1911 was so influential that within a generation Kraepelin's original terminology was forgotten, and for the last fifty years schizophrenia has been recognized throughout the world as the most important single cause of chronic psychiatric disability.

The subjective experiences and observable alterations in behaviour which characterize schizophrenia are both very variable; but there is a central core of symptoms which, though occasionally seen in the presence of brain disease of various kinds, are in practice highly specific. The subject ceases to experience his mental processes and his will as under his own control; he may insist that thoughts are being put into his mind or removed from it by some alien force, or suspect that he is being hypnotized. He hears voices telling him what to do, commenting on or repeating his thoughts, discussing him between themselves, or threatening to kill him. In the acute stages of the illness other hallucinations and delusions of varied kinds may be present. His thought processes also develop a characteristic vagueness and illogicality. At first he simply keeps wandering off the point, but in some chronic patients there eventually ceases to be any logical connection between one idea, or phrase, and the next; so their speech becomes almost incomprehensible. Although intelligence and memory remain relatively intact, the whole personality is affected by the illness. Above all, the patient loses his vivacity and drive; he loses his interest in and capacity to respond emotionally to other people; and he becomes increasingly more apathetic, eccentric, and isolated.

Schizophrenia is a relatively common condition, affecting nearly 1 per cent of the population. Although its onset is usually in adolescence or early adult life, it may develop in childhood, or be delayed until middle age or even later. There is no good evidence that its incidence has changed in the past 150 years, and it occurs in much the same forms and with much the same frequency throughout the world, regardless of environmental differences or differences in language, creed, or social structure. Neither do wars nor other catastrophic events appear to influence its incidence. Although it is well established that some people may, even in the absence of treatment, have a single attack from which they recover completely and permanently, it is more common for a series of psychotic episodes to lead to some degree of lasting emotional impoverishment, even though the subject may still be capable of supporting himself and earning his living.

Of all mental illnesses schizophrenia is the most feared, and the most fascinating, and it is the model for the layman's concept of madness. It causes great suffering, not only to the patients whose lives and personalities it slowly destroys but also to their families, and its high incidence and chronicity make it a greater burden on health services than any other single illness. The fears and frustrations it engenders are also a fertile breeding-ground for worthless treatments and fanciful theories of causation. In the last twenty years there have been claims that schizophrenia can be cured with novel forms of psychotherapy, by special diets, and by massive doses of vitamin B. Others have asserted that it is not an illness at all. To R. D. Laing it is the only rational way of coming to terms with an insane world; to some sociologists it is merely a convenient label used by society for coping with troublesome deviants; to Thomas Szasz (*Schizophrenia. The Sacred Symbol of Psychiatry*, 1979) it simply 'does not exist'.

Despite much research, the cause or causes of schizophrenia remain elusive and no specific neuropathology has ever been identified. It is well established that the lateral ventricles of the brain are often modestly enlarged, but it is still unclear whether this is a direct manifestation of the disease process, or merely a predisposing factor. It has also been established, by postmortem studies, that the number of dopamine receptors in parts of the basal ganglia of the brain is increased in chronic schizophrenia, but again it is uncertain whether this is a fundamental abnormality or a secondary consequence of neuroleptic treatment. Psychological and psychophysiological researches have not been any more successful, though it is clear that the eye movements of schizophrenics are abnormal, and also that there is often a disturbance in the distribution of functions between the two cerebral hemispheres.

There is also evidence to suggest that schizophrenics have difficulty processing incoming information, both auditory and visual; they find it hard to distinguish the relevant from the irrelevant, and their performance on a variety of perceptual and other psychological tests differs from that of other people. But the range of variation is wide and there is always a considerable overlap between them and normal people. There is no doubt, however, that schizophrenia is, at least in part, transmitted genetically. Several studies in Europe and North America have shown not only that the illness runs in families, and that the concordance rate is consistently higher in uniovular (identical) than in binovular (non-identical) twins, but also that the offspring of schizophrenic parents have a high risk of developing the illness even if they are separated from them soon after birth and adopted by other people. The mode of transmission remains uncertain, but is probably polygenic, like height and hypertension.

There is also no doubt that environmental factors are important. Uniovular twins, being derived from a single fertilized ovum, are genetically identical, but if one of the pair develops schizophrenia, there is less than a 50:50 chance that the other will do the same, and this fact alone is proof of the importance of environmental influences. But we have little idea what these environmental factors are, or whether they act in childhood or shortly before the onset of the illness. In the 1960s there were claims that the childhood relationship between the patient and his mother, and emotional strains within the family as a whole, were the crucial factors—that some mothers or families were so pathological that they eventually drove their children into madness. However, the few established facts in this area are all capable of alternative explanations, and it is irresponsible and heartless to suggest to a distraught parent that she is responsible for her child's illness, when there is no real evidence to that effect. There is evidence, though, that the onset of the illness is often preceded by stressful events (like being called up for military service or spurned by a girl-friend) and also evidence that relapses are commoner in schizophrenics living with relatives who nag or criticize them than in those living in more tranquil settings. So it is clear that emotional or psychological factors must be involved, directly or indirectly, in causation.

Because so little is known about its aetiology, schizophrenia has to be defined, and diagnosed, largely on clinical grounds. In consequence, as with other diagnoses which cannot be confirmed by laboratory tests, usage of the term is liable to vary from place to place. Indeed, major international differences in usage were identified in the 1960s, American and Russian psychiatrists, in particular, using the term much more freely and loosely than psychiatrists elsewhere. (It was mainly in these same two countries, and this was probably no coincidence, that psychiatrists were accused of abusing the diagnosis and labelling as schizophrenic people who were really perfectly sane, but who were a nuisance to their families or the state, and incarcerating them in hospitals to receive treatments they did not require.) In the last decade, the adoption of unambiguous operational definitions, at least for research purposes, has reduced the confusion; though the coexistence of several alternative ways of defining the term still means that a diagnosis of schizophrenia may have a somewhat different meaning in different centres.

In the past, most schizophrenics spent most of their lives in hospital, but since the 1950s the course of the illness has been greatly improved by the discovery of the tranquillizing effects of the phenothiazines. The efficacy of these and other neuroleptic drugs, both in controlling the acute illness and in reducing the risk of relapse, is well proved and almost certainly depends on the fact that they inhibit transmission in dopaminergic neurone systems in the brain. Unfortunately, because dopaminergic neurones (i.e. brain cells which use dopamine as their transmitter substance) are also involved in the extrapyramidal motor system, these drugs are all liable to produce troublesome restlessness in the legs (akathisia), involuntary movements (tardive dyskinesia) and Parkinsonism as side effects.

There have also been important social changes in the last thirty years which have probably contributed as much to the improved outlook as these neuroleptics. Partly as a result of legal changes embodied in the Mental Health Act of 1959, partly as a result of increased public tolerance, and partly because of the growing realization by psychiatrists themselves that life in the huge asylums (which they inherited from their Victorian predecessors) increased rather than reduced the disabilities of their patients, the last two decades have seen a substantial change in policy. Instead of being allowed, or compelled, to remain in hospital as long as their illness persisted, patients are now discharged as soon as possible, and if they relapse and have to be readmitted they are discharged again as soon as their acute symptoms are controlled. In this way the evils of 'Institutionalization' are avoided, and many schizophrenics who in the past would have spent forty or fifty years in an asylum are now able to live useful and even happy lives. There are times, however, when contemporary enthusiasm for 'community care' (and for closing hospitals in order to save money) is taken too far and the emotional and practical burdens which a chronic schizophrenic may place on a family are too readily overlooked. There are still situations in which the most humane course is to provide the patient with asylum from a world he can no longer comprehend or cope with.

R. E. KENDELL

STRESS. Why has the problem of stress become a major issue of our time? Can it really be that life conditions in our society are more stressful, more taxing, than those experienced by our ancestors? From a material standpoint the answer to this question is, of course: no. The conditions in contemporary society are less stressful than those that have been experienced by any previous generation. But our age has its own problems, many of them psychological and social in nature; and we do not need to be starved, or cold, or physically exhausted for stress to occur. Life in technologically advanced societies imposes new demands which trigger the same bodily responses that helped our ancestors to survive by making them fit for fight or flight—responses that may be totally inappropriate for coping with the stresses of life today.

Stress may be regarded as a process of transactions in which the resources of the person are matched against the demands of the environment. The individual's appraisal of the importance of the demands is reflected in the bodily resources mobilized to meet them.

Man as a 'stressometer'. One of the notions underlying the use of physiological and chemical techniques in human stress research is that the load that a particular environment places on a person can be estimated by measuring the activity of the body's organ systems. Technological advances, together with progress in the biobehavioural and biomedical sciences, have made new methods available for investigating the interplay between mental and physical processes.

Much of what was previously the subject of speculation can now be recorded and measured, and as more of what happens in the different bodily organs becomes accessible to measurement, the effects that mental and physical processes have on one another become increasingly clear. We can record changes in heart-rate that accompany changes in the environment. We can show how psychological processes are reflected in the activity of the brain, in cardiovascular functions, in hormonal activity, etc.; and we can see how hormonal changes reflect changes in mood, how blood-pressure rises to challenge, and how the alertness of the brain varies with the flow of impressions transmitted by the sense organs.

Since feelings and perceptions are reflected in the activity of many of the body's organ systems, individuals can themselves be regarded as 'stress-ometers', instruments which help to identify factors in the environment that tell hard on their mind and body. The environmental factors may be physical or chemical, such as noise or smell; or social and psychological, such as monotonous work, excessive information flow, or interpersonal conflict.

With the development of chemical techniques that permit the determination of small amounts of hormones and transmitter substances in blood and urine, neuroendocrinology has come to play an increasingly important part in stress research. Two neuroendocrine systems, both of which are controlled by the brain, are of particular interest in the study of stress and coping with stressful situations. One is the sympathetic-adrenal medullary system, with the secretion of the catecholamines adrenaline (epinephrine) and noradrenaline (norepinephrine). The other is the pituitary-adrenal cortical system, with the secretion of cortisol. These substances have several important functions: as sensitive indicators of the mismatch between the person and the environment, as regulators of vital bodily functions, and—under some circumstances—as mediators of bodily reactions leading to disease.

What do we know about the environmental conditions that activate these two systems?

Underload and overload. Stimulus underload and overload are typical features of modern society, and both of them trigger the adrenal medullary and adrenal cortical response. In order to function adequately, the human brain requires an inflow of impulses from the external environment; but both lack and excess of stimulation threaten the homeostatic mechanisms by which the organism maintains an adequate degree of arousal. The optimal level of human functioning is located at the mid-point of a scale ranging between very low and very high levels of stimulus input. At the optimal level, the brain is moderately aroused, the individual's resources are mobilized, and full attention is given to the surroundings; he is emotionally balanced and performs to the best of his abilities. At low levels he tends to be inattentive, easily distracted, and bored. Conditions of extreme understimulation, involving both sensory and social deprivation, are accompanied by a state of mental impoverishment with loss of initiative and loss of capacity for involvement. When the brain is over-aroused, on the other hand, the ability to respond selectively to the impinging signals is impaired. Feelings of excitement and tension develop, followed by a gradual fragmentation of thought processes, a loss of ability to integrate the messages into a meaningful whole, impaired judgement, and loss of initiative.

Helplessness. Psychological theories of helplessness emphasize the role of learning in the development of active coping strategies. A sense of hopelessness, paired with a reduced motivation to control, is likely to develop when people realize that events and outcomes are independent of their actions. Empirical evidence from many sources, including both animal and human experiments, shows that the organism responds differently to conditions characterized by controllability on the one hand, and lack of control on the other. On the whole it is consistent with the view that increased controllability reduces physiological stress responses, such as adrenaline and cortisol secretion, thus presumably decreasing bodily wear and tear.

Is stress dangerous to health? There is general agreement that mental stress may increase the risk of ill health and affect the course of both somatic and mental disorders. But the biological mechanisms by which stress translates into disease are still obscure. Relationships exist between stress and diseases such as myocardial infarction, high blood-pressure, gastro-intestinal disorders, asthma, and migraine; however, it is only occasionally that a particular mental factor can be identified as the specific cause of a disease. As a general rule the psychological aspect is merely one thread in a complex fabric in which genetic components, environmental conditions, and learned behaviours are also interwoven.

This lack of a clear picture of the links in the causal chain between stress and disease hampers our efforts to prevent harmful stress responses. However, we know a great deal about the mobilization of stress hormones under conditions of underload and overload, and although it is still not known when such stress responses lead to ill health it is agreed that they should be treated as early warning signals. Moreover, we also know a great deal about how stress that is liable to impair health can be counteracted. Stress responses can be dampened, for instance, by providing opportunities for personal control, which can then serve as buffer, warding off potentially harmful effects of, for example, overload at work.

In short, stress research has already contributed knowledge that can be used to shape the external environment so as to fit human abilities and needs. Such insights are being utilized more and more, particularly in working life, both in the organization of work and in the application of new technology.

MARIANNE FRANKENHAEUSER

SUICIDAL BEHAVIOUR. Man's ability to kill himself has been a source of fascination since the beginning of human society. Philosophers from Marcus Aurelius and Seneca to Camus, writers (especially poets) from Virgil to Sylvia Plath, and sociologists from the beginning of the nineteenth century to the present day, have all contributed voluminously to its study. This widespread preoccupation has, if anything, obstructed the scientific investigation of suicide in two distinct ways. Firstly, the long-standing theological taboo against suicide, still discernible in many legal phrases and public attitudes, has tended to make the rational consideration of the subject difficult. Secondly, speculation on the theme has tended to spread over all forms of human activity which are potentially harmful or self-defeating, with a consequence that there is remarkably little that people can do which has not been interpreted as concealing some measure of suicidal intent. Clearly for scientific purposes it is necessary to use a much more precise definition.

In the first place, attention is confined to acts in which self-destruction is the essential component and not simply a hazard incurred in the course of pursuing another goal. Thus the religious martyr, or the soldier who has volunteered for a dangerous mission during which he dies, are not usually considered as suicides. Secondly, suicide is taken to refer to the behaviour of an individual and not a group, so that expressions such as a suicidal policy being pursued by a nation are to be understood as metaphorical. And lastly, present-day usage restricts the term to human beings; the notorious lemmings are firmly excluded.

Though often difficult to assess, intention thus becomes a central issue in categorizing deaths in which the deceased was an active agent. The law in most European countries requires clear demonstration not only that an individual caused his own death, but that he fully intended to do so. Psychiatrists and behavioural scientists would in general assert that this criterion is too narrow and that assessment should be made on the balance of probabilities, recognizing that a certain number of deaths will be unclassifiable. The important practical point is that official statistics tend markedly to underestimate the incidence of suicide according to psychiatric criteria. Additional reasons for under-reporting are a desire by families and general practitioners to conceal suicidal deaths in some cases, and a reluctance of coroners to reach the decision in an open court for fear of causing offence or having their verdicts challenged in, or reversed by, a higher court. Various studies suggest that the order of magnitude of under-reporting is in the region of between 50 and 100 per cent. Nevertheless, official statistics have been widely used and have proved valuable for certain types of enquiry.

A great deal of literature exists on the epidemiology of suicide. Virtually throughout the world the rate for men exceeds that for women, with the former tending to use more violent methods such as shooting or jumping from heights, and the latter more passive procedures such as taking an excess of drugs. However, these differences are rapidly disappearing in most European countries. Where the rate for males is falling, that for females tends to remain stationary or fall more slowly; conversely, where the rate for males is increasing, that for females increases even more rapidly. Either way the net effect is towards equality, often interpreted in a rather vague way as reflecting the tendency in recent decades for the social roles of the two sexes to become more similar.

The effects of age are complex and interact with those of sex. In the United Kingdom the rates for males rise linearly with age, though in most developed countries, the curve resembles an inverted U, with the peak in the late fifties or sixties. For women, both in the United Kingdom and elsewhere, this latter pattern has always been the one most commonly reported. In general, suicide is very much a phenomenon of later life, suggesting that Shakespeare was correct in asserting that 'men have died . . . and worms have eaten them, but not for love'. Furthermore, old age is often accompanied by painful illness and chronic impairment of health. Such misfortunes may well precipitate a state of severe depression, when suicidal thoughts and acts commonly occur.

But what is currently true for Europe is not necessarily true for all times at all places. In Japan before the Second World War, for example, there was a distinct peak in the suicide rates for people in their late twenties and early thirties, which then fell away before the rate increased again among the elderly. Commentators ascribed this early peak to the complex and often contradictory social obligations which befell young married Japanese *vis-à-vis* their respective families. With the Americanization of Japan following the war, this early age peak virtually disappeared, and the general shape of the curve now approximates that of the United States.

In the United Kingdom suicide became increasingly common from 1945 until the early 1960s. There then followed a decline in the rates for all age-sex groups, entirely attributable to the progressive elimination of carbon monoxide from domestic gas, and the virtual disappearance of suicide by this method. This dramatic decline was unexpected. One might have supposed that anyone intent upon killing themselves would use any method to hand and that lack of availability of one particular agent would scarcely make any difference. The facts, however, point in the contrary direction. Extensive research, including for example studies on immigrants from different countries to Australia, has shown that the mode of suicide is strongly influenced by cultural attitudes which appear to favour one method in preference to others. More recently the UK rates have resumed their upward trend.

The role of cultural proscription or prescription has already been hinted at, and a number of sociological theories have been proposed which might account for the differences between societies in their suicide rates, differences which often remain surprisingly stable for sustained periods of time. Of the numerous hypotheses that have been advanced, the social cohesion theory developed by Durkheim and his followers still retains the widest support. On this view social cohesion minimizes the risk of suicide, whereas situations in which individuals are dissociated from their groups (leading to *egoistic* suicides), or live in communities that have no adequate normative values and beliefs to meet current social realities (*anomie*), conduce to suicide. The precise meaning of notions such as social cohesion or anomie is debatable, but it is empirically true that the suicide rates are particularly high among the divorced, among childless women, among those living alone, the retired or unemployed, and where populations are highly mobile or subject to economic uncertainty. Conversely, situations which promote social cohesion tend to lower suicide rates, and of these the classical example is the threat of war. In both World Wars suicide rates fell in practically all countries, both belligerent and neutral.

While social factors undoubtedly influence suicide rates, patients with conditions such as severe depression, alcoholism, or epilepsy all have increased risks of dying by suicide. Reviews of comprehensive series of suicidal deaths have now established that the great majority of such individuals were suffering from a clearly recognizable psychiatric illness at the time of their death. In England and Wales the commonest such disorder is the depressive phase of manic-depressive psychosis (see **mental illness**), often triggered by bereavement. In Scotland and in the United States alcoholism is almost as prominent as depression. It also appears that social factors act as additional determinants *within* groups of depressives or alcoholics. Thus among all depressives those who are socially isolated, etc., have an appreciably higher risk of suicide than the remainder. It appears that social and psychological factors are necessary (though not sufficient) causes of suicide.

Such a sweeping statement begs the question of whether there exists such a thing as a rational suicide. The formulation which comes nearest to such a possibility is Durkheim's description of 'altruistic suicide', which he believed occurred only in communities that had extremely rigid codes of conduct, such as the army in the nineteenth century. The notion that death was to be preferred to dishonour, a sentiment which goes back at least to Roman times, was not simply an empty phrase. It is also said that elderly Eskimos kill themselves in times of food shortage to help preserve the family. However, it appears that under normal circumstances rational suicide is exceedingly rare, if indeed it exists at all. The nearest approach is possibly the not uncommon phenomenon of an individual who kills himself during the course of a painful terminal illness in order, presumably, to put an end to intolerable suffering. Even so, many such individuals show an impaired ability to adjust to their disorder as compared with the majority of sufferers. Severe depression (or alcoholism) may of course also be features of a painful and chronic illness.

Whatever the social and clinical context, the meaning of the suicidal act may vary considerably between individuals. For some, death represents simply a termination. For many others the situation is more complex; suicide notes frequently reflect a theme such as reunion with someone who has already died, or imply that the individual will in some way continue and be able to monitor the activities of his survivors. A desire to inflict revenge on others through their guilt and remorse over the death is often evident. Indeed, a multiplicity of motives which, from a narrow logical point of view, may be mutually incompatible may be displayed. The supremely 'personal' action of suicide may, at the same time, be intensely 'interpersonal' or social. (Some psychologists would aver that ultimately there is no distinction between the two.)

Nothing has been said so far of so-called 'attempted suicide', which in the United Kingdom, at least, is overwhelmingly represented by drug overdoses. The term 'attempted suicide' is profoundly misleading; for the majority of such patients suicide is not what they are attempting. Indeed, advances in the study of the phenomenon have only become possible since it was realized that these individuals do not represent failed suicides, but rather something which, though having a loose behavioural analogy with suicide, should be viewed as a more or less distinct variety of behaviour. To this end the term 'parasuicide' has been introduced.

From the epidemiological point of view suicide and parasuicide are markedly different. Whereas suicides tend to be male, and in the second half of life, the great majority of parasuicides are female and in their teens or twenties. Suicide is prevalent among the widowed and the single, whereas parasuicide tends to be commonest among the married. Suicide is notable among the physically infirm and the socially isolated, whereas parasuicide has no such association with physical illness, and tends to be commoner among those who are living in congested, overcrowded conditions. Depressive illness and alcoholism certainly figure prominently among parasuicides, but are usually much less severe than among suicides; while lesser emotional disturbance, induced by interpersonal conflicts and other intercurrent events, assumes a much greater significance: an appreciable minority of parasuicides appear to be free of any kind of psychiatric disorder, unless of course the act itself is taken as sufficient evidence of disorder. Whereas, according to the latest figures, suicide shows no obvious social class gradient, parasuicide is very much less common in the upper than in the lower social classes.

Parasuicide is vastly more frequent than completed suicide, and from what has been said it will be appreciated that the magnitude of the ratio varies by age and sex. Thus, among men aged 55 and over, the excess is approximately threefold, while for young women below the age of 35 it is in the region of two-hundredfold.

From a clinical-descriptive viewpoint, the typical parasuicide tends to have had a disrupted and disadvantaged childhood, often in a broken home. She will be living in a state of conflict with her family of origin, or of procreation, or both; among men a story of trouble with the law and of interpersonal violence is common, as is excessive drinking. In association with these difficulties the patient becomes anxious and depressed, and in response to a crisis or a quarrel takes an overdose of pills (or more rarely deliberately causes self-injury).

The details of the psychological processes involved in the genesis of the act are still unclear, and often the patient herself is confused as to what, if anything, she intended. But certain broad themes can be discerned. A wish for a temporary respite, analogous to getting blind drunk, is one common component. In a minority, a desire to die or an indifference to survival will be reported, or may be inferred. Another very important aspect of parasuicide is its communication function, the much-cited 'cry for help'. Unfortunately the cry so produced may or may not lead to the hoped-for response, since families and friends may as readily pick up the aggressive overtones of the act—the hint of 'I'll die, and then you'll be sorry'.

Parasuicide may, thus, serve a number of purposes; but it is perhaps the communication aspect which is of particular interest. If the act does indeed serve as a means of conveying information, then it can be argued that it is a form of 'language' of a rather special kind. Consequently it could be predicted that the patient would commonly be found among a group of individuals who share a propensity to parasuicide when under stress. This supposition has been empirically confirmed. The concept also points the way to the study of parasuicide as a social institution, and here too the evidence suggests that communities exist in which parasuicide appears to have a more or less standard preformed 'meaning'.

Finally, having stressed the numerous differences between completed suicide and parasuicide, it is necessary to point out that there is also an important overlap between the two. About half of all completed suicides are preceded by a parasuicide. Conversely, if a representative sample of parasuicides is followed up, about 1 per cent would be found to die by suicide in the ensuing year (which is about a hundred times greater than would be expected for the general population), and the increased risk of an eventual suicide persists for many years. Subgroups at high and low risk of later suicide can be identified, but no parasuicide should be dismissed a priori as trivial. N. KREITMAN

TERROR is the specific fear that some evil event or action is going to occur. Its origins go back to the notion of trembling. Strictly speaking, it should be distinguished from horror in that horror implies something disgusting and negative, whereas terror does not.

In the field of myth, terror has often been associated with visitations from an all-powerful god controlling life and death in a seemingly indiscriminate manner. The Delphic oracle went into a kind of trance or frenzy, during which the awesome god spoke through the prophetess. All this, even the ambiguities of the prophecies themselves, was designed to inspire fear of the god in the onlookers.

Terror appears to fit into the category of instinct-response which humans share with most animals. For example, most humans and animals fear the sight of mutilated bodies. Experiments with chimpanzees during which the animals were shown pictures of chimpanzees with their heads or limbs cut off elicited instinct-responses of extreme trepidation. This fear of violence done to the body is at the basis of the terror process.

In the ancient world terror was the basis of tyranny, as in Rome under Marius and Sulla. Historically many political leaders have chosen to rule by terror tactics rather than customary, legal means—that is, by the systematic use of violence to inhibit political opposition. Present-day acts of 'terrorism' bear a different sense, as they are designed to disrupt a given system by violent actions.

While the causes of terror have changed over the centuries, the human mind continues to be highly susceptible to it. Our ancestors gathered round lighted fires not only to keep warm but to ward off 'the terror by night': there were terrifying animals lurking in the darkness. The 'night-light' in a child's room reflects this fear of darkness, of the unseen and the unknown. Even so, most humans seem to enjoy the feeling of terror under controlled conditions. Grandmothers have traditionally told tales of terror around the fireplace to countless generations of children, in a role which today has been supplanted by the so-called horror film. Perhaps the monsters who march across the screen are designed to purge the real monsters within the human psyche.

Contemporary science and technology have created new sources of terror, such as the threat of nuclear annihilation and highly sophisticated means of electronic surveillance and control of human behaviour. Modern adult human beings may no longer fear the presence of huge animals in the darkness, but most humans experience terror born from technology.

RAYMOND T. MCNALLY

6: MINDS IN ACTION

1. Driving a Car

Accident proneness	Learning and learning theory
Attention	Memory for skills
Automatization	Skill
Fatigue	Time-gap experience

For most of the adult population driving a car is a simple activity that can be undertaken while holding a conversation, listening to the radio, or reflecting on the day's activities. But it was not always so simple, and an analysis of the component skills reveals just how remarkable it is that so much of our driving is error-free. Such an analysis suggests that the demands of performing multiple activities must exceed our abilities and that driving is theoretically impossible—a conclusion supported by the impressions of many learners.

During the process of **learning** to drive we are only too aware of attending to the acquisition of information while making simultaneous responses. The problem is overcome, with practice, in a number of ways. First, experienced drivers can allocate their **attention** according to learned priorities. There are critical times when it is necessary to look in the driving mirror, for instance, and the experienced driver will tend to be selective in allocating attention to the events displayed in the mirror. When priority tasks such as steering and keeping the engine running are more demanding, the experienced driver will not allocate attention to non-priority tasks such as environmental adjustments (heating, radio, seat position). These are voluntary actions that we can choose to make at any time, and with the acquisition of **skill** the driver will perform actions according to their priority. Skilled drivers are likely to be reminded of the difficulties of learning to drive when, having become familiar with the instrument and control layout of a car, they first drive a different car. New configurations must be learned and errors will appear as a consequence of old and now inappropriate stimulus-response relationships. We may attempt to indicate a change of direction and find ourselves, embarrassingly, turning on the windscreen wipers. In an extreme case of a changed configuration, we may find ourselves driving on the wrong side of the road with our first experience of a right-hand road traffic system (as on mainland Europe), after a driving experience that has been based exclusively in Britain. The transfer of training from one car to another, or from one traffic system to another, can be rapid, showing learning gains from previous experience, but it is not without its face-reddening moments (see also **memory for skills**).

The second way in which competing tasks can be performed simultaneously also comes with extensive practice. Actions that are performed frequently will also be less disruptive because they have become automatized and can be initiated and executed without attention (see **automatization**). This is sometimes described in terms of the distinction between controlled or conscious activity, and automatic or attention-free activity. Automatic activities develop with extensive practice; they are performed smoothly and efficiently; they are resistant to modification through further learning; they are unaffected by other concurrent activities; they do not interfere with other activities; they are initiated without intention; and they do not require mental effort. One consequence of behaviour being executed automatically is the appearance of **time-gaps** during which our minds are so completely engrossed in other thoughts that complex activities are performed without leaving a memory record. Time-gaps are particularly familiar to experienced drivers who travel the same routes regularly. There is some argument over the question of whether individual activities fall into one or either category of being under automatic or conscious control, or whether all activities fall along a continuum. It seems unlikely that all activities are either one or the other, and although a whole activity may not be automatic (like driving) there may be component processes within the skill that are (like changing gear). The appearance of time-gaps also suggests that an activity that is usually under conscious control can be automatic on occasions.

Driving can be thought of as a multi-level activity. At a micro-level we must control the vehicle from moment-to-moment, acquiring visual information from the road environment and from the vehicle instruments, acquiring information about the vehicle itself (such as engine speed and positions of the controls), and using this information to make changes. Responses at the micro-level include steering, changing gear, initiating the direction indicators, and using the foot pedals to effect changes in speed and as part of the gear-change routine. At this level there are also a number of less essential activities such as making adjustments to the driving mirror, to the car radio, and to the heating controls. Each of these responses depends upon spatial co-ordination of the senses, using micro-level knowledge of the effects of movements of our limbs, as well as higher level knowledge of the position of the vehicle relative to the road environment. In both cases we need to learn the effects of our actions on the actions of the vehicle, but in the case of position in the road environment the vehicle itself can be thought of as an extension of the driver's body. The problem of sensorimotor co-ordination then becomes one of calibrating what actions (within the vehicle) are necessary to take the vehicle from its current position to the desired position. To optimize control, vehicles are ideally designed according to principles of ergonomics that enable the driver to extract information from the instruments and adjust the controls easily and without error. For instance, rarely used instruments should not be positioned in the line of sight, and non-essential controls should not be positioned at the driver's fingertips. The internal design of the vehicle's cockpit can incorporate important safety features such as side-impact protection bars and anti-lock braking systems; ergonomic designs result in reduced driver **fatigue** and consequently reduced accident liability.

An analysis of the causes of road accidents must be as complex as the analysis of the skill of driving itself. A list of potential contributory causes would include ergonomic factors, such as an arrangement of controls and instruments that diverts attention away from the road for a long period. Individual driver differences are also related to accident liability. For instance, a driver may be easily distracted, or have long reaction times, or fail to recognize potentially hazardous situations; each of these factors depends upon the extent and type of training received, and upon the extent of driving experience. Drivers are sometimes labelled with the contentious characteristic of **accident proneness**. In addition, if a particular road layout makes demands of drivers that exceed their psychological abilities, then a number of accidents will appear in one location, and an accident black spot will be identified. In this case the design of the environment would be considered a contributory factor—as when, for example, a road with a high speed limit admits traffic from an occluded side road. The current development of research on driving behaviour by psychologists is not only an indication of a theoretical interest in the analysis of a complex skill, but is also of importance in reducing the number of road accidents.

ACCIDENT PRONENESS is a deceptively easy term. We all know what it means but we do not all mean the same thing. Since the ambiguities arise partly because of the way we speak about accidents, it may be helpful to clarify this term.

An accident refers to the results of an action, generally to an unplanned, even an unexpected result. It has been described as 'an error with sad consequences', but the relationship between the preceding behaviour and the consequences is not at all simple. A time-honoured example of an accident is a person falling flat as he slips on a banana-skin—an act, incidentally, that few have ever witnessed and which conveys the impression that the world at one time must have been littered with banana-skins. In such an example the person who slips has the accident for which he was partly responsible. But we also speak of someone having an accident when something falls on him. *A* spills a cup of tea over *B* and we say that *B* has suffered an accident. To add to the confusion, different kinds of action result in similar accidents, while the same act often has very different results. Hence, if we are to understand accidents we need to understand the preceding behaviour. But accident data are usually only records of the outcome of actions.

There is a further complication. It is a feature of accident statistics that the more severe the accident (particularly a fatal injury), the more accurate is the record. But the majority of accidents are relatively trivial, and in our society the greatest number occur in the home and often go unrecorded. The basis for extrapolation, therefore, is somewhat shaky. Nevertheless we can be confident that over the years the trend of incidence in different kinds of activities has shifted. Industrial accidents are no longer the major component; rather, the home and transport make up the bulk of the total. This shift is important, for a quick inspection of a nation's annual accident data shows such regularity from year to year that it might be concluded that accidents were an inevitable consequence of man's mobility. Closer scrutiny reveals that within the total of accidents the pattern has shifted from one class of accidents to another.

Within this general framework, it is accepted that the risks inherent in some activities are greater than in others and that the chances of accident also fluctuate with varying environmental conditions: changes in lighting, humidity, temperature, for example. The behaviour of the individual is the common factor, and inevitably explanation has been sought of the proneness to accident. The direct question has been asked: in the same circumstances, do individuals differ in their liability to accident? In everyday thinking about skilled actions, some individuals would be more proficient than others; conversely, some individuals would be less so, and to that extent they would have more accidents. This straightforward and rather simple line of thought presumed that a single measure of overall performance provided a reliable index of the skill of a performer. But a performer's degree of skill is not necessarily an index to his liability to accident. A palpably poor driver of a car may be aware of his fallibility and drive more cautiously, with the result that he has fewer accidents than a skilful but over-confident driver. It is necessary to analyse the skill in some detail if it is to provide a guide to accident liability.

Even so, accepting for the moment that we may use an overall measure, it is easy enough to demonstrate in statistical data that some individuals over a limited time-period incur more accidents than others. It is tempting to infer that this identifies those who are more liable to have accidents—the accident-prone. But, of course, such an inference is not necessarily justified. In a normal distribution of random events over a sample time-period, some will occur more frequently than others.

Early research workers, such as Greenwood and Yule (1920), were well aware of these attractive fallacies and, though their data indicated that some individuals had incurred a high proportion of the accidents in situations where other factors were equal, they stressed the need for caution. But in 1926 Farmer and Chambers suggested the term 'accident proneness' for this liability to incur accidents, and such is the power of an attractive label that it was universally accepted, not as a tentative guess to be examined by further research, as they proposed, but as an established fact. The concept of accident proneness was taken a stage further by Flanders Dunbar in America who claimed that a personality trait of accident proneness was proven fact. She gave psychodynamic interpretations which claimed that persons involved in repeated accidents had some unconscious need for physical trauma. Later she had to modify her original views about accident proneness being an enduring personality trait when it was pointed out that some of these so-called accident-prone personalities ceased to have accidents as they grew older.

The history is typical of what happens when scientific ideas are accepted on too little evidence. For a time accident proneness became the major explanatory concept in its field; then in the 1940s doubts began to creep in and by the 1950s careful assessments were pointing out that the evidence was insufficient. Soon opposition swung well beyond this point, as in the highly critical major review of Haddon, Suchman, and Klein (1964). During the 1960s, the fact that the statistical evidence failed to demonstrate the existence of accident proneness was interpreted as a refutation of all hypotheses relating to it. The pendulum had to swing back, and in 1971 Shaw published her comprehensive analysis of accident proneness. She avoided an extreme position. She conceded that many characteristics of behaviour change with age and that it is not true that most accidents are sustained by a small number of people. But she examined in detail earlier studies and demonstrated the importance of certain factors such as attention (defined as the ability to choose quickly and perform a correct response to a sudden stimulus), the stability of behaviour, and the involuntary control of motor behaviour. She supported the study of car drivers—'a man drives as he lives'—and the finding that a bad civil record tends to indicate a bad accident risk.

Where does this leave accident proneness? In spite of, perhaps because of, much contentious writing the problem is still with us and becoming of increasing importance as accidents, the twentieth-century disease, assume an ever greater significance in mortality rates. Now, if accident data are not recording behaviour directly but its consequences, then the less the probability of an accident following an action, the more insensitive the data as an index of behaviour. Little can be inferred about, say, the behaviour of pedestrians at railway level crossings from accident data for, fortunately, there is little data—but what if behaviour could be recorded directly? In general the problem would be lessened, given guidance on the kinds of behaviour that cause accidents, or if the number of situations that have to be studied were reduced. Some beginnings have been made with detailed examinations of the behaviour of drivers on the roads, and these should be extended into the home and to other everyday situations. An understanding is required of the basis of human skills, and fortunately advances have now been made in this field of study. When a human operator is carrying out a skill, he is receiving signals from several sensory modalities and initiating responses to them. The whole process is conceived as an information loop. The operator is in the centre and the information is measured statistically in terms of the probability of the signals. Though this concept may seem at first sight a little removed from everyday thinking, a moment's reflection will show that it is not. We expect to see certain things under certain conditions and we know how we shall respond. For example, it is no surprise to drive round a corner and see another car; it would be to see an elephant. And evidence shows we respond more quickly to the car than we would to the elephant, or, to put it another way, the more certain the signal, the less information in a statistical sense it carries. If, then, we conceive of a skill as processing information, one essential is for the operator to reduce the amount of information by anticipating the probability of different signals. It is a truism to say that accidents occur when the operator has too much information to process in too little time. One way to handle such situations is to know which events are likely to occur.

But although a sensitive analysis may be made of human skills, and insight gained into how a person's propensities vary with different tasks and at different stages of his life, knowledge of how performance is affected by the personality of the individual is still sketchy. Over and above the psychomotor skill itself, there is further influence reflecting the personal qualities of the performer, and exactly how this affects accident proneness is not known. The influence differs according to the state of fatigue or the vigilance of the operator, to the difficulty or length of the task, to the importance of the occasion, and so forth This area requires much more study, but we see its importance exemplified in the case of age. It is often said, 'Tell me a person's age and I will tell you what accidents he may have'. The under-25s contribute disproportionately to road accidents the world over (seen even when experience is held constant over different age-groups). Similarly the over-65s contribute a large proportion of the psychomotor accidents in the home, which are generally due to falls as control deteriorates. It is a question of coming to terms with the varying skills we possess as life advances. Finally, there is the puzzling and recurring example of accidents that turn out to be anything but accidental. Investigation into the antecedent history of the individual in these cases suggests that the behaviour causing the accident was highly predictable and that the accident had the inevitability of Greek tragedy. It was fitting that Michael Ayrton added a new dimension to the classical myth of Daedalus and his son Icarus; under his interpretation it was no mischance that Icarus flew too close to the sun god, Apollo, and thereby caused the wax of his wings to melt: it was his act of challenge and defiance.

HARRY KAY

ATTENTION. The nervous systems of living creatures are subjected to far more stimulation than can be used. On the one hand, the sense organs receive stimuli of great variety. On the other, memories, images and ideas arise internally and must be considered from moment to moment. Yet it is a commonplace that we are consciously aware of only a limited amount of this information at any moment. The operation by which a person selects information in attention, and its study, have twice been seen as central to research on our understanding of how information is processed by humans and animals.

The first great period was around 1900, when James, Titchener, Wundt, and Pillsbury all wrote of attention at length. William James, on this as on so many other topics, described the main characteristics of attention with precision. Attention was, for him 'the taking possession by the mind, in clear and vivid form, of one of what seem simultaneously possible objects or trains of thought'. Titchener and his students, in particular, carried out an extensive experimental programme into such topics as 'prior entry' and the conditions of binocular rivalry and fluctuations of attention. The first of these was the observation that of two simultaneous events, the one to which attention was diverted appeared to occur earlier than the other.

The fundamental property of attention was, for those workers, to make the contents of consciousness appear clearer. It would have made little sense to them to discuss effects of attention of which the observer was not aware. Pillsbury's book *Attention*, published in 1908, contains many observations which modern work has confirmed, and is a remarkably insightful volume in many respects.

With the rise of behaviourism, attention was relegated to the status of a mental function which could not be admitted as a suitable object for research. Indeed, for some thirty years it disappeared from indexes and reviews. The second golden age of attention research dates from the early 1950s, and received a particular impetus with the publication of *Perception and Communication* by Donald Broadbent in 1958. A major reason for the renewed interest was the need for the solution of new practical problems, such as the design of control towers and communication networks in the Second World War. A controller might receive several messages at once from different aircraft or ships, and be required to make appropriate responses to each. With an attempt to understand how humans behaved in such situations, modern work on attention began. It was aided by the invention of the tape recorder, which for the first time allowed the ready control and replicability of speech signals, while the phenomenon of stereophony provided an easy way of varying the content and amount of information in competing messages.

Broadbent's filter theory tried to explain how the brain coped with the information overload caused by having many sense organs receiving information simultaneously. Drawing an analogy with electronic communication theory, he proposed that there is in the brain a single central information channel whose rate of information-processing is rather limited. This channel could select only one sensory input channel at a time, and could switch no more than about twice a second between input channels. To accept an input was equivalent to paying attention to that source of information, and information on unattended channels could be held in a short-term memory for a few seconds. Broadbent called the selection mechanism 'the Filter'. While he drew on many fields of research, the most direct line of evidence was the split span experiment. If three digits are read, at a rate of two per second, to the left ear of a listener, and another three to the right ear, so that the listener receives three synchronous pairs, he will recall them ear by ear, not pair by pair. Broadbent interpreted this to mean that the listener attended to one ear first and then switched to the memory trace of material in the other ear. By finding the fastest rate at which the listener could repeat the message as pairs, he believed he had measured the rate of switching of auditory attention. This concept of a single-channel, limited-capacity information processing system was central to much research in the next twenty-five years.

From about 1953 to 1963 speech shadowing was widely used by Broadbent, Neville Moray, Anne Treisman, and others. This technique had been introduced by Colin Cherry, and required a listener to repeat aloud a prose message in the presence of one or more distracting messages. It was found that major factors which aided selective attention included separation in space of the speakers, difference in voice timbre, and the statistical structure of the messages. In a series of elegant experiments Anne Treisman greatly extended our knowledge. Certain features of a distracting message proved to be potent sources of distraction, including emotional words (such as a listener's own name), contextually probable words, and—for bilingual listeners—the presence of a translation of the message to which they were listening.

However, these experiments also showed that some material, such as emotionally important words and contextually probable words, was perceived even when in the 'rejected' message. This led to a series of modifications to Broadbent's Filter theory, notably by Anne Treisman, Anthony Deutsch, and Don Norman. Although differing considerably in detail, they all attempted to account for the fact that the Filter apparently did not block all information from the rejected channels, and that selection could be not only of sensory inputs, but of such features as language, class of word, colour (in the case of visual stimuli), and even classes of responses. Attention came to be seen as acting in a variety of ways, at a variety of levels, and on a variety of operations in the nervous system.

By the middle 1960s interest had grown greatly, and a wide variety of experimental techniques were developed. In addition to speech shadowing, simultaneous auditory messages were used, requiring much simpler responses than speech. In a series of studies Moray showed that, contrary to what the early shadowing experiments seemed to indicate, attention acted in the same way on non-linguistic as on linguistic material. Others found conditions where little or no interference between two messages occurred. These arose especially when messages were presented in different sensory modalities where long practice had made performance almost automatic rather than conscious and voluntary, and when no competition between responses was required.

Visual attention was investigated by means of eye movements in such tasks as reading, by Paul Kolers, and in car driving and piloting aircraft, by John Senders. Very spectacular results were found using the 'Stroop test', in which attentional and perceptual conflict is induced by the nature of the stimulus. If the word 'red' is written in green ink, the word 'blue' in yellow ink, and so on, it is possible to read the word rapidly without the colour of the ink causing interference, but almost impossible to name the colour of the ink. Analogues of this effect provide a way of discovering which 'analysers' in the brain can be selectively biased by voluntary attention. (The word 'analyser' originated in a theory of learning and perception due to Anthony Deutsch, but its use in attention theory is largely due to Anne Treisman.)

Some attempts were made to investigate the physiological mechanisms underlying attention. For example, the 'Expectancy wave', or CNV was discovered in electroencephalographic records, a change in electrical brain activity which appears when the observer is concentrating on the imminent arrival of a signal he knows is probable. In the late 1970s Emmanuel Donehin and his colleagues began work on the 'P-300' component of the brain-evoked potential, and this seems very likely to be intimately connected with attention in the sense of decision-making. But to date our understanding of the physiological basis of attention lags a long way behind behavioural research.

More than a dozen theories of attention have been proposed since 1958, most of them strongly influenced by communication theory and computer technology. Their variety to some extent is due to the variety of phenomena which may be subsumed under the heading 'attention'. In addition to our ability to listen selectively to one message and ignore another, or to look at a picture in one colour in the presence of other colours, one may cite vigilance (or watch-keeping), in which an observer looks for very rare events, such as detecting the presence of a sonar or radar target. Some studies have been made of mental concentration on cognitive problems. The interference between internal images and incoming stimuli has been investigated, as has the ability of the brain of a sleeping person to respond selectively to the sleeper's name, even though the sleeper is not aware of the response.

Although no single theory has emerged as completely dominant, the influence of Broadbent's Filter theory remains strong, and what follows is a conflation of theories based on his suggestions. He assumed that an observer can block or weaken the strength of incoming messages to the brain, and there is ample evidence that this can happen. It is not known whether this is done by reducing the intensity of the messages or by switching them on and off rapidly. But some such blocking definitely occurs. In vision it can be done by closing the eyes or averting the gaze. In hearing the mechanism is not so clear. It seems probable that all information which impinges on the receptors of the sense organs reaches the pattern-analysing mechanisms of the brain. The Filter perhaps acts to prevent the output of these analysers from reaching consciousness, although behaviour may still be produced, as when we become aware that we have driven for some time 'without being aware of it' (see **time-gap experience**). It seems likely that information from different sense modalities, or from different dimensions within a modality (such as colour and shape), can be attended to simultaneously, at least after practice; while tasks which are very similar (such as judging the loudness of two tones) cannot. One should note that in making these assertions we are far from William James's definition. Very often the observer is conscious of only one message, but it can be shown that the second is producing behaviour simultaneously with that produced consciously.

A second way in which attention can operate is by biasing the interpretation of information proceeding from pattern analysis to consciousness. Thus a person expecting to see a bull in mist will see one, while a person expecting to see a rock will see a rock. This kind of bias is set by the probability of events, their subjectively perceived value, and contextual information derived from recent inputs and from memories. In earlier days this kind of bias was called 'mental set'.

The contents of consciousness as filtered by attention are very limited: attention is frequently modelled as a 'limited-capacity information channel'. But with practice, quite dramatic increases in performance are seen, and some writers, among whom Daniel Kahneman is particularly influential, have proposed a 'parallel processing' model of attention, in which the main limit is on the total effort available, rather than on competition between separate analysers. Such models make extensive use of the concept of arousal.

Recently, renewed interest in applications of attention has become apparent. Most of the laboratory research has been directed to understanding the internal mechanisms of attention in the brain. But as large and complex man-machine systems appear and more and more automation is introduced, there is a tremendous need for a good understanding of man as a monitor of complex systems. How should the latter be designed so as to optimize the use of attention? (It is fairly clear that in real-life tasks attention is never switched more than about twice a second.) How should a man be trained so as to combine to best effect his limited conscious attention with his unconscious control of skilled behaviour? The solution of such questions is necessary if accidents in power stations, aircraft, and industry are to be avoided. Attention theory has advanced to a point where it can give a real insight into the solution of practical problems, and there is likely to be a third age in which the precise experimental work of the 1950s to the 1970s is extended in more complex ways to solve the problems of man-machine system design in the 1980s and 1990s. We have come to see attention not merely as a single process concerned with enhancing the clarity of perception. Rather, it is a complex of skills. These include selecting one from several messages, selecting one from several interpretations of information, selecting one from several plans of action, and selecting one from several actions. But in our interactions with the rich dynamics of the world in which we live and to which we adapt, attention also models that world, and provides us with strategies and high-level control of our tactics of information sampling, optimizing our information-processing in the face of our limited processing capacities.

Developments in research since Donald Broadbent's work in the 1950s have emphasized both the conceptual richness of the concept of attention and the practical importance of an understanding of its properties. One cannot do better than conclude with an early claim of Edward Titchener's: 'The doctrine of attention is the nerve of the whole psychological system, and that as men judge of it, so shall they be judged before the general tribunal of psychology.'

NEVILLE MORAY

AUTOMATIZATION may be defined as a state in which the individual performs simple or complex actions in a skilled or relatively uncoordinated manner without having full awareness of what he is doing. Such a definition excludes purely reflex motor responses but includes well-developed skills, such as playing a musical instrument, where the individual carries out highly complex movements without detailed awareness of what he is doing. This kind of normal automatization increases with practice and the more expert the performer is, the greater will be the degree of automatization displayed.

Related to the phenomenon of automatization, which is the release of attention when we practise extensively, is the phenomenon of automatism, which is associated with psychopathological conditions. In examples such as sleep-walking and post-hypnotic states the subject may respond to signals in a manner suggested to him during the hypnotic trance. Of greater importance are post-epileptic automatisms. This term was introduced by Hughlings Jackson to describe 'all kinds of doings after epileptic fits'. These are most often witnessed following psychomotor seizures and may take the form of continuing an action being performed before the onset of the fit, or of new behaviour, simple or complex, which may although very rarely, be of such violence that serious harm is done to bystanders or any one going to the patient's help. In cases where homicide has been the outcome of a post-epileptic automatism, a plea of non-insane automatism may be accepted in place of insane automatism (a circumstance when an individual, suffering from a disease of the mind, does not know the nature and quality of the act of which he is accused). With a plea of insane automatism, the accused is likely to be found not guilty on the ground of insanity, and sent to a special hospital.

Sane automatism might be adduced in persons committing offences following an epileptic fit or during a post-concussional state. It would have to be shown that the defendant was not suffering from mental illness—disease of the mind in legal parlance.

But in a recent case the accused, an epileptic, attacked an individual who came to his help when he was recovering from a seizure. He inflicted injuries sufficiently severe to warrant a charge of causing grievous bodily harm. A plea of not guilty on the basis of his automatism was offered, but the judge directed the jury to the effect that on the evidence given a verdict of not guilty on the ground of insanity would be appropriate. In this instance the judge considered that psychomotor epilepsy had to be classed as a disease of the mind. Although his ruling was challenged it was upheld by the higher Court of Appeal. The case was further considered by the House of Lords, which concluded that a person who committed an offence while in a state of post-ictal confusion, so that he did not know what he was doing and had no recollection of the event on recovering, was insane at law. This seems to rule out pleas of sane automatism in the future but one might surmise that more will be heard of this decision as it hardly makes sense to insist that a brief disorder of brain function as in epilepsy, is equivalent to a 'disease of the mind' in the 'McNaghten Rules' (diminished responsibility) sense of words.

F. A. WHITLOCK

FATIGUE in living beings refers to deterioration of their performance with the passage of time. It is associated with feelings of tiredness, slowing down, and making simple errors. More severe effects include disturbance of reasoning and judgement, depression, and disturbances in perception (mainly visual) leading to florid hallucinations. A broad view of fatigue in people involves consideration of the extremes of physical and psychological hardship, when they are trying to accomplish some task.

Fatigue most commonly occurs from lack of sleep. A deterioration in the performance of (albeit dull) laboratory tests after one night with only two hours of sleep, or after two consecutive nights with only five hours of sleep each can be reliably demonstrated. Highly motivated people—such as doctors on duty, soldiers in battle, adventurers in hostile environments—are able to keep going longer, but after one night without sleep most of them will be functioning inefficiently, although they may not realize it themselves.

The effects of fatigue. The effects are increased by adverse conditions such as cold, excessive heat, hunger and thirst, noise and vibration, isolation, lack of oxygen, being wet or seasick, or being under the influence of alcohol or drugs. They may also be increased by anxiety, which can occur in people who doubt their ability to perform a task in hand, or who have worries about separate matters such as money, employment, or relationships. The effects include:

Simple errors, poor concentration, and forgetfulness. The initial slowing down is not usually noticed by the individual, though it is plain to observers who are rested. Later on, tasks are started but not completed, things are put down and cannot be found afterwards, a cup of coffee is made and the fatigued person forgets to drink it. Doctors who have to work excessive hours can be shown, for example, to make errors in their interpretation of laboratory reports and electrocardiograph tracings.

Faulty judgements and perceptions. In practice it is not possible to determine whether an error of judgement exists directly as a result of, say, tiredness, or whether it is the consequence of a faulty perception. At a traffic junction where there are tired and frustrated motorists about, a driver wants to go straight ahead but the light is red. A green arrow lights up, permitting traffic to filter off to one side. The tired driver very much wants to see a green light, and so misperceives the filtering light as the signal for going straight ahead, and drives off. He will correct the error in a shorter or a greater time according to the degree of fatigue. Other such circumstances are the overhead railway gantries that carry signals for several adjacent tracks, and harbour lights with many opportunities for 'seeing' the lights a ship's navigator wants to see, indicating a particular channel.

As a second example, a driver when rested and relaxed takes in all relevant information—his car's speed and position in the road relative to other traffic, the condition of the road, proximity to junctions and other hazards, the mechanical state of the car, and weather conditions and visibility—and then responds in a logical manner, having evaluated the relative importance of the different factors; but the fatigued driver may instead concentrate exclusively on one aspect—such as his position in the middle lane—to the neglect of the other factors, and drive remorselessly along the middle lane without regard for speed, visibility, or other vehicles.

Either poor or extremely good visibility, moonlight, high vantage points (with nothing intervening)—all can lead to perceptual errors, especially among the fatigued, so that distances are overestimated or underestimated. Small objects seem to move in the distance, rocks high up on mountains appearing as people.

Ordinary phenomena can be misinterpreted by fatigued people. For instance, a very tired sailor thought the bow wave of his yacht was a flat fish, like a ray; another sailor, in mid-Atlantic, thought he saw a Ford car which later he realized was a small whale; another thought a sleeping-bag laid out on a bunk to be his wife. These are called misinterpretations because they are in due course corrected by closer examination.

A severely fatigued person will not be able (or try) to correct the initial impression. A dramatic example of an uncorrected illusion concerned Shackleton and his two companions as they struggled across South Georgia. All three felt there was a fourth person with them, a presence that was felt to be friendly and supportive. Such experiences are indicative of the limits of endurance.

Ecstasy, depression, and frustration. These are states which can afflict those who are fatigued, and increase the risk of danger.

Ecstatic states of mastery over, or of oneness with, all things are to be treasured, but they can lead to over-confidence if experienced, say, while climbing a mountain or piloting an aircraft. Depression is part of ordinary experience and commonly accompanies fatigue, especially if the person is isolated at the time, and can lead to lethargy and carelessness. Frustration, like depression, can be induced by inactivity, especially among the normally energetic. People accustomed to solving problems by increased effort can become very disturbed when no amount of physical effort is of any avail, as when becalmed in a small boat on the ocean or marooned in a tent in a blizzard. Then the ability to relax and go with events, rather than try to combat nature, has great survival value; the art is to cultivate a kind of alert inactivity.

Disorganization and psychological breakdown. Deprivation of fifty hours or more of sleep at one stretch is likely to lead to visual hallucinations and paranoid delusions, and to render the deprived person incapable of effective action. Experiments in which subjects are given impossible tasks—such as trying to fly a particular course in a trainer cockpit programmed to make the course impossible to steer—bring most subjects, eventually, to a state of complete incapacity.

A traumatic event such as seeing a relative or companion killed may lead to a period of shock-induced inactivity followed by acute distress or engagement in some activity which is useful only in that it distracts. Another response to traumatic crisis is denial of its happening at all: a ship may be sinking but the distressed person simply denies that he is at sea at all. These are instances of the psychological process compensating for circumstances to which the individual cannot adapt.

Panic is not a common reaction to a crisis unless there is imminent danger, as in the case of risk of escape routes closing in the event of fire or flood, or there is repetition of a crisis that has occurred.

Lessening of effects. Exceptional people (such as Shackleton) and ordinary people at times of extreme need can accomplish quite extraordinary physical feats. Most people on most occasions—say, those who have to make accurate observations, exercise rational judgements, or carry out complicated tasks over prolonged periods—can do something to maintain their efficiency. It helps to observe strict routines for rest and eating, especially when any prolonged activity is called for; and when in the middle of intense activity, to take every opportunity to rest and eat, rather than make a kind of virtue of keeping going. It is also useful for people to monitor themselves—to remain aware of how tense, tired, frightened, or hungry they are—and to make due allowances by taking extra care with observations and decisions.

GLIN BENNET

LEARNING AND LEARNING THEORY. The study of learning has been prominent in psychology for more than eighty years. Since the pioneering work of Ivan Pavlov and E. L. Thorndike, its importance has consistently been reflected empirically through experimental investigations and conceptually through interpretative theories.

Pavlov demonstrated empirically the ways in which dogs develop acquired reflexes, and thus identified the basic phenomena of what is now termed classical conditioning. As the result of a temporal association with a stimulus which already elicits a response, a previously neutral stimulus comes to elicit a similar, conditioned, response. Thus, for example, a bell paired with food elicits conditioned salivation. At an empirical level, Pavlov's extensive research was remarkably effective in producing robust data relating to a psychological phenomenon. At a theoretical level, Pavlov introduced an important element of plasticity into the Russian reflexological tradition which interpreted all behaviour, including that of humans, as the result of environmental stimuli. Pavlov regarded conditioned behaviour as a reflection of higher nervous activity set in train by stimuli.

Thorndike also used experimental methods and animal subjects, studying 'intelligence' by investigating, for example, how cats learned to escape from a puzzle box to obtain food. He too obtained pleasingly orderly behavioural data which indicated gradual changes in behaviour rather than sudden 'insightful' changes. Thorndike argued that the gradual changes occurred because the 'satisfying state of affairs' which followed the correct response made it progressively stronger or more probable. Through his law of effect Thorndike emphasized that patterns of behaviour can be selected by their consequences, rather as advantageous taxonomic form is selected by evolutionary pressures on species. In both cases, apparent purpose can be reinterpreted in terms of the effects of consequences. Thorndike originally believed that behaviour followed by an 'annoying state of affairs' became weaker; but his own research, here largely with human subjects, did not demonstrate this. Thorndike therefore retained a truncated form of his law of effect which emphasized the selective strengthening effects of what are now termed reinforcers in instrumental conditioning.

The impact of subsequent empirical studies of learning was for some time largely reflected by theories which were in effect general theories in psychology. This is illustrated in J. B. Watson's writing. He exploited his familiarity with early empirical studies which related changes in behaviour to environmental conditions in order to advocate that psychology as a whole should be reformulated as the science of behaviour rather than of mental life and experience. Watson's behaviourism has contributed to the widespread adoption of behavioural studies in psychology, but his more negative views about the relevance of mental life to the refocused discipline of psychology have been less influential. Like subsequent theorists, Watson used the empirical data of studies of learning as a platform for his approach to psychology in general. In particular, he extended the principles of classical conditioning to emotions in humans through his famous studies with 'little Albert', and emphasized environmental influences on behaviour to the neglect of inherited differences.

Edward Tolman carried out ingenious experiments on learning in animals, and demonstrated patterns of behavioural change which were not so readily interpreted in simple stimulus-response terms. For example, he showed that rats learned to run to a particular place for food rather than to make a stereotyped response such as turning right at a choice point. He also investigated latent learning, shown through savings when animals were allowed simply to explore a maze before being required to run through it to a specific goal box. Tolman used the methods of behavioural investigations, but extended the complexity of the environmental arrangements whose effects on behaviour were studied. He was drawn to use intervening concepts, such as expectancies or cognitive maps, to deal with the relationships he observed between environment and behaviour. In this regard, Tolman was a precursor of contemporary cognitive psychology.

The most detailed and systematic account of learning yet developed was that of Clark Hull. Yet again based on controlled experiments with animals, Hull's theory was presented in formal terms, with postulates giving rise to precise behavioural predictions expressed in quantitative terms through equations with intervening variables. These variables, which in Hull's theory were such concepts as drive, habit strength, and reaction potential, were more tightly tied to empirical measurements than were Tolman's more cognitive terms. Hull's theory is often cited as the best example in psychology of the hypothetico-deductive method of scientific enquiry, and in this sense it is a further example of a learning theory which has implications for psychology reaching far beyond the empirical studies of learning on which it is based. The theory also strove for a general explication of learning, emphasizing similarities between classical and instrumental conditioning and across species, though incorporating quantitative differences.

In the thirty years 1950–80 the emphasis on formal global theories of learning diminished. Empirical research on conditioning and learning has continued to flourish, however. The methods of free-operant conditioning developed by Skinner have been extremely beneficial in this respect, making it possible to study more effectively the effects of intermittent reinforcement, discriminative control, punishment, and so on. Indeed operant conditioning has become a technology for the experimental analysis of behaviour. One systematic use of the data of operant conditioning has been to support the general behaviouristic approach to psychology favoured by Skinner, with its emphasis on explanations of behaviour couched in terms of its relationships with environmental events in applied contexts with humans as well as with animals in the laboratory (functional analysis of behaviour). However, the behavioural data obtained from operant conditioning may be evaluated in terms of other theories.

In recent years a number of trends have emerged from empirical studies of conditioning. First, conventional distinctions between classical and instrumental conditioning have been further challenged. One important factor here has been the suggestion that activities of the autonomic nervous system such as heart-rate and blood-pressure, previously thought to be affected only by classical conditioning procedures, can be modulated by instrumental reinforcement, a possibility that encouraged the use of so-called biofeedback techniques with patients in clinical practice. Secondly, greater interest has been shown in biological or phylogenetic influences on conditioning and learning. It seems that some patterns of behaviour are more readily affected by conditioning procedures than others: animals appear, for example, to be biologically prepared to associate novel tastes and nausea, no doubt because of the implications of such preparedness for survival. Similarly, species-characteristic patterns of behaviour may intrude even in the controlled environment of the conditioning laboratory. These findings have raised some doubts about the generality of the laws of learning established thus far, but they emphasize that behaviour must be interpreted in terms of interactions between inheritance and experience. Thirdly, the increasingly complex relationships between environment and behaviour studied in conditioning experiments have led some contemporary learning theorists (e.g. N. J. Mackintosh) to reintroduce cognitive explanations even of animal behaviour.

The field of learning has consistently been one of the most active areas of experimental psychology. The empirical data which have been produced have consistently demonstrated the power of experimental and comparative methods in psychology. In turn they have given rise to theories which, though designed primarily to accommodate the phenomena of animal learning, have implications for psychology in general, in terms of human as well as of animal behaviour. These theories have therefore reflected (or perhaps led) changing perspectives in psychological science. Learning and learning theory can be said to offer an insight into the empirical and theoretical development of psychology as a whole.

DONALD E. BROADBENT

MEMORY FOR SKILLS. One apparently never forgets how to swim or ride a bicycle. Is this really the case? If it is, does it mean memory for skills is in some fundamental way different from other kinds of memory?

What is the evidence? The fact that one does not immediately fall off a bicycle when remounting after an interval of several years does not necessarily mean that no forgetting has occurred, it simply means that *something* has been retained. Fortunately we do have an answer to the question, based on studies of specialized skills under relatively controlled conditions.

The answer turns out to depend on the type of skill involved. Here we must distinguish between continuous and discrete skills. A continuous skill involves the performer in continually varying his response to a continuously varying stimulus. An example of this would be the steering response involved in driving a car, or the balancing involved in riding a bicycle, or for that matter simply maintaining an upright posture while walking. Such skills can be contrasted with discrete skills in which a discrete individual response is made; typing or manually changing gear in a car would be examples of such skills.

There was a good deal of interest in the acquisition and retention of continuous skills during the Second World War, since the skill of flying a plane clearly has a continuous component, as indeed does learning to control a missile using a joystick. Over the years, a number of experiments have studied the retention of continuous tracking performance, typically using a task in which the subject is given a joystick and required to control the movement of a spot of light on a cathode ray tube. Usually an analogue computer is used to simulate the control characteristics of the plane or missile. With a movement of the joystick changing the velocity of the missile or its acceleration, and producing a response that may be immediate or may follow only after a lag.

Fleishman and Parker (1962) studied a very difficult version of such a task. It involved three-dimensional tracking under conditions which simulated the problem of flying a plane on the attack phase of a radar intercept mission. They trained their operators over a six-week period, giving them 357 separate one-minute trials, by which time they were performing the task well. The operators were then split into three groups and given no further access to the apparatus. Retention of the skills was then tested, with one group returning after nine months, one after fourteen months, and one after two years. In all conditions, after a single warm-up trial to refamiliarize the subjects with the situation, performance was virtually as good as it had been immediately after the end of training. A number of subsequent studies have replicated this and shown that even the warm-up decrement shown on the first test trial can be reduced if the subject is sufficiently highly practised.

In the case of discrete motor skills, forgetting does occur. Consider, for example, the study by Baddeley and Longman (1978) in which a large number of postmen were trained to use a typewriter. The purpose was to familiarize them with the typewriter keyboard, which was subsequently to be used as part of a letter-sorting machine. Since the equipment was not ready at the end of the training experiment, it proved possible to study the retention of the skill under conditions where no subsequent practice was occurring, an unusual situation in the case of typing. Even after a warm-up period, clear forgetting occurred, with the average rate of keying dropping from about 80 strokes per minute at the end of the training session to about 70 per minute after one month, and to about 55 per minute after a nine-month delay. At the same time errors increased from about 1 per cent of keystrokes to somewhere in the region of 3 per cent.

Why the difference between the two types of skill? At present we can only speculate, but one possible interpretation is as follows. One source of forgetting is that of retroactive interference. A person learns to associate a particular stimulus with a particular response or action: for example, he learns that a bathroom tap with the letter C on it is likely to produce cold water if turned on. After a while such an association will become relatively automatic. If the situation then changes—for example, if he goes on holiday to Italy where C stands for *caldo*, 'hot'—then he will probably make a number of mistakes before adjusting. On returning to 'English-speaking' bathrooms he is likely to find that, to begin with, the previous habit interferes with his response, causing him to make at least one or two initial errors, although the massive amount of prior learning will mean that it takes very little time to revert. In brief, what has happened is that the person has learned two separate responses to the same stimulus, and at times he will recall the wrong one.

It seems likely that at least some, and some theorists would claim all, forgetting occurs because of interference from other learning. In the case of a discontinuous or discrete skill, the same stimuli probably occur in a range of situations where the relevant motor response cannot or should not be made. For example, our trainee typists would clearly go on being in a situation where they were responding to printed text by reading or writing rather than by hitting the appropriate key. This would be expected to cause some interference and hence some forgetting, although the amount of interference would depend very much on the precise conditions involved in the two interfering tasks. One might contrast this with a continuous skill in which the operator is functioning as if in a closed loop, with his own responses and their interaction with the environment producing the stimulus for further response. In any situation other than that of performing the skill, the essential stimulus situation is simply not evoked, and hence no interference can occur.

Having presented this view, it should be pointed out that there is very little evidence either for or against it, and our knowledge of the detailed operation of interference effects is certainly not sufficiently great to allow one to regard it as more than a speculation. The basic phenomena, however, are reasonably well established, so you can assume with some degree of confidence that you will not forget how to ride a bike, or perhaps even more importantly, how to swim.

ALAN D. BADDELEY

SKILL. In everyday parlance, 'skill' is used to denote expertise developed in the course of training and experience. It includes not only trade and craft skills acquired by apprenticeship, but high-grade performance in many fields such as professional practice, the arts, games, and athletics.

The psychological study of skills came to the fore during the Second World War with the need to match the demands of new equipment such as radar, high-speed aircraft, and various sophisticated weapons to human capacities and limitations. More recently, the growth of sport as highly lucrative entertainment and as a medium of national pride and international diplomacy has raised competitive standards and led to studies of human performance at games and athletics in order to extract maximum physical and mental effectiveness.

The common feature running through all these types of skill is that the performer has to match the demands of a task to his capacities. He does this by applying some *method*, or, as it is often called, 'strategy' of performance. For example, a tradesman will select tools and manipulate them in ways which match his capacities for exerting force and exercising fine motor control to the requirements of the metal, wood, or other material he is using. Similarly, a barrister or negotiator will order the questions he asks in a manner which he judges will best enable his powers of persuasion to secure the outcome he desires. These strategies, it should he noted, are not typically concerned with single responses to stimuli, but with chains or programmes of action which look ahead from the situation that initiates them to a future goal or end result. Some strategies are more efficient than others, in that less capacity, time, or effort has to be deployed to obtain the results required. *Skill consists in choosing and carrying out strategies which are efficient.*

Almost every skilled performance involves the whole chain of central mechanisms lying between the sense organs and the effectors, but different types of skill can be distinguished according to the link in the chain where their main emphasis lies. For this purpose, the central mechanisms can be broadly divided into three functional parts: perception of objects or events; choice of responses to them; and execution of phased and coordinated action giving expression to the choice made. An example of perceptual skill is the ability of musicians to judge 'absolute pitch'. It depends upon the possession of a conceptual scale against which any note heard can be placed. The ability is sometimes claimed to be inborn, but studies have shown that it can be acquired, or at least greatly improved, with practice. Analogous skills occur in other occupations which require the making of fine discriminations, such as dyers distinguishing subtle shades of colour, steel furnacemen deciding when the colour of molten metal indicates that it is ready to pour, wool- and other fibre-graders assessing thickness by 'feel', cheese-graders judging softness by pressure, and wine- or tea-tasters using a 'sensitive palate'.

Skills in making choices, or, as they are sometimes termed, 'decisional' skills, include the expertise shown in various intellectual pursuits, and also in games such as chess and cards. In all these cases, the perceptual data are usually clear and the precise manner of executing the actions required is unimportant: the essential for success is to decide upon the correct actions to take.

Examples of motor skills include sitting on a horse, riding a bicycle, or manipulating the controls of a car. Their essential characteristics lie in motor coordination and timing. They have attracted somewhat less research than other types of skill, probably because the knacks involved are largely unconscious.

Industrial and athletic skills display the characteristics of all three types. Perceptual factors enter into trades and crafts in the assessment and judgement of materials, and in observing the effects of tools such as drills and lathe-cutters. In ball games they are concerned in the observation and assessment of the flight of the ball and of the moves made by other players. Motor skills are obviously involved in the fine manipulation of tools in trade and craft work, and in bowling, catching, or kicking and making strokes with bat, racquet, or club in various games. However, the core of all these skills, especially at higher levels of expertise, lies in processes of choice and decision. Thus high-level skill in craft and trade work lies less in the ability to execute particular manual operations, such as shaping clay on a potter's wheel or cutting cleanly through a piece of metal with a hacksaw, than in deciding what shape is needed or exactly where the cut should be made. Similarly, high-grade athletic skill lies more in the strategy of the game than in the ability to make accurate individual strokes or in sheer muscular strength. Again, in music, the soloist's skill transcends the mere playing of the instrument to the interpretation of the score.

Strategies are developed and become more efficient in the course of practice, and it is these rather than basic capacities that are amenable to training. Four points should be noted.

1. For improvement to occur with practice, some knowledge of results achieved by previous action (feedback) is required, and, broadly speaking, the more precise and direct this is the better. Early in practice feedback needs to be detailed, but when comprehension and action become organized into larger units the need for feedback within these is reduced. In extreme cases the units become 'automatic' in the sense that conscious attention to feedback no longer occurs and the performer has little awareness of what he is doing. When this stage is reached two results follow. First, because each decision covers a larger unit of performance, fewer need to be made, so that action becomes smoother and less hurried—the skilled performer 'seems to have all the time in the world'. Secondly, performance becomes highly efficient, but may also become rigid in the sense that it cannot be adjusted to meet changing circumstances. A high-grade yet versatile expertise involves a nice balance between such efficiency and flexibility.

2. Strategies and information acquired in training for one task may *transfer* to others: for example, techniques learnt when mastering a foreign language can be applied again when studying another language. Such transfer usually results in the later task being mastered more easily than it would otherwise be, but occasionally the reverse is true: for instance, the co-ordination between tilt and movement needed to ride a bicycle leads to gross oversteering if applied when riding a tricycle, and must be inhibited before the tricycle can be ridden successfully.

3. Improvement with practice is typically rapid at first, then more gradual but continuing over long periods: for instance, the speed of some repetitive work in factories has been shown to rise with time on the job over several years.

4. Once high levels of skill have been attained, they are usually well preserved over periods of many years. The fine edge of performance may be lost without continual practice, but can usually be regained relatively quickly.

Most discussions of skill have been concerned with men or women interacting with machines, tools, or other objects in their environment. It has recently been recognized that the concepts of skill can be applied also to the interaction of one human being with another. Social *skill* includes all the three types already distinguished. It includes perception of the needs and desires of others and of the effects upon others of one's own actions; decisions about how to react to the behaviour of, and communications from, others to achieve rapport and to influence them in ways desired; and on the motor side it includes the making of gestures, kissing, and modulations of the voice in expressing feelings such as sympathy. Social skill applies not only to relationships between individuals, but is essential for efficient leadership and communication in industry and other organizations, and is indeed necessary for living satisfactorily in any society.

A. T. WELFORD

TIME-GAP EXPERIENCE. Quite frequently, during the course of a long-distance journey, motorists reach some point—a crossroads for instance—and find they have no conscious recollection of covering the miles since the last village. They usually interpret this in terms of time, reporting, for example, a 'lost half hour'. Having consulted their watches, they may reflect, bemusedly, 'How did it jump to three o'clock?' For this reason, the term 'time-gap experience' has been coined for discussion of the phenomenon.

The sudden awareness of a 'time gap' is usually experienced as 'waking up'; part of the puzzlement felt by the individual is due to the experience of 'waking up' when one is already awake. But more perturbing is the belief that there has been an inexplicable blank in one's awareness of the passage of time. In part this is due to the strict temporal structuring of our civilization. For most of us, our workaday lives demand continual reference to clock time, and assessment of temporal duration. Only in certain occupations or during holidays can we enjoy release from the constant need to be aware of the passage of time. But more importantly, our sense of self is intimately related to the subjective awareness of the continuity of life. Any break in personal time is alarming because it suggests some disintegration of psychic synthesis.

There is considerable evidence to suggest that our awareness of temporal duration is determined by *events*. These can be of both external and internal origin. What the time-gapper describes as his failure to register a period of time is really a failure to register a series of external events which would normally have functioned as his time-markers. The problem is primarily one of *attention*. The question, then, is how he could fail to register so many sequential events. How can a person completely fail to 'pay attention' over a prolonged period while successfully performing a very complex task like driving a car, which itself is largely dependent on reactions to external events?

The answer may be found by considering the nature of skilled behaviour. This is hierarchically organized so that its elementary components become progressively automatized. The skilled driver does not need to pay conscious attention to such basic matters as the position of the controls, or the movements of his hands and feet. He can afford to reserve his attention for the assessment of input at a strategic level. If the situation is relatively undemanding, and external events routine or predictable, he may require only a low level of conscious attention. He will deploy his attentional resources elsewhere—typically to his own thoughts. In one sense, he has 'switched to automatic pilot'. But any significant change in the situation will involve the processing of new information, the assessment of probabilities and the making and implementation of decisions. All this requires heightened conscious awareness, a switching back to 'manual control'. The crossroads, for example, introduces a sudden increase in information load, which demands the sharp refocusing of our motorist's attention. And this is the moment when the time-gapper describes himself as 'waking up'.

GRAHAM F. REED

2. Solving Problems

Appeal of problems	**Intelligence**
Calculating geniuses	**Lateral thinking**
Creativity	**Problem-solving**

The hallmark of an intelligent, adaptive mind is the ability to solve problems. Successful species are those that achieve well-defined goals within well-defined constraints. In the case of humans, **problem-solving** is not only pervasive across our professional and vocational lives, but is also the focus of much of our recreational activities. On a day-to-day basis we encounter a range of mundane difficulties, from those that we would not ordinarily classify as problems ('where is the nearest post office?' or 'which TV programme shall I watch next?'), to more interesting questions that require some thought ('what can I cook for dinner tonight, with the things in the fridge?' or 'if my car makes a peculiar noise when I try to accelerate, what is likely to be wrong with it?').

As well as solving these kinds of everyday problems, perhaps without even recognizing that they are problems as such, we engage in activities that are more explicitly problem-solving in nature, as diversions of the mind. Card games, board games, and crossword puzzles all involve well-defined goals and well-defined constraints, and occupy a large proportion of recreational time, but it is less clear why we spend so much time attempting to solve such problems. Theories of the **appeal of problems** have posited a homeostatic need to maintain a certain level of arousal, and alternatively have considered the importance of mental exercise, using the metaphor of the brain as a special kind of muscle that would atrophy unless used. We do not have a definitive account of the biological function served by curiosity, but the ability to solve problems is an indicator of **intelligence**, which has a clear biological purpose. An extremely intelligent person, otherwise described as an extremely proficient problem-solver, can be described as a genius, although such individuals usually have extreme abilities in a restricted domain. On the other hand, intelligent individuals within the normal range tend to perform well over a range of problems. One specific extreme ability that gives us some insight into genius is seen in form of the **calculating geniuses**, who are able to perform numerical calculations that prove either impossible or very difficult for the rest of us (for example, in your head, multiply 123 by 456). Many of the mental acts performed by these individuals appear to be extensions of acts that others perform effortlessly, whereby regularly performed operations become automatized. For most individuals the 'problem' of multiplying 3 by 6 (say) is so straightforward that it is, quite literally, not a problem. When the problem is presented the solution appears in the mind, in much the same way that when asked 'what is the capital city of Italy?' the answer appears. No effort is required in either case, and the same appears to apply to the calculating geniuses, but on a very impressive scale. In addition to well-rehearsed routines, these mental gymnasts also use arithmetic short cuts and can organize their operations to optimize their use of short-term memory.

Some of the mental processes that constitute thinking can be learned, as can any other skill. In learning how to solve problems there are a number of components that one person can describe to another. For example, we can learn constraints (or rules, in the case of an artificial problem), and heuristics—general principles that take the operator closer to the goal state. For example, in playing chess one useful heuristic is to use one's own pieces to protect each other, and another important heuristic is to control the four squares in the centre of the board. Such guiding principles can be stated explicitly and can therefore be taught. It is less clear whether we can improve our performance in solving problems by the development of intuition, although contemporary views of intuition as a convergence of association of ideas would perhaps lend themselves to training. The related concept of 'incubation', whereby the solution to a problem may appear after a period of non-directed thinking, has received some recent support from laboratory investigations, and may prove to be a learnable skill. We can be taught **lateral thinking**, but this is only useful with certain kinds of problems, and is more helpful with multi-solution problems than, for example, with numerical calculations. At the opposite extreme to logical calculation, where **creativity** is demonstrated, the definition of the problem itself may be called into question. When an artist displays creativity it may be difficult to identify the nature of the problem being solved, and our criteria of well-defined goals with well-defined constraints may be the very aspects of the exercise that are denied. When losing a crucial chess game, creative solutions may go beyond the rules of the game and might include destruction of the board or distraction of the opponent, but then the problem solved is no longer the well-defined problem that was initially addressed.

APPEAL OF PROBLEMS. People enjoy the mental stimulation of a good problem, and for some it becomes a powerful need—a cerebral restlessness epitomized in fiction by Sherlock Holmes. It makes little odds whether the problem is trivial or profound, vague or precise, so long as it tempts us to resolve a state of puzzlement or contradiction. Harlow et al. (1950) have shown that even monkeys spend considerable time in the manipulation of puzzles without any extrinsic reward when left to their own devices. Does curiosity constitute a biological need? White (1959) and Berlyne (1971) have developed the theory that one reason for seeking the stimulation of novelty is to ward off boredom. The challenge of the problematic is manifested in a wide variety of forms, and here we contrast the response to two problem situations of a very different kind in order to see what they have in common.

The solution to a formal problem generally demands the postulation of a hypothesis, the assumption that something is true without knowing whether it is true. Its consequences can then be tested to see whether they fit the facts. The following is a very precise problem which critically requires this ability (Wason, 1977). (For a fascinating development of this problem, see Smyth and Clark, 1986.) If the individual does not think about it hypothetically he finds himself in a looking-glass world where everything seems the wrong way round. In front of you imagine four designs made up of two colours and two shapes:

Blue diamond   *Blue circle*
Red diamond   *Red circle*

The problem is this: 'In these designs there is a particular shape and a particular colour such that any of the designs which has one, and only one, of these features is called a THOG. If the *blue diamond* is a THOG, could any of the other designs be THOGS?'

The problem hardly seems difficult. The *red circle* obviously could not be a THOG, and the other two could be THOGS because each has one feature of the *blue diamond*. That is the common-sense solution and it is wrong; it is the mirror image of the correct solution. If the *blue diamond* is a THOG then the *red circle* is a THOG, and neither the *blue circle* nor the *red diamond* could be THOGS.

There is more than one path to the solution, but the following one is probably the clearest. Postulate a hypothesis about the pairs of features consistent with the *blue diamond* being a THOG. It could not be ['blue' and 'diamond'] and it could not be ['red' and 'circle']. These hypotheses have both, or neither, of the features contained in the *blue diamond*, and the problem states that a THOG has just one. Try ['blue' and 'circle'] as a candidate. It would stop the *blue circle* being a THOG (it has both features) and also the *red diamond* (it has neither feature), but it would make the *red circle* a THOG because 'circle' is one of its features. The only other hypothesis compatible with the blue diamond being a THOG is ['red' and 'diamond']. By the same argument it would rule out both the *red diamond* and the *blue circle* but it also would make the *red circle* a THOG because 'red' is one of its features. The solution is rather elusive because the reasoner has to keep clear the distinction between the designs and the features which constitute them.

Elsie Mimikos showed that students with a science education do better on this problem than students with an arts education. A subsequent experiment convincingly replicated this result. Twenty-five out of thirty-two science graduates solved it compared with only three out of thirty-two arts graduates. It would seem that the precise hypothetical thinking which is involved may be alien for the latter group, although there is no imputation that the problem is in any way a test of intelligence.

The formal elegance of the 'Thog problem' prevents it from resembling most of the problems we encounter in daily life. It tests a highly specific skill—that is all. Problems do not generally come like this, in neatly packaged form. They have to be discovered, and it is difficult to investigate this process experimentally. Moreover, the problems used by the psychologist to study thinking usually have one right answer. In real life problems are seldom like this; they have many different grades of adequate answer. Art, furthermore, provides a realm in which problems do not have right answers at all. It may be objected that this is to stretch the meaning of the word 'problem' metaphorically, but artists (and poets) do often discuss their work in these terms.

In a unique longitudinal study of artistic creativity, Getzels and Csikszentmihalyi (1976) were struck by the fact that students of fine art seemed primarily motivated by self-discovery. It might be expected that they would discuss the rewards of the artist in aesthetic terms, in terms of 'beauty', 'harmony', or the creation of 'order'. Instead they talked about them much more in terms of 'discovery' and 'understanding', and this suggested that their work was structured around 'discovered problem situations'. The investigators developed an ingenious technique to test this idea. Thirty-one fine-art students were asked to compose a still-life drawing based on a selection from a number of objects which were placed on an adjacent table. The first task of each student was to choose some of these objects, and arrange them on another table to form the subject of his composition. The investigators made the assumption that the choice of objects corresponded to a 'problem-finding' stage. They observed the number of objects chosen, the way in which the student explored and handled them, and their uniqueness, i.e. the extent to which each had been chosen by the other students. These indices were assumed to reflect the characteristic ways in which a person approaches an unstructured aesthetic task. They were used to test the hypothesis that individuals who considered more problematic elements, explored problematic elements more thoroughly, and selected the less common among them, would formulate a visual problem which would result in a more original drawing. Five art critics, who knew nothing about the experiment, then independently rated each drawing for originality, aesthetic value, and craftsmanship. The main result confirmed the prediction. The problem-finding process results in drawings which are judged to be more original, but not necessarily of higher craftsmanship. In fact, the correlation between the problem-finding scores and 'originality' was highly significant.

This result is really surprising: the quality of the final product is related to behaviour *before* the drawing started. It was corroborated by subsequent interviews. Those artists who stated that when they started to work they had no clear idea about what they would do, produced drawings which were highly rated for aesthetic value and originality; those who stated they already had a problem in mind when they approached the task were rated low on the same dimensions. It was corroborated by measures of time taken during the experiment. The only such measure significantly related to the quality of the drawings was time spent in choosing objects, as opposed to time spent in arranging or drawing them.

In science the result would hardly be surprising because its theories are based on explicitly formulated problems, while the products of art are based on the attempt to come to grips with unformulated private problems. Copernicus's questioning of the common-sense observation that the sun revolves around the earth was also highly original. But in the long run his doubts would have had no more value than a delusion had they not also been shown to be true. After problems have been discovered in science the testing of possible solutions can proceed deductively in order to see whether they can be falsified. It is precisely this ability which the 'Thog problem' attempts to catch in a small way. A scientist would probably regard it as trivial because skill in solving it involves no imagination. And yet this skill involves an analysis of the structure behind the surface of things. Without it, a person finds the solution incredible in its outrageous assault on common sense—the *red circle* has *nothing* in common with the *blue diamond*. How different it is from the production of a work of art subject only to aesthetic appraisal! We should not allow the difference to conceal a more fundamental similarity. In both science and art the individual is driven by an insatiable curiosity which refuses to accept things as they are, and which forces us to think about them in a new way. The origin of this curiosity is manifest in the appeal which artificial problems exert upon us.

PETER C. WASON

CALCULATING GENIUSES. The term 'calculating genius' describes anyone strikingly more able than normal to do numerical calculations mentally. Since the term is relative to what is regarded as normal, it is applied to people of three different types. (i) Children whose ability is precocious, i.e. exceptional for their age but not necessarily by comparison with many adults. (ii) Mentally retarded people in whom mental calculation is an 'island of ability'. Their ability is not usually outstanding by normal standards but contrasts with their general lack of ability in other respects. (iii) People whose ability is exceptional relative to the adult population at large, and among whom calculating geniuses, in the strict sense, are to be found.

In studying calculating geniuses, four general points merit emphasis. First, the ability rests on the individual's knowledge of numerical facts and short-cut methods. To illustrate, you can multiply by 25 by dividing by 4 and multiplying by 100: for example, 16 times 25 is 4 hundreds. The answer, 400, is attained so rapidly that it seems miraculous to anyone unfamiliar with the shortcut. Now, there is literally no end to the numerical facts, interrelations, and short cuts that may be discovered; and when these are deployed in mental calculation, the resulting performances can be impressive, especially to the uninitiated. Mental calculators of high calibre skilfully deploy extensive, recondite knowledge of facts and methods which are largely unknown to, and unsuspected by, most people, and which have usually been discovered by the calculator himself.

Secondly, people who have acquired a small amount of numerical knowledge can go on by themselves to discover and elaborate new facts and methods, and progressively build calculating ability that is out of the ordinary. Self-taught and with no need for external equipment, they can, unaided and unobtrusively, build an ability which may be well developed before it comes to public notice or before they themselves become aware that they can do something unusual. It may easily be supposed that the ability blossoms abruptly and fully formed. However, there is no evidence that ability develops other than by prolonged, cumulative experience. Furthermore, ability atrophies with disuse.

Thirdly, calculating procedures taught at school are designed for use in conjunction with a written record of the various steps taken, and are not serviceable in mental calculation. To illustrate, multiply 123 by 456 using your accustomed paper-and-pencil method. Now repeat exactly as before but, this time, try to do the entire calculation in your head without writing anything. You lose track, don't you? So would mental calculators. They would use other methods—of which there are many—that lend themselves better to mental working. They would, also, generate the answer (56,088) in natural left-to-right sequence, not right-to-left as happens with your paper-and-pencil procedure. In brief, the numerical language needed for mental calculation is, in many respects, different from that taught in school. This explains why the unschooled are not necessarily disadvantaged in developing talent in mental calculation and why such people often claim, in retrospect, that schooling would have been a positive hindrance.

Fourthly, it is difficult to discover in minute detail how any individual calculates. A certain amount can be inferred from objective characteristics of performance; but reliance must also be placed on subjective reports which, apart from their inescapable limitations, encounter certain difficulties. When the calculator is highly educated and articulate, he may take his numerical knowledge so much for granted that he neglects to make it explicit, even if able and willing to do so, once the need for communication becomes apparent. When young or uneducated, he may lack vocabulary to describe his self-taught knowledge. George Parker Bidder (1806–78), for example, was a calculating genius who became a distinguished engineer and gave an autobiographical account of his talent. At six, when he began seriously to calculate, he could not read or write, had no notion of written numbers, and had never heard the word 'multiply'. He remarked, 'The first time I was asked to "multiply" some small affair, say 23 by 27, I did not know what was meant and it was not until I was told that it meant 23 times 27 that I could comprehend the term'.

The difficulties are worse confounded when the calculator is a public entertainer who contrives theatrical effects and deliberately conceals the tricks of his trade. He may, for example, give the square roots of numbers called out by the audience. His swift, accurate answers are impressive because we all know how cumbersome it is to calculate square roots. What we do not realize is that he has no need to calculate at all. He assumes that the audience will, to save labour and be able to check his answer, take some number, square it, and give him the result. So assuming a perfect square he applies special numerical knowledge and, by merely inspecting the number and especially its last two digits, detects what the square root must be. With cube rooting, the inspectional technique is even easier, granted knowledge of certain numerical facts and the assumption that the given number is a perfect cube. Such an entertainer would be embarrassed if given a number which is not a perfect cube and asked to express its cube root to several decimal places.

Fairly full and reliable information exists about the biographies and abilities of several people who properly deserve to be called calculating geniuses. Of these, the ablest and best documented is A. C. Aitken (1895–1967), an outstanding mathematical scholar with exceptional all-round intellectual accomplishments. At the age of 13 he became fascinated by mental calculation, and then spent years exploring numerical facts and calculative methods. In middle age, mental calculation lost its intrinsic appeal, and for certain calculations, such as multiplication by very large numbers, he used electric calculating machines which had, by then, come on the market. However, he still found it convenient, in his mathematical research, to do some calculations mentally, and so he never lost his ability. His nimble deployment of deep numerical knowledge is illustrated by the two following commentaries, both transcribed from a tape-recorded session. After expressing 1/851 as a decimal, he reported as follows

> The instant observation was that 851 is 23 times 37. I use this fact as follows. 1/37 is 0.027027027, and so on repeated. This I divide mentally by 23. 23 into 0.027 is 0.001 with remainder 4. In a flash I can get that 23 into 4,027 is 175 with remainder 2. And into 2,027 is 88 with remainder 3. And into 3,027 is 131 with remainder 14. And even into 14.027 is 609 with remainder 20. And so on like that. Also... before I even start this... I know that there is a recurring period of sixty-six places.

He was asked to multiply 123 by 456, and gave the answer after a pause of two seconds. He then commented as follows

> I see at once that 123 times 450 is 55,350. and that 123 times 6 is 738; I hardly have to think. Then 55,350 plus 738 gives 56,088. Even at the moment of registering 56,088, I have checked it by dividing by 8, so 7,011, and this by 9 gives 779. I recognize 779 as 41 by 19. And 41 by 3 is 123, while 19 by 24 is 456. A check you see; and it passes by in about one second.

The study of calculating geniuses gives insight into how people develop and deploy their varied talents, and how development depends on the interplay of potential ability, interest, and opportunity. It also shows how intellectual skills must be organized differently in order to meet special requirements, such as calculating mentally rather than by using external recording devices. It reminds us that there are many ways of calculating—for example, logarithms, electronic calculating machines, and several forms of abacus, among which the Japanese *soroban* is especially efficient in expert hands. Each of these calculative systems has its own balance of strengths and weaknesses, and each requires its user to master a distinctive repertoire of skills.

Much of the literature about calculating geniuses is patchy and regrettably unreliable. This is not always because people are inclined to exaggerate, but because it is so easy to gather false impressions when care is not taken to consider each calculator individually and to make precise observations about his ability. We go seriously astray if we assume that every calculator works in exactly the same way, or by conventional procedures that are somehow speeded up. Each uses a knowledge of numerical facts and methods which is, in its details, largely self-taught and uniquely his own.

IAN M. L. HUNTER

CREATIVITY is one of those terms (intelligence is another) that psychologists use as though they refer to single human characteristics, but which direct us in practice to a number of concerns that are rather separate. Some of these, like 'innovation' and 'discovery', have a bearing on the ideas or objects that people produce; some, like 'self-actualization', refer more to the quality of the life an individual leads; and some, like 'imagination' and 'fantasy', point us, in the first instance, to what goes on inside a person's head. Despite its air of vagueness, the notion of 'creativity' has none the less served an important function among psychologists and teachers, acting as a banner under which ideological battles have been fought; and indicating, too, a somewhat disparate body of research, some of which is of real value.

What is now thought of as the 'creativity movement' had its first stirrings in America in the years after the Second World War. At one level, it was psychology's response to the challenge of

Sputnik, and to the fact that little of the best space research was being done by home-grown American scientists—the implication being that there was something deadening about the education that clever young American scientists had received. At another level, it represented a liberal reaction, within psychology, against values which were seen as excessively manipulative and bureaucratic. Translated into the classroom, this concern for creativity expressed itself in a desire to shake education free of rote-learning and the set syllabus, multiple-choice examinations, and the IQ test, and to give children the opportunity to make discoveries for themselves.

Although hints of its existence were detectable as early as 1950, this movement was not in full swing until the early 1960s. It seems, in other words, to have been a portent of the liberal and anti-authoritarian mood that dominated university life towards the end of the 1960s, and which, in its turn, provoked its own reaction. By the early 1970s, the more self-consciously scientific psychologists had already begun to reassert the virtues of the IQ test, and to argue in favour of genetic rather than cultural explanations of individual and racial differences.

This symbolic war between 'soft' and 'hard' psychologists has tended to obscure genuine advances in our understanding of the ways in which the human imagination works. The founding fathers of psychology were keenly interested, Francis Galton no less than Sigmund Freud; and research has proceeded quietly for a hundred years or more. Two sorts of enquiry have been especially fruitful: straightforwardly descriptive studies of the lives that highly original men and women have led; and research on the processes of thinking itself.

In a sense, the evidence of the biographical studies has been largely negative. It has been found, time and again, that those who display great originality as adults were often, like Charles Darwin, only mediocre as students. British scientists who become Fellows of the Royal Society show roughly the same distribution of good, mediocre, and poor degree results as do those who go into research but achieve little. The same holds for intelligence-test scores: above a surprisingly low level, there is little or no relationship between IQ and achievement in any sphere of adult endeavour yet studied. As a result, we would expect future Nobel prize winners to show roughly the same distribution of IQ scores as their fellow students at university. In the American context the budding scientist of high renown seems typically to be a 'B+' student: one who works hard when a topic captures his (or her) imagination, but otherwise does the bare minimum. Science springs to life for such individuals when they discover that instead of assimilating knowledge created by others, they can create knowledge for themselves—and are hooked from that moment onwards.

It is the more detailed studies of thinking that indicate the tensions which underlie such creative effort. Some of the most vivid have concerned mathematicians; and a feature of them is the stress they place on the process of 'incubation'. Often, having struggled with a problem and then put it aside, mathematicians find that the solution comes to them quite unexpectedly in a flash. The clear implication is that our brains are at their most efficient when allowed to switch from phases of intense concentration to ones in which we exert no conscious control at all.

There are many instances of such 'unconscious' work, one of the more dramatic being that of the German poet Rainer Maria Rilke. In 1912, in the midst of a long poem, the *Duino Elegies*,

Rilke ran out of inspiration, and lapsed into a long period of frustrated depression. Interrupted in any case by the First World War, he was able to write little for a decade. When utterance and release came to him in 1922, it took the shape of a series of poems, the *Sonnets to Orpheus*, that he had no intention of writing whatever. Eighteen days later when he had finished both these sonnets and the *Duino Elegies*, he had produced some 1,200 lines of the pithiest and most carefully poised poetry ever written, and had done so largely without correction, as if taking dictation.

Such evidence encourages us to reconsider the popular idea that genius and madness are closely allied. It is not true, of course, that great poets, painters, scientists, and mathematicians are mad; far from it. On the other hand, it may well be that they work as intensely and imaginatively as they do in order to remain sane; that they have access to aspects of the mind's functioning from which those who live more staid and conventional lives are excluded, and that it is this access which gives their work both its flair and its sense of risk. Rilke's lengthy depression may well have been necessary for the extraordinary burst of creative but also highly disciplined work that followed it.

It is such tensions as these which explain a remark once attributed to Einstein. He suggested that the creative scientists are the ones with access to their dreams. Occasionally a dream will actually provide the solution to a problem—as in the case of the chemist August Kekulé and his dream of the snake swallowing its own tail, the clue to the nature of the benzene ring. Einstein's point was less specific, though. As Freud realized in establishing his distinction between primary and secondary process thought, the mind is capable of functioning both intuitively and according to the dictates of common sense. The implication of Einstein's remark is that in order to innovate the scientist, like anyone else, must break the grip on his imagination that our powers of logical-seeming story-telling impose. We must be willing to subvert the conventional wisdom on which our everyday competence depends.

It is here that the research done by the advocates of creativity in the 1960s now seems most relevant. Rather than straining to see whether tests of creativity can be devised, to stand side by side with IQ tests (a largely barren exercise it seems), we can concentrate on an issue that Francis Galton identified over a century ago: the extent to which each individual can retrieve apparently irrational ideas, sift them, and put them to some constructive use. We know that individuals differ in their ability to free associate, to fantasize, and to recall their dreams. We also know that these differences have a bearing on the kinds of work people find it comfortable to do: among the intelligent, it is those who are relatively good at free associating (the 'divergers') who are attracted towards the arts, while those who are relatively weak in this (the 'convergers') are drawn towards science and technology. What we do not yet know is how the abilities to think logically and to free associate combine to produce work of real value: what qualities of mind, for example, a genuinely imaginative solution to an engineering problem demands, or how a sustained contribution to one of the arts is actually achieved. LIAM HUDSON

INTELLIGENCE. Innumerable tests are available for measuring intelligence, yet no one is quite certain of what intelligence is, or even of just what it is that the available tests are measuring. There have been any number of attempts to resolve these uncertainties, attempts that have differed in their approach to the problem, and in the outcome of applying each given approach.

One time-honoured approach to discovering the meaning of a construct is to seek expert opinion regarding its definition. This is exactly what the editors of a major psychological journal did in 1921, when they sought the opinions of experts in the field of intelligence regarding what they 'conceive "intelligence" to be, and by what means it can best be measured by group tests' ('Intelligence and its Measurement', 1921, p. 123). Fourteen experts replied, with definitions of intelligence such as the following: (i) the power of good responses from the point of view of truth or fact (E. L. Thorndike); (ii) the ability to carry on abstract thinking (L. M. Terman); (iii) having learned or ability to learn to adjust oneself to the environment (S. S. Colvin); (iv) the ability to adapt oneself adequately to relatively new situations in life (R. Pintner); (v) the capacity for knowledge, and knowledge possessed (V. A. C. Henmon); (vi) a biological mechanism by which the effects of a complexity of stimuli are brought together and given a somewhat unified effect in behaviour (J. Peterson); (vii) the capacity to inhibit an instinctive adjustment, the capacity to redefine the inhibited instinctive adjustment in the light of imaginally experienced trial and error, and the volitional capacity to realize the modified instinctive adjustment into overt behaviour to the advantage of the individual as a social animal (L. L. Thurstone); (viii) the capacity to acquire capacity (H. Woodrow); (ix) the capacity to learn or to profit by experience (W. F. Dearborn). The other experts did not answer the question directly.

Viewed narrowly, there seem to be almost as many definitions of intelligence as there were experts asked to define it. Viewed broadly, however, two themes seem to run through at least several of these definitions: the capacity to learn from experience, and adaptation to one's environment. Indeed, an earlier definition often cited by these experts viewed intelligence as general adaptability to new problems and conditions of life.

If one is dissatisfied with the heterogeneity in these definitions, one can attempt to answer the question of what intelligence is by begging the question. Edwin Boring (1923) did just that when he defined intelligence as whatever it is that the tests measure. This definition tells us no more than we knew when we started, and it may tell us less: no two tests measure exactly the same thing, so that one is left with as many definitions of intelligence as there are tests (which is certainly a number greater even than that of experts in the field!).

A more recent and sophisticated version of the definitional approach to discovering what intelligence is has been suggested by Neisser (1979). According to Neisser, the concept of intelligence is organized around a 'prototype', or ideal case. One is intelligent to the extent that one resembles this ideal case:

> There are no definitive criteria of intelligence, just as there are none for chairness; it is a fuzzy-edged concept to which many features are relevant. Two people may both be quite intelligent and yet have very few traits in common—they resemble the prototype along different dimensions . . . [intelligence] is a resemblance between two individuals, one real and the other prototypical (p. 185).

If there is a single prototype, or ideal case, Neisser's notion will give us a concept of intelligence validated by consensus, if not a concrete definition. There are at least two problems with Neisser's approach, however. First, there exist multiple prototypes, or ideal cases, not just a single one. Different groups of people have somewhat different prototypes. Which one do we use? If we use all of them, including those of various groups of experts and laymen, we end up with as many ideal concepts of intelligence as there are different prototypes, and we are no better off than we were when appealing to experts' definitions. Secondly, the 'ideal case approach' seems to be an excellent way of discovering what people mean by 'intelligence', but not of discovering what 'intelligence' means. Neisser would argue that the two are indistinguishable, but I suspect they are not. Suppose, for example, that people in some culture view their ideal case as able to harmonize with Kron, the god of nature. This description tells us what these people think intelligence is, but it doesn't tell us much about the nature of intelligence: we still have to find out what it means to harmonize with Kron. In our culture, an analogous notion might be the ability to adapt to natural events. Again, we still need to find out what kinds of mental events and physical behaviours result in the ability to adapt. What is it that people who are able to adapt well do that people who are not able to adapt well do not do?

Questions such as this one have led some theorists of intelligence to seek the nature of intelligence by the analysis of individual differences. The question asked here, as above, is what aspects of mental functioning distinguish more intelligent people from less intelligent ones. The nub of this individual-differences approach is to have people perform a large number of tasks that seem to predict intelligent performance (in school, on the job, or wherever), and to analyse patterns of individual differences in task performance. These patterns of individual differences have usually been analysed through the use of a method of statistical analysis called 'factor analysis'. The idea is to identify the 'factors' of human intellect.

The earliest factorial theory of the nature of intelligence was formulated by the inventor of factor analysis, Charles Spearman. Spearman's (1927) analysis of relations among the kinds of mental tests he and other psychologists had been administering led him to propose a 'two-factor' theory of intelligence. According to this theory, intelligence comprises two kinds of factors—a general factor and specific factors. General ability, or *g* as measured by the general factor, is required for performance of mental tests of all kinds. Each specific ability, as measured by each specific factor, is required for performance of just one kind of mental test. Thus, there are as many specific factors as there are tests, but only a single general factor. Spearman suggested that the ability underlying the general factor could best be understood as a kind of 'mental energy'.

Godfrey Thomson's (1939) reassessment of Spearman's individual-differences data led him to accept Spearman's hypothesis of a general factor running through the range of mental ability tests; however, it led him to reject Spearman's interpretation of this factor. Thomson disputed Spearman's claim that the general factor represented a single underlying source of individual differences. Instead, he proposed that the appearance of a general factor was due to the workings of a multitude of mental 'bonds', including reflexes, learned associations between stimuli, and the like. Performance of any particular task activates large numbers of these bonds. Some bonds will be required for the performance of virtually any task requiring mental effort, and these bonds will in combination give rise to the appearance of a general factor.

L. L. Thurstone (1938), like Thomson, accepted Spearman's hypothesis of a general factor. But he disputed the importance of this factor. He argued that it is a 'second-order' factor or phenomenon, one which arises only because the primary or 'first-order' factors are related to each other. What are these primary factors, or, as Thurstone called them, 'primary mental abilities'? Thurstone suggested that they include verbal comprehension (measured by tests such as knowledge of vocabulary), word fluency (measured by tests requiring rapid word production—for example, a listing of as many words as a person can think of that have C as their third letter), number (measured by tests of arithmetical reasoning and computation), spatial visualization (measured by tests requiring mental manipulation of geometric forms), perceptual speed (measured by tests requiring rapid visual scanning, for example, proof-reading), memory (measured by tests of recall and recognition of previously presented information), and reasoning (measured by tests such as number series, which require people to say which of several numbers should come next in a given series).

J. P. Guilford (1967) parted company from the majority of factorial theorists by refusing to acknowledge the existence of any general factor at all in human intelligence. Instead, he proposed that intelligence comprises 120 elementary abilities, each of which involves the action of some operation upon some content to produce some product. An example of an ability in Guilford's system is 'cognition of verbal relations'. This ability involves recognition of a conceptual connection between two words: for example, recognition that a *caboose* is often the last car in a *train*.

Probably the most widely accepted factorial description of intelligence is a hierarchical one. A good example of this class of descriptions was proposed by P. E. Vernon (1971). He proposed that intelligence can be described as comprising abilities at varying levels of generality: at the highest level of generality (the top of the hierarchy) is general ability as identified by Spearman; at the next level are 'major group' factors, such as verbal-educational ability (the kind of ability needed for successful performance in courses such as English, history, and social studies) and practical-mechanical ability (the kind of ability needed for successful performance in courses such as draughtsmanship and car mechanics); at the next level are 'minor group' factors, which can be obtained by subdividing the major group factors; and at the lowest level (the bottom of the hierarchy) are specific factors, again of the kind identified by Spearman. This description of intelligence may be viewed as filling in the gaps between the two extreme kinds of factors proposed by Spearman: in between the general and specific factors are group factors of intermediate levels of generality.

The factorial views of intelligence are unlike the definitional ones in that they are based on the analysis of intelligent functioning (on ability tests), rather than merely on the speculations of one or more psychologists or laymen. The factorial views are like the definitional ones, however, in their potential number and diversity. Is it the case that one of the factorial descriptions is right and the others wrong, or is it possible that a single entity or complex of entities, intelligence, can conform to all of these different descriptions? In other words, is there some level, or common denominator, at which these various descriptions all reduce to the same thing? It is here suggested that such a level of description exists, and that it can be found by analysing the ways in which people process information when solving problems of the kind found both on intelligence tests and in everyday life.

Information-processing psychologists have sought to understand general intelligence in terms of elementary components (or processes) used in the solution of various kinds of problems. Let us distinguish five kinds of components that people use in the processing of information. *Metacomponents* are higher-order control processes that are used for planning how a problem should be solved, for making decisions regarding alternative courses of action during problem-solving, and for monitoring one's progress during the course of problem solution. *Performance components* are processes that are used in the actual execution of a problem-solving strategy. *Acquisition components* are processes used in learning, that is, in the acquisition of knowledge. *Retention components* are processes used in remembering—that is, in the retrieval of previously acquired information. *Transfer components* are used in generalization—that is, in the transfer of knowledge from one task or task context to another.

Consider, for example, how each of these five kinds of components might be applied in the solution of an arithmetical problem.

> Mrs Smith decided to impress Mrs Jones. She went to a costume jewellery shop and bought three imitation diamonds of equal value. She received £4 in change from the ten-pound note she gave the assistant. (But as Mrs Smith was receiving her change, Mrs Jones walked into the shop!) How much did each imitation diamond cost?

Metacomponents would be used in setting up the equations for solving the problem, for example, in deciding that the problem can be solved by subtracting £4 from £10 and dividing the difference by three; the metacomponents must also decide what information is relevant to the problem at hand, and what information is irrelevant. Performance components would be used in the actual solution of these equations to obtain, first, £6 as the price of the three imitation diamonds and, then, £2 as the price of each item. Acquisition components were used in the problem-solver's past to learn how to set up the equations, how to subtract, how to divide, and so on. Retention components are used to retrieve this information from memory at the time that it is needed. Transfer components are used to draw an analogy between this problem and previous ones: the problem-solver has never learned how to solve this particular problem, and must generalize his or her learning from similar problems previously encountered to the problem presently being encountered.

How can this scheme account for the various factorial views of intelligence described earlier? According to this view, the general factor that appears in various theories of intelligence results from the operations of components that are general across the range of tasks represented on intelligence tests. For the most part, these are metacomponents—mental activities such as deciding upon the particular components to be used in the solution of problems, deciding upon a strategy for problem solution, monitoring whether the strategy that has been chosen is leading to a solution, deciding upon how quickly the strategy can be executed and still lead to a satisfactory result, and so on. Major group factors of the kind found in Vernon's theory, and primary factors of the kind found in Thurstone's theory, are obtained in factor analyses primarily as a result of the operations of performance, acquisition, retention, and transfer components. For example, verbal comprehension, as tested by vocabulary, is the product of past executions of acquisition components to learn new words, and of present executions of retention components to retrieve the meanings of these words. If vocabulary is tested by presenting the words in unfamiliar contexts, transfer components may also be involved in applying previously acquired information to the new contexts that are presented. Reasoning, as tested by problems such as numerical series completions (say, 3, 7, 12, 15, 18, 25, ...), requires the execution of various performance components, such as encoding the terms of the problem, inferring the relations between the given pairs of numbers, applying these relations to the last given number to obtain the next number, and the production of a response.

This information-processing view of intelligence seems to unify what were formerly a number of disparate views regarding the nature of intelligence. A number of important questions still need to be answered, however, and it is possible to consider only a small number of them here.

First, is the meaning of intelligence the same across different societal and cultural groups? On the view proposed, the answer is both yes and no. On the one hand, the components that would be applied to the solution of a given problem in one culture or society probably overlap to a large degree, although perhaps not completely, those that would be applied to the solution of the same problem in a different culture or society. On the other hand, the kinds of problems that need to be solved may differ widely from one culture or society to another. The mental (and physical) processes needed to corner game in a hunt are very different from those needed to balance accounts. Hence, the kinds of persons who are considered intelligent may vary widely from one culture to another, as a function of the components that are important for adaptation to the requirements of living in the various cultures.

Secondly, if intelligence tests measure, in greater or lesser degree, the components of information-processing, why are they so imperfectly predictive of real-world performance? One reason is that they are fallible as measuring instruments: they measure only imperfectly what they are supposed to measure. Another reason is that they do not necessarily weigh most heavily those aspects of intellectual functioning that are most important for intelligent functioning in a given environment. Metacomponential functioning is probably under-emphasized, for example, in the measurements made by most of these tests. Yet another reason, and probably the most important one, is that there is a great deal more to everyday living than what the intelligence tests measure, or even than what can reasonably be called intelligence. The tests fail to take into account such important aspects of functioning as motivation, social skills, persistence in the face of adversity, and ability to set and achieve reasonable goals. The tests provide reasonably good measures of limited aspects of functioning for most people. But even here a qualification is necessary, since there are some people whose anxieties, or inability to take tests, render their test scores meaningless or even deceptive.

Finally, is intelligence largely inherited, as has been claimed by some, or is it largely or exclusively determined by environment, as has been claimed by others? Few bodies of evidence are more confused and confusing than that dealing with the heritability of intelligence. The probability is that heredity, environment, and the interaction between heredity and environment all play some role in intelligence as it has traditionally been measured, but it is not at all clear what the relative extents of these roles are. Nor is it clear what it means, in practical terms, to assign proportional values to the influence of each. No matter what the proportions are, there is good evidence that at least some aspects of intelligence are trainable, and theoretical interest in the heritability of intelligence should not divert attention from questions about how intelligence can be modified in individuals of all levels of measured intelligence.

ROBERT J. STERNBERG

LATERAL THINKING. There may not be a reason for saying something until after you have said it. That statement does not make sense in the world of logic, where each step has to rest securely on the preceding step: reason must come before a conclusion, not after it. Yet the statement makes perfect sense in the world of lateral thinking, of perception, of patterning systems, of poetry, and of hypothesis. Philosophers and scientists have always complained that we have no logical way of generating hypotheses. We do have such a way, but it cannot be logical for logic involves analysis of what we know. Instead of analysis we need provocation, and that is what lateral thinking is about.

Suppose we are looking for a new idea for a cigarette product. We use one of the more provocative lateral thinking techniques and we bring in a random word as provocation. The word can be picked from a dictionary with a table of random numbers so that no unconscious selection takes place. Does this mean that any word whatsoever may be used as a provocation with any problem whatsoever? It does. There is no connection at all between the random word and the problem. The word is 'soap', and from this comes the idea of freshness, and of spring, and of putting flower seeds in the butt of cigarettes so that when the butts are thrown away a flower will grow from each one and beautify the surroundings instead of polluting them. It is very difficult to see how such an idea could ever come purely from *analysis* of a cigarette since there is no part of it which would suggest this type of idea. Another time the provocation is 'traffic-lights' and from this comes the idea of putting a red band round the cigarette about two centimetres from the butt end to indicate a danger zone and so give the smoker a decision point. Now this idea is very logical in hindsight and could possibly have come through analysis. In hindsight it is often difficult to tell how an idea actually came about since the aim of lateral thinking is to produce ideas that are logical in hindsight.

The first stage of thinking is the perception stage: how we look at the world, the concepts, and perceptions we form. The second stage of thinking is the processing stage: what we do with the perceptions that have been set up in the first stage. Logic can only be used in the second stage since it requires concepts and perceptions to work upon. So what can we do about the first or perception stage? We can rely on chance, circumstance, experiment, or mistake to change our perceptions, or we can try to do something more deliberate. That is where lateral thinking comes in.

A perception is a particular way of looking at some part of the world. It is the grouping together of certain features or the isolation of a certain relationship. Perceptions are the patterns which form in our minds after exposure to the world at first or second hand. These patterns are only some among the *many possible patterns* that could have formed. Moreover, because of the nature of patterning systems, we may be unable to use one perception because we are led away along another. So the type of processing we want to do in the first stage of thinking is concerned with *changing perceptions*. It is concerned with forming new perceptions and with uncovering the perceptions we have but are unable to use.

If we accept that the mind is a pattern-making and pattern-using system, at least in the perception stage (and all the evidence suggests it is), then we need to develop some deliberate habits of provocation if we are to move from established patterns to open up new ones. Our usual mode of thinking is, quite properly, based on judgement. But judgement only serves to reinforce existing patterns, not to change them. Instead of judgement we need something more provocative. Instead of judgement we need movement, and that is what lateral thinking is about.

There is nothing mystical or magical about lateral thinking. As soon as we accept that perception is based on patterns (rather like the streets in a town) then we need some method for getting out of the familiar patterns—some jotting or provoking system. If our ideas are only a summary of what we already know, then how are we to get new ideas? Certainly we can get some by analysing more fully the implications of what we do know, but the really new ideas depend on new hypotheses, on new conceptual jumps. In a patterning system it is perfectly logical to be illogical. In the example given earlier there is no connection between a cigarette and soap, but one quickly forms along one of the many association pathways we have. Our ideas about cigarettes can now start to move out along this track—and it is a different track from the one they would otherwise have moved along. So the reason for juxtaposing cigarette and soap only appears after the juxtaposition has been made and has proved useful.

We need some indicator to show that we are not operating in the usual judgement system. Otherwise, if we make a statement like 'The hands of a watch should move backwards', we would be judged as unhinged. So from *po*etry, hy*po*thesis, and sup*po*se we extract the syllable *po* which indicates that we are using an idea in a provocative manner in order to open up new ideas. So we now say, 'Po the hands of a watch should move backwards', and using that as a stepping-stone we might come to consider the idea of having the numbering of the hours running from twelve down to one so that by glancing at our watch we can tell how many hours are *left* to the day rather than how many have passed.

The use of random juxtapositions and provocative stepping-stones is only part of the process of lateral thinking—there are many other techniques, some of which are more analytical than provocative. With all the techniques the aim remains the same: the changing of concepts and perceptions. Occasionally the changed perception gives a solution or a valuable new idea. More often lateral thinking only gives a new starting-point which has then to be developed in the usual logical manner. For instance, in a fish-processing plant the starting-point that it might make more sense to take the bones away from the flesh instead of the more usual method of taking the flesh away from the bones led to a new process which saved a great deal of money.

In general our mental tools for judging and processing and analysing are very good. But we have been very poor at generating new ideas and hypotheses because we have failed to realize that in a patterning system provocative methods are required. It was necessary to invent the term 'lateral thinking' because creativity is too vague a word, simply meaning the production of something new. Lateral thinking is concerned with changing concepts and perceptions. Some of artistic creativity has to do with lateral thinking but much of it does not. The term 'divergent thinking' only covers a small part of lateral thinking: that is to say the generation of alternatives as a method for changing perceptions. Indeed some of the lateral thinking processes are not divergent at all. Lateral thinking is concerned with the changing of concepts and perceptions by provocative and other means.

A young toddler is upsetting granny's knitting by playing with the ball of wool. One suggestion is to put the child into the playpen. Another suggestion is to leave the child outside and put granny into the playpen.

EDWARD DE BONO

PROBLEM-SOLVING. A great deal of the art of problem-solving is to understand the kind of question that is posed and the kind of answer that is demanded. It is for this reason that psychologists prefer problems with unique solutions, and that they try to ensure that individuals understand what they have to solve.

There are several theoretical points of view about problem-solving, but none are really complete because each tends to be restricted to different problem domains and there is little definitive agreement about what constitutes a problem. The Gestalt theorists believed that a problem occurs because of the way in which a situation is initially perceived, and that its solution emerges suddenly from reorganizing it in such a way that its real structure becomes apparent. On the other hand, many contemporary psychologists have been impressed by ideas borrowed from research on artificial intelligence. They conceive the mind as analogous to a computer program which operates in discrete steps ('information-processing') to reduce the difference between existing states and 'sub-goals'. Their pioneering efforts were devoted mainly to a small number of computable games and puzzles, and they were not deterred by the fact that computer programs played poor chess. My own interest has been to devise problems in which the initial response may ensnare the capacity to see the point.

The difficulty of writing about problem-solving is that one may either insult the reader's intelligence, or create states of frustration. Hence I shall not report the solution to my first problem. Instead I shall take the reader by the hand (if he will pardon the condescension) and ask him to solve with me two related, simplified problems. These may alter the way in which he conceived the original problem. Of course, he may find the first problem trivial, but then I hope his boredom will he alleviated by the knowledge that others find it rather puzzling. I could say a lot more at this point, but that would be to lay all my cards on the table. Consider the first problem.

Problem 1. I formulated this problem in 1966, and the present version was devised for the 1977 Science Museum Explorations Exhibition in London. Earlier versions contained some confusing features. The problem is generally known as 'the selection task'.

You are shown a panel of four cards, A, B, C, D (Fig. 29), together with the following instructions:

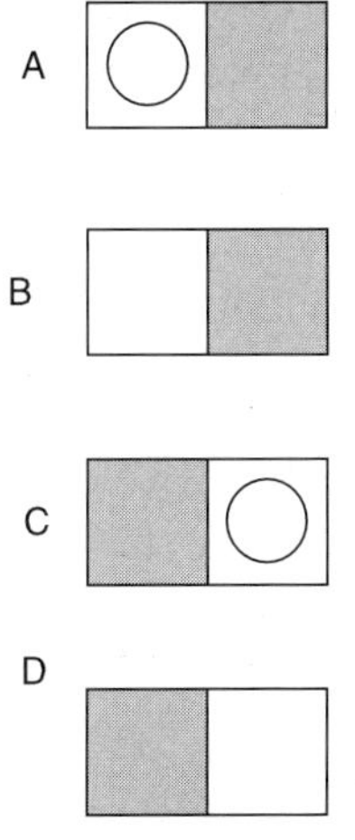

Fig. 29 Problem 1: the Science Museum Problem.

'Which of the hidden parts of these cards do you *need* to see in order to answer the following question decisively? FOR THESE CARDS IS IT TRUE THAT IF THERE IS A CIRCLE ON THE LEFT THERE IS A CIRCLE ON THE RIGHT? You have only one opportunity to make this decision; you must not assume that you can inspect cards one at a time. Name those cards which it is absolutely necessary to see.'

Please record your solution, and then consider *Problem 2*. This problem is based on Johnson-Laird and Wason (1970). A more recent, intensive investigation of the issues may be found in Wason and Green (1984). In front of you are two boxes, one labelled WHITE and the other labelled BLACK (Fig. 30). There are fifteen white shapes in the white box and fifteen black shapes in the black box, and the only shapes are triangles and circles. Your problem is to prove the following sentence true, as economically as possible, by requesting to inspect shapes from either box: IF THEY ARE TRIANGLES, THEN THEY ARE BLACK.

The students who were tested in this experiment tended to ask first of all for a black shape—they were handed a black triangle. The task turned out to be fairly easy; on average only six black shapes were requested. Of course, when individuals asked for a white shape they were always handed a white circle. Somebody in my class said recently: 'The best strategy is to alternate your choices between the two boxes.' This would have been a perverse strategy, especially if one were to apply it consistently by exhausting the contents of both boxes. In fact, insight came rapidly, and all the individuals exhausted the supply of fifteen white circles, and requested no more than nine black shapes. Moreover, they tended to do so with a broad grin, as if they had penetrated a secret, or seen the point of a joke. In order to prove the truth of the sentence 'If they are triangles, then they are black', it is merely necessary to establish the absence of a white triangle. The contents of the black box are gratuitous.

WHITE	BLACK

Fig. 30 Problem 2.

What is the connection between problems 1 and 2? In the first place, problem 2 is only concerned with half the amount of information in problem 1. In problem 2 no decision has to be made about 'triangles' and 'circles' which corresponds to the presence and absence of a 'circle on the left'. Secondly, problem 1 involves a single and ultimate decision for its solution, but problem 2 involves a series of decisions so that an earlier error can be corrected. Thirdly, problem 2 involves a number of concrete objects rather than the consideration of symbols positioned on cards. Are you still satisfied with your solution to problem 1?

Problem 3. This problem is based on Wason and Shapiro (1971). There are four cards on the table in front of you, showing (respectively) 'Manchester', 'Leeds', 'Train', 'Car' (Fig. 31). The students who were tested in this experiment had first of all examined a larger set of cards (from which these four had been selected), each of which had on one side a town (e.g. Chicago), and on the other side a mode of transport (e.g. aeroplane). They had been asked to satisfy themselves that this condition obtained on every card. The four cards were then placed on the table, and the individuals were instructed to imagine that each represented a journey made by the experimenter. They were then presented with the experimenter's claim about her journeys: EVERY TIME I GO TO MANCHESTER I TRAVEL BY TRAIN.

The problem is to state which cards

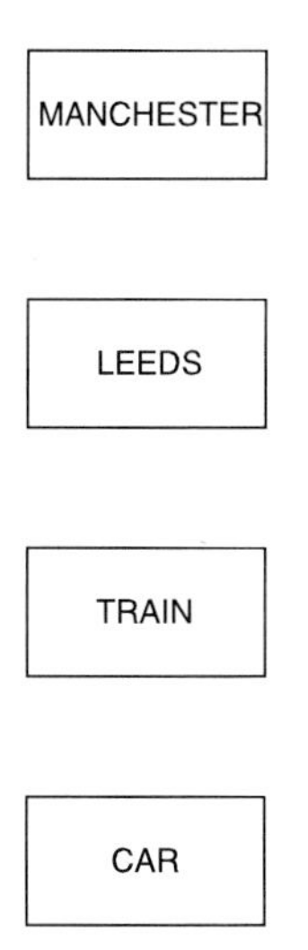

Fig. 31 Problem 3.

need to be turned over in order to determine whether this claim is true or false. The solution is 'Manchester' and 'Car' because only 'Manchester' associated with a transport other than 'Train', or 'Car' associated with 'Manchester' would disprove the claim. This thematic problem proved much easier than a standard, abstract version which was structurally equivalent to problem 1. However, recent attempts to replicate this effect have not been at all clear. For a general discussion, see Griggs (1983).

What is the connection between problems 1 and 3? In both a single decision has to be made about four cards, so in this sense they are both unlike problem 2. But in problem 3 the cards are not simply cards. They represent four different journeys and their two sides are connected intrinsically in this respect. This means that the material of the problem is intimately related to experience, and the solution can be guided by it. For a more detailed account of these, and similar, experiments see Wason and Johnson-Laird (1972).

Still happy about the solution to problem 1? If it did cause any difficulties, it seems fairly likely that any error will now have been corrected because that particular problem has been broken down into two much simpler ones, each of which eases the original burden of thought. But suppose, just for the sake of argument, that the solution to problem 1 is still wrong—for instance, it might be cards A and C. In the original experiments based on it I devised therapies which induced contradictions between the first attempted solution and a subsequent evaluation of the material. The card, corresponding to A, which everybody had (rightly) selected, would have been revealed thus:

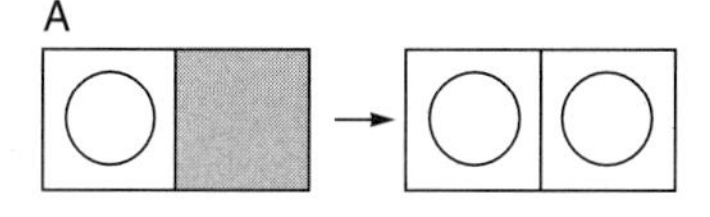

'What does this tell you about the answer to the question?' ('For these cards is it true that if there is a circle on the left there is a circle on the right?') Everybody said that this told them the answer is 'yes'.

Then the card, corresponding to D, which nearly everyone had (wrongly) omitted, would have been revealed thus:

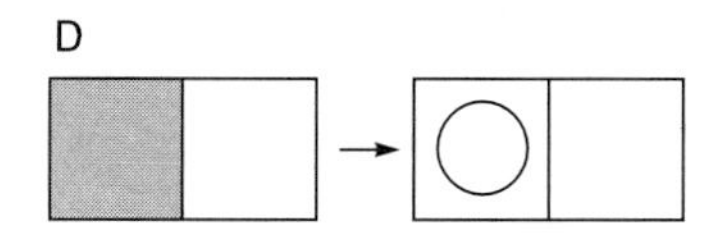

Conflict: a card which had been chosen allowed the answer 'yes', but now a card which had been ignored indubitably forces the answer 'no'. The majority of individuals remained unmoved—they refused at this point to incorporate D into their solution. When prompted, they made remarks like, 'It's got nothing to do with it', and 'It doesn't matter'. All the available evidence is present, but the correction tends not to be made.

We went on informally to discuss the potential consequences of B and C which were never fully revealed. B had nearly always been omitted (rightly) and C selected (wrongly).

'Can you say anything about the answer from this card [B]?':

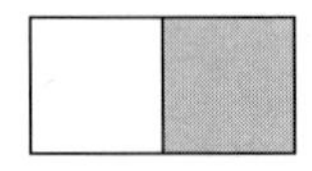

'It's got nothing to do with it because there's no circle [on the left].'

'Can you say anything about the answer from this card [C]?':

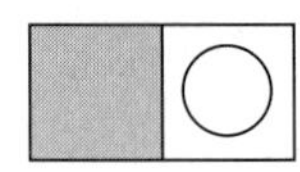

'There has to be a circle under it for the answer to be "yes".'

'What if there is no circle?'

'Then the answer would be "no".'

What could be the selfsame card has a different meaning according to whether it had been selected initially. The individual is confronted with the possibility of both cards being like this:

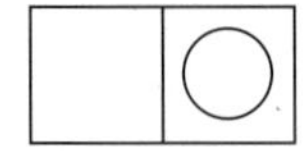

But only when this contingency derives from C is it assumed (wrongly) to be informative. It is evidently the individual's intention to select a card which confers meaning on it.

Reality, for the individuals who made these kinds of error, is determined by their own thought. That is not, perhaps, surprising. What is very surprising is that this reality is so recalcitrant to correction. See Wason (1977) for further discussion. For a recent and much more comprehensive account of the issues raised by this problem, see Wason (1983). It is as if the attention mobilized in the initial decision is divided from their subsequent attention to facts, or possibilities. The solution, cards A and D, is systematically evaded in ways which are not yet properly understood. There is even the finding that the origin of the difficulty might arise through differences in the functioning of the two hemispheres of the normal brain. When corrective feedback is induced in the left ('analytic') hemisphere it is more effective than when it is induced in the right ('synthetic') hemisphere.

Our basic paradigm (problem 1) has the enormous advantage of being artificial and novel; in these studies we are not interested in everyday thought, but in the kind of thinking which occurs when there is minimal meaning in the things around us. On a much smaller scale, what do our students' remarks remind us of in real life? They are like saying 'Of course, the earth is flat', 'Of course, we are descended from Adam and Eve', 'Of course, space has nothing to do with time'. The old ways of seeing things now look like absurd prejudices, but our highly intelligent student volunteers display analogous miniature prejudices when their premature conclusions are challenged by the facts. As Kuhn (1962) has shown, the old paradigms do not yield in the face of a few counter-examples. In the same way, our volunteers do not often accommodate their thought to new observations, even those governed by logical necessity, in a deceptive problem situation. They will frequently deny the facts, or contradict themselves, rather than shift their frame of reference.

Other treatments and interpretations of problem-solving could have been cited. For instance, most problems studied by psychologists create a sense of perplexity rather than a specious answer. But the present interpretation, in terms of the development of dogma and its resistance to truth, reveals the interest and excitement generated by research in this area.

PETER C. WASON

INDEX

P

Q–R

S